Wal... in the Wilderness

Sierra Club Outdoor Adventure Guides

Land Navigation Handbook

The Sierra Club Guide to Map, Compass & GPS
By W. S. Kals
Completely updated, with new text by Clyde Soles

Simple Foods for the Pack

More than 200 all-natural, trail-tested recipes
By Claudia Axcell, Vikki Kinmont Kath, and Diana Cooke

Walking Softly in the Wilderness

The Sierra Club Guide to Backpacking

John Hart

Fourth Edition • Completely Revised & Updated

Sierra Club Books
San Francisco

The Sierra Club, founded in 1892 by John Muir, has devoted itself to the study and protection of the earth's scenic and ecological resources—mountains, wetlands, woodlands, wild shores and rivers, deserts and plains. The publishing program of the Sierra Club offers books to the public as a nonprofit educational service in the hope that they may enlarge the public's understanding of the Club's basic concerns. The point of view expressed in each book, however, does not necessarily represent that of the Club. The Sierra Club has some sixty chapters throughout the United States and in Canada. For information about how you may participate in its programs to preserve wilderness and the quality of life, please address inquiries to Sierra Club, 85 Second Street, San Francisco, California 94105, or visit our Web site at www.sierraclub.org.

Fourth Edition

Published by Sierra Club Books
85 Second Street, San Francisco, CA 94105
www.sierraclub.org/books

SIERRA CLUB, SIERRA CLUB BOOKS, and the Sierra Club design logos are registered trademarks of the Sierra Club.

Book and cover design by Lynne O'Neil
Composition by David Van Ness

Library of Congress Cataloging-in-Publication Data

Hart, John, 1948-

    Walking softly in the wilderness : The Sierra Club guide to
    backpacking / John Hart.– 4th ed., complete rev. and updated.
      p. cm.– (A Sierra Club outdoor adventure guide)
    Includes bibliographical references and index.
    ISBN 1-57805-123-1 (alk. paper)
      1. Backpacking. 2. Backpacking–United States. 3. Wilderness areas–
    Environmental aspects–United States.
      I. Sierra Club. II. Title. III. Series.
    GV199.6.H37 2005
    796.51–dc22   2004056554

Printed in the United States of America on New Leaf Ecobook 50 acid-free paper, which contains a minimum of 50 percent post-consumer waste, processed chlorine-free. Of the balance, 25 percent is Forest Stewardship Council certified to contain no old-growth trees and to be pulped totally chlorine-free.

09 08

10 9 8 7 6 5 4 3 2

To Helen

Contents

Making & Managing the Camp

Variations

Trouble & How to Deal With It

The Places & Their Future

Acknowledgments

The author of a book of this kind is less creator than compiler, assembling the knowledge of an unthanked many; but I must thank a few.

I've learned much from fellow wilderness travelers. For this edition, I must single out Steve Roper and Gene and Betsy White. Many people involved with Sierra Club outings have shared their expertise, including Dennis O'Connor, Susan Drayne, Gordon Peterson, and Carol Vellutini. Other companions and critics include Carlisle Becker; Eric Brand; Lew Gardner of the Boy Scouts of America, Bay Area Council; Bob Golden; Jon and Gail Hall of the Boy Scouts of Canada, Northern Region; John Harlin of *Backpacker* magazine; Nancy Kittle; Lelia Loban Lee; John Lewis; Linda McMillan; Julie Manson; Allen Steck; Mary Anne Stewart; Nicholas Van Pelt; and Wes Wagnon.

On the always-ticklish medical side, I'm grateful for the generous assistance of Dr. Gordon Benner, Sierra Club medical officer. Thanks also to Drs. William Epstein, Michael J. Franzblau, and Buck Tilton and to Oscar V. Lopp of the Mountain Medicine Institute.

On wilderness impact and management questions, I've gleaned from researchers like David N. Cole of the Aldo Leopold Institute, bear expert Stephen Herrero of the University of Calgary, impact researcher John Stanley, and longtime Sierra Club national outings leader Jim Watters. Thanks also to Elizabeth Rieben of the Environmental Education Office, Bureau of Land Management, and to Marit Sawyer of Leave No Trace.

For help in understanding the status of various wilderness conservation battles, my thanks to Bruce Hamilton of the Sierra Club; Fran Hunt of the Wilderness Society; Michael McCloskey of the Sierra Club; Alice Chambers of the Sierra Club of Canada, Prairies Chapter; Steve Gatewood of the Wildlands Project; Mary Granskow of the Canadian Parks and Wilderness Society; Elizabeth May of the Sierra Club of Canada; Ray Payne of the Smoky Mountains Hiking Club; Juri Peepre of the Canadian Parks and Wilderness Society; conservation biologist Reed Noss; Will Skelton of the Tennessee Chapter, Sierra Club; Rob Smith of the Sierra Club's Southwest Regional Office; Caryl Terrell of the John Muir Chapter, Sierra Club; and very especially to Alaska crusaders Peggy and Ed Wayburn.

When it comes to the ins and outs of gear, I've taken my questions to helpful people like Mary Abbott of A&H Enterprises, Rich Davies and Gary Klein of Recreational Equipment Inc., Maria Frederiksen of Sun Precautions, Richard J. and Beverly Garcia of Garcia Machine, Chard Lowden and Mark McCartney of Marin Outdoors, Mark Randall of Yosemite Concession Services, Jim Reid of Peak 1, Mike Scherer of Kelty, Buck Smith of Marmot Mountain Works, and Bob and Ted Wallace of Polar Equipment.

I've had the assistance of numerous folk at the agencies who manage public land: federal, state, and provincial. Please don't dismiss these good people as "bureaucrats." They know what they're talking about, and they care.

A Note to the Reader

Welcome to the fourth edition of *Walking Softly in the Wilderness*.

If you are new to backpacking, I hope it will smooth your entry into a fascinating wild world. If you're an old hand, and maybe familiar with prior editions of this book, you'll notice how much has changed. These pages reflect the continuing evolution of the field: the enticing new option of ultralight travel; the continuing refinement in all forms of gear; the emergence of new tools and toys, such as the Global Positioning System; and much more. Yet the essence is delightfully unchanged.

The experience of many is more than the experience of one. I'm grateful to all the readers who have chimed in over the years with suggestions, comments, experiences, gripes. I welcome such nudges and will certainly respond. I can be reached by e-mail at jh@johnhart.com.

Of course, no book of manageable length and decent clarity can explore all the possible choices in wilderness gear and methods. Instead, a book must simplify such choices. It must select among them. Often, it must present only one way of doing things when there may be other ways that are equally good. Every backpacker works out a personal style, and yours is, or will be, your own.

I hope, however, that you will take very seriously what this book has to say about "walking softly" in the wild places: about the skills of using but not injuring the vulnerable land. These are not merely points of backcountry manners or "wilderness etiquette." Not optional finishing touches. Low-impact methods are twenty-first-century necessities. While there are legitimate disagreements about some of the details, the outlines are clear enough. There is little doubt about the things each hiker needs to know and do. I hope you will help.

The Land Beyond the Roadhead

Where do the six trails go?
What are the mountains named
That are colored like Iroquois?

–Jeanne McGahey, "Journey"

1

Backpacking in the Twenty-first Century

In Nevada, a man is striding across a stony plain toward a row of seven sharp, black peaks. His pack is heavy with water, and he sloshes a little as he walks.

In Virginia, a pair of hikers takes advantage of an opening in the trees to steep themselves in a world of fall color. The baby, sound asleep in a carrier on the man's back, is not impressed.

In Oregon, an elderly woman finishes her lunch and rises from the pine log she has been sitting on. She shrugs on her light pack, gazes one more time at the icy gleam of a distant volcano, and sets out on the next leg of her walk from Mexico to Canada along the Pacific Crest Trail.

In Minnesota, a group from a local outing club is settling down in their tents. The murmured conversations stop as the twilight is split by the laughing call of a loon.

In California, a line of hikers turns into a clump at the top of a granite pass, sharing food, unfolding maps, and looking over into the lake-strewn basin beyond.

Today there are millions of them, heading out from the roadheads: the backpackers. They are the people who don't mind a long day's walk, who are willing to carry moderate loads on their backs, who take pleasure in self-sufficiency. Where others might see just work, they find a superior form of play.

During the 1960s, backpacking became established as one of the major American outdoor pursuits. About 15 million people, surveys indicate, camp out away from their cars at least once a year; about 3 million do so frequently. Numbers rise and fall from year to year, but from decade to decade the trend is only upward.

It seems the most innocent of pleasures, this manner of approaching the natural world. And surely it is a good thing that more people make this connection and by doing so may be moved to join the effort to preserve what can still be preserved.

But the popularity of backpacking has brought some problems as well.

Backpackers pursue their sport, for the most part, in very special environments: on the roadless, unscarred, unexploited lands that we call *wilderness*. In a sea of landscape shaped and controlled by human activity, these areas stand out as primitive islands. On a planet threatened with ecological collapse, these lands are vital refuges. Here the webs of life are more or less intact, not torn and rearranged by our ceaseless, overwhelming activity.

And yet—in the form of the backpackers—here we are. And our presence is not without cost.

The Impact Problem

Some of our wilderness is unmistakably, jarringly *crowded*. And some of it is trampled: certain especially accessible or scenic places have gotten the worked-over look of run-down city parks.

In the Appalachians from the Smokies to the Catskills, the woods around popular campsites have been stripped of dead branches and young growth by hikers hunting fuel.

At popular lakes in any western range, you may find shorelines beaten bare and spotted all around with blackened fire rings.

On the famous High Peaks of the Adirondacks, the trampling of thousands of boots is destroying the moist alpine tundra that makes these peaks so much of another world. In Colorado, the flanks of 14,000-foot peaks are webbed with eroding paths.

Such signs of wear and tear are most frequently seen in wild areas near cities, or in remoter landscapes so celebrated that they draw travelers from far away; yet hardly a wilderness anywhere is free of recreational scars.

This kind of physical damage, disturbing as it is, is in fact just one of three dimensions of the impact problem. It may not even be the most important one.

A more profound type of damage, which may accompany the first, is ecological rather than aesthetic. It is long-term disruption of natural systems. It may be invisible. Unlike the eroded trail, the overfertilized, subtly polluted lake may still look good. Nor is it obvious when native birds and animals disappear from a well-used area, or when a grizzly bear, tempted into aggression by backpackers careless with their food, becomes a menace that must be destroyed.

A third type of damage overlaps both of the others. It is the effect of people on people, what we do to one another's enjoyment of places.

When backpackers are asked what they desire most of all from wild places, the answer comes back: solitude. Not, to be sure, the total solitude of the single traveler; most backpackers move in groups of two, three, or four, and like it that way. "Solitude," for them, means that they should meet not too many other groups, and that they should have no company at camp. Four or five meetings a day, for some people, begins to cheapen the experience. There are exceptions. People who walk such celebrated pathways as the Appalachian Trail fully expect company, and the participants in large groups obviously value it. Yet by and large we backpackers, while we are backpacking, are antisocial, or, anyway, anticrowd.

Physical damage to the land, subtler damage to the ecosystem, the diminution of solitude: these are the three dimensions of "impact." All are controllable. If every hiker entered the wilderness resolved to make no mark on the country, to do no harm to its creatures, and to intrude on the experience of other people as little as possible, the threefold problem would be on its way to control.

Conscience, or Quotas?

Government agencies manage most of our protected wilderness, and it is their charge to keep it authentically wild. In the 1980s, shocked by the explosion of backpacking and its impacts, the authorities moved to regulate use as never before. Visitors to popular regions were required to secure "wilderness permits" for their trips, and in some well-used areas and seasons they were subject to daily quotas.

These rules aroused some resentment. After all, one of the chief pleasures of the land beyond the roadhead has always been the independence of the traveler there, the freedom from formal rules. Because of what might be called consumer resistance, quota systems have not spread beyond a few regions. Lately, the agencies have put their hopes on education, on getting each visitor to understand the need and to cooperate in keeping impact down. It's in the interest of every wilderness user to make this voluntary approach a success.

Each backpacker must make certain that his or her own way in the wilderness is a gentle and a thoughtful way. Each of us must make a game, an ethic, a matter of pride, of walking softly in the wilderness world. Each of us must develop a personal, knowledgeable code, subtler and perhaps stricter than any set of standardized rules can possibly be. We have to grasp the fact that no change we inflict on the wilderness is trivial: each of us now is a thousand.

In addition to watching our own ways, we can serve as eyes and ears for the deskbound people who work, in one way or another, for the wilderness cause. We can call the managers' attention to the gullied trail, the misleading sign, the cattle grazing where they aren't supposed to be. We can praise or criticize, suggest, kibitz, and influence for the better how wilderness areas are cared for.

There is another contribution that some may want to make. We each have the chance to speak out for the protection of wilderness, and of near-natural areas in general. If every second or third backpacker did so, the future of the wilderness would be considerably brighter. For more on this, see Chapter 31.

What we hope to experience, when we go to the wild places, is wideness, freedom, *room*. The more wilderness we manage to preserve, the roomier it will be.

Walking Softly: First Points

The principles of low-impact hiking and camping are not complex. There are, indeed, varying problems from region to region, from landscape to contrasting landscape. There are questions different experts answer differently. There are subtleties to wander in. Yet for conscientious backpackers, certain imperatives are clear.

We don't camp on vegetation. This is a hard one; it seems to run against some instinct out of the Stone Age. The novice hurries to make camp on the grass at the edge of the water or—a second choice—on the grass at the edge of the forest. Most experienced hikers have gotten the word that lush meadows are fragile (also damp, cold, and full of mosquitoes). It's not so widely recognized that some other types of vegetation are even more vulnerable. Short of learning a lot of botany, you can fall back on a simple principle: don't camp on green things at all. You can almost always find bare ground to settle on. Even in steep terrain, three or four people can usually locate a flat, pleasant, unvegetated spot.

We take the landscape as we find it. The perfect camp is found, not made. If you want a developed campsite, choose an established one. If you pitch a tent, find a site with natural drainage. Don't cut limbs, dig ditches, pound nails, pile stones. The game is preservation, not pioneering.

We carry out all our trash, including uneaten food. Hikers are pretty careful these days about outright litter, but some still think it good practice to bury or scatter food they cannot consume. Not anymore. Whatever isn't readily, completely burned must go out the same way it arrived—in your pack.

We carry stoves and are sparing with fire. This is one of the more complicated matters: see Chapter 18. But note that in many wild areas, fires are allowed only at certain sites or in certain zones or in certain seasons. A light, portable stove gives you much more freedom to camp where you like.

We go along with agency advice. All land management agencies have lists of recommended practices and are anxious to promote them. Whether or not you need to secure a "wilderness permit" (see Chapter 11), make it your business to get the official guidelines. Comply with these; ask courteous questions when the rationale is less than clear. The agency workers aren't just hassling you: they are the people who watch the country from year to year; they see it changing. Play along—or go them one better in your efforts to spare the land.

Backpackers are anxious to do the right thing. In fact, as studies show, it would be hard to find another group of people so inclined to be conscientious. They just need to know the score.

This book is one source of sound information. Another is the Leave No Trace (LNT) campaign. LNT, an offshoot of the private National Outdoor Leadership School, also involves researchers and managers from all the land agencies. You'll see LNT guidelines, and often the organization's distinctive spiraling logo, in all kinds of wilderness information. Advice from this source is thorough, subtle, based on current research, and inflected for conditions in each separate region. LNT maintains an excellent Web site (see the Resources section).

Beyond Rules

It's easy to get hung up on rules, but the key is a new attitude. The era of fighting the wilderness, of subduing it, is long over. Rather than wanting to change it, we ask it to change us. We may still test our powers in it, but not at its expense. If we enter these regions with a certain humility, leaving behind our more aggressive tools and approaches, we experience there a joy different, perhaps, from the conquering verve of the pioneer, but every bit as heady.

This pleasure is one we are entitled to. What the wilderness needs from us today is not our absence. It needs our presence, our advocacy, and our knowledgeable care.

2

Breaking In

The way is open.

Wilderness travel is not for the experts only, nor just for the well-to-do, nor just for the young. It is not only for the people who love to travel hard and count the miles behind them. It is not a competition. It is not a proving ground.

The way is open; yet it can be hard to know just where and how to begin. How do you find out where to go? How do you learn just how much you can do? How do you make sure you have the right gear?

The key to starting smoothly is to start rather slowly, accumulating knowledge bit by bit.

The easy first step: *start hiking close to home.* You need not walk far at first, nor seek out rugged terrain. Just start taking short walks, as easy as you like, on any available parkland trail. You will need no special gear at the beginning, and later only a light daypack and a pair of boots or hiking shoes. If you would like to go with a group, get in touch with a local hiking club. These are found all over the country: the Appalachian Mountain Club, the Mazamas, the Mountaineers, the Carolina Mountain Club, and the Colorado Mountain Club are just a few. The Federation of Western Outdoor Clubs and the Appalachian Trail Conference (see addresses in the Resources section) can give you information on their member organizations. The Sierra

Club has chapters all over the United States and Canada; most of these run local outings. Inquire also at gear stores. With an Internet-connected computer, you can check out numerous Web sites containing such information and tap into newsgroups, ongoing electronic mail discussions full of good (and bad) advice. (See the Resources section for a few starting points on the World Wide Web.)

There are advantages to hiking with a group. For one thing, it hooks you into a grapevine, with constant chatter about gear, experiences, places to go, and problems encountered and solved. It also allows you to watch how experienced hikers handle themselves. And though most backpackers eventually choose to travel in family-sized parties, larger groups are good social fun.

Now, as gradually as you like, begin building up your stock of gear and the skills that go with it. A good pair of boots or trail shoes will be about the first item on your list (see Chapter 4). As soon as you have these, set out to break them in. Wear them for short distances, then for long, until boot and foot have adapted each to the other. Try out the combinations of clothes you have in mind to wear on later overnight trips (see Chapter 5). When you buy your first full-sized pack (see Chapter 6), get accustomed to it by carrying it on day hikes with increasingly realistic loads.

Spend time working with a compass and a topographic map on local, familiar ground; learn to translate from map to land and from land to map. This is important: even if you never plan to step off plain trails, you are bound to want to do a little navigation, and you might conceivably find yourself someday in a situation in which map and compass could save your life. You don't need to master the higher-tech tool called a *Global Positioning System receiver*, but it's an entertaining adjunct.

If day hiking is step one, step two (which many skip) is the overnight backpacking trip run by an organization. Most hiking clubs offer these; in national parks and some other wild areas, you will find trips run by concessionaires as well. In such a group you have the support of experienced people, and if you've arrived without some small, crucial item, you can usually count on the party having a spare.

These sizable, organized groups have a very special function. For many hikers they are the indispensable bridge into a wilderness that seems at first a bit strange and incalculable. Organized groups, some studies suggest, have more middle-aged people than you find elsewhere in the wilds and more children; unlike smaller parties, where males still predominate, larger ones are made up about equally of men and women. They also can do a good job of demonstrating low-impact practices.

Step three, for those who wish to make it, is the first independent trip with family or friends. The first time you head out, you may want to choose a well-known corner of the wilderness; inquire around the grapevine, seek information online, or check one of the thousands of trail guides sold in backpacking stores and in general bookstores (see also Chapter 30). With that first trip behind you, you have known real self-sufficiency; you are no longer "breaking in." You are on your way.

Getting or Staying in Shape

Hiking with a pack is not, of itself, very strenuous. Many people—especially young, or older but physically active ones—start backpacking without any kind of preliminary training. But not everyone is young or active. To people who have accustomed themselves to a life of physical leisure beyond the limits of what is healthy, backpacking can seem hard. And when you have limited time, it's a pity to waste any of it on aches, pains, and breathlessness.

There are several ways in which one can be "fit." One kind of fitness matters most on the trail: the kind known variously as stamina, aerobic conditioning, or just plain wind. This is not a matter of bulging muscles but a matter of efficient heart and lungs. When you are fit in this way, your heart will beat relatively slowly, even when you are working hard; you will be taking deep, satisfying breaths; you won't feel pressed for air. You get this stamina from lots of walking, lots of cycling, or from briefer periods of running or swimming. Anything that makes the heart and lungs work will strengthen them. If you don't have such activity in your life already, you need to begin it several months before even a modest backpack trip. Three bouts of such aerobic exercise a week are recommended.

The specific training for backpacking is backpacking; the second-best preparation is hiking without a pack. Make sure that you can hike pretty vigorously without ill effects before adding the stress of an overnight load. As a transitional stage, you can carry an empty or very lightly loaded pack on local hikes and build up to full weight. (Don't overload a little daypack for this purpose, though; a heavy pack without a hip-belt is hard on the shoulders; see Chapter 6.)

The important muscles for backpacking are those in the legs and, to some extent, in the arms, and those that support the back. The habit of picking things up by squatting and then straightening the legs—good because it does not stress the spinal column—also strengthens the quadriceps muscles in the thighs. Bicycling is excellent training. So is climbing stairs.

If you already have a program of weight lifting or other muscle-building exercises, you can easily adjust it to support your backpacking. Focus on routines that work the abdominal muscles and quadriceps, and don't neglect stretches, notably of the hamstring muscles in back of the thighs. Where you're going, endurance matters more than peak strength and infinitely more than how you look in a mirror; do many repetitions with fairly light weights.

There's a less methodical, more typical, and perfectly reasonable approach to muscle conditioning: do it only as your body complains and tells you what your weak points are. You can think of each persistent ache as an order from some part of your anatomy: "Strengthen me." The older you are when you hit the trails, the more such messages you will receive. To interpret them correctly, you may need the advice of a physical therapist, orthopedist, or family doctor with some understanding of sports medicine. If the first advice you get is to quit an activity you love, seek a second opinion.

Sore knees are a frequent problem with beginners of any age; knee braces, available in stores that sell athletic equipment, can be a temporary help. If the problem is at all persistent, you will need to work all the more diligently on the muscles that stabilize the knee.

It goes without saying that not *all* bodily complaints can be trained away. In particular, you need a doctor's advice if you suspect a heart problem or any other condition that might truly limit your backpacking; older people who have been sedentary should start very slowly and keep the doctor posted on what they're undertaking. But the chances are good that your physician will enthusiastically approve. The backpacker's kind of fitness is the kind that doctors most welcome in their patients, and nobody who is basically healthy needs to deny himself or herself the pleasure of the trails.

Gearing Up

*Naturally, we also carried all the standard mountain
climbing equipment: cleated shoes and nails of all
kinds, ropes, screw rings, hammers, snap hooks, ice
axes, crampons, snowshoes, skis and all accessories,
as well as instruments for observation like compasses,
clinometers, altimeters, barometers, thermometers,
range-finders, alidades, and cameras. And arms: rifles,
carbines, revolvers, short sabers, dynamite—in other
words, enough to face any foreseeable obstacle.*

—René Daumal, *Mount Analogue*

3

The Gear You Need & How to Choose It

No matter how gradually you get into backpacking, you will soon have to start acquiring gear—*objects*, and quite a few of them. Even the lightest pack will contain seventy or eighty separate items. The novice, looking at a typical pack list like the one on the next few pages, sees a sizable job ahead.

What do you need in order to travel safely and in comfort?

You need *boots or shoes* sturdy enough, and heavy enough, to support and protect your feet—and not one bit heavier than that.

You need *clothing:* garments to protect you from sun, from wind and cold, from rain and snow, from scratching brush and irritant plants, from mosquitoes and stinging flies.

You need *sleeping gear* for warmth at night and *shelter* to keep you dry.

You need *water and food*, and the *tools of eating and cooking.*

You need a *knife, a flashlight or headlamp*, plenty of *matches*, and a good length of *cord*.

You need *navigation tools*—at a minimum, maps and a compass.

You need *emergency, medical, and repair gear* for the minor problems you will certainly meet and the major ones you have to be prepared for, just in case.

You need *personal items*–toilet paper and a tooth-brush for starters.

And you need *containers*–mostly bags, big and small, and a pack to put it all in.

The Buying Process

In buying gear, there's a Rule Number One: *Make haste slowly.* There is no reason to purchase everything at once, and unless you are unusually sure of yourself you should not try to. Borrow and rent equipment whenever your can. Some tricky items like stoves and tents are normally shared, so you may be able to rely at first on better-equipped companions; or you can begin with organization-sponsored trips where these items are part of the package. The longer you delay, the better chance you have to find out what truly suits you.

The gear buyer's Rule Number Two: *Go shopping with particular trips in mind.* Where do you plan to go in the near future? In what climates? At what elevations? For what length of time? Always on trail, or sometimes off? If you are clear about your ambitions, salespeople can tell you clearly what your likeliest choices are.

By far the best source of gear is an outdoor specialty shop–or several. Department stores, surplus outlets, and general sporting goods stores also carry wilderness gear, some of it adequate; what you almost never find there is information you can trust.

To find appropriate stores, take a look in phone company yellow pages or similar directories: first under "backpacking and mountaineering," then under such headings as "camping equipment," "ski equipment," and "sporting goods." You probably have several competing specialty shops in your area, carrying similar but not identical gear. Visit as many as you can find time for. The salespeople in most of the specialty shops are knowledgeable, easy to talk to, and generous with their time. Many stores also rent such major items as packs, tents, sleeping bags, and stoves. Renting is not a waste of money–it's a valuable series of lessons in the merits of different brands and designs.

An Economical Summer Pack List

Item	Weight in Pack (Oz.)	Cost
Clothing, Worn		
nylon pants with web belt		$100
briefs		$16
synthetic T-shirt		$28
nylon overshirt		$78
sunhat		$21
sunglasses		$39
socks		$17
liner socks		$5
hiking boots		$210
watch		
Clothing, Packed		
spare socks, one set	4	$22
hiking shorts	10	$35
rain pants, urethane-coated	8	$35
spare sunglasses	1	$15
balaclava	2	$10
wind-resistant polyester pile jacket	18	$150
waterproof-breathable wind/ rain parka	24	$250
Sleeping Gear		
mummy sleeping bag in stuff sack	43	$220
closed-cell foam pad	9	$12
Kitchen and Basic Tools (Individual)		
headlamp with batteries	5	$33
spare batteries, bulb	2	$3
matches	1	trace
two cups	6	$8
two spoons	1	$1
pocketknife	2	$20
bandannas, two	1	$5
50-ft. nylon cord	4	$4
iodine for water treatment	2	$5
Office		
notebook, pencils	2	$1
topo map	4	$8
compass	1	$10

Item	Weight in Pack (Oz.)	Cost
Personal		
tooth-care items	1	
toilet paper	1	
lip balm	1	$2
sunscreen	2	$5
other toiletries	1	
Miscellaneous		
first-aid kit	14	$30
sew and repair kit	8	$37
whistle, mirror	1	$8
toilet trowel	2	$2
antibacterial gel	4	$4
Haulage		
pack	64	$230
pack cover	9	$24
stuff sacks	12	$40
plastic bags and closures	1	$5
water bladder (2 liter)	1	$7
Shelter (Group)		
hoop tent	77	$170
matching ground sheet	11	$37
kitchen (group)		
white-gas stove (burner, pump)	9	$90
fuel bottle	5	$11
windscreen	2	$10
two pots, gripper	18	$35
scouring pad	1	$1
Consumables (Group)		
food (two people, four days)	192	$80
reserve food	16	$10
fuel (1 pint)	12	$2
reserve fuel	6	$1
water (in packs at one time)	67	$0
Total Pack and Contents		
Personal gear	272	$1,755
One-half of group gear	61.5	$177
One-half of consumables	146.5	$47
Total Weight (in ounces)	**480 oz.**	
Total Weight (in pounds) **and Cost**	**30 lb.**	**$1,979**

You can also study and order gear via printed or online catalogs. All manufacturers and large retailers have Web sites; gear advertisements include Internet addresses. The "reader service cards" bound into outdoor magazines make it easy to order numerous sample catalogs at one blow. Some good, specialized gear is sold primarily by mail. See the Resources section for a partial list of makers.

However you approach the gear-buying business, you face a long series of choices. For every type of equipment there are not just competing brands but competing, fundamentally different, designs. The days are gone when a mere backpacker can keep track of the changing technological scene, and the glossy ads of the makers are designed to sell, not to inform. This confusion makes the advice of the salespeople, opinionated though it naturally is, more important than ever.

For further help, you can turn to equipment-rating articles published in such magazines as *Backpacker*, *Outside*, and occasionally *Consumer Reports*. Read the comparative studies and ignore the short reviews on single, often newly introduced items; these tend to be uncritical endorsements. It's worth noting that a negative comment on a product often causes the manufacturer to alter the design—thus all such studies date quickly. Nonetheless, reviews can help the buyer navigate the equipment labyrinth.

In addition to its reviews, *Backpacker* devotes one issue a year to a "gear guide" that simply lists the specifications of boots, packs, sleeping bags, and so on—*as supplied by the manufacturers*. These useful compilations should not be confused with critical assessments. Even the simplest data may be measured, by different makers, in different, incompatible, and sometimes downright nonsensical ways; the makers' estimates of the uses to which their gear is suited may be wildly self-serving. The industry is working to rationalize assessments in a few areas—sleeping-bag makers, for example, are trying to agree on a standard method for measuring the insulation value of their bags. But there's a long, long way to go.

Much comparative product information is available online. A *Backpacker* Web site at www.gearfinder.com permits you to search out gear with particular characteristics—for instance, packs of a certain price, weight, and capacity.

Whether you are buying in person or via remote control, you may not get every item right the first time. Clothing and boots, notably, may turn out not to fit as well as first thought. Most major items can be returned if an indoor test convinces you that you need to try again. Some stores take back even well-used gear, no questions asked.

Gear makers at last seem to be catching up to the fact that women, the fastest-growing part of the backpacking population, are different from men. Not only clothing but also packs and sleeping bags now come in models proportioned and otherwise designed for the female body, rather than for smallish males. This development is long overdue.

Beware of Hype

Backpacking gear by reputable makers is good, and getting better. It is becoming lighter, tougher, and more convenient, sometimes all at once. (One thing it is not becoming: cheaper.) Innovations are announced almost month by month. Some fade away; others survive and become, by imitation, standard features of design. The evolution in the last twenty years, even in the last five, has been remarkable.

The competition that has brought these benefits, however, has a predictable by-product: hype. Immerse yourself in the gear pages of an outdoor magazine, and you will soon feel under siege. Every choice of gear is advertised as a life-or-death decision. There can be only one right answer, and Our Company has it! Enjoyment, comfort, survival itself are at stake. Top climbers, thousand-mile walkers, Antarctic trekkers are called upon as witnesses.

Writers and reviewers, who might be asked to give us information to weigh for own purposes, often seem part of the sales team. Their function seems to be to make us afraid of being out of step. As I write this, for instance, the pressure is on to go "ultralight," reducing pack weights to previously unheard-of levels. This is one excellent backpacking style among many, and one I tend toward myself; but I don't like to be bullied about it.

Similar angst is generated by the makers of "hydration systems," water containers that ride in your pack and sprout accessible hoses so that you can sip all day. "Hydrate or Die," the slogan goes. But lately we learn that water needs have been overestimated for years. Indeed, a not infrequent medical complaint on today's trails is *hyponatremia*, a condition that results from too much water intake combined with a shortage of salt. Of course a hiker must drink a lot, but hydration systems are a useful option to consider, no more.

Then there's the hype surrounding GPS, the satellite-based Global Positioning System. The GPS navigation units that many hikers now carry are wonderful tools, especially for special, rarely encountered conditions of low visibility and maximum possible confusion. But the industry wants us to feel that we can't walk around the block without a GPS. This is nuts.

So let's take a deep breath and remember:

The backpacker does the work, not the backpack. The brain does the thinking, not the GPS.

People outfitted with the gear of 1970 moved in the wilderness just about as well as we do.

Gear is only a set of tools: a means to a pleasant end.

And backpacking is actually pretty simple, most of the time.

How Much Will It Cost?

Let's start with the first weekend trip. How little can you spend and still be safe and comfortable your first time camping in the wild?

This depends, of course, on where you are going, how much useful junk you have around, and how many people you have with you to share common expenses. By renting some of the major pieces of gear and buying the cheapest adequate versions of other items, you can probably reduce the tab to about $500 the first time you go out. Lower than that it is difficult to go.

What about the total tab for building your permanent stock of good equipment? It can no longer be said that backpacking gear is cheap. A pretty complete set of well-made summer gear will set you back at least $2,000, in 2004 prices, before you are through. About one-third of the price tag is likely to be for three major items—your *boots* (Chapter 4), your *pack* (Chapter 6), and your *sleeping bag* (Chapter 7). A *tent*, which not everyone needs, is another major purchase (Chapter 8). *Clothing* (Chapter 5) can also be pricey. *Kitchen gear* (Chapter 9) is relatively cheap.

There are ways of beating down the entry cost. By shrewd shopping, you can get perfectly good gear at a discount. What you lose out on is the advice that goes with "normal" pricing; you may also be forgoing standard guarantees, so be careful here.

- You may be able to find seconds—items that come from the factory with harmless imperfections and are sold at reduced prices, in the parent stores, at factory outlets, or in special "seconds shops."

- You can pick up excellent bargains at end-of-season sales that gear stores hold.

- You can draw on large mail-order houses, which are likely to be cheaper than your local mountain store. Three to check out are Campmor, Recreational Equipment, Inc. (REI), and Sierra Trading Post.

- You can buy used gear. A few stores handle second-hand items; many have bulletin boards where sellers advertise. Sound items may turn up at flea markets and in thrift stores. And shops that rent gear eventually sell those items at cut prices. As for Ebay and similar online auction services, they are risky sources for serviceable gear.

Whether you buy high or low, remember the principle of buying for the trip. There's no point spending money on gear that's intended for a different use than you plan to give it sometime soon. The sleeping bag you could use in the winter in the Never Summer Range of Colorado is only hot and clammy in a normal wilderness July. And a Himalayan-scale backpack is a poor container for a weekend's worth of gear.

Please bear in mind that all prices given in these pages are both approximate and liable to change. They reflect the situation in 2004 and are best used for comparative purposes.

The shopping never stops entirely. There are always items to add or replace. But once you are past the major purchases, backpacking becomes a delightfully cheap hobby. Trip by trip, the cost of gear, food, and fuel for the trail is typically overshadowed by the cost of transportation to the trailhead.

Minimum Cost of First Three-Day Trip

For party of two. Reflects search for bargains and near-maximum use of rentals.

Individual

rent pack	$52
rent sleeping bag	$45
rent air mattress	$36
buy ground cloth	$12
buy cheapest good boots	$100
buy hiking socks, 2 sets (outer + liners)	$44
buy cheapest rain gear, hat	$80
buy other items	$40
buy food (plus any restaurant meals)	$25
Individual total	**$434**

Group

rent tent	$52
buy cartridge stove	$30
buy fuel	$8
bring pans (found at home)	$0
Group total (plus shared auto costs)	**$90**

How Much Will It Weigh?

Let's say you have a pack load without too many extras: no paperback novels, no ropes, no cameras, no games. Assume your load is for a lightweight summer trip. Forget for a moment about water, food, and fuel. And forget about shelter, stove, pots—the gear you will be sharing among companions.

Thus limited, the *basic dry weight* of your pack—including clothing, bedding, first-aid kit, various oddments, and the pack itself—should not be more than 18 pounds. This does not count your boots or the clothes you start out wearing, but it does include clothes for rain and moderate cold, which will, with luck, be stowed away much of the time.

To get a notion of what the rest of the pack load will weigh, you can apply these rules of thumb:

- For food, figure on 2 pounds per person per day, tops. With expensive freeze-dried foods and an average appetite, you may find yourself happy with less. Women may eat somewhat less; teenagers may eat more.

- Add 1 pound for each pint of water you expect to be carrying during a typical hiking day. (You always want to have some water on board.)

- Add 6 ounces for each cup of white gas or kerosene you will start out with. An economical allowance is one-quarter cup, or 1.5 ounces, per person per day. It's a little harder to estimate fuel needs for the popular "cartridge" stoves burning gaseous fuel, because you can't carry a fraction of a cartridge, but approximately the same ratio applies; see Chapter 12.

- If your group will use a tent or tents, figure about 3 pounds per person. But allow just 1 pound per person if shelter is a tarp or tarps.

- Finally, a group of two or three hikers will carry 2 to 3 pounds of cookware and stove.

So, say two of you were heading out for five summer days, in, say, the Adirondacks; if you carried, as you should for that trip, both stove and tent; and if each of you had a pint of water in a canteen, your theoretical share of the load would be something like this:

17.5 pounds of personal gear

10 pounds of food

1 pound of water

1.5 pounds of cooking gear

0.5 pound of fuel (1.5 ounces per person per day)

3 pounds of shelter

for a theoretical total of 33.5 pounds.

This, like the detailed list a few pages back, is merely an illustration. But it makes the point—on a trip of less than a week in a place and month not extraordinarily hostile, you won't need a load of more than 35 pounds.

Is this a lot or a little? It depends.

An old rule of thumb says you can carry a third of your body weight. And indeed, if you have to, you can; climbers and winter campers may wind up toting that or more. But for most people on today's trails, such heroics are quite unnecessary. With light, modern gear, it should be possible to limit your pack to a fifth of your own weight on trips of a few days.

So a 120-pound woman might have a comfortable limit of 24 pounds; a 190-pound man, by this formula, would be limited to 38. (If you are seriously overweight, however, go by your target body weight, not your actual one.) With loads of this order, experienced hikers may almost forget that they have packs on their backs. If you hike with companions, as most people do, you can split up food, fuel, and community gear according to body weight. Lighter people often insist on toting an arithmetically equal share that puts them at a disadvantage; if this is you, reconsider. As to your purely personal gear, you're stuck with the weight of your choices. If you travel alone, your pack will include all "community" gear and will ride a little heavier.

The one-fifth guideline is only a starting point. It is possible to cut down this standard load, easier still to build it up. Older backpackers, in particular, may find themselves torn between comfort in camp, which implies more equipment, and comfort on the trail, which depends on toting less.

After years of stealthy pack bloat, the pendulum is now swinging the other way. Hikers and gearmakers are now challenging old habits in the pursuit of the lightest possible load. A whole new discipline of ultra-light backpacking, or "fastpacking," has developed as an alternative to, and influence on, the traditional sport. For more on this option, see Chapter 22.

The Wilderness Regions and the Gear You Take

From region to region and season to season, your needs will change. One list of gear won't serve for all landscapes, all weathers, or all the different demands of the American wilderness.

Some places are pretty dry in summer; some are very wet. In the dry-summer mountains of the West, shelter and rain gear can be simple and light; the occasional thunderstorm may be more an entertainment than a piece of serious weather. Quite a few people here rely on tarps and bivouac sacks for staying dry in the normal hiking season. But in the Smokies or the northern Cascades, summer rain is serious, and tents are the norm. Tents are also strongly recommended in grizzly bear country; see Chapter 29.

Humidity counts, too. If the air is dry between rains, classic down sleeping bags can be efficient. But in the Catskills or the Blue Ridge, even a cool, clear night may be damp enough to saturate your bag; in such places, sleeping bags are usually synthetic filled or equipped with water-resistant shells.

In the deserts, and on some ridge routes in less-arid ranges, water is a problem in another way. Springs and convenient streams may be far apart and unreliable. In the Sonoran Desert of Arizona, for instance, two-thirds of your pack load might be water; see Chapter 23.

In areas where winter brings snow, a whole new kind of wilderness, a white and challenging wilderness, appears with the first cold storm. Travelers in that world need considerably more gear; see Chapter 24.

Hassles with Gear

Backpacking equipment is certainly better made, on the average, than other consumer goods today. It is not perfect, however, or indestructible: sleeping bags and tents get torn; stoves balk and have to be tinkered with; waterproofing wears off and must be reapplied; zippers fail; plastic buckles age and crack; stitching frays; flashlights let you down. While some items and some brands hold up better than others, none are trouble-free or immune to wear.

When you shop for gear, ask questions about durability and the details of construction. Look also for generous warranty policies. Some stores will take back and replace an item that has failed even after years of use.

When gear goes bad on the trail, minor repairs, of a rough-and-ready sort, can often be made on the spot. More substantial work can be done at home, with a certain amount of instruction and patience. A superb guide for the fix-it-yourselfer is Annie Getchell's *The Essential Outdoor Gear Manual*.

For problems that surpass the home workshop, you can turn to the general repair services at many gear stores, not restricted to items sold or under warranty there. Shoemakers are also very helpful: they will sew on leather patches, replace grommets, and handle many other problems with leather and heavy fabric.

Gear and Low Impact

The modern need to go gently in the wilderness has brought about changes in the gear we take. Because it isn't permissible to build shelters or mattresses of boughs any more, we carry tents and sleeping pads. Because of the damage fires can do in some environments, we carry stoves. Because our food can attract bears and turn them into pests that must be killed, we tote the means of keeping it out of their reach.

One matter the gear buyer has to think about is *color*. Wilderness gear is sold today in every shade, aggressive or subdued: various blues, reds and yellows and explosive iridescent oranges, leaf greens and olive greens, rust browns and earth browns, and compound colors in between. Color is part of the pleasure of handling good gear and is one of the things that gives a stack of fine equipment that curiously valuable look.

But there's more than personal taste to consider here. Simply put, do you want to stand out or blend in? Unless you're hiking in the eastern woodlands in October, a bright-colored tent, pack, or parka makes you highly visible. Indeed, it can make you *too* visible: the more fellow hikers you see and are seen by, the more crowded the wilderness landscape must appear. This is a doubly true above timberline. A dozen hikers in an alpine basin, carrying gear in muted colors, may give you no hint of their presence—three outfitted in screaming shades can make the same place seem busy. To walk softly, then, you choose the softer tones.

There is a counterargument, of course, and that is safety. Maybe you do a lot of traveling in popular hunting areas at just the wrong time of year and *want* to be seen. Or maybe you're thinking about a time when you could conceivably need to be rescued. Standing out as it does, bright gear can draw searchers to a lost or injured hiker.

If you're very concerned about the rescue angle, I would suggest this compromise: pick subtle hues for major items of gear, but carry something brightly colored in your pack—rain gear, perhaps, or a ground cloth. This you can spread on the ground, or drape on your pack, or wear on your back, if you badly need to be seen.

Like all consumer products, backpacking gear has a history before it ever reaches you. Its manufacture represents a greater or lesser amount of pollution and resource cost. The plastics used in modern clothing fibers and some pack frames, for instance, can be made of "virgin" petrochemicals—or recycled from soft-drink bottles. Companies that do the latter, a lengthening list, rightly pride themselves on it. There is increasing use of recycled materials in gear of all sorts, and the customer should notice and reward it.

There may be a social cost, too, to the manufacture of gear. More backpacking products than not, especially items of clothing, are now assembled in what used to be called the Third World. Tags on gear usually tell you where. You may want to apply your own "screen" here and avoid buying goods made under regimes, or working conditions, of which you particularly disapprove.

4

Boots

About the first thing you'll have to acquire for back-packing is a good pair of boots. At $125 to $250, this is big-ticket-item number one.

The choice is wide. About forty manufacturers make boots and specialized shoes, and every one of them claims special virtue for its product. You can get lost in the clamor of competing features and learned arguments for this or that cunning design.

And yet there are just two things you require from a backpacking boot or shoe. The first is comfort: the footgear should be as light, well fitting, and easy on the flesh as it possibly can be. The second is protection: it must shield the foot from incessant jarring, bruising stones, encroaching water, and the coldness of the ground, and it must support the ankle against twisting. Comfort and protection compete, and every boot or shoe is a compromise between them.

The trick is to choose footgear that is heavy enough for the kind of hiking you will do—and not one ounce heavier. Only experience will tell you just where that balance point lies for you. For years, people wandered around the wilderness wearing vastly excessive amounts of leather, simply because it was the expected thing. Then the pendulum swung toward very light footwear. What you actually need will depend on the type of hiking you do, the kind of loads you carry, and your personal steadiness of ankle.

Kinds of Boots

The lightest boots that backpackers use weigh as little as 2 pounds for a pair in a man's size 9, which is still the conventional basis of comparison (see "Shopping and Fitting," below). The heaviest pairs approach 5 pounds. The spectrum can be divided into three parts.

General trail boots are relatively light and flexible. Their uppers often incorporate materials other than leather: nylon cloth, nylon mesh, and even canvas. They are fine for travel on smooth trails when the weather is not too cold, and some backpackers find them adequate for rougher terrain as well. Typical weights, for a middle-range size, lie between 2 and 3 pounds per pair. Prices presently run from about just under $100 to just under $200.

All-terrain boots are heavier and stiffer. Although constructions vary, you'll see lots of leather. These are suitable for heavier loads on the trail, for cross-country travel, and for cold weather. But there's a penalty in off-the-shelf comfort and in weight: these boots run 3 to 4 pounds per pair. Prices run from $135 to about double that. Lighter is not necessarily cheaper: the harder the maker has worked to create a boot both light and strong, the higher the cost is liable to be.

All-terrain boots overlap with another category, *light mountaineering boots.* These are defined by excellent waterproofing, a rather rigid shell, and a groove where the sole meets the upper, which permits the wearing of crampons. Most are made of leather, some of tough plastic. You can also recognize them by their cost, up to $500. Boots heavier than 5 pounds per pair—no longer "light" by any standard—can safely be left out of your backpacking calculations.

Let's mention here some other types of footwear you may see in stores but can rule out for basic travel. *Ultralight shoes* are of various types called cross-trainers, trail runners, or approach shoes; they are meant for

Lightweight and low-cut boots, like the one at left, are best suited for trail use with light loads. Higher, thicker boots give more protection and support at a cost in weight and break-in time.

hiking, scrambling, and trail jogging under very light loads. They don't offer much ankle support and usually lack the protective flaps or bellows that full boots have at the tongue. *Rock-climbing boots* are light, tight, fragile, and completely unsuited for plain walking. *Shoepacs* are high boots with waterproof rubber around the foot and leather rising up the ankle; they are used in very soggy places and for snowshoeing, especially in the East. *Backcountry ski boots* are built to attach to skis with one of several types of specialized bindings. For more about winter footwear, see Chapter 24.

So: how heavy should your first pair of general-purpose boots be? The decision depends partly on your experience and partly on your ambitions.

Day hiking should already have given you some ideas. If you've hiked in sneakers, running shoes, or other light footgear, what do your feet tell you? Do you find that you keep your balance easily, or do your ankles tend to turn under you? At the end of the day, are your soles bruised and sore from the hardness of the ground? If you've felt comfortable in soft shoes, you can reasonably consider boots toward the lighter end of the range. If you have felt tentative and vulnerable in light shoes, then a somewhat heavier boot, probably all leather, makes sense for you.

As for ambitions, do you expect, for the time being, to hike well-maintained trails in warm climates? Or do you plan to branch out soon into cross-country travel and cold-weather hiking? Lighter boots fit the first case, somewhat heavier boots the second.

Still undecided? Then start with a boot in the middle of the spectrum, something under three pounds per pair for a woman and around three pounds for a man. Choose one of the lighter and more pliable all-leather boots. Or go with one of the stouter models that mix leather and fabric, with a good stiff heel area, a good stiff toe, and a high top that supports the ankle well. Such boots can hardly fail to be useful in quite a range of conditions, and you won't have to take out a loan to buy them. After a season or two, you will have a better idea of what your real requirements are. Then you can replace your starter pair or add other, more specialized gear to your collection. Many backpackers wind up owning (and using) a whole row of diverse clodhoppers.

Anatomy and Features

Boot soles today may look like those of traditional running shoes, like those of traditional hiking boots, or like something in between. Always, there is the tread layer, or *outsole,* next to the ground; one or several *midsoles*; and the *insole* next to the foot. Hard-rubber outsoles have various patterns but are more or less toothy; some are made of "sticky" rubber for good gripping on (dry) rock. Midsoles may be of various materials, including nylon, rubber, and urethane. Ethyl vinyl acetate (EVA), found in some cheaper boots, is not very durable. The midsole layer may contain a *shank*—a flexible band of metal, plastic, or carbon fiber—to add support and springiness. Some midsoles incorporate air-filled pockets.

All-leather boots, durable and supportive, are still the choice of many hikers. The typical leather boot has much the same structure today as it did a generation ago.

The *insole* is what your foot actually rests on. In boots of the most traditional design, it may be just a piece of thin, smooth leather; more often it is a "footbed," a curvy piece that can be removed for washing or replaced with a thinner or thicker version to refine the fit (see "Shopping and Fitting," below).

The margin where the sole joins the *upper* is called the *welt*. Uppers are fastened to soles with glue or, in more traditional boots, with stitching. In glued or "cemented" boots, the joint between sole and upper will be protected by a waterproof rubber *rand* that overlaps the latter. Some boots have soles that climb well up the side of the boot, joining the almost vestigial upper several inches from the ground.

Uppers, as noted, are made of various materials. You will see boots built of nylon packcloth or the textured nylon called Cordura; of cloth with leather reinforcements; of leather with cloth "cutouts"; and of leather throughout.

The advantages of the nonleather materials are clear. Lightness. Lower price. Coolness on the feet. Instant comfort (if the fit is good). There is a cost, however, in support, and also in durability: an active cross-country hiker can demolish a pair of ultralight boots in a season. I would rule out as a primary pair any boot that does not contain considerable leather.

Modern light boots blend elements of hiking boot and running shoe design. Compared to traditional leather boots, such footwear is cheaper, more comfortable, somewhat less supportive, and much less durable.

On a rack of leather boots, one cosmetic difference will jump out at you. Some models have a rough, feltlike surface; others are smooth and shiny. This really doesn't matter, and all finishes give way to the same battered look after a few journeys. More important is the distinction between top-grain, split-grain, and full-grain leather. Full-grain leather, the heaviest and toughest, uses the full thickness of the tanned cowhide, including the rugged, pliable, naturally oily, water-repellent surface that was next to the hair. ("Nubuk" is full-grain leather with a suedelike finish.) Commonly, however, the hide is split into several layers. Off the outer surface comes top-grain leather, including the weather-resistant epidermis. The lower regions of the hide yield split-grain leather, more permeable and not so strong. Fine for trail hiking, such boots do stretch and get a lumpy look, and they wear out more quickly than boots of top-grain or full-grain leather. Not surprisingly, they are also cheaper.

There are other differences among leathers. Some pieces are tougher and cost more. Large chunks also cost more. Some boots are made from several pieces of hide and have many seams; some are made of few pieces or even just one, with a single seam down the heel. These one-piece boots are the most expensive, the most durable, the easiest to waterproof, and the hardest to break in.

Many boots of all weights now incorporate linings or layers of special materials designed to block the penetration of water from the world to the foot while still permitting the evaporation of moisture from the foot to the world. See Chapter 5 for generalities about these waterproof breathable fabrics. Gore-Tex and Sympatex are two brands used in boots. They work as advertised, and boots so equipped are nice to have in mud, shallow snow, and sodden grass.

Whatever material makes up the body of the upper, both heel and toe must be quite rigid for protection and proper fit. Some models have rubber toecaps. Some have a molded plastic heel cup that is actually integral with the sole.

The collarlike opening around the ankle should be stiff enough to provide support when a foot threatens to turn but soft enough in back to avoid bruising the Achilles tendon. Some boots have plastic *scree collars* here, designed to keep the tiny rocks of "scree" from bouncing into your boots, but perhaps more functional as tendon padding. Because women's calf muscles are thicker at boot-top height than men's, boots built for women have relatively wider and softer ankle openings, perhaps with a notch in back. A nice feature on heavier boots is a well-anchored finger loop at the back of the heel opening: hauling on this makes it easier to insert the foot in the morning.

Boot interiors are lined with thin leather or with cloth, sometimes treated with antimicrobial agents to discourage mildew and the buildup of odor. Between the lining and the main wall of the boot, most makers put at least some areas of protective closed-cell foam. Such padding makes boots comfortable sooner.

Lacing hardware varies but should be of metal, perhaps plastic-coated, but not plastic throughout. There may be grommeted *eyelets*, *D-rings* that rivet onto the upper, or *hooks*. Most often there is some combination of these. Eyelets break less frequently than the other fittings but are a little harder to lace, especially with cold hands. Rings and hooks tend to break off, but any cobbler can repair them for a small charge. Sometimes, midway in a row of hooks, one pair of normal hooks is replaced by a pair of "lace hooks" or similar friction devices that grip the laces and prevent them from sliding through. Using these, you can tighten the laces firmly on one side of the clinch while leaving them loose on the other. You can get much the same effect, however, by tricks of lacing (see Chapter 15). The laces themselves should be nylon.

Beneath the lacing is the *tongue* (sometimes two tongues). It is more or less padded, to protect the top of the foot from bruising under the pressure of the laces. On either side of the tongue are spaces that, in a backpacking boot, must be closed off in one way or another. Some boots have overlapping flaps; others use fanlike, flexible bellows or gussets. Light mountaineering boots may have a set of inner laces on the tongue itself.

Socks

Before choosing boots, you need to know what else you'll be wearing on your feet. Most people these days wear a single thick sock (per foot!). Socks can be synthetic, wool, or a mix, but not cotton. Avoid coarse weaves and bulky seams, especially at the toe. Socks made especially for hiking (around $17 and worth the price) may offer extra cushioning at various points: underfoot, around the toes, behind the heel, and along the upper surface, where the laces press. Some people like to add a very thin, smooth liner sock of polypropylene next to the skin. Me, for instance. I also find that I get fewer blisters in all-synthetic hiking socks than in the popular wool blends.

Shopping and Fitting

Except as a last resort, buy your boots in person in the specialty outlets. With the proliferation of gear stores, mail purchase is no longer really worth discussing. What can hardly be discussed enough is the challenge of getting the right fit. Make up your mind to insist on something near perfection.

Before you head for the stores, trim your nails as they will be for the trail: short, but not so short that they fail to protrude past the surrounding skin. Take along the combination of socks you plan to wear when you hike (see "Socks," above). Veterans recommend shopping for boots in the afternoon or later, when your feet will have expanded a bit with the day's activity.

Before you enter a store, you should already have an idea of the type and weight of boot you want, or at least of the conditions you want to hike in soon. Will you be going on-trail or off? Under what loads? In what likely weather? Tell the salesperson these things, along with your street shoe size, and let him or her take it from there. You'll soon be standing on a "Brannock device," the familiar tool that measures total foot length, heel-to-ball length, foot width, and height of arch. Then come the boxes of boots.

Slide on your first candidate pair. They will feel a bit roomier than your street shoes, especially in front. They should be at least ½ inch longer than your stockinged foot, but less than 1 inch. Before you lace up, push your foot forward inside the boot as far as it will go. You should just barely be able to fit an index finger all the way down between your heel and the back of the boot. (Two fingers is too much room.)

Now kick back in the boot to settle the heel into the socket and lace the boots tightly. In tightening, it is natural to pull the lace ends across the boot, so that the topmost hook or eyelet pair is tugged toward the mid-line. This is hard on the fittings, however. Instead, pull the laces outward, on each side, away from the boot, until you've pulled out all possible slack; only then cross the laces to begin your actual knot. If the laces draw the sides of the closure so close together that they almost touch, the boot is too loose.

Have the salesperson hold your heel to the floor and do your best to lift the back of your foot. The heel should rise no more than ¼ inch inside the boot. (That's not much. It should feel very firm.)

To check the fit of the toe, hook your heel over a rock, a wooden shoe rack, or a street curb so that your toe points sharply downhill. Kick forward inside the boot. If your toes feel stubbed against the tip, the boot is too short. (You can also kick against something hard, if the store will let you.) You must be able to wriggle your toes freely when you wear the boot, or you risk cutting off blood circulation. On the other hand, if a boot is too long, the normal flexing of the front end will occur too far forward, over your toes rather than over the ball of your foot, and give you blisters.

Besides length, the overall volume of the boot is important; your foot should feel snugly contained but not compressed or pinched. In traditional sizing, width is the indicator of volume; some makers have substituted explicit volume sizing. To make sure the boot is not too sloppy, have someone hold it to the floor while you try to rotate your foot inside it. Neither the ball nor the heel of your foot should shift appreciably sideways. In some lines of boots, volume is adjusted, within an overall size, by choosing among thicker and thinner footbeds.

You may hear it said that it is better to have a boot too large than too small, on the theory that you can always add socks or correct the fit with padding. Better not count too much on this. Although a slightly too narrow leather boot will adapt to your foot, a boot that is sloppy in the store will only get sloppier. And a loose fit is almost bound to give you blisters.

If the boots or shoes seem to pass these various initial tests, make sure you have them laced up firmly and spend ten or fifteen minutes "hiking" around the store. Speed up, slow down, go up and down stairs, swivel, do knee bends. Watch again for a feeling of tightness in the toes or of sloppiness in the heels. As foot and boot warm up, the fit may change.

Do you like the stiffness or flexibility of the sole? Boots vary. Generally, heavier people need soles that are stiffer to start with; lighter people will be more comfortable on somewhat softer soles.

Undecided between two sizes or models? Try wearing one of each. In a few minutes, one foot should start feeling markedly better than the other. Double-check by repeating the experiment with the two types on opposite feet. If you have a third model on your final list, compare it with the survivor of your first elimination round, using the same method. The process takes patience, but the time spent is worthwhile. No competent salesperson will try to hurry your decision.

If you're almost but not quite sure of the fit, you can go ahead and make the purchase—but confirm that it's okay to return the boots after further indoor trial. At home, live in them a little. Walk around indoors, perhaps up and down stairs in a city building, until you have a clear opinion. Then, if necessary, take the boots back and try again.

If you find nothing that fits you properly in the stock of a particular store, go to another. Keep looking. Different brands of boots can be quite different in configuration. Boots are built on standardized patterns called *lasts*. A last is nothing but a model foot—a hypothetical, average foot. Somewhere out there, somebody is probably building boots on a last that matches your foot shape reasonably well.

Women's feet are different from men's. They tend to be proportionately narrower at the heel, lower in overall volume, and less well padded with flesh. Arches tend to be higher and toes longer. There is now, finally, a good range of boots designed to respect this anatomy. If female, be sure to try at least one. If male and hard to fit, consider that "women's" boots may provide the variation you are looking for. The only thing that matters is what fits *you*.

If you don't find the right fit in reasonably local stores, you may have to turn, after all, to mail order. The Resources section is a starting point. Look up sources online or phone for catalogs. You may be asked to send an outline of both your feet (or the larger, if there is an obvious difference). Be sure that you can return boots tried out indoors.

Hikers with fitting problems often discard the footbeds that come with their new boots and replace them with new ones purchased separately and trimmed to match their feet. So, increasingly, do hikers without fitting complaints. The separate footbeds, podiatrists say, are simply better. They have deep, rounded heel cups, arch supports, raised rims to keep the foot centered, and layers of cork and plastic for shock absorption and support. Older hikers, who have lost some spring in their arches and some natural padding under their soles, may especially benefit.

For extremely nonstandard feet, a podiatrist can prepare customized footbeds called *orthotics*, at a price that may rival that of the boots themselves.

Breaking In

Whatever sort of boots you buy, you want to be well acquainted with them before the Big Trip starts. With boots that are largely of fabric, the fit and feeling won't change much with wear. Leather boots are another matter. They do indeed adjust to your feet—with time. Light split-leather boots, especially those with generous inside padding, settle in fairly soon; heavier leather boots need deliberate, rather lengthy breaking in. It may take 10 miles for the first stiffness to disappear and 50 before the adjustment is complete.

Allow several weeks for this process. Start with easy walks and short distances. Don't be discouraged if you get a blister or two—better now than later. You may find that you can help tender skin to toughen by massaging it with rubbing alcohol every day. Some people use tincture of benzoin for the same purpose. Walking barefoot when you can helps also. If you know you blister easily at the heel, try leaving the upper hooks or eyelets in the lacing pattern unused for the first 5 miles or so; some find this helps.

Water softens leather and can help it adjust at this stage. The old advice to fill your boots with water, empty them, and "hike them dry" is overly drastic, but you needn't be shy of walking in the rain.

You can also take some corrective action on the boot. A slightly rough spot on the lining can be taped over or rubbed smooth with something like a knife handle. A dose of silicone spray can make an older boot lining slippery and easier on your skin. Again, a change of insole or footbed may help.

When you first start wearing leather boots, make sure that the tongue lies straight under the lacing. If it gets twisted or lopsided at this stage, it will have a tendency to stay that way—forever.

If you're heading out on a long trail with blisters already started, or with leather boots that aren't really broken in, bring along some tennis or running shoes. They will be worth their weight many times over.

Boot Care

A top-grain leather boot should last five years or more and carry you across some 1,500 miles of the world. Light fabric boots wear out much faster, as do lightweight leather boots made of split leathers. Whatever kind of boot you have, you can get more wear out of it with a little care and the application of some protective compounds.

Except for cleaning, don't do anything much to your boots until they are somewhat broken in. For one thing, they may have been coated in the factory with short-lived polishes that could interfere with what you are applying.

Then treat external seams with beads of urethane sealant (available under various brand names at outdoor and shoe stores). The best application tool is a blunt-tipped plastic syringe. Before sealing, scrub the seams with water and something like a toothbrush; let them dry completely; and clean again with rubbing alcohol. When this has evaporated, use the syringe to lay a thin bead of sealant. Seal also the welt, or the upper margin of the rand. Let the treatment dry overnight.

Next, treat leather surfaces, whether these are just strips and patches or make up the entire boot. Just what to treat them with is a matter of some controversy. Most boot makers advise you to steer clear of pure greases, fats, and oils, which soften leather unduly. Some widely used preparations are Sno-Seal and Bee-Seal, which are based on beeswax; Ultra-Seal by REI; Biwell; and Nikwax. If care instructions accompany the boot, by all means be sure to use the treatment that's suggested. Leather takes treatment best when warm (not hot), and two thin applications are better than one. Some preparations are applied to wet leather. When done, thoroughly wipe to remove the excess.

The fabric portions of mixed-construction boots can be treated with spray-on water repellents like those used on clothing. Nikwax is one brand.

Some ultralight boots can be resoled; some can't. This is a good thing to find out and consider when you shop. In the very lightest models, the uppers are unlikely to outlast the soles in any case.

On the Trail

Moisture, whether it comes inward from the outside world or outward from your own feet, is bad for boot materials. Keep boots as dry as you can. Take them off when you have an opportunity. Keep them under cover at night. If your pair has removable footbeds or insoles, remove these in the evening and wring water from any absorbent materials. When boots are seriously wet, the quickest way of drying them is to wipe them inside and then wear them with a pair of dry socks. In winter, try to keep damp boots from freezing. Often that means taking them inside your sleeping bag with you (in a plastic bag).

Heat and ultraviolet rays are bad for boots. Don't dry them at the edges of a campfire or even leave them in the hot sun any longer than you can help. Leather, for all its ruggedness, is as burnable as skin. Cemented soles are vulnerable to heat as well.

Dirt and grit are bad for boots. The cleaner you can keep them, the better. Wipe off surface grime each evening. Caked mud left on a boot draws natural oils out of leather and can also damage glues. If you expect mud on a trip, carry a small, stiff wire brush.

Make sure that the laces continue to run smoothly through hardware, and file off any snags. Broken laces? Substitute your nylon utility cord.

Especially in light boots, soles will sometimes begin splitting apart layer from layer. These delaminations can be fixed temporarily with one of the superstrong instant-hardening glues, or with duct tape (the ubiquitous fallback resource of wilderness repairs) wrapped around sole and upper.

Between Trips

When you get home, brush crusted dirt from your boots. Clean leather boots with a sponge and a little cool water; saddle soap is nice for leather surfaces. Fabric may be cleaned with nondetergent soap and water. Let the boots dry gradually but completely. (You can stuff them with newspaper to draw dampness out, and replace with fresh paper for storage.) Finally, treat the leather portions once more with whatever product you have been using.

Resoling and Repairs

Regardless of construction, most boots can be resoled. The price is currently $45 to $70—probably a fraction of the cost of your boot and very much worth it. Consult a gear store or cobbler. All but the lightest boots are likely to make it through two soles. Take this step before the soles wear so thin that the midsole—the second layer up—is exposed, which makes the process much more difficult. Thinned soles are also hard on the feet, reducing cushioning and insulation. One brand, Vibram, dominates the market in neoprene rubber lug soles; a sole that's not Vibram is probably "proprietary," made by one maker for the boots of its own line.

A cobbler can also make minor repairs on your boots—restitch a fraying seam, replace a grommet or a hook, reglue a separating sole—for a small charge.

Accessories

Gaiters ($24–$85) are fabric coverings that fasten around the tops of your boots when you slog through snowbanks or shallow water, wade through ankle-deep scree, or simply walk in the rain. They protect your feet and prolong the life of the boot. They are also of safety value in rattlesnake country. For summer use, a short, relatively inexpensive gaiter is the most you might need.

Other extras go directly on your feet. A real necessity is some sort of *patch material* to stick on at need; it may be "moleskin," "molefoam," adhesive tape, or duct tape. Apply the appropriate layer whenever you suspect an irritation that could lead to a blister. Spenco's 2nd Skin is an excellent patching material when it's too late for prevention (see Chapters 10 and 15). A few hikers take *foot powder to* fight both blisters and athlete's foot.

Camp shoes–tennis shoes, river sandals, moccasins, or whatever–are sometimes taken for use around camp, especially if the trail boots are heavy; besides being comfortable, these may reduce wear and tear on the local environment (see end of chapter). Light and cheap will do, but you can spend up to $90 for specialized models. Sandals should be the slipper type that accepts the stockinged foot, rather than the thong type that is worn barefoot. Light shoes are also sometimes useful for crossing streams and may replace boots altogether in beach hiking (see Chapter 23).

Waterproof socks can be useful on very wet trips, like those involving many fords of streams, and also keep feet warmer in very cold conditions; they cost $30 to $50.

For warmth at the end of the day, there are thick *fleece socks* and more substantial *booties,* high-topped slippers stuffed with insulation ($30 and up). A luxury in summer, they can make the difference between achingly cold feet and pleasantly warm ones on a cold winter night. Booties with heavy fabric soles cost more. These grade into *mukluks*, constructions of fleece and felt that are unmatched for living in extremely cold temperatures (see Chapter 24).

Lug Soles: A Question of Impact

There is really only one impact question when it comes to boots: are lug soles bad for the land?

Common sense suggests they might be. The lugs of the typical boot sole, projecting like so many rows of teeth, dig in and grip. That's what they're for. It seems reasonable to suspect that they break up the soil surface, leaving fragments that runoff can carry away. Critics of lug soles have stated this suspicion as fact; in earlier editions of this book, I agreed.

But this commonsensical idea may be wrong, or at least not demonstrably right. The few controlled trampling studies so far have shown no significant difference between the effect of toothy soles and flat ones.

Common sense still suggests that lighter boots (which tend also to have less-ferocious soles) may produce a gentler stride simply because the people who wear them have to place their feet a bit more carefully: they are less likely to plow through a bog, for instance, or to drive their weight down hard on their heels when descending a slope. On the other hand, this same caution may encourage them to step off an unpleasantly muddy trail and establish a damaging new track alongside it. For trail travel, then, the balance of evidence seems most unclear.

What about in camp? There are certainly anecdotes to suggest that heavy boots can cause more damage there than light shoes do. But conscientious behavior—determination not to expand the total trampled zone within the wilderness—would seem to be the real key.

The wild country can be thought of as a green expanse webbed with brown lines and patches: trails and campsites where the ground has been compacted, probably eroded, and effectively sterilized by human traffic. The first goal of low-impact travel is to avoid expanding the brown territory, to leave the enveloping green intact.

Until solid data can replace the conflicting impressions, I'm just not convinced that footwear has much to do with it, either way.

5

Clothing

Clothing is the fundamental wilderness gear. You can survive in remote places without a pack, a tent, a stove, a sleeping bag, a compass, a flashlight. You can even do without specialized boots. Naked, in typical hiking climates, you wouldn't last long.

Wilderness garments today are mostly made of cunningly crafted synthetic materials—that is, ultimately, of oil. There is limited use of silk, wool, and waterfowl down. Cotton is seldom seen anymore—at least it is seldom recommended—because it becomes cold when wet, serving as a conductor and pulling heat from the body.

Broadly speaking, wilderness hikers have two sets of clothing. First, there is a basic fair-weather outfit: underwear, pants or shorts, shirt, hat and sunglasses, and of course boots and socks. Second, there is a set of *reserve* clothing, more often in the pack than on the back, for dealing with cold, wind, rain, and snow. In spring, summer, and fall hiking, this reserve may be rather small, but it is always there. In winter travel, the basic outfit gets thicker, and the reserves are more formidable.

The Basic Outfit

There are two ways to go with the innermost clothing set. Some people dress as they might at home, starting with light underwear, and adding pants and shirts on top. Others combine these layers in one, and meet the world in a more rugged and more presentable version of their skivvies.

Fabrics in contact with the moister parts of the body need to "wick," or carry moisture outward. The favorite wicking fabric today is polyester, alone or in combination with other fibers like acrylic, rayon, and stretchy Lycra. Polypropylene appears mostly in loosely woven "net" garments. Silk and fine merino wool, modified to minimize scratchiness, are also used. To discourage odor, synthetic materials are commonly treated with antibacterial agents; these aren't very effective and may actually prove to be bad for skin health. Wool is by nature less odorous.

At its simplest, underwear may just consist of short-sleeved shirts above and bikini briefs, jockey shorts, or boxers below. Panties for women should be cut high on the legs for striding. On the other hand, "long-handled" versions are now worn top and bottom in many hiking climates. These garments come in various thicknesses and degrees of warmth; except in winter, most backpackers choose the light end of the spectrum.

Long-underwear bottoms should be simple, snugly fitting tights with wide waistbelts and elasticized cuffs that can be rolled up. They should have smooth outer surfaces that resist snagging and slide easily under outer layers. Seams should be flat and smooth. A gusseted crotch is good for freedom of movement. Men's versions will have a fly opening; at least one maker offers a model that allows women to relieve themselves without pulling the inner garment down.

Underwear tops are more variable. You can get plain round crew necks; turtlenecks with short zippers; or three-button "henley" models. Long sleeves should push up when you want them to (but not creep up when you don't). Tails need to be long, for ready tucking in.

Prices per item, depending on thickness and cut, run $15 to $65. A few top $100.

Winter travelers started the trend; now many summer backpackers meet the world in close-fitting base-layer garments rather than traditional pants and shirts.

Various companies make sports bras ($25–$40) that work well for women on the trail. Good ones are made of moisture-wicking fabric and have a minimum of seams on the top of the shoulder, where pack straps will press.

In the 1970s, cross-country skiers started using their long johns as trousers, with a pair of shorts added for modesty. This is how a whole wardrobe of "base layer" garments evolved, similar to underwear in fabric and fit but huskier and equipped with such outerwear features as pockets and ankle zips. Many people swear by them. Cost per garment is $30–$50.

More commonly, though, separate outer pants and shirts are worn.

Made-for-hiking trousers are commonly made of ripstop nylon, alone or blended with other synthetic fibers. Most today are "stretch-woven," giving slightly with the body's movements. These materials are wind resistant and somewhat water resistant, too. Schoeller fabric is a common brand.

Fit varies, but pants must in any case be generous enough to wear over long johns if you like and trim enough to wear under rain gear. There will be several pockets, with openings low enough so that the pack belt doesn't block access. There may be gussets, added panels of fabric set into the basic tube shapes, at the crotch and perhaps down the leg to knee or ankle; these make movement freer. For the same purpose, there may be "articulated knees" tailored in a slight bend. Instead of conventional belt loops, which are awkward under the hipbelt of your pack, specialty pants have elastic gathers, built-in belts of flat, wide webbing, or both. I find a belt essential; elastic waistbands alone get dragged up and down when you put on or take off your pack. Ankles are tapered, to avoid snagging and flapping, but should be wide enough to fit over the top of your boot. Some models have zippers up the leg, permitting you to put them on over footwear.

Specialty pants go for $50 to $100 or more. At the other extreme, you sometimes see old nylon slacks on the trail.

Hiking shorts are a nice luxury; in hot, wet places, everybody wears them, but sun exposure is a concern. You should always have longer leg coverings along as well. You'll need these at least when the sun is highest, for any hiking through brush, and wherever irritant plants are a problem. Mosquitoes, too, can make bare-legged walking unappealing. Shorts can cost from

This hiker is wearing specialized pants made of weather-resistant synthetic fabric and tailored for freedom of movement, a loose nylon shirt with vents for coolness, and a hat that shades the neck.

nothing (something you have around) to $50 or so; some specialty pants, equipped with zip-off legs, can shrink into shorts at need. (Give such a model a good walking trial in the store to be sure that that zippers don't bother your skin.)

Shirts made to be worn over undershirts are commonly of ripstop nylon; light wool is also a possibility.

Gearing Up

They must have long sleeves, high collars, and pockets that button, zip, or close with hook-and-loop patches (Velcro is the familiar brand). There may be vents with inset mesh panels for ventilation. You'll spend $40 to $85 for a specialty trail shirt.

Altogether, basic clothing has become a pricey proposition since the days when hikers wore denims and cotton work shirts. Of course, some of us cheapskates still do.

Cotton, as noted, has a terrible reputation, because of the way it chills you when wet. It is no fabric for damp climates. But the case can be overstated. In dry regions, especially in California and the Southwest, very experienced backpackers happily wear jeans, cotton "chamois" shirts, and cotton underwear. In desert travel, it would be silly to avoid the fabric. If you're unsure what you're facing, by all means go with the noncotton options. But if you're better equipped with knowledge—consider, and choose.

You need a broad-brimmed hat to protect your face and neck from the sun, your head from heat, and your eyes from glare. The best protection is the type that has a long front visor and protects the back of the neck with a sort of curtain (called a "havelock"): a Lawrence of Arabia look. There must be a drawstring "keeper" that snugs up under your chin. A suitable hat will cost $15 to $35. In the Pacific Northwest, water-resistant rain hats are worn. You also need effective sunglasses ($30–$100), with a keeper strap or cord to prevent loss. On snow and at high altitudes, carry not just one pair but two, in case you lose or break your primary pair. For more about the hazards of ultraviolet radiation, see Chapter 28.

There are places where mosquitoes are so tormenting that some hikers add to the basic outfit a head net: a veil of mosquito netting ($8–$20). There are even full suits of netting. Most people make do with insect repellent and netted tents.

Bathing suit for swimming? Possibly. Depending largely on the company you're hiking with, underwear, shorts, or nothing at all may suffice.

Into the Reserves

So much for the dry, pleasant day. Now suppose the temperature begins to drop: from 70 to 50 to 40 degrees Fahrenheit or lower. Clouds move across the sun; a cold air is stirring. Or maybe it has been cool all along. You were warm when you were walking, but when you sit down to eat lunch, you feel a chill.

Or maybe the mists of a temperate morning are congealing into rain.

What do you pull out for what conditions?

It is useful to split the problem into parts. One environmental challenge is *cold,* and you respond to that by adding one or more layers of *insulation.* Another set of problems is posed by *wind and rain* (or snow), and you deal with that by adding *shells.* Some garments, called soft shells, usefully combine a degree of insulation with a degree of weather protection; see "Insulating Garments," below.

Insulating Garments

The first essential for warmth is a wool or polyester stocking cap ($10–$30). More than a third of the heat the body loses into the air is radiated from the head. Conserve some of that, and you'll feel warmer all over. Some stocking caps are thick and fuzzy; others are thinner and less formidable looking. For most purposes, the simplest will do. For colder places and times, get a longer cap that rolls down to cover the neck, with a gap left for the face, helmet-fashion (called a *balaclava*). Hands also radiate a lot of heat; on chilly summer evenings, gloves or mittens ($10–$50) can be nice. Gloves for women need to be of slimmer cut than men's. The more expensive caps and gloves incorporate wind-blocking layers.

For the torso, the most traditional armament is one or two wool sweaters, or an extra wool shirt and a sweater. In sweaters you have a choice between the pullover type and the type that opens at the front. The pullover is simpler and lighter, but a front closure lets you cool off without taking off the garment. For closures, zippers, not buttons, are standard.

A good substitute for wool is polyester fabric, the same stuff found in underwear, woven in nappy textures known as pile, fleece, and microfleece. Polyester garments can be thought of as heavy sweaters or light jackets; $90 to $200 is typical. Like wool, polyester has the great virtue of retaining its insulating power when it gets wet; of the two, polyester absorbs even less moisture and dries more readily. Pile garments now account for most of the insulating outerwear you see. More expensive versions incorporate wind-blocking layers.

Still available, however, are *insulated jackets and vests,* stuffed either with waterfowl down or synthetic insulations. Down is the luxurious choice for dry, cold conditions but loses its warming power when wet, so synthetics are more generally used. A versatile alternative to the full-scale jacket is the insulated vest or armless jacket, with or without collar. You can expect to pay $100–$200 for a good insulated jacket; a vest may cost as little as $70.

Many light insulating garments now incorporate wind-blocking layers, which keep the breeze from stealing the warmth you're trying to conserve. These layers may also deal with light rain. Such compound garments, borrowing some features from the next category, are known as *soft shells.* They are not suited to extremes.

Shell Technology

If the human body didn't sweat or need to dissipate heat, rainproofing it would be a cinch: just wrap it in plastic. Unfortunately, we do sweat, and when we hike we sweat a lot. If we feel more or less dry, it's because evaporation whips the water away as fast as we produce it. If this doesn't happen, we get hot and sticky. Thus the shell maker's problem: How do you protect the hiker from moisture coming in while still allowing moisture to get out? Despite recent advances, the perfect garment—completely waterproof against the storm, completely open to evaporation from the skin—does not exist. What we have instead is a range of cunning compromises, ranging from very waterproof (but clammy) garments at one end of the spectrum to very permeable (but only briefly waterproof) garments at the other.

At the waterproof end of the scale are garments coated inside with an impermeable polyurethane, impregnated on the outer surface with silicone, or both. These waterproofs are simple, effective, and fairly cheap. But it is never fully comfortable to hike in such clothing. Even if the air is cold, you're likely to find it hot and damp inside. A partial solution is to design garments with as much ventilation as possible.

At the opposite, permeable end of the spectrum are garments that make little claim to block rain but are effective against wind. They do resist water to some extent because they are treated with a chemical called durable water repellent (DWR), as indeed all foul-weather gear is treated. Of course, such garments are very comfortable when it's not raining.

The rest of the spectrum of rain gear, the great middle, uses what are called microporous fabrics. These contain a layer peppered with extremely tiny openings. Liquid water, which sticks together in bulky droplets, can't get through the microscopic holes. But water vapor, which travels in separate molecules, can pass. Wrap a microporous layer around a human body, and sweat will tend to evaporate and escape outward; rain will tend not to get in.

There are rival means of achieving microporosity. The longest-established technology uses Gore-Tex, a thin, fragile Teflon film originally developed for kidney dialysis. To make a strong fabric with Gore-Tex, the film is bonded to a layer of ordinary cloth, which faces the weather, and protected on the body side by a lining (which may be bonded or loose). Numerous variations on the same idea—Stormshed and Klimate are two—have appeared more recently. Alternatively, the micropores can be created directly in shells made of urethane, the same stuff used in fully waterproof rainwear; Ultrex and Helly-Tech are two brands that use this technology.

The microporous fabrics have many applications. They are used in tents, sleeping bags, and boots. However, their most significant use, by far, is in clothing. Never before have water-resistant garments been so comfortable to wear while actually hiking.

The new fabrics neither exclude water nor pass vapor perfectly, let alone both. There is still an unavoidable trade-off between water resistance and breathability: the more of one you achieve, the less of the other you have. Different products now offer different compromises. There are even microporous garments "calibrated" for maximum breathability and designed to be used only against wind and the occasional light drizzle.

If you don't choose the expensive microporous garments, an old solution is still very practical: take a set of light waterproofs and a separate set of coverings to block a dry but chilling wind (if that's a kind of weather you expect to encounter).

Kinds of Shell Garments

The simplest, cheapest, and best-ventilated piece of rain gear is certainly the *poncho*. This is simply a big rectangle of urethane-coated nylon with a hole for the neck and a hood, so long in back that it hangs over the pack and protects the load as well as the porter. Generous ponchos can double as tarps for shelter if the rain is not too serious (see Chapter 8). Because the pack is inside with you, so to speak, a poncho isn't pinched in around your body by shoulder straps and hipbelt. Thus ventilation is excellent. Good nylon ponchos cost about $25. To be practical, they must be worn with rain pants or rain chaps.

But if the rain is heavy, especially if there is wind, no poncho will be protection enough. Rain always works its way in at the sides. When the mist comes down in the hills and the sky closes over in a slow-arriving, slow-departing storm, you need a regular raincoat and a separate cover for your pack.

Next up the line in cost are coats of urethane-treated or silicone-treated nylon, designed to be simply impermeable. These usually come with full front openings and hoods, the *jacket* style. A longer hooded jacket is a *parka*. You may also see the *anorak,* a short, hooded nylon shell that has a short zipper at the neck opening and pulls on over your head, like a sweater. Perhaps the most total protection possible is the full-length anorak, or *cagoule,* which covers you down to the knees. The more vents there are to help you deal with the body-moisture problem, the better. Impermeable raincoats cost from $30 to $65.

The typical weather protection today, heavier and bulkier, is the *parka* built of microporous fabric. It has a rugged front zipper, with a flap of fabric covering it and a line of snaps or hook-and-loop tabs that can be used instead. Some high-end parkas come with "waterproof" zippers, coated with a springy substance that forms a kind of gasket when the teeth interlock. There are usually several enormous pockets, which should be arranged so that pack straps don't block access to them. A drawstring in the lower hem allows you to tighten the coat down below when it's cold and windy. Parkas intended for winter use may also have a "powder skirt" inside at waist level, an elasticized strip that clings to the body and keeps you drier if you take a tumble in a snowdrift. Most hoods are integral, but some are detachable. (Having once had a detachable hood blow off my head in a snowstorm, I greatly prefer built-in.) Drawstrings snug hoods up around the face.

Ventilation is achieved by various means. The main front zipper should open from the bottom as well as from the top so that you can crack it either way. Most parkas have zippers under the armpits, which you can open to let some unwanted heat and body moisture escape. Some have instead "gill" zippers, which angle from chest to lower back. Pockets may also be floored with mesh, providing another exit for warm, moist air.

Some microporous parkas are made of two-layer laminate with a loose inner lining; others are of three-layer laminate with the lining bonded in place. Loose linings make a softer fabric that drapes better, but

Gearing Up

bonded liners make the coat tougher, more packable, quicker to dry, and indeed more water resistant; these are preferable. In a newer variation in Gore-Tex, the bonded lining is reduced to a galaxy of tiny bumps or dots on the surface of the membrane. It is not clear whether these will be a sufficient abrasion shield.

You'll pay $200 or more for a heavy-duty micro-porous parka; high-end garments using Gore-Tex, with such features as waterproof zippers and glued or "welded" seams, approach $500.

What about your legs? In warm country, many hikers wear shorts and let their legs get wet. In cooler climates, you'll need waterproofing all the way down. Many people who wear waterproof, breathable garments on their torsos find that they can wear cheaper waterproofs on their legs without discomfort. Urethane-coated *rain chaps* come in literal pairs, a separate tube for each leg, and tie onto the belt at the top; they are rarely seen these days. Full *rain pants* protect the crotch and waistline better. There may be zippers up the leg so that the garment can be put on over boots, or even full-length zippers allowing it to be put on over skis. Whatever combination of coat and leg protection you work out, make sure there is a generous overlap at the waist. Pant cuffs should be loose, not elasticized, as the latter design channels rain into your boots. Impermeable rain pants cost $20 to $40; rain pants with microporous fabrics run anywhere from $75 to $280.

Another item to consider for the south end is a pair of *gaiters*. These tough nylon sheaths fasten around the ankle, closing off the gap at the top of the boot where rain, snow, rubble, or mud could otherwise get in. They also protect against snakebite and ticks. Gaiters for occasional summer use are simple and collarlike. For winter snow travel you need the fitted or spat type that covers the upper half of the boot and rises well up the leg. For best convenience, the closure should be in front; it may be a zipper (backed up with snaps or hook-and-loop fabric) or consist simply of a wide hook-and-loop overlap. A cord or strap, running

This woman is outfitted for cold and snow, with base-layer garments, tall gaiters, fleece vest, gloves, and stocking cap.

under the boot, keeps the gaiter from creeping up out of place. Gaiters may be waterproof or not, waterproof only in the lower part, or of waterproof breathable fabric; some wearers find that completely waterproof ones are clammy. Prices range from $24 to $85.

Seams, where holes are poked through fabric, are zones of potential leakage. In almost all rain gear, these lines are sealed in the factory with melt-on plastic strips: shiny and recognizable on the inside surface, unless concealed by a lining. You can also see the strips, on some garments, by holding them up against the light. If in doubt, confirm with the store before you buy. On high-end garments, the seams are not sewn at all but "welded," which simply means glued.

Clothing Care

Specialty wilderness clothing, for all its toughness, can be finicky to care for. One of the first things to do when you get a new garment home is to check the washing instructions on the labels, and record them somewhere in case the originals fade. As a rule, you'll use gentle soaps that contain neither detergents nor surfactants. Dreft and Ivory Flakes are two familiar brands in powder form; Nikwax makes an expensive liquid cleanser for gear. Bleach should never be used.

If you use a washing machine (sometimes appropriate), it should be the front-loading, drum type; top-loading, agitator-type machines are to be avoided. You will rarely use the "hot" setting. Some items can be tumble-dried at low heat; some can't. Polypropylene fabric can't stand even minimal dryer heat. Silk never goes in machines. No wilderness clothing gets dry-cleaned, period.

Insulated garments, whether they contain down or synthetics, are best hand washed and air dried, with one exception: down garments actually need a warm-air tumble to fluff up properly. Let them drain well first. Throw into the dryer with them a clean, dry towel—maybe several, and maybe several towels in succession—to absorb water and hasten drying.

Polyester fleeces machine wash perfectly in cold water and emerge almost dry. Zip the zippers (as you always do when you put a garment in a machine) and turn items inside out to reduce pilling.

The care of shells is a little more complex. Coated-nylon garments (including some waterproof breathables) should be rinsed off, inside and out, to remove sweat residue that can attack the coating. If further cleaning seems necessary, follow the manufacturer's suggestions. Never wash in a top-loading, spindle-type washer.

For garments incorporating Gore-Tex or similar membranes, machine washing is usually okay or even preferred. Again, zip zippers and mate pieces of hook-and-loop tape: if unattached, these rasp at fabric and pick up mats of threads and lint. To keep sleeves from twisting or turning inside out, link opposite cuffs with their hook-and-loop tabs or snaps.

Tumble drying at low or even medium heat (check your label) is actually beneficial for some shells because it rejuvenates the chemical coating known as *durable water repellent*, or DWR.

Just about any shell garment, whether nominally waterproof or not, comes from the factory impregnated with this fluoropolymer, a kind of dispersed Teflon. DWR causes water to bead up and prevents the outer-most layer from becoming saturated. This makes a difference: waterlogged outer fabric can make a garment *feel* like it's leaking even when it's not.

DWR loses effectiveness over time. Moderate heat, as in a dryer, remelts and redistributes it, freshening it up. You can also revive it by ironing the outer surface of the garment with a steam iron at moderate setting.

There comes a time when DWR needs a more thorough renewal. The chemical is available as a liquid and as a spray. A widely distributed brand, essentially the same stuff used in manufacture, is TX-Direct by Nikwax. DWR is best applied in the liquid form to a freshly cleaned garment in a washing machine whose cycle can be interrupted for a long soak. After the drum has filled with water, pour in the DWR; after about five minutes, stop the action for a quarter of an hour, then let the machine finish its routine. Complete the process with a thorough tumble-drying.

Spray-on DWR treatments (not to be confused with silicone sprays) are considered less effective. In one situation, however, they are required: Gore-Tex or similar garments with loose-hanging inner linings should not get wash-in DWR treatment, as the lining is supposed to wick sweat, and you don't want that action interfered with.

There is also a wash-in DWR treatment specifically for down; this helps the plumules stay springy in humid (but not too humid!) conditions. For a manageably small garment, the washing-in is best done by hand, with the usual finish in a commercial dryer.

When the main waterproof layer of urethane-coated rain gear starts peeling, most people write the garment off. It can, however, be given a second life by painting the outer surface—not the inner one that is peeling—with any of several liquid, water-based polymers. Any factory-sealed seams that peel are defective; return such a garment to the manufacturer.

In the field, fabric tears are usually repaired with sticky tape designed for the purpose (and possibly even matched by color). There are even microporous fabric patches for waterproof-breathable gear. The area around the rip should be cleaned thoroughly (use an alcohol-soaked towelette). Before applying the patch, trim off any square corners, which tend to lift. Duct tape too, is often used, but it leaves a stubborn, gummy residue.

6

The Pack

The pack makes the backpacker. Without it you remain a hiker, confined to a circle with a car at its center and a radius as long as you can walk in half a day. But with your pack on your back, you are a *traveler on foot*; you can go for a week or longer and cover, if you wish, several hundred wilderness miles. There is something formal, almost ceremonial, in the way an experienced packer hoists the load on the first morning of a trip.

And that moment should be a pleasant one. A properly fitted pack, not overloaded, is comfortable. Nobody who goes on a wilderness trip of normal length and difficulty should have to feel like a pack animal, struggling forward under a painful burden. Although almost any pack is likely to seem heavy at the end of a long day, no pack should make you groan sincerely when you put it on (some people groan for show). If it does, something is wrong. Either you've filled the pack too full, or you have it wrongly adjusted, or—just possibly—you have the wrong pack in the first place.

Buying a Full-Sized Pack

There are several hundred different models of full-sized packs on the market, and new variations are turning up each year. You needn't rush to choose among them.

This is a large and important purchase, and the chances are you'll be traveling with the thing for many years.

Many gear stores have packs for rent. Take advantage of this if you can. Only experimenting on the trail permits you to know for sure what you like best, especially if you are deciding among fundamentally different designs. A three-day rental is $50 or so. Since there are acceptable packs as cheap as $100, that may seem hefty; but I think this first hundred is better spent renting than buying what may turn out to be "disposable" gear.

Now, more on the anatomy of backpacks, and the choices to be made.

Internal and External Frames

Modern full-sized backpacks are a genus with two species. First, there are *internal-frame packs*, which appear to be one-piece towers of fabric. Second, and now less commonly seen, are *external-frame packs*, with obvious rigid frameworks to which separate packbags are attached.

Both types contain rigid members that transmit the weight of the load down to a padded hipbelt; the pressure comes to bear, not on the weak shoulders and back, but on the robust joints and powerful muscles of the hips, buttocks, and thighs. When you wear a properly adjusted backpack, your shoulders take only a small share of the burden.

Do you want a pack with an external frame, or an internal-frame design?

Internal-frame packs are general-purpose carriers, useful both on and off the trail. Their frames are somewhat flexible, and their outline is narrow. They fit closely against the back. Thus they tend to move with you, not to shift around like independent beings. They also tend to be warm on the back in hot weather.

External-frame packs are comfortable tools for carrying massive loads on trails. Their packbags are wider and flatter, with a higher center of gravity and less inclination to bulge out behind; thus they permit a more upright posture than do internal-frame packs.

They have an advantage in warm weather: standing well out from the back, except at shoulder and hip, they give sweat plenty of chance to evaporate. Finally, exoskeletal packs are considerably cheaper than the internal-frame variety. Price and adjustability make them the preferred packs for kids (see Chapter 25).

On the negative side, rigid frames tend to bounce and swing whenever the wearer makes a quick motion. When the hips swivel and dip, as they do when you hike downhill, the frame pack does the same—but in its own competing rhythm. Externals are miserable to carry when, for instance, you stride and leap across the boulder fields called talus. They may also creak and squeak in a manner that some people find annoying.

You might relate the choice to your ambitions like this:

- If you plan to spend much time off the trail, going cross-country, especially over rugged ground; if you want to use the pack for scrambling or for climbing; or if you want a pack that you can carry when skiing, there's really no choice: the internal-frame pack, with its flexibility and closer fit, is almost certainly for you. (For snowshoeing, too, an endoskeleton is preferable, though a frame can be managed.)

- If you plan to carry oversized loads, as for very long trips—and if you will do nearly all your travel on the trail, or in very easy cross-country—then a frame pack is a reliable choice.

- If you expect to carry moderate loads and to do most of your hiking on the trail—a description that fits most backpackers, most of the time—then either an external-frame or internal-frame pack will make sense. All you can do is rent differing kinds for a trial, and trust your experience.

Also consult your wallet. Two hundred dollars is quite expensive for an external-frame pack but just middling for an internal frame. A few very elaborate internals cost more than $500.

Internal-Frame Packs: Frame and Suspension

These apparently "soft" packs get their rigidity from long bars of aluminum, graphite, or polycarbonate. The bars may be arranged parallel, one on either side of the spine; in an X design, in which case the pack must stand out a little farther from the back; in a U design, with a crossbar at the bottom; in a V design; or in still other variations. There may also be a wider piece of molded plastic called a *framesheet*, which adds some support and prevents items in the pack from poking into your back. A pack with a framesheet may have just one vertical bar.

The bottom of the frame connects with, and transmits weight to, the hipbelt. The key connection may take several forms, each a compromise between the rigid linkage that would transmit the pressure best and the soft linkage that would allow the pack to follow best the movements of the torso. Some belts are solidly pinned to the frame at a point behind the lumbar pad; at the other extreme are models in which adjustable webbing loops form the entire connection.

The hipbelt itself is an elaborate padded structure, more or less sculptured to grip and cradle the hips. Typically, you have soft open-cell foam against the body and firmer closed-cell foam behind, backed up again, in some models, with a plastic stiffener. Softer isn't better for everyone: some people prefer a firmer feel. Open-cell foam has the drawback of soaking up the rain. Some makers use a "slow memory" foam that's supposed to adapt itself to the shape of a particular wearer. Others build in cunning adjustments that let you tilt the belt to match your anatomy, or change the angle at which the essential webbing belt emerges from the enclosing pads. Hipbelts adjust for length with buckles and close in front with heavy plastic snap-in clamps.

From either side of the hips, straps rise to the shoulders, over them, and down to an attachment point or points just behind your shoulders. As with all

An internal-frame pack rides close to the back and moves well with the body. You can adjust the fit at the shoulder straps, load lifters, sternum strap, hipbelt, and load stabilizer straps.

packs suitable for backpacking, the shoulder straps function more to keep the load upright and steady than to support its weight. Their design can be quite elaborate, however, with plenty of padding and sculpting, a skin-sparing lining on the underside, and perhaps as many as four possible adjustments for each shoulder. Where the straps go down the back, they may converge in what is called a yoke or remain separate; to allow variations of fit, strap origins can usually be shifted up or down.

To add to stability, most packs will have *sternum straps* and *load lifters* (also called *lift straps*). Sternum straps buckle across the chest, linking the two shoulder straps. Load lifters rise from a point just in front of the shoulders to the upper corners of the packbag, about at ear level; when tightened, they pull the pack's weight closer to your body, thus permitting you to stand more nearly upright as you carry it.

The part of the pack that lies against the back will be padded. Some makers build in slots or channels designed to increase ventilation and keep things cooler back there. Usually there is a thick *lumbar pad* where the weight of the pack comes to bear on the sloping base of the spine.

At the bottom corners of the pack, short *load stabilizer straps* may be provided; these tug the packbag firmly against the belt, in hopes of reducing sideways sway.

Packs used to be regarded as unisex, but, as with other kinds of gear, they were really designed for the male body; sometimes they suited women just fine, sometimes they didn't. Now there are many packs engineered specifically for shorter and narrower torsos, slimmer shoulders, narrower waists, and broader hips. Check that shoulder straps stay put on your shoulders, and that overly wide pads do not pinch at your armpits or encroach on your breasts. Hipbelts for women are especially carefully contoured to place the weight equally on all parts of the pelvic flare.

Internal-Frame Packs: Packbag

Most packbags are made of a smooth, tightly woven nylon duck. Others are made of a rougher nylon called *Cordura* or of ultrastrong fabrics known as *ballistics cloth* and *Spectra*. Fabrics are almost always coated for water repellency, with factory-sealed seams.

The space within the internal-frame pack can be variously organized. There may be a single major compartment, or an upper and a lower one. Some packs open only at the top, others at the front of the pack (that is, on the side away from your back), others in both places. Frontal zippers may be horizontal, vertical, diagonal, or shaped like an upside-down U, allowing you to lay the whole compartment open like a suitcase. If there are upper and lower compartments, the divider between them may be a solid floor or a sleevelike arrangement that closes with a drawstring. There may be smaller internal pockets: possibly a slab *pocket,* inside next to the back, for stowing heavy gear, or a netting pocket for small, easily lost objects. Little pockets for wallets and *lanyards* for keys are likely to appear somewhere.

Top-opening packs usually have drawstrings at the mouth. Often they have *extension sleeves,* tubes of lighter fabric that, once pulled out, rise well above the original top of the pack and increase its capacity. The vulnerable opening is protected by a *storm flap,* a long tongue of fabric that arches over it, runs partway down the front of the pack, and cinches securely there.

You'll see *compression straps* arranged on the outer surface of the pack. Tightening these, you draw the center of gravity closer to the back and take pressure off bulging zippers. If you're carrying an undersized load, the same straps will neaten it by cinching up unused volume. And they will hold your pack together if a panel-loading zipper has failed. The larger the pack, the more of these tighteners it is likely to have.

For storage on the outer surface of the pack there is always a large top pocket; in top-opening packs, this rides on the storm flap. Frequently, this pouch can be detached and used as a *fanny pack* for day trips (see "Daypacks, Rucksacks, and Travel Packs," below). There may or may not be some smaller outside pockets, either built in or strapped on and detachable. The typical pack-bag is also fairly decorated with attachment points for tying things on: slotted plastic patches through which straps can be passed, built-in belts or elastic bungee cords, ice ax loops, *daisy chains* of webbing with many openings. *Ski sleeves* may be formed by the space behind side pockets. There may be a *shovel flap,* a long tongue of tough fabric on the pack's front that can be secured around a snow shovel, wet clothing, or anything else that's awkward to store inside.

Many hikers today like to sip water as they walk, drawing it through a little hose out of a bladder housed in the pack. Many packs have pockets designed for such bladders, and some have the bladders and hoses built in. In packs meant for winter use, the hose may be placed inside a shoulder strap, where body heat will keep it from freezing shut. Accessible water bottle holders may also be built into hipbelt, shoulder strap, or anyplace on the pack that you can reach while wearing it. Each such refinement, of course, adds its bit of weight.

External-Frame Packs: Frame and Suspension

The exoskeletal pack is a simpler creature than its internal-frame counterpart. Its two basic components—the suspension system and the packbag—are distinct. The classic frame is a structure of metal tubing shaped like an H with several crossbars, to which hipbelt and shoulder straps are attached. The packbag itself—tall, wide, flat, and boxlike—is attached to the frame in any of several ways, most often with metal skewers called *clevis pins*. Though you buy packbag and frame as a unit, you may be able to exchange components by one maker, and to some extent between brands.

Frame materials vary. The traditional stuff is tubular aluminum, but plastics are increasingly used, in addition to metal or in place of it. Any joints are usually welded. All frames are curved from top to bottom and from side to side to match the shape of the body.

Not all frames are of the basic H pattern. Some close off the H at top or bottom. Some frames rise extra high, creating a sort of shelf above the packbag where things can be strapped on. Some curve backward at the bottom in a sort of curl, creating a shelflike space down there. Some have an hourglass shape, like a rectangle pinched in at the sides. Off your back, some frames will stand up unsupported on the ground; most won't.

When you wear a properly fitted frame, none of the rigid structure touches your body. The three parts of the pack that actually touch you are the hipbelt, the shoulder straps, and the backbands or lumbar pad.

The hipbelt attaches at the bottom tips of the H and runs around the body just below the waist, buckling securely at the front. Some belts are heavily padded, like those on internal-frame packs, and some aren't—experiment to find out which you like best.

STORM FLAP

SHOULDER STRAPS

BACKBAND

PADDED HIP BELT

External-frame packs are still the best containers for carrying large and awkward loads on trails. Their simplicity, adjustability, and price make them good packs for children, too.

Shoulder straps rise from the same bottom points of the H, cross your shoulders, and converge to join the frame at a point near the back of your neck. A buckle in front of each shoulder adjusts for length. Straps are more or less elaborately padded where they rest on the body.

Belts and straps are usually attached to the frame with clevis pins that run through grommets in fabric and holes in metal, and lock in place with retaining rings.

The pack also touches your back toward the rump, at the lumbar spine. Here you may find a mesh *backband* or a thick, soft *lumbar pad* like those found on internal frames. The pad is cushier and keeps the load a bit more stable, but simple backbands are cooler.

External-Frame Packs: Packbag

Packbags can be attached to external frames in several ways but are most often joined with clevis pins like those used elsewhere in the design. A few bags clip or strap to plastic frames.

Gearing Up

Most frame packbags are *three-quarter length*—shorter than the frames on which they are mounted. The sleeping bag, stuffed in a storage sack and strapped to the lower crossbars of the frame, fills the remaining space. Some packbags are so designed that you can shift them up or down to change the center of gravity (a low-slung load helps in cross-country scrambling). In packs with extra-tall frames, a second slot for tying things on exists at the top.

External-frame packbags lend themselves to subdivision. In the most common design, there is a large upper compartment held open at the top by a light metal framework. You may be able to expand this compartment upward for bulky loads by unfolding an *extension sleeve.* The top opening is protectd by a *storm flap,* usually with a big top pocket mounted on it. Underneath the upper compartment there is commonly a smaller bottom chamber, with its own zippered opening to the world. Most people seem to use this area for clothing.

Some bags aren't divided at all but have a single deep compartment. This is less convenient for getting at things, easier for packing bulky or odd-shaped items. Some packs have zip-out dividers so that you can have it either way. Some have permanent dividers but leave corner gaps so that you can stick long objects down through.

As with internal-frame packs, panel loading is also found, with the same advantage—suitcaselike convenience—and the same disadvantage—that gravity isn't helping you keep the contents in place if a zipper creeps open or fails. Modern zippers are pretty tough, but problems do occur.

Outside pockets are numerous on frame packs. It's a luxury to have so many places to put objects you may need during the hiking day. Pocket zippers, like the heavier zippers on the major compartments, may run straight across the tops of the spaces they open; or they may be vertical; or they may be arc shaped or inverted-U shaped (opening around three sides). I personally prefer straight-across zippers.

Selecting a Pack

Once you have decided on an internal or an external frame, some other questions arise.

How much capacity to do you want? If you expect most of your trips to be weekend affairs, you can get by with as little as 3,000 cubic inches, or about two standard brown supermarket bags' worth (the bag holds about 1,400 cubic inches). In metric terms, that's about 23 liters. More flexibility is provided by what might be called three-brown-bag and four-brown-bag packs, holding between 4,500 and 6,000 cubic inches; that's plenty for a week's worth of gear in summer. Packs over 6,000 cubic inches are really for expeditions or winter mountaineering. If you are shopping for one of these "load monsters," look for generous padding in the shoulder straps and for a hipbelt engineered with a very soft exterior and a very stiff, supportive layer somewhere in its makeup.

Bear in mind that capacity figures include only the inside space of a pack and its pockets; thus they understate the volume of frame packs, which lend themselves to strapping things on the outside, and especially of packs with three-quarter-length frames, where the sleeping bag *always* rides outside. Bear in mind too that manufacturers compute volume in different ways and have been known to overstate it.

The pack's own *weight* needs consideration. It is, after all, part of the load you carry—the part you can never leave home. The trade-off isn't really between weight and volume, nor is it always between weight and durability. Rather, it's between weight and convenience: every added pocket, strap, zipper, and gizmo adds its ounce or two.

Packs large enough for a weeklong trip can vary from 4 pounds to almost 9 pounds, which is way too much; many solidly built packs can be found that are less than 5 pounds. Ultralight enthusiasts can go even lighter (for instance, by substituting a folded sleeping pad for a built-in frame): see Chapter 22. Not surprisingly, very light packs that are also rugged are among the most expensive.

Fitting a Pack

Fitting a pack correctly is less exacting than fitting a pair of shoes, but only just.

You know how tall you are, but do you know how tall your back is? More accurately, do you know the length of your torso? Before venturing to the pack store, better find out. You need a fabric tape measure and a friend. Stand with your feet in a natural position, about shoulder width apart. At the sides of your body, locate the tops of your hipbones and have your friend imagine (or even draw) a line connecting them across your back, close to the small. Tilt your head forward and find, at the back of your neck, the obvious bony protuberance (the seventh vertebra). Now have your friend measure between these markers, following the actual contour of your back. As a general rule, if the measurement is less than 18 inches, your size in packs will be "small"; if it's 18 to 20 inches, you want a "medium"; if you're longer of torso than that, you need a "large."

Not all packs have sizes as such. Some makers achieve good fit by offering a range of interchangeable belts and harnesses for the same packbag. And some packs, highly adjustable, are supposed to be "one-size-fits-all." (Be skeptical if you are very short or tall.) On adjustable packs, the anchor point behind your back, where the shoulder straps converge, can be shifted up or down. The hipbelt attachment may slide up or down as well. But there are limits to adjustability, and a very adaptable pack adjusted to your body will feel a little sloppier than a pack that adjusts in a narrower range—if the latter is sized correctly for you.

In the store, a salesperson can help you locate the right size and harness, show you how to shift a movable harness anchor point, and make obvious adjustments to the hipbelt and shoulder straps. In preparation for the next step, load the pack with 20 or 30 pounds. Most stores offer you sandbags or climbing ropes for weights; bringing gear of your own in stuff sacks will make a more realistic test—and also give you a practical idea of pack capacity.

Get the pack on your back, close the hipbelt, and tighten it firmly. It should lie just below the upper edge of the hipbone, not so high that the belt is really around your waist, but not so low that it slips off below the widest part of the bone. The lumbar pad or backband should fit snugly just beneath the small of your back, where your body starts to swell toward the rump. As you tighten the hipbelt, the whole pack should shift upward on your back. If this doesn't happen, the pack is probably too short for you.

Now for the shoulder straps. Tighten them to feel the load come onto the shoulders, then ease off to feel it settle back onto the hips. Adjust lift straps so that they rise at about a 45-degree angle on their way back to their attachment points on the packbag. On the rare frame pack that lacks lift straps, the main shoulder straps should run straight back from shoulder to attachment point, or even slightly upward. In front, the padded portion of the shoulder strap should end 1 or 2 inches below your armpit. If there is a sternum strap across your chest, it should be a couple of inches below your collarbone; on most packs, it can be adjusted up or down.

In addition to hipbelt, shoulder straps, load lifters, and sternum strap, there are typically two more adjustment points: a load stabilizer strap on either side of the waist to snug the load into the belt. Tighten these last.

Continue tinkering until you have reached the point of maximum comfort: a state in which the weight is plainly on your hips, but the upper part of the pack seems pleasantly firm.

Now, take an indoor hike with your load. Climb stairs, bend, sit down, stride. Make sure that the hipbelt is comfortable and that it shows no sign of slipping down, or up, from its proper position. (Exception: with some frame packs, the belt always shifts when you sit down.) Satisfy yourself that the hard parts of a frame don't touch your back at any point. Check that the buckles on straps and belts do not slip (on some cheap models they may). If anything seems inclined to loosen in the store, it will be far worse on the trail.

Also try tilting your head back, as though you were tracking a bird or reaching for a hold. Does the back of your head bump the frame or top pocket? Better look for another model.

The more adjustments your model allows, the longer you need to spend working out the arrangement most comfortable for you. When in doubt between sizes, go to the larger one. As with boots, keep looking until you are very satisfied. Women should try on at least one pack designed specifically for female proportions.

Internal-frame packs, with their flexible, close-fitting supports, allow and occasionally require a special type of adjustment: actually bending metal stays to match your back's own shape. A knowledgeable salesperson will be willing to spend some time helping you tweak the supports just right.

The question of fit is only part of the larger question of comfort. Makers are constantly trying new variations in hipbelts, shoulder straps, and lumbar pads. The design that works for somebody else, even somebody else with similar proportions, won't necessarily work for you. For example, some people like straps and pads quite soft, whereas others prefer a harder feel. (On a few internal-frame models, lumbar pads or hipbelts contain air bladders and can be pumped to different degrees of firmness.) Don't let yourself be talked into somebody else's idea of comfort.

Although packs don't need "breaking in" in the sense that some boots do, a basically acceptable pack will probably grow a little more comfortable with time. Some hipbelts, for instance, use a foam that adapts to your hips—but not right away. Your hips will get a little tougher, too; if you don't have much natural padding, you may want to apply tape or moleskin there at first. And you'll learn by experience how to adjust all those straps.

Care of the Pack

The best packs are pretty reliable objects, designed and built to endure years of hard use. Some are more fragile, though; accidents do happen; and even good gear gets old.

Besides the usual sewing kit and tape (see Chapter 10), your repair kit should include a few items for the pack: a clevis pin, if it's a frame pack; a spare slider or two for the most important zippers; maybe a spare buckle (see Chapter 10). On a long trip, you may want to supplement your ordinary sewing things with an awl and a few squares of packcloth.

When packing, avoid overstuffing, which stresses both seams and zippers. On the trail, avoid fuel spills on pack fabric and clean them up promptly if they happen; insect repellents containing DEET (see Chapter 29) also attack nylon. Keep your pack free of food crumbs and don't leave food in it at night. On a long trip, it's a good idea now and then to rinse the part of the pack that adjoins your back, and also the shoulder pads, to wash away the salty residue that can attract gnawing animals. For more about protecting your food, your gear, and yourself from scavenging wildlife, see Chapters 18 and 29.

If your pack fabric gets damaged in the woods, you can patch it initially with duct tape or sticky repair tape. But the likeliest thing to fail is one of the large molded-nylon buckles, especially the big one that closes the hip-belt in front. The hollow "female" side is especially prone to cracking if walked on. It helps to leave buckles joined when the pack is off. Some people carry a spare buckle set; there are many incompatible makes, so you need both halves. You can usually do a temporary repair by wrapping the split area with duct tape.

The second familiar trouble area is zippers. Keep them free of grit and don't force them if they catch fabric; rather, back off gently and try again. If fraying threads are caught, tug these out with pliers. If a zipper slider moves freely but doesn't close the tracks behind it, it is probably worn. It's a little tricky but quite possible to replace it in the field; if your pack is so designed that a major zipper failure would spill your stuff all over the landscape, carry a spare slider and learn how to install it. In a pinch, large safety pins can make a temporary closure.

Frame packs have some specific weak points. The lock-ring that holds a clevis pin in place can get broken or lost; replace it with a spare or with a piece of wire. If a lock-ring goes missing, its clevis pin may follow it; replace this, also, with a spare. Grommets can sometimes pull out of straps; you can make a temporary hole with a hot stick or a heated awl. A bent or broken frame can be splinted with a stick and cord, or more elegantly with a section of split tubing and hose clamps from a well-stocked repair kit (see Chapter 10).

After the trip, give your pack a good shake and a good wipe and check it over before stashing it till next time. Stains in general don't matter, but food stains should be scrubbed away, and any sticky spots, as from pitch, need to be removed. Any grit in seams or zippers should be chased out by brushing or with the pressure nozzle of a garden hose. Check for any fraying fabric along seams and especially near zippers; trim loose threads, and neaten the edge by melting with something like a lighter flame. If the stitches that actually hold a seam together seem to be getting abraded, you can protect them with a bead of urethane; any cut threads need to be oversewn with an awl. Tiny punctures can be sealed with dots of polyurethane; slightly larger ones can be patched, if you're handy with thread and awl; gaps larger than 3 or 4 inches need professional care. In frame packs, check to see if any grommets are tearing out of the straps they are set in. Replacement straps and backbands are available. If any field repairs need to be replaced with permanent ones, do this, or have it done, while it's on your mind. When the pack is thoroughly dry, store it in a cool, dry place. Humidity breeds mildew.

Daypacks, Rucksacks, and Travel Packs

Even before you buy a full-sized pack, you will need a *daypack*—a small, uncomplicated bag just big enough to carry a lunch, a camera, a canteen, and the essential safety items you should never leave behind (see list,

Daypacks can be simple or elaborate. Hydration packs (left) have water bladders and hoses. Waist packs (bottom) are also known as lumbar or fanny packs and handle smaller loads.

Chapter 15). You'll use such a pack, of course, for trips near home, but also on long wilderness trips if you want to be able to shuck your main pack and take off on a side excursion. Some large packs are designed to shrink to this purpose, and some have detachable pockets that will serve.

The traditional daypack is simple. A tough fabric bag and a couple of wide shoulder straps, and you've about got it. Slightly more luxurious models will have padded shoulder straps, padding against the back, leather-reinforced bottoms, and stabilizer straps across the belly. Though desirable in themselves, these features make the auxiliary pack a heavier, bulkier item. Whatever you buy, look carefully at the points where the straps attach to the basic bag: reject any pack that lacks good sewing and some kind of reinforcement here.

The packbag is usually nylon, coated inside with urethane. Typical dimensions might be 12 inches wide and 6 inches front to back, with a depth of 1 foot or more. Since a loosely loaded bag fits more comfortably to the back than one stuffed to the limit, be generous. Some bags open and close with zippers, variously placed; others use drawcords. Some have outside pockets; some don't. Some daypacks are set up as hydration packs, with much of the load space occupied by a water bladder and a hose near the mouth for easy sipping. Shoulder-hung daypacks will cost $20 to $90, weigh a pound or two depending on features, and handle loads of 15 pounds or so.

A daypack can also serve as a backpack for a young child. (For more on packs for kids, and baby carriers, see Chapter 25.)

Larger and more elaborate daypacks are known as *rucksacks* or *summit packs*. Still lacking hipbelts, these have well-padded shoulder belts, padding against the back, and sometimes rigid framesheets like those in internal-frame packs. They may have compressor straps to snug up an undersized load. Such features make it possible to use a rucksack for overnight trips in the ultralight style (see Chapter 22). They also make the unit too heavy and bulky to bring along as a mere accessory, as a true daypack can be. Such packs can cost up to $170.

Some daypacks, known as *waist packs*, *lumbar packs*, or *fanny packs*, hug the waist instead of hanging from the shoulders. When a pocket of a large pack detaches for daypack use, it usually takes the waist-pack form. Capacity is markedly less than in a standard daypack. Skiers like these rigs on short trips because they don't bounce. Some packs are amphibian: they start as fanny packs but unfold into full-size daypacks with shoulder straps, if you need the room. Prices range from $20 to $100 or more.

Yet another corner of the backpack warehouse contains "travel packs." These are compromises between packs and suitcases. Some are really just luggage with hipbelt and shoulder straps; at the other extreme are a few quite credible packs modified for urban travel convenience. All variations provide a way of stowing the harness out of harm's way, usually behind a zippered panel, while airport personnel are doing their worst. Features vary widely, and so do prices, from $100 to $300.

A better option for travel is to place your no-nonsense wilderness pack in a duffel bag. Duffels come in all sizes. Some have rugged linings and generous padding and can be used to carry vulnerable external-frame packs or sharp-edged climbing gear. There are models with wheels. Prices for the simpler sort run from $20 to $100. For more about taking gear on aircraft, see "Packing for Air Travel" in Chapter 13.

Accessories, Bags, and Carriers

If your basic pack is on the small side, you may find yourself cramped for space when you take a trip of unusual length or difficulty. Several things can be done to make a minimal pack carry a big load.

Most packs come equipped with *tie-on patches,* squares or strips of tough plastic with slits. Running thin nylon webbing through the slits, you can fasten various objects securely outside. If your pack doesn't have patches where you need them, you can buy them cheaply and sew them on (with an awl); but a cobbler does a neater job for a small price. Whenever objects have to be tied on, elastic *shock cords* are invaluable to keep things stable. Extra *pack pockets* may also be purchased for some models and either strapped or sewn on.

Although most packs are made of water-resistant fabric, this built-in protection isn't really enough for hiking in the rain. For short summer storms, a multipurpose *poncho* may serve ($25 or so). For extended rain or snow, you just about have to have a waterproof *pack cover* ($24), a coated-nylon shell that snaps on over the pack. Once on, it's a nuisance because it blocks access to the outer pockets, but items inside stay dry.

For storage inside the main pack, the common containers are nylon stuff sacks, usually urethane coated, that close with drawstrings and cordlocks. Netting stuff sacks allow you to see at a glance what's in them, and can double as food coolers in a stream or lake; but pointy things tend to snag in the weave. Zippered pouches may also come in handy. Padded bags can be had for sensitive items of gear, and compressor bags for bulky things that need to shrink. Depending on size and features, cloth container prices run anywhere from $5 to $25. Zipper-locking plastic bags in various sizes are indispensable. So are large plastic garbage bags—I usually have a couple. Except possibly for a few food items, rigid boxes are not used.

A useful accessory is the *beltbag*—a zippered cloth pouch that rides on the packbelt. You can use it for ski paraphernalia; for film and camera; for pencil and paper; for lunch; for anything you want close at hand. A variation is the *bottle carrier*, which converts any liter bottle into an accessible canteen. Water bladders with hoses can be added to packs that don't already have them. These various add-ons cost anywhere from $12 to $35.

7

The Bed

Being out in the wilderness is one thing. *Sleeping* out in
the wilderness, and on the ground, and with the lightest equipment, is quite another. For people unaccustomed to it, it can take some getting used to. For
anybody, it takes some pretty good gear: ground cloth,
pad, and above all, sleeping bag.

How do you set about choosing the right bag? You
need to decide *how warm* a bag you need; *what kind of
insulating material* you want in it; and *what shape and
design* are best suited to your use. Then there are certain features you should look for in any bag.

How Much Bag Do You Need?

First things first. How cold will it get where you plan to
go? The bag you choose should be about right for the
temperatures you expect to encounter frequently during the next few years. Don't think in terms of an eventual dream trip to the high Arctic. Don't even buy for
the coldest possible night in the place and season you
will visit; rather, think of a night somewhat below the
average. You can make a light bag do very nicely for the
occasional chillier time, and you won't be carrying
needless weight when it's warm.

On summer trips in temperate North America, you
are unlikely to see many nights below freezing, even in

the high country, and in some regions, summer nights are in the fifties and above. Even three-season backpacking—spring, summer, and fall—is unlikely to take you below the twenties Fahrenheit. If you have an idea where you will go most often—New England mountains, say, or the Sierra Nevada—you might check trail guidebooks or talk to experienced local hikers about the conditions they have found. Online newsgroups are good sources of information.

How warm-blooded are you? People vary a good deal. Some are obvious cold sleepers—they shiver in sleeping bags that look like they belong on the Greenland ice. Others find it unusually easy to keep warm. It depends pretty much on your metabolic rate. Women on average seem to sleep a little colder than men.

Sleeping bags of a sort can be gotten for less than $50. Department stores everywhere sell rectangular bags that look like thick zippered blankets. They have quilted seams and generally use the cheapest synthetics for fill. These bags may serve for car camping, but they are either too cool for backpack camping, or too heavy and bulky to tote, or both.

The backpacker's sleeping bag is a much more highly engineered object. As a rule, it has no sewn-through seams; there is insulation all around you.

Bags come in a range of weights and degrees of warmth. The medium-weight *three-season bag*, good to about 20 degrees Fahrenheit, is the most versatile. It should weigh no more than about 4 pounds if a good synthetic filler is used, or not much over 3 pounds if the insulation is waterfowl down. Prices range from under $100 to over $400, depending largely on the fill material used. The archetypal three-season bag is a mummy bag filled with down (see "What Kind of Insulation?" below), weighing about 2 pounds and costing about $200.

As the amount of fill increases, three-season bags grade into *winter* sleeping bags, marvelous constructions intended only for conditions down toward 0 degrees Fahrenheit and below. In the other direction lie *summer* and *ultralight* bags, designed for warm weather travelers or fanatical weight-savers and weighing as little as 1 pound; see Chapter 22 for more information about these variations.

Judging the Warmth of a Sleeping Bag

How do you tell how warm a given bag will keep you? The answer is not as simple as you might expect. How warm you are on a particular night depends on half a dozen things besides your sleeping bag itself: the padding under you, wind, humidity, protection from the open sky, how much you ate for dinner, and of course your own warm-bloodedness. Even if we forget all these variations and speak of an "average" sleeper in "ideal" conditions, it can be hard to judge the insulating power of a bag.

You have three things to go by: manufacturers' temperature ratings, weight and kind of fill, and visible loft.

Manufacturers make predictions for their bags: this one is supposed to be comfortable to freezing, that one perhaps to 10 degrees above 0. Unfortunately, these ratings are variable and subjective. Better makers are cautious, afraid to claim too much, but some assertions are still out of line. No guarantee is ever implied. Manufacturers' assessments are best used to compare bags within one brand: a maker's bag rated to 20 degrees may or may not deliver, but it will certainly be warmer than the same maker's 30-degree bag.

The frustrating thing is that the relative warmth of bags can be precisely measured in the laboratory. Using a metal mannequin, researchers can determine exactly how well a sleeping bag retains heat. All that's needed is an agreement on how to express these test results as standardized ratings. Such a "protocol" has already been established—in Europe. North American bag buyers are still waiting.

The second consideration is fill. Every sleeping bag has a fabric label attached that states the type and weight of the insulating material used. (In a three-season bag, that weight should be under 2 pounds for down and not much over 3 pounds for other materials.) Now if the same material is used in bags of the same design, more fill means a warmer bag. But seldom is the comparison so straightforward. More often you are looking at bags of different shapes filled with different substances, or with down of different grades (some insulate twice as well as others). So weight is not the key.

The third factor is one you can check for yourself: *loft*. Loft is the height to which a sleeping bag puffs up when it is nicely shaken out. It used to be said that loft was the sole determinant of warmth, but the cleverness of the designers has overtaken that statement. Certain insulations have credible claims to be warmer, inch for inch, than their competitors; shell materials and other components can change the picture, too. All you can really say is that, of two bags with the same fill material and the same shell fabric, the loftier bag is going to be the warmer. Some manufacturers provide loft figures for their bags, but you can make your own estimate with a couple of rulers. Lay one ruler on top of the bag, to compress it just slightly and give you a reference point; use the second ruler to measure the distance from the floor to the first. Again, the best use is comparative: other things being equal, each added inch of loft adds about ten degrees of warmth.

In the end, of course, your comfort is the only accurate measure. Once more, it may be a good investment to rent several bags (under $50 for a weekend). Each time you try a bag, make a note of its materials, its loft, and of the temperatures you encounter. When you find out how comfortable you are in a particular bag on a particular night, you will have more than theory to go on. You can extrapolate, at least, to others of similar construction.

What Kind of Insulation?

What is it that keeps you warm outdoors in a sleeping bag? Nothing but your own body heat, trapped by the material around you. Heat escapes by traveling through solids (conduction), through space (radiation), and, most important, through moving air (convection). Insulation creates a layer of still air, blocks convection, and holds heat in. The thicker the barrier, the less heat will escape. Thus, the importance of insulation thickness: loft.

There are now just two filling materials in wide use that are light enough and lofty enough for wilderness sleeping bags. These are *waterfowl down* and *polyester* in half a dozen cunningly crafted forms.

Top-quality goose down is the gold standard of sleeping bag insulation. Nothing else gives so much warmth for so little weight. Nothing else compresses into such a tiny volume in your pack. Nothing else lasts so long. Nothing else costs so much.

What counts is the down's springiness or ability to loft. "Lofting power" can be measured precisely in cubic inches filled by a single ounce of puffed-up material. Grades vary; 900 cubic inches per ounce is tops.

All synthetic insulations are attempts to imitate and ultimately to catch up with down. Progress is being made, but even the newest synthetics insulate less well than any decent down. The synthetic bags are not only heavier but also clumsier—they won't compress as well. And they are less durable.

They have, however, two powerful selling points. First, they are very much cheaper. Second, synthetic bags are safer when it's wet and cold. It would be difficult to overstate how important this can be.

Down, like cotton, turns on you when it gets wet, losing nearly all its loft. A waterlogged down bag is not just a nuisance, it's a horror. Anyone who has spent a night in a wet snowstorm, two days' walk from a roadhead, with a couple of hundred dollars' worth of wringing-wet goose down, can make the case for a synthetic bag. A synthetic bag loses only part of its loft when wet. You won't be exactly happy in a wet synthetic bag, but you'll make it through the night. You can squeeze the bag out like a sponge and dry it completely, once good weather returns, in a few hours.

As noted, all synthetic fills are forms of polyester. Most are made in short fibers, in emulation of down;

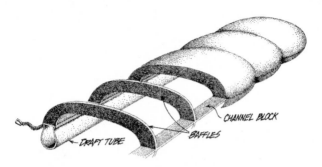

In a classic down bag, baffles create compartments to stabilize insulation. The draft tube covers the gap made by the zipper. The channel block keeps down from shifting into the bottom of the bag.

current competitors are LiteLoft by 3M; Thermolite Extreme and MicroLoft by DuPont (the latter with ultrafine fibers); and two versions of Primaloft by Albany International. The short-fiber fills are fairly light and compressible but tend to break down quickly, losing their loft after several years of use. There seems little reason for preferring one of the current leading types to another. Two fills that were standard a few years ago, Hollofil and Quallofil by DuPont, are now economy products.

Polarguard Delta by Hoechst-Celanese, the latest version of one of the oldest good synthetic fills, is different: it is a continuous hollow filament spun like cotton candy. This quite new material seems at present to be down's closest competitor (and is priced to match). Its predecessor, Polarguard 3D, is still used in cheaper bags. The Polarguards retain their lofting power a good deal longer than short-fiber synthetic fills.

Various bag makers have developed their own house-brand insulations, which may be either short-filament type or long.

Different fills are arranged in different ways.

In a down bag, the fill is loose. There are internal netting walls, called baffles, to keep the down from shifting and opening up cold spots. These walls run the short way around the bag, leaving the outside seams that give down bags the familiar caterpillar look.

Ways of organizing insulation. Slant-box baffling (left) is giving way to trapezoidal baffling (center), which stabilizes down better. Synthetic fills are often packaged in overlapping battings (right).

The compartments created may be parallelograms (slant-box baffling) or trapezoids, with nonparallel walls (trapezoidal baffling); the latter seems to stabilize better. Synthetic fills come in blocks, called *battings;* these are usually arranged to overlap like shingles, slanting from outer to inner shell like slant-box down compartments, and leaving the same outside seams.

What Kind of Shell?

Sleeping bag shells are made of nylon or polyester. Ripstop nylon is the old standard. Nylon taffeta is the same fiber woven to be softer and more flexible, but not quite as resistant to tearing. Polyester also comes in ripstop and taffeta weaves; it deteriorates more slowly in sunlight than does nylon, prolonging bag life if you virtually live outdoors; it also tends to shed water. "Microfiber" shells are very tightly woven, which helps water repellency and wind resistance; Pertex is a brand.

Then there are shells built of water-resistant "breathable" fabrics. The makers of Gore-Tex have developed a material called DryLoft specifically for sleeping bag use; some makers use their own proprietary fabrics. Such shells make excellent sense when the stuff inside them is vulnerable down; they are also used widely with synthetic insulations, to which they add some warmth. Some users complain that high-tech shells ice up and grow ineffective in cold conditions.

Whatever the fabric, a dark-colored shell is best, because it helps a damp bag dry faster in the sun.

Design and Construction

When you know how much warmth you want, and what kind of filler and shell you prefer, you are halfway toward buying the right bag. What's left to consider is shape, design, size, and the finer points that show that the maker has done a good job.

Shape. The standard is the mummy bag, a close-cut design that starts wide at the shoulders but narrows with the body to the toes. The snuggest mummies are more like sleeping garments than portable beds: when you roll, they roll with you. Mummies give the greatest warmth for the least fill. At the head there is typically a hood that can be closed around the face to leave only the tiniest of openings.

Some people find mummies unpleasantly confining. Other designs give you more room: modified mummies with and without hoods; barrel-shaped bags; semirectangular and fully rectangular models. But the broader the bag, the more mass it must have to provide the same uniform loft, and the more air your body has to keep warm in order to maintain its local comfort zone. Wider bags do work well for couples, who can zip two together to form a luxurious bed; a small child can be tucked in alongside.

Length and proportions. Most models come in three sizes: short, regular, and long, for people over six feet. When you lie in the bag with the hood (if there is one) tightened over your face, you should be able to stretch your neck and point your toes without compressing the insulation at head or foot. Bags designed specifically for women are built a bit narrower at the shoulders and a

The mummy-style sleeping bag (top) is the most efficient type for a single sleeper. Rectangular or semirectangular bags, opened out and zipped together, work well for couples.

bit wider at the hips. They also have a little extra insulation, especially for the torso and at the feet.

Channel block. In most down bags an internal partition runs the length of the bag, on the side opposite the zipper, to prevent the fill from shifting between the topside and the underside. Some makers leave out the barrier, arguing that you can shift the down yourself to make the bag warmer or cooler. I prefer the stability of the channel block.

The foot end. A good bag won't simply pinch out at the foot. Instead, it has an elaborately constructed bulge, a sort of a box, with room for your toes and a good thickness of insulation beyond. In a woman's bag, the foot end may be lined with polyester fleece.

Zipper. Most bags have them, typically down the sleeper's right side to about the ankle. Some near-rectangular bags zip all the way to the foot and along the bottom. A few lightweight bags have just a short zipper down one side or the top. The zipper should work in both directions, so that you can open the lower end while leaving the upper end closed. Massive nylon sliders are standard and pretty reliable. In better bags, each track of the zipper is set in a strip of stiffer fabric, to discourage snagging. Another nice feature is a snap or hook-and-loop fastener at the zipper's top, to discourage its working its way open. Bags of the same or compatible models can be zipped together to form a single, larger bed (but one of them must have its zipper on the *left*). In a very narrow bag, you need to reach across your body to work a zipper, so it should be on the opposite side from your favored hand.

Draft tube. This long flap of insulation shields the inside of the zipper and keeps heat from leaking out along this line. At the foot of the bag, the tube should extend a bit beyond the zipper end, so that no cold gap is left.

Draft collars. Bags intended for very cold conditions will also have an insulated collar or sill that clings to the body at neck or chest level to prevent warm air from escaping. This may be a simple ruff, or may be elasticized or adjustable.

Pockets. Some sleeping bags have pockets built into their shells: a little one for stashing the stuff you may need at night; a larger one for a pillow.

Mattress holders. There may be straps to hold your sleeping pad in place (see "Between You and the Ground," below), or even a full-length pocket underneath into which you slide the pad. In some ultralight bags that have pockets, built-in insulation under the body is omitted entirely.

Buying a Sleeping Bag

In the store, spend some time with the available sleeping bags that fit your general specifications. Lay them out and crawl in. Thrash around a bit. Does the bag seem long enough when you are stretched out inside with the hood closed up around your face? Is it roomy enough for your personal taste? If you plan cold-weather camping, is there room at the foot to tuck in a water bottle or anything else you want to keep warm? When in doubt, favor the longer size.

Consider the hood. Different makers tailor these differently. Do you like the way your model drapes around your face when you snug it up? Does the hood opening stay put in front of your face when you change position—for instance, to lie on your side?

Consider the shells. The fabric next to your skin should be pleasant to the touch. If the fill is down, shells must be woven very densely, or down particles will work their way out between the threads. A few plumules always escape from a new down bag, especially at the seams—no cause for alarm unless the leakage continues.

Work the zipper up and down to see that it doesn't tend to snag, and that its draft tube is generous.

Especially in a cheaper bag, it's not a bad idea to check detailing. How good is the stitching? Examine a lot of it, especially where stress comes on the seams: along the zipper and around the hood where the drawstring runs in its sleeve. Double stitching, and of course strong bar-tacking, are important at these places. Turn the bag inside out and examine the foot end, the hardest part of the bag to sew. You can't get at everything, but a bag well made where you can see it is probably sound clear through.

Finally, stuff the bag into the stuff sack it comes with. Instead of rolling it, mash it, handful by handful, starting with the foot end. Consider how much room the resulting package will take in your pack. If you will be wearing a traditional three-quarter-length external-frame pack, which carries the sleeping bag outside and below, the bulk of the bag hardly matters. If you're working with an internal-frame pack of modest capacity, it matters a great deal. If the bag is bulky, you may want to buy a *compression stuff sack* with straps that squeeze it down farther. If by any chance the original stuff sack isn't waterproof, get one that is.

Adding Layers

Lately, the concept of the "sleeping system" has attained a certain vogue. Essentially, the idea is to supplement the insulating power of the basic bag with an assortment of shells and layers that act, in one way or another, to increase warmth and protection. The result is a layer system like the one applied to clothing. There is an element of hype in all this (when a heretofore simple piece of gear is redefined as a "system," watch out: the price has just gone up). Nonetheless, there is value in the concept.

Here are some of the possible added layers:

Bivouac sacks. Some bags, as noted above, have waterproof breathable outer shells. You can also carry a separate bivouac sack of the same high-tech fabric, perhaps in place of a tent. These "bivy sacks" cost $90 and up and weigh something over a pound. In very cold conditions, however, these separate shells have some tendency to ice up, losing the breathability that makes them different from ordinary urethane-coated cloth; they are more likely to suffer this effect than are microporous fabrics built into the sleeping bags themselves.

Overbags and liner bags. You can beef up your basic bag for a colder trip by adding to it a second light sleeping bag, inserted inside or wrapped without. You'll gain ten or twenty degrees of warmth. Some makers offer two-in-one bags, with an outer layer you can zip off.

Bag liners. Cleanliness, not warmth, is the main reason for using a simple inner sheath of cotton, flannel, or silk. The readily washable liner intercepts the grime that otherwise winds up on your not-so-readily washable sleeping bag (see "Storage, Cleaning, and Care," below). This addition strikes most people as inordinate fussiness, but a liner can add years to the life of a down bag that is frequently used. Liners weigh as little as 4 ounces and cost $20 to $60.

Radiant heat barriers. Ordinary sleeping bag insulation is not very good at blocking heat loss due to radiation: the infrared waves that pour from your body pass right through. A radiant barrier is a piece of reflective fabric designed to turn back these rays. Backpackers first came to know of this tool in the form of the "space blanket," a rectangle of fragile reflective cloth for use as cloak, shelter, or groundsheet. Tailored reflective liners are also available and can add ten or fifteen degrees of warmth to an existing bag.

Vapor barrier. Every few years there's a surge of interest in this variation. By putting a waterproof layer next to the skin, you can prevent body moisture from migrating outward through the insulation and evaporating into the night air. Since this evaporation takes away a good deal of heat, you will sleep warmer if it doesn't take place. Won't you also sleep wetter? No, say the advocates: you simply stop sweating. Yes, say many people who have tried it, you do get uncomfortably wet. If vapor barriers have a place, it is in bitter cold.

Between You and the Ground

Ground is hard. Ground is cold. Ground is often moist. To deal with these things, you need some defenses beneath you.

Undermost goes a ground cloth—just a rectangle of coated nylon or vinyl, available for a few dollars in any store that handles sporting goods. The more expensive ones last longer. Reflective "space blankets" are popular but easily torn. When you use a tent, you will want the same sort of sheet next to the ground under it, to protect the waterproof floor.

On top of the ground cloth you'll want a mattress or pad. This cushions, which is important; it insulates, which is vital. If your bag is down filled, the part beneath you will collapse almost to nothing under your weight. Bags with synthetic fills do not compress so totally, but a pad underneath is still part of what keeps you warm.

That protection may be a simple foam pad, or an air mattress.

Closed-cell foam pads (Evazote, Ensolite) are compact, durable, impervious to water, and unaffected by all but the coldest temperatures. The simplest form is the rectangular sheet, 18 to 22 inches wide and in varied lengths. Weight-conscious summer backpackers may choose a length of less than 4 feet or cut a longer rectangle down. Thickness varies from ¼ inch to ¾ inch; the thinner style will do in summer for warmth, but thicker is softer. More elaborate brand-named versions come with textured surfaces, cloth covers, and rounded outlines. A hinged, folding model by Z-Rest is very popular.

Air mattresses get their softness from air but their warmth from insulating materials that keep that air from moving around and robbing you of heat. Blow-up mattresses may be filled with down or polyester insulation. The popular "self-inflating" type, pioneered by Therm-A-Rest, uses blocks of open-cell foam. When the pad is rolled up tight, the foam is compressed: when the mattress is laid out and the valve opened, the foam expands by itself and pulls air in. It's tidy, elegant, and sort of magical. Lengths, thicknesses, and features of air mattresses vary. All of them have two drawbacks: greater weight and bulk, and, despite tough shells, a certain vulnerability to puncture.

The prices of pads vary widely, according to length, thickness, and construction. The cheapest good pad is still a closed-cell slab, ⅜ inch thick; even full-length ones can be gotten for about $12. The most expensive might be a self-inflating mattress, full length and 1¾ inches thick: about $80. Weights vary from ½ pound for a short, closed-cell pad to about 3 pounds for a maximum self-inflatable version. With the appropriate kit, a self-inflatable pad can be made to serve as a camp chair, luxurious sometimes for the older back. Another useful accessory is the yokelike arrangement that joins pads side by side into a sort of double bed.

The ultimate air mattress is a *hammock*. Since most hammocks for wilderness use are set up as tents, with rainflies and netting, these are discussed in Chapter 8.

What about a *pillow*? Most people use clothing, stuffed perhaps into a cloth bag or a pillow pocket in the sleeping bag. Air mattresses may have built-in pillow segments. Separate inflatable pillows can also be had.

Storage, Cleaning, and Care

A down bag should last ten or twelve years, a synthetic bag perhaps a third that long. But all sleeping bags have enemies: rough handling, compression, moisture, heat and sunlight, certain chemicals, and body oils.

The baffles of down bags and the battings of synthetic bags are fragile structures. Avoid twisting them or yanking on them. You have to be much gentler pulling a bag out of its stuff sack than pushing it in.

Between trips, bags must get room to breathe. Stuffed for weeks or months, down loses part of its springiness and thus its all-important loft. Synthetic fill collapses even more dramatically. Any bag can be stored safely in a very large cotton sack. Bags that have built-in loops for the purpose, at the foot end, may be hung. The ideal storage area is dry, cool, and dark. In the wilderness, too, it's good to leave a bag unstuffed as much as you can. (Exception: when the air is very moist, a loose bag with nobody in it will just get damp.)

Dampness is the third enemy, though not of all bags equally. Synthetics don't mind water, but down that is continually damp will disintegrate, and any bag can mildew. Make sure your stuff sack is waterproof. On the trail, if a bag is moist and bedraggled when you put it away in the morning, you can dry it out, weather permitting, at lunch. After the trip, air your bag thoroughly. A seriously wet bag should be treated as though it had been washed (see below).

A sleeping bag shouldn't be left in the sun for more than the minimum time necessary—sunlight eventually damages nylon shell material. Heat attacks both shells and fills, including synthetic fills; a synthetic bag locked in a very hot car trunk can be ruined. And campfire sparks can give you a pox of melted holes in a hurry.

Certain chemicals are bad for down, or for synthetic materials, or both. Insect repellents containing DEET are death on nylon. And sleeping bags should not be dry-cleaned, period.

Which brings us to the question: How *should* they be cleaned, when the time comes?

The best way, clearly, is by hand, with the help perhaps of a big tumble dryer. Do the washing in a tub with Ivory Snow soap flakes or a similarly gentle soap (never detergent or bleach). The water should be copious and warm, not hot. Ease the bag into the soup gradually (some like to leave it in its cotton storage sack for first submersion). Once the bag is saturated, work the suds through it by gently pressing. When the suds have turned dark, drain the tub and start over. Do this as often as you need to until the suds are white. Then rinse again several times, making sure to get all the soap out of the material. Let gravity drain most of the water from the bag; press gently to extract a little more.

Now comes the crucial move. Lift the wet bag with all the care you can. Cradle the whole soggy thing in your arms. No part should hang unsupported. If you simply grab an end and haul, the heavy, sodden fill will macerate baffles or battings, and you'll be out your two hundred bucks or so.

The drying process can be started outdoors. You can hang the bag on a clothesline, but lengthwise, so that the dividers run vertical. To finish the job, you can tumble it in a public laundry dryer—the bigger, the better—at very low heat or no heat at all. (Down is very sensitive to heat; the resins that hold polyester battings in place are even more so.) If there's lots of room, throw in a couple of dry towels to help absorb water (you might replace these once along the way). Forget the once-traditional tennis ball or shoe. Every 15 minutes, check that the fabric is not too hot, and if you feel any clumping in the fill, knead it out. You can pull gently across clots of down; synthetic batts that seem to be sticking together can be teased cautiously apart.

Too laborious? You can shorten the job somewhat by using a large front-loading washing machine (never a machine with an agitator) set on the coolest, gentlest cycle and using the usual gentle soap. The machine must be one you can shut down, once the soap is dispersed, for a good, long soak. Wash a second time soapless to get a thorough rinse.

When you wash a bag, should you take the opportunity to wash in a specialized water repellency treatment? There are variations on durable water repellent meant specifically for down. But Annie Getchell, gear care guru, recommends against this treatment, except for a very old bag, or one that has suffered dry cleaning. Reason: the treatment can hamper the breathability of the shell.

Plainly, washing your sleeping bag is no joke. You don't want to do it more often than you have to, and in the case of down, you shouldn't. Down loses a certain amount of insulating power every time it is laundered.

Mattresses, too, need to relax between trips. Closed-cell pads are virtually indestructible but lose thickness eventually; prolong their usefulness by storing them flat or loosely rolled. Air mattresses should be stored flat with valves open. Punctured shells can be fixed like rain gear, with a dab of urethane sealant for a pinprick and sealant plus a coated-nylon patch from your repair bag for a slightly larger opening. Specialty mattress repair kits are also available. A major rip requires professional attention.

8

Shelter

When you head into the wilderness—no matter how fine the weather at the roadhead—you must have some plan for *shelter*. And that means something carried in your pack. Such old woodcraft techniques as building huts of green boughs are now reserved for survival situations. You can't count too heavily on trailside huts or lean-tos, either; some regions have them, but they afford little privacy, and when they are empty you may find them dirty or in disrepair. In another category are full-service backcountry hostels, like those in Yosemite or the White Mountains of New Hampshire: delightful, but not part of what this book is about.

The basic requirement, of course, is a roof to shed rain. It will incidentally keep dew off your sleeping bag and keep you a little warmer. It can also protect you from hot, bright sunlight, which, in treeless landscapes, can itself be a problem. Most though not all shelter types ward off the bugs as well.

What kind of roof should it be? In the eastern United States, in the coastal Pacific Northwest, and in the northern U.S. Rockies, the case is good for carrying a full-scale tent, a diminutive fabric building with walls and a floor, at any time of year. So too for Canada and Alaska. In the southwestern third of the United States, by contrast, many people make do with tarps or floorless tents, at least past the peak of mosquito season.

All shelters must deal with moisture from two sources. They have to shed water that comes from the sky; they also must somehow get rid of water that comes from within, from the breath and sweat of the occupants, so that it does not condense on the cool canopy and produce an internal drizzle. Broadly, there are three solutions. Some shelters are made of waterproof fabrics and simply rely on copious ventilation to take body moisture away. Tarps and pyramids (see below) work this way, and you find some fully enclosed tents of this impermeable type as well. Second, a number of tents utilize microporous, waterproof-breathable fabrics like those in rain gear. Shelters of the third group, known as "double-walled" tents, come in two parts: an inner enclosure built largely of permeable nylon, not waterproofed, so that moisture can escape; and an additional, fully waterproof *rainfly* that is stretched just above the vulnerable structure underneath. Regardless of design, ventilation remains the key to staying comfortably dry.

Less Than a Tent: Tarps and Other Options

With the new interest in ultralight backpacking, minimalist shelters have come back into fashion.

The simplest possible roof is also an item of clothing: the *poncho*, a rectangular piece of waterproof fabric with neck hole and hood. Although some ponchos are made just large enough to cover the hiker's body, others are long enough in back to drape over the pack as well; these, called *backpack ponchos*, can be pitched as minimal one-person shelters. A few people use bivouac sacks, discussed in Chapter 7, as shelters; some of these, equipped with frameworks that lift the fabric off the face, can be thought of as tiny one-person tents.

The classic Southwestern rain shelter, for elevations below tree line, is the *tarp*. This is simply a piece of water-repellent cloth. Good tarps are made of nylon coated inside with polyurethane and perhaps treated outside with silicone; if silicone is applied, less

You may never pitch a tarp the same way twice. This simple A-frame pitch, nice if you can get it, depends on having just the right pair of trees.

polyurethane is needed and overall weight drops. A 10-by-10-foot square (really a shade smaller because of hemming) will serve for one sleeper; a nominal 10-by-12-foot rectangle suffices for two. Some have scooped outlines, allowing for a tighter pitch. Edges are reinforced and grommeted. Weights range from 1 to 3 pounds. Prices run $40 to $120. The fly of a double-walled tent (see below) can also be used alone as a tarp. Avoid tarps made of polyethylene, which are cheap but too fragile for this use.

A tarp can, in theory, be pitched with nothing but cord. Actually, you may be glad to have a tent pole, trekking pole, or staff together with several stakes; natural anchors don't necessarily come just where you'd like them. In pitching a tarp you may wish for a grommet where one is lacking, even in the middle of the sheet. You can improvise an attachment by bunching the fabric around a small, smooth stone and looping a noose of cord around it. There are commercial gimmicks that do the same thing with a plastic or rubber "rock" and a plastic or metal "noose." Tailored tarps may have mid-sheet attachments and "pole patches."

A step up in coverage and weight is the waterproof *pyramid*, shaped as the name implies but lacking a built-in floor. It is supported by a single central pole (again, perhaps your staff). You pitch it so that its bottom edge is a foot or more above the ground, allowing substantial ventilation—though not as much as a tarp. Pyramids are even used in snow camping, though not by me. Prices start at $100 and weights at about 2 pounds.

Tent Basics

Though tents are built in many sizes, the one you take backpacking won't be a palace. Anything offering less than 27 square feet of floor space, a space about 4 feet wide by 7 feet long, is strictly a one-person model; 32 square feet is a snug fit for two. At about 40 square feet, two-person tents grade into lodgings for three. Though shapes vary widely, the smallest tents tend, like people, to be oblong; larger ones are more likely to have square or hexagonal floors. Roofs rise 2 or 3 feet in shelters intended for one, 3 or 4 feet in most two-person models, and almost 6 feet in the largest family-sized backpacking tents.

Tents vary widely in weight and ruggedness. At the light end of the scale are what might be called *bug tents*, built largely of netting and designed mainly to exclude insects, but equipped with (sometimes rather scanty) rainflies. *Three-season* models, the norm for backpacking, can fend off serious rain; they vary in their ability to handle high winds. *Winter* tents are stoutly supported, carefully tailored, and strong.

Some tents, known as *convertibles*, allow adjustment for differing seasons. For instance, supplemental poles can be used or left home depending on the conditions expected; or netting windows can be exposed or hidden under zip-on, solid-fabric shutters.

A three-season backpacking tent for two shouldn't weigh much more than 7 pounds including stuff sack, cords, and stakes; you can get that down below 5 pounds with clever design and at a cost in roominess and features. As space for additional people is added, weight climbs too, but more slowly; a three-person, three-season model weighing more than 9 pounds, accessories included, is distinctly heavy.

Prices vary even more widely: you may pay as little as $50 or as much as $200 per person sheltered. REI and Coleman are about the cheapest specialty makers; Bibler and Stephenson, both makers of innovative single-wall tents, are about the most expensive.

Most backpacking tents are made of nylon, either ripstop or nylon taffeta. Some use polyester, which holds up better against the ultraviolet radiation in sunlight, or nylon-polyester blends. There may be larger or smaller areas of mesh. Tent floors are always waterproof (with the coated side up), and the waterproofing extends 4 inches or more up the sides of the walls and up the door or doors. This "tub floor" cannot be built without seams, but the fewer there are, the better. In high-end tents, seams are not sewn but "welded," that is, glued. A few convertible tents have removable floors.

The upper reaches of the tent may be made of waterproof-breathable fabric, or they may be simply waterproof, coated with urethane and perhaps impregnated with silicon. More commonly, the canopy is ordinary permeable nylon, *not* waterproofed. This allows moisture to escape from the inside. To prevent water from invading from the outside, the double-walled tent has its second roof: the waterproof rainfly.

The rainfly is usually a separate, detachable piece of material. It drapes over the tent's supporting framework in such a way that it never touches the inner, permeable wall. It should overhang the sides enough to prevent slanting, wind-driven rain from reaching uncoated fabric. At the lower edges, this upper roof attaches to the main body of the tent, often with snap-in buckles. There may be added attachment points for greater stability.

The flies of many tents are designed to create a patch of rain-sheltered ground, a *vestibule*, just outside the inner entrance. This is a sort of porch area where you can park some gear or even cook. Some vestibules are walled and quite weatherproof, lacking only the floor.

At one end or facet of the tent is a triangular or hemispherical *door*. In long narrow tents, entry at one end is most convenient for two people, but a door on the long side can be larger, helping ventilation. Doors sometimes hinge at the bottom, sometimes at the side. Each arrangement has advantages. If a door is bottom hinged, with zippers running up to the apex on either side, the top can be opened easily for ventilation; but the loose flap of a fully opened door is prone to get trampled and dirty. If the door hinges at one side and opens along the bottom, it zips to a raised, waterproof sill. Many tents have two doors on opposite ends or sides; when both are open, this may give you a cooling breeze.

Ventilation is exceedingly important in any tent. Besides the entrances, there must be at least one opening high up near the ridgeline. Two vents are better. Some tents have large areas of mesh. In flyless, single-wall tents, openings must be protected by waterproof hoods; doors may create their own rain shadows by leaning out at the top.

Any tent to be used in warm weather needs *mosquito netting* over every opening. Doors are commonly split-level, with netting above and a solid panel below. Complete inner doors of netting are also occasionally found.

Two or more *pockets* of netting, hanging from the sidewalls, are essential for keeping track of small, losable objects.

For the vital connection to the ground, all tents are equipped with *stakeout loops* at the corners and perhaps other points around the floor. You will also find attachment points for added cords called *guylines*, and perhaps the lines themselves. These add stability in wind.

Holding Up the Roof

Tent canopies are supported by poles. In the very lightest models, you can use your trekking pole to provide a single, central pillar, which saves enormously in weight and is much more convenient. General-purpose tents have elaborate pole systems.

Poles are made of aluminum or, increasingly, a variant called tempered aluminum; both are found in excellent tents. Distinctly a second choice is tubular fiberglass. Poles come in sections, each 12 to 18 inches long, linked by elastic shock cord running inside. When the pole is set up, the base of each section nests in a socket in the end of the one below. Fiberglass segments are linked by metal sleeves. For packing, the sections pull apart, and the pole folds into a manageable bundle.

Poles are seated in grommets or pockets at the margins of the tent floor and pass through fabric sleeves on the outside of the canopy; or they may be attached to the canopy only by elastic cords and clips; or they may even run inside the canopy. Most poles are curved (when pitched) and form tensioned arcs. Rounded shapes and tension combine to pull the fabric tight, making surfaces that don't flap much in the wind.

The simplest layout to visualize is the hoop or *tunnel tent*, with a long, rounded roof held up by two or more half circles of tensioned poles. The effect is a little like a Conestoga wagon. Some tunnel tents slope sharply down from head to foot; some hump up in the middle. The poles do not intersect, and the tent must be pulled taut between ground anchors at either end before it is self-supporting. A two-pole tunnel tent is a pleasantly light design (under 5 pounds for two), and several enormously popular tents use this arrangement. At the other end of the spectrum, rugged mountaineering tents are also built on this plan.

Another design is the *modified A-frame*. At each end of such a tent, a pair of poles forms a rounded A with no crossbar. There may be a third A or arc amidships. Linking these supports from end to end is a ridgepole. This arrangement is a hybrid between a tunnel tent and an older, almost vanished design, the basic A-frame (which is all straight lines and lacks the middle pole). Unlike either of its parents, the modified A-frame will stand up by itself, without guylines.

The majority of tents today, however, are of *dome* or *modified dome* design. They rely on arcing poles that

Tents of this tunnel or hoop design are light and somewhat short of head-room. To create the shelter, the two ends must be staked.

The modified A-frame design resembles a tunnel tent but has nearly trian-gular ends and often an additional pole running the length of the canopy, for maximum stability in wind.

cross each other, intersecting in sometimes ingenious ways. In one simple variation, poles connect the diago-nally opposite corners of a rectangular floor, forming an X. A popular refinement adds a third arc, like a cap on one end of the X, at the front door. Again, two poles may lean toward one another without touching, like a pair of parentheses turned wrong way around, or lean together and overlap at the top. The combinations mul-tiply from there. Generally speaking, added poles bring greater stability at a cost in higher weight. All tents of the extended family of domes are freestanding.

Dome tents are very popular. Erecting the poles creates a freestanding shelter; guylines add some stability in wind.

Tents for Wind and Winter

A winter or "all-season" tent may have to resist 80-mile-an-hour gusts or bear a weight of several hundred pounds of wet, clinging snow. Compared to three-season models, such tents are built of thicker materials, with extra reinforcements at stress points. They have more and stronger poles; there may be a means of locking poles together where they cross. Also, they typically have somewhat more room than comparable three-season tents. All this gives winter tents an average weight per person of over 3 pounds—unless the canopies are made of waterproof breathable fabric, in which case they can be lighter. Unsurprisingly, winter tents are more expensive than three-season types—the midrange is about $450 for a two-person model.

Buying a Tent

The ideal place to shop for a tent is one of those barn-like stores where many different designs can be pitched side by side. If you have access to such a display, start with a get-acquainted visit. Send some time crawling in and out of tents, stretching out experimentally inside, and getting to know their features. Then go away and mull the choices.

At this stage, renting is an excellent idea. Rental tents are affordable (about $50 a weekend), and the experience will help you to clarify your preferences before you spend perhaps five times that amount on a purchase.

Questions to ask yourself: First, do you really need a full tent at all, or will a tarp or pyramid give you protection enough? If you do need a tent, where will you use it most often—in rainy, mosquito-ridden woods? On summer treks above timberline? On ski or snow-shoe trips? How many people should it be able to sleep? How long might you need to spend in it at a time? And, of course, how much are you willing to pay?

Every shelter is a compromise. The roomiest tent won't be the lightest nor the most stable in a wind. The cheapest tent won't be the most durable nor the easiest to pitch. And the harder the tentmaker has worked to combine different practical advantages in a single model, the higher the price is likely to be.

Size. You have a choice of shelters for one person, for two, for three or more. If your tent will be only a now-and-then shelter, it need only be large enough to stretch out comfortably in. But if you expect to spend days in it, during long rains or snowstorms, with much of your gear inside, you need a good deal more room. A generous vestibule—the area under a rainfly but not under the main canopy—helps house your stuff.

Height. Some shelters are high enough so that you can sit up in them without brushing the roof; some aren't. Some people get claustrophobia from low ceilings. In grizzly bear country, too, it may be a good idea to have some extra room between you and the canopy (see Chapter 29). Higher profiles, though, don't do so well in wind.

Wind stability. For typical backpacking, especially in the West, you need a tent that can take a pretty good gale. If you will be camping mostly in sheltered woods, high stability may not be worth the sacrifice in money and headroom.

Convertibility. If you plan to camp in varied conditions, you might consider a tent that can change to match, with such features as zip-out windows. These, however, add some complexity and weight.

Durability. An obvious value, durability comes from heavy materials, lots of reinforcement, and very careful workmanship (see "Detailing" below in this list). For example, some poles are thicker than others; some waterproof coatings are thicker than others. Such desirable extras cost you something in weight and something in money.

Lightweight. The ultimate good—or is it? Most of the other things you value in a tent add some ounces. Tent innovations are mainly aimed at getting more advantages from less mass, but you can pay a great deal to shed just a handful of ounces.

Back in the store, you can look at the offerings again with your criteria in mind. As you begin to zero in on a choice, look at three more factors: ventilation, ease of pitching, and detailing.

Ventilation. Is there plenty? Make sure there is at least one vent high up.

Ease of pitching. When you consider a tent, inventory the jobs that have to be done. Pitching usually begins with staking out the floor, continues with erecting poles, and ends with attaching the fly. The pole stage is key. Do poles slide into fabric sleeves, or simply run through a series of clips? If poles are different lengths, can you quickly tell which is which? (Color coding is common.) Can you readily see which path each pole is to follow? How hard is the push to get the last pole seated? Must guylines be pulled out to make the tent stand up (true of hoop tents only)? Is this okay with you? How easily does the fly attach? How readily could you do all this with cold hands, or in the dark?

Detailing. Especially if you are shopping for bargains, make sure that minimum standards are met. Most seams should be what the industry calls "lap felled." In such a seam, the two pieces of fabric are folded, each over the other; stitching goes through all four layers. In any seam that is not of this type, make sure that stitching is not too close to the edge of any piece of fabric (such spots are likely to fray). In any seam in the fly, or in a one-layer, waterproof-breathable canopy, make sure that the joining is stable, not tending to gape when you pull on either side. In some expensive tents, seams are now glued together, without stitching. If not thus "welded," seams in the fly and in the tent floor will have been sealed in the factory with melted-on tape

Stitching is crucial. The more places with double or triple rows, the better. There should be no holes without thread in them, no loose, hanging thread ends, and no puckered effect where some stitches, out of line with the others, are taking extra strain.

There should be plenty of reinforcement. Look for it wherever there is a grommet; a loop where a tent peg will seat or a cord attach; a sewn-on strap; and wherever guylines attach to the tent. At a minimum, each stress point should have a heavy, doubled hem. In better tents, an extra piece of material may be added, especially at the peg loops. Grommets and other metal parts should be rust-free aluminum or brass. All points of quality become doubly important in a tent intended for winter use.

Pay attention to the poles as well. If metal, are they smooth and free of burrs and sharp edges? Do the segments join easily and securely? Is the shock cord elastic and firm?

If you must buy a tent you can't look at first, reserve the right to bring it back after setting it up indoors for a closer look. Most stores and suppliers are good about this.

Stakes, Lines, Accessories

A set of stakes may or may not come with the tent. Even if one does, you'll want to own a larger assortment for different conditions. You have a choice of materials and shapes. Of the materials, steel is strong but heavy, titanium strong but costly, aluminum and plastic the most common. The simplest design is the slender, pointed skewer with an eye at one end. Skinny stakes are insecure in soft soil, and aluminum ones will bend in hard ground. Better grip is provided by stakes that are T shaped in cross-section. Channeled stakes are C shaped in cross-section and work well in soft ground or consolidated snow. For winter there's the snow stake, a light aluminum angle, V shaped in section. Some stakes can be pounded in, some can't; there are even stakes that screw into the ground. Weight is generally about an ounce per stake, and prices run from under $1 to as much as $4 apiece (for titanium). If you camp in a variety of places and seasons, you may find yourself choosing a different set of anchors every time you pack.

Your tent may or may not come with a guyline for each possible attachment point. If not, fill out the set using stout parachute cord.

When you rig a tent, you need a way of tightening or loosening the lines without shifting the stakes. The knot called the tautline hitch (see Chapter 19) will serve; plastic gadgets are available to do the same thing. Some tents have tension adjusters built in.

Depending on your tent, you may be able to buy a "footprint" ground cloth tailored to its dimensions: $10 to $70. Important tools in any tent that gets lived in a lot are a superabsorbent towel for wiping up spills and condensation and a whisk broom for brushing out dirt or loose snow; you can even get a tiny broom-and-dustpan set.

Tents come with stuff sacks. Make sure that the tent and anything you want to travel with it—poles, stakes, repair items, ground cloth, whisk broom, towel?—will fit into this bag with a little room to spare; if it's tight in there, buy a bigger stuff sack.

Handling and Care

Few pieces of gear take as much punishment from the elements as a tent. After all, that's what it's for. But by the way you treat your tent, you can prolong its life—or shorten it.

You're going to load your tent into its stuff sack. Is it better for the fabric to fold and roll it around its poles, or should it be stuffed, handful by handful like a sleeping bag, with the poles on the side? It's a surprisingly big and technical argument. If the manufacturer has a preference, follow that. Gear care specialist Annie Getchell recommends rolling when dry and stuffing only when wet. If you do fold and roll, try to avoid creasing fabric at the same places every time.

Ultraviolet light is hard on tent materials, so pitch the tent in shade when you can. Look for a piece of ground without sharp rocks, sticks, or anything else that could puncture or abrade the water-resistant floor. Under the tent, spread out a ground cloth, tailored or folded so that it doesn't extend beyond the tent edges and thus funnel rainwater inward. If you are going to be lighting a fire, don't pitch the tent too close to the fire ring. Some canopy materials burn, though not explosively, and sparks melt nasty holes.

In assembling shock-corded poles, be slow and gentle. Start with the middle sections and work toward the ends. Check for grit and incipient damage as you go. A tent should be pitched firmly but need not be "drum-tight." A flapping shelter deteriorates faster than it should, but so does a hypertaut one.

Keep the inside of the tent as clean as possible. Boots stay outside in the vestibule, or in plastic bags. Cooking inside a tent, or even under its vestibule roof, is a risky business and not recommended. Nevertheless, winter campers routinely do it. Spilled stove fuel can damage the waterproofing on your floor. Citrus drinks are bad for nylon, and so are bug repellents containing DEET (see Chapter 29).

When you break camp, remove the fly first and spread it to dry, weather permitting, with the wetter side up. (After a clear night, that will be the condensation-soaked underside.) Take time to rub off any droplets of pitch or bird droppings. (Cooking oil, peanut butter, or kerosene will help.) Unstake the tent, shake out all grit and debris, and tip it on its side to air and dry. When you ease the poles out of their sleeves, use a pushing motion, not a pulling one: pulled segments will separate and nip the fabric. If the cloth is very wet and the weather fine, you can tie the tent on the outside of your pack in a loose bundle. Nylon is treated to resist mildew up to a point, but the drier you can keep it, the better.

If you get a minor puncture during a trip, wax from a candle, or even lip balm, will caulk it for a while. For a multiday temporary patch, use duct or adhesive tape, applied to the outer surface. Appropriately colored and textured nylon patches are also available; they look nicer but (in my experience) are harder to make stick. Be sure the surface is clean and dry; wipe it with an alcohol towelette from your repair or first-aid kit. Cut a patch a little larger than the problem. Trim it into a rounded shape (corners will peel) and smooth it on. To get a better bond, put something firm inside the canopy and a piece of paper outside, over the patch, and rub the edges of the tape with something like a knife handle. A little urethane sealant, if you have it along, should go on the inside of the trouble spot. A dab of urethane can also close a small tear in mosquito netting.

A broken pole can be fixed temporarily with duct tape and the metal splint that may have come with the tent. A C-shaped stake can also be used.

After a trip, set the tent up and police it. Check for abrasions, bad zippers, pulling threads, overlooked tears—the usual items to fix yourself or delegate to a shop, depending on your patience and skill. Sponge off any especially dirty spots with mild soap and water. Rubbing alcohol is the first home remedy for pitch; nail polish remover will lift it in a pinch. If a tent has been stored wet and has developed mildew, you can stop the damage, but not remove the stain, with baking soda or borax. Never wash a tent in a machine: too hard on coatings, membranes, and netting. If the thing is really filthy, you can take a garden hose to it. Let it dry standing briefly in the sun and for a longer time in the shade.

Check the poles, too, at this point. Make sure they're clean; wipe them thoroughly, especially if you have been camping near salt water. Pay special attention to the joints. Burrs can be gently filed off; flattened circumferences can be gently squeezed back to round. You may notice that once-straight poles are starting to reflect the arc shapes they are pitched in; that's all right. If there are breaks or kinks, you'll have to replace a segment. Weakened shock cords need shortening or replacement as well.

Tent waterproofing is not forever. In time you may have to repaint large areas with waterproof coating. For this you can use liquid, water-based polymers like AquaSeal, Poly Coat, Kenyon Recoat 3, or Thompson's Water Seal. As with urethane-coated rain gear, the treatment is applied to the outer, formerly uncoated side.

Tents and Low Impact

The improper placement of bedsites is one of the principal causes of damage to wilderness lands. *Where* you pitch your tent is much more important than *how*. Avoid vegetation and moist ground. For more on impact considerations in camping, see "Making and Managing the Camp," below.

In cross-country travel, away from established campsites, very low-impact sites may be tricky to find. It helps to have a narrow shelter that will fit in narrow spots. Tarps are the most flexible, because only the actual sleeping area needs to be level and clear. Where trees and stakable ground are scarce, freestanding tents may have the advantage over those that won't set up without guylines.

Does the driving of stakes have a significant impact on wilderness ground? Probably not very, but the matter is worth considering. When you select stakes for a trip, choose the thinnest style the area and season make practical: in summer, thin metal-eyelet stakes, not too flimsy, will work fine. It is often possible to use natural anchors instead of stakes. See also Chapter 19.

Your tent is the most visible item in all your gear. How visible depends on its color. Do you make your campsite obvious with a tent in yellow, orange, or a light, bright shade of blue—or do you blend into the landscape with green or rust or brown? I recommend here the unobtrusive colors. Nothing makes a wild landscape seem so populous as a scatter of highly visible tents—a whole seeming village where you would prefer to see no human presence at all.

The Hammock Option

Every few years there is a burst of publicity concerning a type of shelter we haven't discussed yet: the hammock. By wrapping a hammock in netting and stretching a fly across it, you have a construction that combines the functions of ground cloth, mattress, and tent. Such units—there aren't many makers—cost $120 or more and weigh about 2 pounds; they are designed for one person.

The hammock might seem the ultimate low-impact sleeping tool. Since your weight does not rest on the ground at all, you won't be flattening vegetation and compressing soil.

However, this advantage dwindles on examination. In an established campground, used for years, your body weight on the ground is not going to damage anything that isn't damaged already. If you are camping away from the trail, you can usually find non-vegetated ground, and you won't be using a site repeatedly. The hammock, which requires convenient trees, may even limit your choices. And it brings its own impact concern: you will need to pad the trunks of supporting trees if they are thin-barked or young.

Comfort suggests that the hammock is a fair-weather tool. Given much of a wind, it will rock, as one reviewer puts it, "not like a cradle."

9

Stove & Kitchen

Everybody likes a campfire, but virtually everybody, in the modern wilderness, carries and cooks on a stove.

An evening fire is a presence: almost a pet or a companion. It gives pleasant light, pleasant heat, pleasant noises. It is an event, an entertainment. It draws a group together around it. For many, it is a symbol of camping, a symbol of the wilderness even. "A campfire burns in the submerged memory of the Americans," writes Bernard De Voto, "all the way west from Plymouth Beach."

And yet the fire, in the wilderness today, has fallen out of favor. There are simply too many of us now and too little pristine land for old habits to hold. Fires near timberline, where wood is scarce and the growing season short, are not now defensible. Nor is there any excuse for the building of new fire rings where none has been before. In our more populous wilderness landscapes, firespots mark the ground like so many black sores, and these, more quickly than anything else we leave to mark our presence, make the land look used and overused.

There are situations where a campfire is perfectly acceptable—see Chapter 18. But even parties that now and then build fires must have a stove along. It's no great sacrifice. Stoves suitable for backpacking are light, efficient, and inexpensive.

Known to many as the Bleuet, this classic cartridge stove now goes by the name Camping Gaz. The small fuel canister shown must be left attached until empty; larger canisters are removable.

Stoves fall into three groups. There are *bottled-gas stoves*, which draw fuel from canisters containing compressed gases that, when released, stream out under pressure. More versatile but trickier are *liquid-fueled stoves*, burning white gas and in some cases kerosene and other fuels. A couple of *alternative stoves*, burning nonpressurized alcohol or solid fuel, make up the third group.

Bottled-Gas Stoves

These are also called "cartridge stoves" because their fuel comes in self-contained tanks that you plug in, use up, detach, and discard (by recycling: see "Fuel and Accessories" below). They are attractively simple and very popular. The burners of cartridge stoves are much like the ones you see on kitchen ranges, with many tiny openings, or "ports." The fuel, a mixture of propane and butane, would be gaseous at room temperature if unconfined; it is kept liquid, under pressure, in its rigid-walled container. Open the valve, and the fuel instantly streams out as vapor, ready to burn. There's no monkey business about lighting a cartridge stove under good conditions: a flick of a lighter, probably built in, and you're there. The flame can be adjusted high or low and is silent. In some models you can unplug the burner and substitute a very effective gas-powered lantern.

In the very lightest stoves, the cartridge sits upright and supports the burner on top. These burner assemblies weigh as little 3 ounces. In heavier models, burner and cartridge are separate but linked by a flexible fuel line; these tend to have wider and more stable burners and weigh half a pound or more. The midget stoves are best for ultralight and solo hikers; for general backpack use, the heavier ones make sense. Prices range from $40 to $80.

For all their elegance under good conditions, cartridge stoves have limitations.

The gas streams out so nicely because the pressure inside is greater than the atmospheric pressure outside. But the more fuel is used, the less the inside pressure. After about the halfway point, the flame begins to weaken. It may take twice as long to boil water with a fading cartridge as with a fresh one.

The problem becomes much worse under cold conditions. When the pressurized gas gets chilled, it pushes outward less strongly. To complicate matters, the stove cools itself as it operates—because the evaporation of a liquid consumes energy, the surface of the cartridge actually loses heat as the contents empty. When fuel temperature drops far enough, the stove will simply refuse to work.

Manufacturers are trying to overcome this problem. One solution is to modify the fuel. Ordinary butane, the onetime standard, quits vaporizing at 30

A cartridge stove with a separate burner, the Coleman Exponent Xtreme. The black-topped cylinder is a regulator designed to keep output constant in spite of low temperatures or waning gaseous fuel supply.

degrees Fahrenheit. Most makers now use a mixture of propane and butane, which remains volatile to 20 degrees, or of propane and isobutane, a still more volatile variant. Some stoves also incorporate regulators or preheaters designed to improve the flow. Nevertheless, I wouldn't count on any cartridge functioning well at temperatures below freezing.

Oddly enough, this advice must be modified for high altitudes. As you gain elevation, there's less competing pressure from outside to block the exit of fuel from the cartridge. At 10,000 feet, even a stove burning ordinary butane should work below freezing; above 15,000 feet, bottled-gas stoves are reliable standard equipment.

The MSR WhisperLite, a typical white gas stove, consists of burner, connecting tube, and pump, which screws into the mouth of a metal fuel bottle.

Liquid-Fueled Stoves

At $90 to $150, a liquid-fuel stove costs a bit more than a bottled-gas type. It also has a good deal more anatomy. There is a *fuel tank*. There is a *fuel line* linking the tank to the business end of the stove. Next comes a *generator* or *vaporizing tube* in which the fuel is preheated and mixed with air to form a vapor suitable for ignition at the *burner* itself. In some burner designs, a single jet of gaseous fuel emerges from a tiny orifice and strikes a *burner plate*; in others, the vapor issues from many openings in a *ported burner* like those on cartridge stoves. Fuel flow is controlled by an adjustment knob and also by a *pump* that forces air into the fuel tank to maintain pressure there.

In classic stoves, the burner sat on top of the fuel tank; now only Coleman builds on this plan. In most current models, burner and the fuel supply are separate, with a fuel line connecting them; the pump simply screws into a bottle. Stoves of this type are made by Mountain Safety Research (MSR), which invented them, and also currently by Brunton, Snow Peak, and Primus.

A few liquid-fueled stoves, like the Coleman Exponent Feather 442, have built-in fuel tanks. Start-up is simpler and simmering easier than on many rival stoves, but refueling is more of a chore.

When a stove is running, its own heat keeps the vaporizing tube hot enough to do its work. (In some models, the tube actually loops through the flame.) To get things started, however, you may have to supply some initial heat, a process called priming. Typically, you release a trickle of cold stove fuel from the pressurized fuel tank through the burner into a *priming cup* and light it. Once this starter dose has flamed away, the works should be hot enough to vaporize fuel for normal operation.

A couple of stoves, by Peak 1 and Snow Peak, work differently. When you pressurize such a stove and open a valve, the fuel emerges as a spray of droplets, ready to ignite; once it does, actual vaporization ensues. Under less-than-ideal conditions, however, you may still need to intervene. For much more about priming and lighting liquid-fuel stoves, see Chapter 18.

Any stove that uses liquid fuel will burn "white gas," the highly refined camp-stove fuel found in sporting goods and hardware stores throughout the United

Some stoves, like this MSR XGK Expedition, burn a variety of liquid fuels. Kerosene is the usual alternative; automobile gas is not recommended because of the additives it contains.

States and Canada. White gas burns very cleanly and leaves less residue than other fuels.

A few stoves are built to accept one or more other fuels, including ordinary automobile gasoline, kerosene, diesel oil, and methyl alcohol. Among other refinements, multifuel units tend to have thicker-bored fuel lines. Some such stoves require work on your part, like swapping one jet or vaporizing tube for another, before they will burn products other than white gas.

Overseas travelers must learn local terms. U.S. kerosene is "paraffin" in Britain, "pétrole" in France. U.S. gasoline is British "petrol," French "essence," German "Benzin." "Gas" and "gaz" usually mean propane or butane.

Even the North American traveler may choose multifuel stoves for either of two reasons. When they burn white gas, their generous bores make clogging unlikely; when they burn kerosene, they are safer.

Gearing Up

Spilled kerosene won't flare up in a flash fire, as can happen with spilled white gas. Leaders of organized groups, including Sierra Club outings leaders, tend to favor this fuel, and cherish old-fashioned kerosene-only stoves that, unfortunately, are no longer on the market.

Kerosene is found in hardware and sporting goods stores. It costs a bit more than white gas, weighs slightly more, and stretches slightly further. As for automobile gas, it tends to contain nasty additives and should be used in a stove only as a last resort.

Alternative Stoves

A few stove designs don't fit into the categories above.

Some people swear by the Trangia line of alcohol-burning stoves. The liquid fuel simply burns in a cup under a housing that is windscreen and pot support in one. The package is elegant and windproof but rather heavy and noticeably slow to boil water; nevertheless, you see Trangias used even in winter camping. These are the safest stoves around, especially in a tent or in the company of children.

You will just occasionally see a minimal solid-fuel stove consisting of a platform over a can of Sterno (jellied alcohol) or a fuel pellet. The units are cheap and simple but lack the heating power to be of much use in wilderness cooking. Nevertheless, ultralight hikers are giving them another look.

Then there is the small family of wood-burning stoves. The oldest entry in this category is the curious Sierra solid fuel stove by ZZ Corporation, a cross between a stove and a miniature fireplace. Priced like the cheapest white-gas stove, it burns twigs, pine cones, or any small dry wood, with the help of a battery-operated fan. Long-distance and ultralight hikers find these stoves more efficient than fires and lighter, when the weight of fuel is considered, than conventional competitors. Other makers are now entering the field. Note that such stoves may be subject to the same rules that apply to open fires.

Choosing a Stove

What stove is best for you? Start by asking yourself when, where, and for whom you will be cooking. Summer? Winter? High elevations or low? Large or small parties? Then consider these points.

Kind of fuel. Do you want to burn bottled gas or liquid fuel? Cartridge stoves are temptingly compact for short trips, but when you start packing extra cartridges, the weight adds up quickly. And cartridges cost between five and ten times as much as white gas per hour of burning. If you plan to camp in very chilly weather, better go for liquid fuel. If it's to be liquid fuel, do you want the ability to burn kerosene and maybe other products? Child safety can be a large consideration here.

Boiling power. How long does it take the stove to boil a quart of water from room temperature? Under good conditions at sea level, average boiling times range from 3 to 8 minutes. Most stoves boil more slowly in the cold and still more slowly in wind. In bad weather, you want the highest possible boiling power. MSR liquid-fueled stoves are famously good for winter camping.

Simmering ability. If you plan to prepare many dishes that require slow cooking, look for a bottled-gas stove or for a white-gas/multifuel stove with a ported burner and a valve mounted near the burner, not far off near the tank. There are now several good white-gas simmerers.

Stability. Some stoves give very good support to the pot on the burner and have low centers of gravity. Others are quite tippy. Look at each model and ask yourself how easy it might be to lose a pot of goulash. Flexible fuel lines between burner and bottle help here; so do adjustable legs found on some stoves.

Ease of use. Can you see and reach the controls while the stove is running? Do they get hot? Are there any small parts that can fall off and go missing?

Reliability and ease of maintenance. Bottled-gas stoves are the most reliable; but if something goes wrong, there's little you can do about it. Multifuel stoves burning white gas are markedly trouble-free. Straight white-gas stoves are the most finicky. MSR stoves are notably field-maintainable, other brands far less so

Weight. Always a consideration for the backpacker. A weekend's worth of stove and fuel can weigh as little as 6 ounces, with the lightest bottled-gas stove and a single minimum cartridge, or as much as 2 pounds, with a liquid-fueled stove and a generous supply of white gas.

The package. Some stoves come more or less naked, others in packages including cooksets and windscreens. There's no need to buy a combination deal, but you should consider how neatly your stove will pack, how well it will fit your pots, and how it will be screened from the wind.

Fuel and Accessories

How much fuel you need depends on your stove, your cooking style, and your trip. It also depends on altitude; cooking times increase as air pressure drops. For a closer look at fuel planning, see Chapter 12.

Butane/propane, of course, is purchased by the cartridge. These typically weigh about 10 ounces and contain 6 to 8 ounces of fuel. Half-size units are also available. Cartridges cost $4 to $8 and, since each is good for 3 hours at most, get pretty expensive over time. Used containers, which are aluminum, can be recycled easily once every trace of fuel has been burned away; the recycling of partially emptied bottles, however, requires special equipment that even major outdoor stores may not have.

A quart of white gas or kerosene now costs $4. It will cook seven meals or more for two or three campers. Fuel is much cheaper by the gallon, but it deteriorates with time, so you don't want to have too much on hand. After twelve months, you can pour any unused white gas into your car's reasonably full gas tank. On the trail, fuel is carried in cylindrical aluminum bottles matched to your stove. Regrettably, various brands are not reliably interchangeable. These come in several capacities. If you need more fuel than one will hold (see Chapter 12), you might as well store the excess in the same kind of container: when the first gives out you can simply plug in the spare, with no fuss.

A substantial *windscreen* is essential and may be sold as part of a stove-and-cookset package. If not, buy wind protection separately. Mountain Safety Research makes a two-piece screen of thick aluminum foil—ugly but highly effective—that can be trimmed and restapled for use with models other than MSR's. You can also start from scratch with metal flashing. Don't be satisfied with the little wind barriers built into some stove burners: they help, but you want more protection when it really blows.

If you are camping on snow, you will need a *stove pad*: a small piece of wood or closed-cell foam (wrapped in duct tape) about 6 inches across. This goes under the burner, which otherwise could melt a well into the snow. For some two-part stoves, you can get a *stove stand* to which burner and fuel tank clip, making it all nicely stable ($9–$30 and a few ounces).

Instead of MSR's likeably primitive aluminum sleeve, you can install its cunningly fluted *heat exchanger* ($30), which wraps around the pot and captures heat ordinarily lost to the air. It weighs about 6 ounces but earns back its weight, in fuel conserved, after four meals for two.

Some stoves come with cases, or disappear into cookset pots. Others are pretty vulnerable in the pack. For these, a variety of padded stuff sacks and cases are available separately.

Many white-gas stove users, and all kerosene users, bring along a separate fuel to prime with. This may be some form of solid fuel, or it may be liquid alcohol (the denatured solvent form, not rubbing alcohol, which has high water content and burns poorly). Whatever you use, take plenty of it, especially the first time out with a new stove.

A small *butane lighter* can be handy, but also carry several sets of *matches*. Put them in your kitchen gear, in your first-aid or emergency kit, and in at least one other place—perhaps tucked in with some reserve food. Some stoves have built-in sparkers; they're nice when they work, but not cause to leave your matches home.

There are several sorts of matches to choose from. Cheapest, of course, are the ordinary folder type. They have to be dry to ignite, and must be struck on their own sandpapery striker pad. Then there are wooden kitchen matches, which you can strike on any dry, rough surface. Third are waterproof matches, which may or may not require their own striker; but both match and striking surface can, in theory at least, be soaking wet. (You can also waterproof ordinary kitchen matches by dipping them in wax.) Finally, there are waterproof/windproof matches. These burn like sparklers and cannot be blown out. Though they will actually burn under water, they must be dry to ignite.

In dry summer climates, many people favor the strike-anywhere kitchen type, or a mixture of strike-anywheres and waterproofs. If you plan to camp in rainy country or on snow, your matches should certainly be waterproof, and you should have perhaps a handful of the more expensive windproof ones as well.

"Waterproof" or not, protect your matches: in doubled plastic bags, foil envelopes, or (wooden matches) in a plastic or metal *match safe*. The best safe will be brightly colored and also distinctively textured for the groping hand. Some have built-in strikers. Carry, regardless, several extra striker pads for matches that require them.

Auxiliary fire starters must be on your list. In very wet weather, it takes more than matches to light a wood fire—and even a devout stove-user may someday desperately need to do so. The simplest thing you can take is a segment of plumber's *candle*. Some people make little logs of wax-soaked newspaper. A piece of *cork* works well. In an emergency, a nylon stuff sack is excellent. Various fibrous and woody incendiary products are found in gear stores.

Getting to Know Your Stove

When you've purchased your stove, settle down and read the manufacturer's instructions, then read them again. Practice the lighting routine. Burn a full tank or pint bottle of white gas, or a full cartridge of butane/propane, to get an idea of how the stove behaves. Cook some meals while you're at it. Just how long will the stove run between fuelings? If it's a bottled-gas model, when in the life of the cartridge does the falloff in heating power begin?

A bottled-gas stove needs hardly any maintenance, but a liquid-fuel stove is a notoriously tricky item. Before you fire it up the first time, it's a good idea to rinse out the detachable fuel bottle with a little clean white gas. Discard this into your automobile fuel tank. Then make it a habit to pour fuel through a filter-equipped funnel whenever you transfer it from one container to another.

Review what's in the parts kit you may have gotten with the purchase. If the stove boasts of "field-maintainability," take it apart and put it back together again. Identify the parts that are likely to need replacing somewhere along the line, especially the jet, the several O-rings, and the pump leather. Parts and instructions, of course, should go in the kit you take along with you on the trail.

For more about the care and feeding of stoves on the trail, see Chapter 18.

Back home again, take a close look at the stove before forgetting it until next time. In stoves with a single, pin-prick-sized fuel jet, examine this closely. Has it become enlarged from cleaning? Maybe it's time to replace it. To head off trouble, O-rings should be replaced about once a year. Check the flexibility of the piece of leather at the business end of your pump; if it's sound but a little dry, you can lubricate it with light machine oil. You can test for leaks by submerging the fuel bottle, pump in place, in water. If there's more than a trace of bubbles, quickly dissipated, you have a bad seal.

If you need more help, own a tinker-resistant stove, or would just rather not mess with the thing, many gear stores do stove overhauls: $15 or so. They have tools you don't, like sonic cleaners.

Cookware

Backpack cookery is mostly boiling things in pots. A single hiker can get along with a single small pot (or none, if you choose to eat cold food). In a small group you need a couple of cooking vessels. Common sizes are 1.5 and 2.0 liters; nothing smaller is very useful, and larger is often welcome.

Backpacking pots are made of aluminum, stainless steel, steel masking an aluminum core, or titanium. Uncoated aluminum is simple, light, cheap, and easily dented. Stainless steel is more durable and more handsome but also heavier, 12 ounces or so per piece. Titanium is very light, strong, and expensive; but it's so conductive that food is easily burned.

Most pots are wider than they are tall; a few are deep and cylindrical. The tall, narrow pots are inefficient for cooking on most stoves. Top edges should be "lapped," folded over to make a rigid rim that resists distortion and is easily gripped. Inside, the bottom should merge with the sides in an easily scrubbable curve. Pots should nest, and it is nice if two work together as a double boiler. As for support, most backpacking pots are "naked," but some have folding handles or strip or wire bails (very useful if you cook much over fire).

A nonstick inner surface is handy for quick cleaning. Materials now in use are less vulnerable to scratching than earlier versions, but care is still required. A black outer surface makes for faster heat absorption. Few makers coat their ware in the factory, but you can paint pot bottoms yourself with flat black stove paint (available at any hardware store). In the days of campfire cookery, many chefs just let their gear get sooty and stored it proudly in a special, spectacularly grubby bag.

Snugly fitting lids will shorten cooking time. If you want to go really light, you can substitute aluminum foil.

You'll need a light aluminum *pot lifter* compatible with your pots. A bandanna or glove will do in a pinch. When it's very cold, a pair of light cloth gloves will take some of the sting out of the touch of freezing metal or spilled fuel.

Many people buy *cooksets*. The typical package includes one smaller and one larger pot, one or two lids (typically usable as frying pans), and a gripper. Some include windscreens and are matched to particular stoves. Tailored or no, it's handy if your stove can fit inside your largest pot.

Bought as a unit or assembled from scratch, your basic cookset will probably cost $25 to $60 and weigh under 2 pounds—barely over 1 pound if you go with titanium and pay $90 or so.

What about other cooking tools? Some people like bacon and eggs enough to carry *frying pans* (some pots come with lids designed to double as fry pans). Separate pans weigh 12 to 15 ounces in steel or Teflon-coated aluminum and cost $10 and up. With a pan, you need an appropriate *spatula.*

Baking isn't easy on the trail, but it is possible. By placing a piece of metal on the flame of a not-too-vigorous stove, you can spread the heat enough to bake after a fashion. You can also produce a reasonable facsimile by boiling dough in a heat-proof plastic bag, though of course you don't get a crisp top. To produce that top crust, you can light a tiny fire on the lid of a pot that is simultaneously being heated from below by your stove. One maker offers a specially indented lid for this purpose. More elaborate rigs are essentially little ovens that mount on top of the burner. For larger groups that build fires, there are full-size reflector ovens (2.5 pounds and $35). Campfire users may carry light *grills* ($8–$35; cheap cake racks will serve). A fire grate with legs is a low-impact tool. Besides its convenience, it improves ventilation, prevents spills, and encourages complete combustion of the wood below.

As you gain in altitude, cooking takes longer. For one thing, most stoves become less efficient in thinner air; for another, the boiling point of water declines. At 10,000 feet, the boiling point is about 192 degrees Fahrenheit, 20 degrees below the normal 212 degrees, and it takes more than 6 minutes to cook a "3-minute" egg. Similarly, some teas won't steep properly at altitude. Instant and just-add-water foods are less affected. Tight lids help a bit.

One way of speeding up mountain cooking is to use a *pressure cooker*: a 2-quart cooker weighs over 2 pounds and costs about $30. Cookers are mainly taken to very high altitudes or on trips so long that the saving in fuel makes up for the weight of the appliance many times over.

For the simple cooking that most backpackers do, about the only other important utensil is a ladle or *serving spoon*. For pastas and such, a light substitute for a *colander* can be useful; a piece of cheesecloth works. Some people take *coffee filters* and a light plastic *cone* to support them, or a cone with filter built in. Some take little *teapots*, which can also serve as colanders because of the screen in the spout. For that matter, tiny *espresso makers* are now seen on the trail.

Your personal mess kit can be minimal. Many people carry nothing more than a plastic or metal *cup* and a *spoon* or a "spork," a spoon with forklike teeth at one end. Others like a plastic or aluminum *plate*, or *bowl*, or both. An *insulated mug* with lid is nice when it's cool. A very deep cup, however, is awkward to eat out of.

For dishwashing you need a wire or Teflon *pot scrubber*, and probably some biodegradable liquid *soap*. Detergents are never used, and wash water is dumped far away from any lake or stream (except in one or two special situations). You need some sort of *strainer* to pour wastewater through, so that solids can be added to your garbage. You can get along without a separate *washbasin*, though light ones of foldable plastic are available. Dish towel? Let things dry in the air. For more on staying clean in the wilderness without polluting it, see Chapter 20.

Containers for Food and Water

The typical water bottle today is made of polycarbonate plastic; Lexan and Nalgene are brand names. Lately some concerns have been raised about endocrine-dis-

The cylindrical plastic water bottle by Nalgene (above right) is the type most commonly seen on American trails, but collapsible bladders like the MSR Dromedary bag take up less room in the pack.

rupting chemicals leaching from this plastic. Alternative materials are anodized aluminum and polypropylene.

Most containers are cylindrical, a few squarish. There are narrow-mouthed or nipple-nosed versions for liquids and large-mouthed ones for liquids and bulk solids; wide mouths are more generally useful. An alternative to the rigid bottle is the soft bottle, or bladder, made of plastic or other synthetic material; it has the advantage of shrinking when empty, and the disadvantage, in most incarnations, of smelling a bit after being filled with anything but water. Some new bladders also impart an unpleasant plastic taste. Bottle prices run from $4 to $12 for a liter size, depending on materials and features, and weights run to 4 ounces.

Large collapsible *water carriers* are often useful. In camp, hanging on a tree or rock, they can reduce the

Gearing Up

number of trips you have to make to the local watering hole, thus reducing trampling: a virtuous thing, especially if you're camping at an unmarked site. They also permit you to camp where there is no waterhole. Carriers hold from 1 to 5 gallons; they cost from $6 to $30. Not all types are leakproof in the pack, so be sure what you're getting. A light and effective in-camp substitute is three large plastic grocery bags, nested one inside the other.

In most wilderness situations, hikers now disinfect the water they find on the land. Boiling will do it, but filters or chemical treatments are often more convenient. For a discussion of the options, see Chapter 20.

Most solid food gets carried in larger or smaller *zippered plastic bags*. Oversized, very tough bags can be found in gear stores. There are also square plastic *boxes* with snap-on tops; flat, round, screw-top *butter dishes*; and plastic *egg carriers*. *Squeeze tubes*, with backs you can open for filling, are handy for things like peanut butter so long as the weather stays warm. Avoid containers with tops that snap on rather than screwing on: they always open and spill. Cheap two-part *shakers* are commonly taken for pepper and salt (or use film containers; just make sure the lids won't come off in your kit). More ambitious cooks carry miniature *spice kits*. If you have steel cans to open, you can use a minuscule GI-style *can opener* or simply a knife blade. Multibladed tools (see Chapter 10) may include a serviceable can opener.

At home, all food and water containers should be washed and stored open with lids off.

Bear Protection

In many North American wilderness areas you have to protect your food from scavenging bears. The traditional method is to hoist it into a tree at night and whenever you leave an established camp unoccupied. So your kitchen gear must include, along with plenty of *cord*, one or more stout *containers* for the hoisting. Sometimes you can use an empty pack, a tarp gathered

Containers for protecting food from bears. The original Backpacker's Cache (left) is from Garcia Machine; its newer rival the BearVault (right) is made of clear plastic.

into a sack shape, or a hammock. The recommended counterbalance method of bearbagging works best with two large stuff sacks, the size you would pack a sleeping bag in. Laundry bags will also serve. Miniature carabiners, like overgrown safety pins, are handy for attachment. For rain protection, you can wrap plastic garbage bags around the cache; if you're headed for really soggy country, you might look for a light backpacker's version of the rafter's drybag, which rolls over itself at the top and fastens shut. For more on bear protection, see Chapters 18 and 29.

Another option is the *bearproof canister*, a rugged plastic cylinder about 1 foot deep and 9 inches across, with a lid it takes a human hand to open. To reduce odors, food goes in a plastic liner. The original Bear Cache by Garcia Machine now has a rival called the BearVault. Canisters can be purchased in specialty shops for under $80 or rented at some gear stores and park destinations. Drawbacks are weight and bulk: the units weigh 2½ pounds or more and do not fit inside slimmer packs.

Obviously, you won't want to carry such heavy defenses if you don't have to. These canisters must be regarded as essential, however, in certain areas. One such is the Arctic tundra, where there are voracious grizzly bears and no trees; the canister was developed for, and first tested at, Alaska's Denali National Park. Canisters are also needed in certain more temperate areas where the bears seem always to be one step ahead of the rope-slinging camper. Their use is mandatory, for example, in Yosemite National Park.

Recently a much lighter bear safe has appeared, the soft-sided Ursack. Instructions call for lashing it firmly to a thick tree trunk or immovable rock. Though effective against most bears (and all smaller animals), the sack form does not have the blessing of bear managers in the most trouble-prone regions.

The protection of your edibles is really only the secondary reason for toting these containers. The primary purpose is to protect the bears themselves. Once the animals become habituated to human food, they all too often must be destroyed.

10

The Rest of the Load

Clothing; sleeping gear; shelter; cooking gear. With these we have covered the bulk of what goes in the pack (for food, see Chapter 12). What remains, though, is important: some essential tools, personal items, and medical and emergency supplies.

Tools

Map and compass. Each member of a party should carry both. Other navigation devices are optional. See Chapter 16.

Knife. Any folding pocketknife will serve. Stainless steel is nice and widely used; plain carbon-steel sharpens more readily. You need at least a 2-inch blade. Suitable knives have locks so that they won't suddenly shut and slice a finger. Basic knives cost $25 to $50 and weigh an ounce or two.

Then there are "multitools," which offer a number of blades or tools in one. Everybody knows the Swiss Army knife, familiar with its imprinted cross and red rubbery handle (though other colors and textures can be had). These knives come with as few as three and as many as nineteen different blades and accessories. Beware of Swiss Army knife knockoffs; the real ones are made by Victorinox or Wenger. Leatherman and other companies also make multitools, some a good deal

Some basic tools. Clockwise from top: LED headlamp; flashlight; single-blade knife; multitool; compass and map; strong nylon cord.

heftier than the Swiss version. It can be handy to have a number of basic items together like this; on the other hand, you may not find exactly what you want on one tool, or may choose to carry separate and more robust versions. Things you may get in a multitool are a second knife blade, a pair of needle-nose pliers, one or several screwdrivers, a wire cutter, bottle and can openers, a pair of scissors, and ruler markings. You can probably do without saws, magnifiers, plastic scrapers, and files. Prices run from $12 to $60, depending mainly on blades, and weights go up to 7 ounces.

A folding knife or multitool needs to be sharp, and it needs to be clean. To remove dirt, make a "knife soup": open all blades and tools, and drop the whole thing into hot, but not boiling, water. In a few minutes, remove and scrub with an old toothbrush. Rinse the tool, fold and unfold the blades several times, apply a little light machine oil, work the blades again, and wipe dry.

For sharpening, the best tool is a whetstone. Though a small stone might be packed for a long trip, usually this job is done at home. Lubricate the stone with water or light oil. Place the blade on it, sharp edge away from you, at a slight angle (23 degrees, if you have a mathematical eye). Now push the blade across the stone, with moderate downward pressure; depending on the composition, bluntness, and roughness of the blade, it may take just a few passes or several minutes to get a sharp edge. For the other side, use the same push-away stroke but work with the opposite hand. Relubricate the stone as needed.

Flashlight or headlamp. Flashlights made for wilderness use usually omit the conventional on-off switch, a perennial problem spot; to turn on one of these lights, you simply twist the lens housing or a basal piece at the other end. Some lights allow you to widen or narrow the beam, or to hood it, producing a lamplike "area light." Prices of better flashlights run from $10 to $40; AA and AAA cells are usually included, but C and D cells are not. Weights without batteries vary from a couple of ounces to half a pound.

For $20 to $75 you can get a battery-powered *headlamp.* The working end of a headlamp straps to your forehead (or clips to your hat) and shines wherever you are looking. Good ones today use two to four LED (light emission diode) bulbs. The batteries may be right behind the bulb, in a case at the back of the head, or even in a shirt pocket, connected by a wire; your hands are free. You can choose several levels of brightness; some models include an ultrabright halogen bulb as well, which can be adjusted in focus from narrow and laserlike to broad but dim.

Along with the original batteries, take a couple of extras and a spare bulb (of the original type). Alkaline power cells are more or less standard. Another kind of battery, the expensive lithium cell, lasts somewhat longer and works better below 20 degrees Fahrenheit. How long any battery holds up in use depends largely on the output of the bulb it is feeding; with efficient

LED bulbs, however, you can typically go 50 hours or more on a battery set.

Since disposable batteries are a form of toxic waste, it would be nice to substitute nickel-cadmium rechargeables. Unfortunately, these don't last long enough for wilderness use. Solar rechargers exist, but they work too slowly to be practical. Let's hope for progress toward a compact sun-charged flashlight whose batteries would never need changing at all.

Modern lights are less prone than their forebears to "turning themselves on" in the pack and draining batteries. However, an old-fashioned sliding switch can be held in the off position with tape or a rubber band.

Inside a tent (or snow cave or igloo) a candle can give you good light. For $20 you can get a candle lantern that protects the flame from drafts. Some lanterns are tall and slender, best suited for hanging; stubby ones with legs are better for setting on things. Bottled-gas-powered stoves can also run powerful lanterns.

Cord. One of the real necessities, anywhere at all. Carry more than you think you'll need. Fifty feet is required for bearbagging (see Chapter 18). Cord is also a repair item. It should be pretty strong; ⅛-inch or 3.5-millimeter parachute cord, 500-pound test or more, is fine. Hard-finished cord is best for bearbagging (less likely to snag or tangle).

Sanitary trowel. Recommended equipment these days, to make sure you dig the perfect "cathole" for human waste (see Chapter 20). A stick or a boot will often do as well. Plastic trowels cost a couple of bucks and weigh a couple of ounces; stainless steel trowels, recommended where soils are stony, weigh and cost more.

Ax, hatchet, shovel, saw. Not ordinarily needed, or even desirable.

Notebook and pencil. For anything you feel like writing down. Could be vital in an emergency, to leave messages, take notes in first-aid situations, and so forth. Some specialty notebooks have waterproof paper you can write on in the rain.

What about a *wristwatch*? Some people make a point of leaving this item behind, but you may need it if your plans involve very early starts or perhaps a closely timed rendezvous. If you really do need a watch, you probably need one you can read in the dark, with a loud alarm. If digital, large buttons are also nice. With microelectronics, very elaborate functions can now be built into a timepiece. Some watches incorporate navigation aids (see Chapter 16).

Staff or trekking poles. Whether it's a found object or an elaborate "trekking pole," a staff shifts some impact of the footfall from the lower body to the upper, an excellent thing for aging or substandard knees. Two poles are often advised, so that each knee gets support and the alternation matches the natural swinging of the arms. I find a single pole easier to handle on narrow trails or going cross-country. You'll spend $60 to $150 for a pair of adjustable telescoping trekking poles with spring-loaded tips that dampen impact; singles cost less. Tips may be pointed, for ice and rock, or rounded, better for general use.

Besides their primary purpose, poles and staffs have endless incidental uses, especially in pitching shelter. Several lightweight tents today come with no poles of their own—your staff is an essential part of their design.

Repair Kit

You need at least a small one. There are excellent prepackaged kits ($5–$40, depending on contents) for general gear repair or for special tasks like fixing zippers and patching self-inflatable pads. These can get you started. Your specific needs will vary with the trip, with your gear, and with your taste for tinkering. The repair kit is also a convenient stashing place for items not strictly used for repair, like extra flashlight batteries and bulb. Here's a comprehensive list of components, some of which I've never actually taken:

Sewing materials. Some very stout "button-and-carpet" thread, and some medium-weight thread. (Dental floss will double for the former.) A couple of needles with large eyes for easy threading. A couple of buttons. A few large safety pins. Twist ties (which will do nicely to hold together an opening that has lost its button). Less-often carried are thimbles and awls for work with leather and thick fabric.

Repair tape. You can use adhesive-backed nylon tape for neat patches on tents, sleeping bags, jackets, and such. Adhesive tape from your first-aid kit will work for temporary repairs. For heavier jobs, the tough stuff called duct tape is unbeatable, though it leaves a sticky, stubborn residue. Duct tape is best carried wrapped around something, like a screwdriver handle or a segment of pack frame.

Alcohol towelettes. Unless you carry alcohol for stove priming, throw in a couple of these for cleaning an area that is going to be taped.

Webbing straps and hook-and-loop (Velcro) tape. Mainly for good sewers who want their field fixes to be elegant.

Urethane sealant. For waterproofing and cementing patches. It comes in several consistencies. The thinnest version is most generally useful; the thick stuff can be used to fix sole problems on ultralight fabric boots. Products by McNett are most often seen.

Glue. Glue sticks get melted over a candle or butane lighter. Epoxy is stronger but, with its two components that you mix, a little finicky. Instant "superglues" are good in the cold and can also be used in first aid, as to stick down a cut flap of skin on a fingertip.

Wire. A foot or more. Stout enough to be strong, pliable enough to bend around corners. Braided steel is the best. Wire has a dozen uses in repair.

Pliers. Many uses, especially with zippers: to tug out pinched fabric or to gently compress a worn slider that is gaping too widely to do its job. Pliers are sometimes found on multitools.

Screwdriver and screws. A screwdriver tends to be used most often as a pry bar for jobs like removing a zipper stop in order to replace a slider. But it sometimes drives a screw as well, for instance to anchor a loose boot sole. A tiny driver may be useful for eyeglasses, binoculars, or cameras. Notice any screws you have in your gear, and bring assorted replacements to match.

Extra sliders for critical zippers. The two that matter most are on the sleeping bag and the panel-loading pack. Replacing a slider on a "separating" zipper, where the two sides of the closure can be taken completely apart, is relatively easy; the same job on a "coil" zipper, where one end is permanently bound together, is quite a chore. You have a coil zipper on your pack and (probably) a separating zipper on your sleeping bag.

Extra cordlocks. These handy gripping devices allow you to snug up cords without knots. Although it's no disaster if one breaks, a replacement is easily carried.

Spare pack buckles. A broken buckle on a shoulder strap or hipbelt can be a major problem. Duct tape can probably get you home, but on a long trip you might be glad to have spare hardware. Take both components of each buckle and be sure they're right for your particular pack. You can't insert a sewn webbing loop into the typical "ladderlock" buckle without either unstitching the loop at the root or slipping it through a slot snipped in the buckle's crossbar; preslotted emergency buckles may be found in commercial repair kits or purchased separately. They are invaluable.

Frame pack fittings. On frame packs, packbags are commonly held to frames by clevis pins and lock-rings. Rings can break, and clevis pins occasionally get lost. A spare pin is good to have; stout wire can replace a ring.

Tent-pole repair sleeve. This can be a custom item from the manufacturer, a C-shaped tent pole, or simply a slit-open can.

Hose clamps. Can also be useful in pack-frame or tent-pole repair.

Stove tools and parts. Likely to include jet and O-rings. A spare fuel-can gasket can be vital. A cork can replace a lost cap. Consult (and bring along) the instructions that come with your stove.

Small butane lighter. To melt glue sticks; to seal frayed nylon; to light a stove or start a fire.

Monofilament (leader) line. For things that need binding.

Rubber bands. Assorted, mostly the thicker kind. You're always wanting one; may be kept in kitchen kit instead.

Personal Care Items

The list starts with some essential skin-protection items and continues, indefinitely perhaps, with personal "must haves" and optionals.

Insect repellent. At certain times of the year, in certain places, this will seem more like a survival item than a mere convenience. The most effective preparations are those that contain the chemical N,N-diethyl-meta-toluamide (abbreviated DEET). DEET is powerful stuff; choose one of the lower concentrations (they vary from 25 percent to nearly l00 percent) and apply sparingly. Various alternatives to DEET are also available; for more about these, see "Mosquitoes and Other Insect Pests" in Chapter 29.

Suncream/sunblocker. Suncreams vary. Almost all preparations, however, are marked with a *sun protection factor (SPF)*, a number from 1 to 50. This indicates how long you can be exposed without burning: a cream with protection factor 5, for instance, would theoretically allow you to stay in sunlight five times as long as you could without protection. For outdoor recreation, use SPF 15 or higher. Above 8,000 feet or so, and on light-colored rock or snow or near open water, Use SPF 30. For more about sun hazards and protections, see Chapter 28. Combination creams combining SPF 15 sunscreen and low-concentration DEET are available.

Lip balm. Most hikers will need this to prevent and treat cracked, burned lips. The best preparations contain sunscreen. Unflavored ones won't get licked off so fast.

Poison oak/ivy/sumac lotion. Blocking creams are available and may be worth having if you're highly allergic, especially for off-trail travel where these irritant plants grow thick. For more about this problem, see Chapter 29.

Toilet paper. Bring a generous supply (even if your use is sparing, you might get diarrhea). It should be white, single-ply, and unscented.

Soap. For personal cleanliness, you'll want a sliver or, more typically, a tube. Should it be antibacterial? Big argument. The overuse of antibacterial products may be breeding resistant "superbugs." A compromise is to carry ordinary soap and a supply of antibacterial gel towelettes to use after taking care of toilet needs.

Other cleanup things. You'll want several *bandannas*, one of which serves as a washcloth. Some hikers like a superabsorbent *towel*. Hikers who do a lot of swimming may splurge and carry a square of terrycloth. Some like a light pocket *mirror*. Everybody takes a *comb*; some also a small *brush*. In larger parties, it can be nice to have a folding personal *washbasin*. A luxurious item is a *shower rig* consisting of a large water bag and a showerhead: leave the bag in the sun for a couple of hours, and serve.

Tooth stuff. Most people take a *toothbrush*; many take *floss*. You can skip the toothpaste, which leaves a white splotch when you spit it out, or substitute *baking soda*.

Deodorant. Some scoff; some can't live without it. Any type with a scent, which can attract mosquitoes and even bears, should be avoided. "Crystal" antiperspirants are good but a trifle heavy. If you are going to territory with grizzly bears, even these should be left home.

Other personals. Tampons and *contraceptives* may be appropriate. Contact lens wearers should carry saline and antibiotic eyedrops, and backup spectacles or extra lenses just in case. You know what you need. If you are traveling with very small children, you'll of course be carrying all sorts of added paraphernalia: see Chapter 25.

The Medical Kit

Every wilderness traveler needs a personal medical kit, which will be drawn on, with any luck, only for minor problems. How much is in it depends mainly on the place and season of your travel. In U.S. wilderness areas south of Canada, where it's pretty hard to get more than 20 miles away from a road, modest "first-aid kits" are carried. In remoter situations, a more extensive kit or a second, better-stocked group kit should be carried. Expeditions (especially with doctors aboard) tote sophisticated medical supplies. Hikers in the great wilderness regions of the far north need to be equipped for more than first aid; this book has little to tell them. In a party with children, the adults are the expedition leaders and have to plan for more contingencies.

What about prepackaged, commercial first-aid and medical kits? There are many on the market; prices for adequate ones range from $20 up. Good kits are the work of MDs experienced in wilderness medicine. Yet these products have drawbacks. For one thing, the selection of items is never quite the choice you would make; second, and more important, there's nothing like putting your supplies together from scratch to teach you exactly what you've got. If you do buy a packaged kit, don't just toss it in and forget it; study it, learn from it, and add or subtract items as your own experience grows.

Let's run down some of the common and not-so-common components of wilderness medical kits. Many of these are available separately, in suitable sizes, at gear stores. Items marked with an asterisk (*) are of special importance.

The container. This can be a stout zippered pouch or a rigid box but should in any case be waterproof. A fairly generous kit should fit in a container of about 50 cubic inches—say 3 inches by 3 inches by 6 inches, though almost any shape will do.

First-aid manual. A step-by-step routine for dealing with emergencies can be useful. There are various portable manuals, from densely printed cram cards to James A. Wilkerson's hefty *Medicine for Mountaineering.* One good packable book is William Forgey's *Wilderness First Aid Manual.* See the Resources section.

Bandage compresses. (Band-Aid is a trademarked brand name.) You'll need several sizes, three or more of each. You can get all kinds of variants: knuckle bandages, fingertip bandages, butterfly bandages; but most odd shapes can be improvised from basic strips.

Gauze pads. Three or four pads, 4 inches square, in sterile envelopes.

Gauze bandage. One inch wide. Not less than 15 feet. Not required to be sterile. Handiest is the self-clinging kind.

Porous cloth adhesive tape. Also 1 inch wide and plentiful—take 10 yards.

Moleskin or equivalent. Stick-on pads to cushion feet when blisters threaten. Moleskin is thin, molefoam thicker. Spyroflex is flexible and less likely to peel. Some people find adhesive tape or duct tape works just as well for prevention. Spenco's 2nd Skin, a clear film developed for burn treatment, is good if you do get a blister. See Chapter 15.

Triangular bandage. An item with many uses; the classic arm sling. Bulky (about 11 square feet) and often missing from the small kits. Improvised substitutes are usually possible.

Elastic bandage. Three inches wide. Reduces swelling in joint injuries.

Antiseptic soap. Betadine (povidone-iodine) is the standard.

Topical antibiotic. Three-in-one antibiotic cream, available in small foil envelopes.

Antifungal cream or powder. For anyone prone to athlete's foot.

Cotton swabs. Various possible uses.

Needle. For draining blisters.

Tweezers. Mainly for splinters, occasionally for tick removal. They must be very sharp and not unmanageably small.

Scissors. Mainly for cutting dressings, moleskin, repair tape. May be on knife.

Safety pins. Like needles, you think of these as sew/repair items, but they have uses in first aid too—for instance, fastening arm slings and bandages.

Razor blade or disposable razor. These have various uses. A blade can substitute for scissors. It is also used to shave skin before applying tape, or the suction cup of the next item.

Venom extractor. A suction device that can reduce the effect of a bite by a venomous snake (see Chapter 29) and also of lesser encounters like bee stings.

Tick remover. Several little devices are available to help you remove an attached tick most efficiently.

Analgesic of choice. Aspirin, ibuprofen, naproxen, acetaminophen. Aspirin is cheapest. Ibuprofen is very popular for muscle and joint pain. Naproxen is a cousin. These three are related: all are anti-inflammatories, and if you're allergic to aspirin, you should avoid the others, too. Acetaminophen is easy on the stomach but doesn't work against swelling.

Topical anesthetic. Various preparations to counter pain, itching, and swelling from abrasions, insect bites, or stinging nettles.

Prescription painkiller. Many hikers carry half a dozen 30-milligram tablets of codeine/empirin, or some other mild prescription medicine for pain. Consult your doctor. Watch the expiration date and replace as needed. Pills can be stored in little vials or, perhaps better, in tiny ziplock plastic bags with instructions inside.

Digestive remedies. Antacid or acid-blocker tablets for indigestion; antidiarrheal tablets for a problem that is rare but miserable on the trail.

Personal medicines. Anything you know you're likely to need: Toothache drops . . . laxatives . . . antihistamines . . . your own prescription drugs. If you have a known medical problem, consult your doctor before you head into wild country.

Other drugs. Many are possible, but few are needed for ordinary travel. Doctors hesitate to prescribe except for immediate need. However, on very remote trips it may make sense to carry a broad-spectrum antibiotic like tetracycline and a heavy-duty narcotic painkiller (oral forms are now available). Drugs should be replaced as required.

Syringe. Not a needle for injections, but a blunt-nosed plastic model that can produce a stream of water under pressure, as for flushing out a wound. A plastic bag with a pinhole can serve the same purpose.

Latex gloves and CPR mask. If you find yourself giving first aid, you may wonder about AIDS and other diseases that may be transferred in body fluids. The danger of AIDS transmission in blood is real, and you should wear latex gloves when pressing on a wound to stop bleeding. There is, by contrast, very little danger of catching a disease when doing cardiopulmonary resuscitation (CPR); some like to carry a protective surgical mask, but this is not essential. See Chapter 26 for more about these matters.

Credit card. Sad but true: if you are injured and evacuated, you may have trouble securing further treatment without a credit card. It happened to a climber friend of mine.

Emergency and Survival

In this group are some special items you might want to have with you if you were lost, if you needed to spend an unexpected night out without normal equipment, or if you hoped to attract the attention of rescuers.

Whistle. You blow it to summon help (three signals of any kind indicate distress, two indicate response). A whistle is most useful when there are other hikers nearby; though better than a shout, the sound doesn't carry that far. Whistles may also help in keeping a large party together, and parents often give them to their kids.

Mirror. A longer-range rescue signal, especially useful in the desert. Doubles as a first-aid item. You may already have a mirror on your compass (see Chapter 16).

Signal cloth. A piece of bright-colored cloth—an item of clothing, a ground cloth, whatever—that you could spread out to attract the attention of aerial searchers.

Waterproof/windproof matches. A special supply in your first-aid kit or emergency kit so that you will never be caught without.

Candle stub or other fire starter.

Snares, fishhooks, and such. Sometimes packaged with commercial "survival kits," these are scarcely necessary in most travel. If you're lost for a short time in wild country, food is by no means your first need: warmth and water are primary. Still, it can be entertaining to learn a few skills for living off the land: how to build a "figure-4" snare or a noose of thread or hair, how to recognize edible and poisonous wild plants, and *so* on. Many books give instruction in these skills, which seem to fascinate people out of proportion to their practical importance.

Manual. Prepackaged kits may contain manuals on how to stay alive. It's far better to have done your reading and thinking in advance; see Chapter 16.

Whenever you leave your main pack behind, as on a side trip, you want to make sure you have with you the basic items, including some of the above, that are often referred to as the "ten essentials." Your personal list is likely to include some twenty essentials, and will vary with circumstances: see Chapter 15.

Winter and Technical Gear

There are various items that you'll need only in snowy winter: snowshoes or skis, waxes and ski accessories, snow shovel and snow saw, avalanche rescue transceivers, and so on. Then there's the endless range of more technical gear for mountaineers: ropes, ice axes, crampons, helmets, protective anchors of various sorts, and such. For more about just a few of these extras, see Chapters 22 and 24.

Specialties and Luxuries

You name it, somebody has probably loaded it into a pack, somewhere, sometime. And everyone has a short list of personal "luxuries" that seem as necessary as boots and cooking gear.

Some optional items frequently taken are camp shoes to put on when the boots come off; camp chairs (adapted from sleeping pads) to lounge in; cameras and accessories; natural history guides; binoculars or monoculars; magnifying glasses; fishing gear barometers; altimeters; thermometers; Global Positioning System receivers; and books and games (things like cards that don't need batteries). Some of these items become near-necessities in certain situations—altimeters for some kinds of navigation, for instance, and binoculars in grizzly bear territory.

Cellular Phones

Wilderness used to be the place where you went to be out of touch, exchanging no information with the outside world. This is no longer automatically the case. Portable weather radios now allow us to get the latest outlook from the National Weather Service. Global Positioning System receivers can pinpoint our location with the help of orbiting satellites. Most of all, cellular phones—in regions well provided with transmitters—permit us to "phone home" at any time. Cell phones, in particular, have caused a sharp debate.

The advantages are irresistible. In a genuine emergency, the ability to summon rescue quickly can be lifesaving; in less serious cases, it would be nice, for instance, to tell your family that you're coming out a day late but that all is well.

There is also an obvious risk of misuse. Rescue workers tell tales of people summoning help for trivial causes. And managers worry that overly easy contact with the outside will make people more ready to blunder into dangerous situations they might otherwise shy away from.

Perhaps most fundamentally, easy communication tears away the veil of isolation that is one of the reasons for being in the wilderness in the first place. It lessens the demand for self-sufficiency. To many people—I am one—it brings a significant cheapening of the wilderness experience.

This cat, however, is well and truly out of the bag.

If you do use a cell phone, it is courteous to be inconspicuous about it.

Preparing for the Trip

Then find in the horizon-round
One spot, and hunger to be there.

—Gerard Manley Hopkins,
"The Alchemist in the City"

11

Designing the Trip

The easiest way to take your first longer trip is to sign on with an organized party (see Chapter 2). But it's when you start setting your own targets and making your own plans that the real fun begins. The whole ritual of preparation—the packing, the planning, the study of the maps that build a landscape in your mind—is not just the dull means to the pleasant end: it is the first part of the journey itself.

Experienced packers—some of them, anyway—can throw a trip together quickly. On a few hours' notice they are packed and gone, needing little time to prepack, prepackage, preplan. But at the beginning, at least, you will need to be a little more methodical.

First Step: Pick a Place and a Time

Most trips seem to start with gossip: "They say it's nice at Stonecup Basin . . . the Big Craggies . . . Silver Falls." But if you're not tied in yet to a grapevine, you may need to do some asking around.

If you live in the West, or on the eastern seaboard, there is probably backpacking country within 200 miles of you. If you don't know just where, there are several ways of finding out quickly.

For computer users, the Internet is the starting point. A search under "backpacking" and the name of a state will yield a voluminous list of individual Web sites to consult. Outdoor publications, clubs, and management agencies all have sites (see the Resources section for a few). Various offices of the U.S. Forest Service, the National Park Service, the U.S. Fish and Wildlife Service, and (in western states) the Bureau of Land Management offer lots of information on the Web. So do state agencies that manage wild land, notably in California, Michigan, Maine, Pennsylvania, New York, and Wisconsin. Backpackers also swap information informally online in newsgroups

Much information is also available, of course, by mail. Once you've narrowed the field a little, regional guidebooks are invaluable. And at some point you'll be on the phone, seeking more specific advice.

In some regions, the focus of backpacking is likely to be not the single large wild area, but the lengthy trail that threads landscapes both very wild and relatively tame. Such long trails as the Appalachian are more celebrated than the individual parks and preserves they traverse, with copious maps and guidebooks.

Such sources tend to lead you first to the well-known, well-used landscapes. That may be just what you want at the beginning—or perhaps much longer—if you don't mind a certain amount of company. It does appear, though, that many backpackers prefer relative solitude. This you can find by going where other people do not, or by going *when* other people do not.

Weekends in the wild are always busier than weekdays; holiday and August weekends, in most regions, are busiest of all. Yet over much of the United States, autumn is a more welcoming hiking season than midsummer. In many regions, September is drier than August; a little later comes the wonderful bonus of fall color. Spring, too, is lovely and not very populous. But it should be noted that the soils in many areas are waterlogged in the spring and easily damaged by human traffic.

In regions where winter brings snow, that clean, white surface covering the fragile meadows and the mountain roads creates a wilderness at once more

In a typical mountain wilderness area, most use occurs in summer, with spikes on weekends and holidays. Backpackers with flexible schedules can plan accordingly.

spacious, starker, and less vulnerable to human abuse: see Chapter 24.

You can avoid the crowds in space as well as in time. Even in summer, and even in the best-known regions, use is anything but evenly spread. People flock to a few favorite lakes, a few peaks, a few trails. This is by no means a bad thing. You wouldn't want all parts of an area to be used equally. But the hiker who is slightly more adventurous, or simply better informed, can take advantage of the unequal distribution and go where others do not.

As a rule, you can be more alone on trails that do not lead straight to peaks or lakes or picture-postcard scenic climaxes. You can also be more alone on trails that are too rugged for horses and mules.

In addition to less-visited parts of popular areas, there are whole wild regions where hardly anybody goes. Some are protected as wilderness; many, though thoroughly qualified, are not. In the western United States and in much of Canada, these unprotected de facto wilderness areas make fascinating destinations. You just don't know what you will find. And you have the added zest of knowing your visit can make a difference. If you visit an unlabeled wilderness area, take a few minutes, when you get back home, to write a letter in defense of what is there. You will be doing an important service to the country you enjoyed (see Chapter 31).

How do you learn where these places—by nature underpublicized—are found? The usual source is the grapevine, but a call to the nearest chapter of the Sierra Club may yield some information. Government land management agencies are of course aware of these areas, too—they have inventoried and studied them repeatedly. A visit to an agency office can net you a rich catch of information, once you get past the front desk (where only the most popular hiking areas will be mentioned).

Then there is cross-country travel; it's more adventurous, more solitary, and more of an exploration. But this, like winter travel, takes preparation and skill (see Chapter 22).

Once you've settled on a general destination, check right away with the managing agency to find out whether a wilderness permit is required and how to get one (see "Fifth Step: Take Care of Any Paperwork"). For very popular areas, six months' lead time is not too much. If your party is larger than a handful, find out about size limits, too.

Second Step: Get Maps and Detailed Information

There is a pleasure in going off to the woods with no firm idea of where you'll wind up. But this is not a pleasure for the beginner. As a rule, planning makes a better trip. Besides, it's fun.

Your basic planning tool is always the topographic map or "topo sheet" published by the U.S. Geological Survey or Geomatics Canada. These are webbed with thin brown lines that show elevation in feet or meters above sea level. For more about these maps and how to use them, see Chapter 16; for ordering information, see the Resources section. Maps can be ordered and delivered through the mail. You can also buy them in CD-ROM form or download them over the Internet, printing them out on your own color printer. Once maps are in your computer, you can play with them on-screen, perhaps adding your own notes and information, and print the customized versions on your own printer.

In addition to government topos, management agencies publish maps for each national park, state or provincial park, national forest, national wildlife refuge, or Bureau of Land Management district. These maps are small scale, representing a lot of country on a little bit of map, and generally lack contour lines, but they usually contain up-to-date information about roads and trails. Such agency maps are indispensable for exploring de facto wilderness, and in regions where there is a lot of private property intermixed with public lands. Of special value are the "recreation maps" published by the U.S. Forest Service for its extensive holdings.

Also very useful is the *Atlas and Gazetteer* series by Delorme. These volumes, extending rapidly across the United States, usually cover one state apiece. Based on topo maps, but on a far smaller scale, the Delorme maps fill the gap between the detailed sheets and ordinary road maps. They are great for general orientation and access roads.

Even if you already have the maps, even if wilderness permits are not a issue, you'll want to be in touch with the management agency office responsible for the region you're headed for. There are things agency people will want to tell you; there are things you will want to ask them. The more well known and populous the area you plan to visit, the more you need to learn about the rules that apply there; the less well known and populous it is, the more you need to learn about its physical realities.

Some questions you may want to ask: Has a certain trail been recently maintained? Which areas get the most recreational use and which the least? Which trails are heavily used by pack stock? Are there routes on which you may meet off-road vehicles or mountain bikes? Are there areas currently being grazed by cattle or sheep? (You may want to avoid these.) How reliable is a certain water source? Are there any extraordinary hazards you should know about? Are there current bear problems? Can bear canisters be rented near the roadhead? Where will hunters be active?

If you are planning something unusual and need specialized information, you may have trouble finding someone knowledgeable. Explain your problem, get the name of the best person, find out when he or she will be in (most likely from 7 to 9 AM), and keep trying to make contact.

Third Step: Plan Your Transportation

Most readers can skip this step. They know already that they will be driving from their homes to the wilderness. Some hikers, bound for distant destinations, will be traveling by air and renting cars locally. It's a little difficult to get to wilderness trailheads without a car in the picture somewhere, but it is possible (see below).

Backpackers sometimes compare themselves smugly with people whose enjoyment of the landscape depends on internal combustion engines: motorcycles, jeeps, or snowmobiles. One implicit argument is that the mechanized recreationist burns a lot more gasoline, and causes a lot more pollution, than the self-powered walker of the trails.

But that is only true if the backpacker has driven a merely moderate distance to the trailhead. If you live, say, in Cleveland, and drive (or fly) to British Columbia for your wilderness vacations, you may be using more fossil fuels than the busiest local off-road-vehicle enthusiast can burn.

Indeed, it can plausibly be argued that the worst thing any of us do environmentally in the course of a wilderness trip is to drive to its beginning.

Extreme? Possibly. Yet I like to avoid, at least, long drives before short hikes. I try to drive no more than 100 miles (one way) for each day on the trail. By this formula, day trips would lead to places less than 100 miles away; a weekend trip would lie within a range of 200 or 300 miles; the weeklong trip, within 700.

You will, naturally, take as few vehicles as possible. Sometimes, though, your party will want more than one. Maybe your hike will end miles from where it began; in the absence of public transportation, you need to spot a second car at the exit point (see "Planning Shuttles," below). Then there's the case of travel in remote areas like the Canadian north or the Great Basin of Nevada and Utah. Here, where driving conditions are brutal and mechanics few, it is a bit foolhardy to depend absolutely on a single vehicle.

Yet one more point about cars. If you're traveling between regions, you risk being an unwitting botanical Typhoid Mary, introducing pestiferous plant species to distant wilderness roadheads. This is a more considerable problem than you might imagine, and authorities plead with roving backpackers to make sure their vehicles (and gear in general) are free of seeds and other plant materials from home (or landscapes they've traversed along the way).

What if you want to avoid the automobile entirely? This is a somewhat daunting proposition. But there are places where buses or even trains can take you directly to trailheads.

The carless backpacker in the eastern United States has relatively good pickings. Bus lines thread the Adirondacks and the Catskills, run through Cumberland Gap and across the Great Smoky Mountains, and intersect the Appalachian Trail at any number of points. There are even rail stops on the Appalachian. In the White Mountains of New Hampshire, too, wildland trails begin on the shoulders of main paved roads where buses run.

Out West, things get sparser. But there is regular transit service along Interstate 80, which runs close to interesting roadless areas in the California Sierra and elsewhere; over Snoqualmie and Stevens Passes in the Cascade Range in Washington; through the Columbia Gorge and past Mount Hood in Oregon; along Interstate 70 and U.S. Highway 40 in the Colorado Rockies; and elsewhere along major western highways. There are also transit services to many national parks: Yosemite and Mount Rainier, Grand Canyon, Rocky Mountain, Yellowstone, and more. Glacier National Park has two Amtrak stations. In Canada, many national parks are reasonably accessible by rail or bus. Once you're in the right neighborhood, local recreational shuttles can be helpful. In general, approaching the wilderness by public transportation will put you in well-known and popular locales.

If you are going by air, be aware that you will not be able to take your stove fuel; you may not even be able to take your empty stove. Contact your airline about this. A duffel bag to encase your pack is a very good investment. For more on this subject, see "Packing for Air Travel" in Chapter 13.

Fourth Step: Map the Trip

Now comes the pleasant job of laying out your trip in detail. You know how many days you have to spend: How many of those days would you like to spend resting, or on side trips out of a fixed camp? How many will you have left to use on moving forward, onward, deeper in? And how far can you walk in that time?

It all depends on the land. A crude but standard rule of thumb makes 10 miles an average day on easy terrain with pack. Some people routinely do much less, others much more. Another formula runs like this: allow 40 minutes for every mile of trail, plus an extra hour for every 1,000 feet you climb. Not as slow as it sounds, this rate is a good one to plan with. So you might allow 8 hours of actual hiking to cover 9 miles of easy trail with 2,000 feet of elevation gain—a longish day. Soon, of course, you'll know better than any book what you actually can do and want to do.

Now study the map for likely routes that take you to the places you want to see. One thing is obvious: you can enjoy a lot more country if you don't repeat yourself. Look for trails that loop back on your starting point or that bring you out to another roadhead.

How long is the line you have just traced? A guidebook may tell you and so may an agency's response to your request for information. You should, in any case, check the distance yourself using the map scale. A ruler won't help you much here, since rulers are straight and trails wander. One good traditional tool is a piece of fine wire (or a pipe cleaner). Lay the wire out along your path, bending it to fit the curves; then straighten it out and compare the length you've used with the scale. This works best on the standard 7.5-minute topo maps, less well on maps of less detail—it's easy to underestimate the bends. At the high-tech end, computerized topo maps can compute precisely the length of any line you indicate on the screen.

Try "walking" your entire route on the map. A skilled map reader can get a clear mental picture of the place to be visited: here there is a sharp drop, there a gentle forested valley; here an easy stretch, there a sustained ascent; here a long view over the plain, here a closed-in canyon. If you like, you can use a computer (or graph paper) to prepare an "altitude profile"—a simple graph relating horizontal distance (horizontal scale) to elevations taken from the map (vertical scale).

Give some thought to your camps. Estimate approximately where you will find yourself at the end of each day's move: Is there reasonably level topography thereabouts? Be sure to consult the managing-agency rules. There may be no-camping zones to be avoided, or even specific sites you have to use. If you plan to build wood fires, you may find yourself limited to established spots, to particular, designated locales, or to lands below a certain elevation. Fires may also be permitted only at some times of year, or even forbidden entirely. If your trip is in the desert away from a perennial stream, or along a high ridge without lakes, springs, or snowbanks, you will have to take note of water points and plan your stops with these in mind. In desert travel it is common to plant water caches in advance (see Chapter 23).

In such eastern ranges as the Catskills, wilderness sometimes lies in narrow mountainous strips between lowland valleys. Often a long ridgetop trail will send short spurs down to roads on either side. This makes trip planning somewhat simpler, because you can make a quick exit to a road and perhaps a bus stop if the weather turns nasty, or if you get blisters, or if you simply run out of time. But in larger wildlands, you can seldom "bail out" except by going back.

If your trip will take you to high altitudes, try to allow time for adjustment to the thinner air. At a minimum, schedule a night's sleep at a high roadhead (see Chapter 28).

Planning Shuttles

Often you can see more country if you start and end your trip at two different roadheads. This requires some sort of a shuttle.

The classic method is to take an extra vehicle and park it in advance at the exit trailhead. Two cars must go to the exit point so that one can bring the shuttle driver back. If entry and exit points are well apart, this process can take many hours.

Given just one car and a slightly larger party, you can split into two groups that walk in opposite directions. Group A, say, can be dropped off at a northern trailhead to begin a southbound hike; Group B drives on to the southern trailhead and hikes northbound. Car keys can be duplicated, or switched when the groups meet in the middle.

In some regions, public transportation or cab service can link the ends of your trip. In some popular areas, there are well-planned recreational shuttles. In California, a local taxi company transports parties, by arrangement, from roadhead to roadhead at the eastern base of the Sierra; a similar service connects the rims of the Grand Canyon (see the Resources section).

A possibly viable alternative is to hitchhike. Even a grubby backpacker may find it easier to get a lift than would someone in street clothes. And you may bump into people on the trail or at the trailhead who will happily give you a ride in exchange for a tall tale.

Fifth Step: Take Care of Any Paperwork

If you are going into a national park, into a much-visited wilderness zone in a national forest, or into certain state parks, you are likely to need a wilderness permit. In some cases you can secure it in advance, by mail; this is convenient and, if you plan to visit a popular area at a popular time, highly advisable. For some destinations, *all* available slots are now offered in advance.

Lacking an advance permit, you may need to stop at a local office—no problem, if the office is fairly close to your trailhead and if you arrive at the proper time of day. (In fact, you may need to make this stop even if you have done advance work, trading a receipt for the permit itself.) If your route goes through two jurisdictions—a national park and a national forest, for instance—a permit secured for the first area will do for both. In a few areas or parts of areas, permits (locally available) are required for day hiking as well as backpacking.

Why permits? Their first purpose is simply to gather information. As wilderness use increases and impact problems grow, managers have a clear need to know more about hikers, their preferences, and their habits of travel. At certain trailheads, permits are further used to limit use: only a given number of people or parties are allowed to enter each day. You want to work the system to make sure you're among them.

When you get your permit in some national parks, you are required to list the general areas in which you plan to camp. A few parks insist that you reserve a specific camping *spot* for each night, but the trend seems to be to dispense with this extra, indeed chilling, bit of regulation.

Want to avoid the whole business? Go to less popular areas, or go off-season. The publicity about wilderness permits gives you the impression that restrictions are everywhere, but they're not. Permits are required in only a minority of wilderness areas, and they are used to ration use in even fewer. If getting a required permit is iffy, it's wise to have an acceptable alternate destination in mind.

One final complication: even in areas that do not now require wilderness permits, you may be asked to produce a *fire permit*. These permits, available at agency offices and often by mail, are commonly required not only for open fires but also for the use of stoves. And in some areas you may have to carry *both* a fire permit and a wilderness permit.

Wilderness access is traditionally free, but this is changing. Charges may be levied for permits, for trailhead parking, or for driving into a national park or other specially designated areas. Under a controversial but expanding program, such charges are kicked back to the local managers for use in local improvements, including trail maintenance.

What About Your Dog?

To begin with the formalities: some backcountry areas (state and national parks, for starters) do not allow dogs at all. Some forbid them at certain places and times (such as during deer fawning season or in bighorn sheep habitat). Some allow them on leash. Some merely require that they be under close control.

Behind the rules lies a big argument. Are dogs an undue impact on the wilderness? Certainly they can be. There are horror stories of dogs that bark incessantly, chase wild animals, get in trouble with bears, and even occasionally bite hikers. On the other hand, a dog's natural protectiveness can be reassuring, especially to a solo female backpacker or in a group with children; and the obvious joy the animals show on the trail can only add to our own.

What strikes me in this debate is that the pro- and antidog people are talking about different critters. A dog that is *very* well trained and supervised can be a blameless member of your party; a dog that is merely a pet on the loose can be a disaster.

If you want to take your dog, regulations permitting, do. But also take on the responsibility this entails. Make sure the animal is trained and also reasonably fit. Give it a load to use up some of its energy (there are many canine packs available). Keep it leashed when other people are near; otherwise, keep under close voice control. Bury its feces as you do your own. Prevent more than minimal barking. On the trail, step aside for oncoming, dogless hikers. Don't let the animal beg food, especially from other parties. Prevent it absolutely from chasing animals. If you and the dog can't manage all these things—you'd better leave the animal home.

Two further cautions. Dogs should not be taken into wild areas where there are wolves or grizzly bears. In the first case, it's for the wolves' sake: dogs carry a parvovirus that is deadly to their wild relatives. In the second case, it's for the sake of dog and owner. Though a specially trained dog can be an asset in dealing with a grizzly bear attack, the typical dog is more likely to provoke than to deter the bear.

12

Planning Food & Fuel

Like many things in backpacking, the matter of food
and cooking can appear more complicated than it is.
Elaborate, time-consuming planning is not ordinarily
required, and you can stock up for any trip of normal
length at the local supermarket, with help, if you like,
from a specialty store or two. Freeze-dried foods are
convenient and, for long trips, essential, but they are
pretty expensive. Most of the time you can do fine without them.

Nutrition

The first thing you require of backpacking food is that
there be enough of it. That means, simply, calories to
keep your body running under fairly heavy work. You
can figure to eat about half again as much on the trail
as you do at home. Plan on 3,000 to 4,500 calories,
depending on your size, or even more. That's quite a
bit of fodder.

Few people bother to compute these things precisely. It's useful to bear in mind, though, that pure
sugars and starches provide about 100 calories to the
ounce in dry form. Proteins are about the same, and
pure fats run 250 calories to the ounce. Most foods are
mixtures of these elements and fall somewhere in
between. Breads, crackers, candies made mainly of

sugar, and dehydrated fruits and vegetables don't get much above the 100-calorie level. Chocolate, nuts, bacon, and dried eggs cluster near 150 calories per ounce. Margarine and oils are over 200.

What proportions of carbohydrates, proteins, and fats should you aim for? The consensus holds that backpackers should get 60 to 70 percent of their calories from carbohydrates, 20 to 25 percent from fat, and the remaining 10 to 15 percent from protein. The carbohydrates are basic running fuel; they don't stick with you, but they keep the muscles working. Fats are energy in concentrated form and burn more slowly. In winter, and on sustained, difficult trips, backpackers carry more fatty foods. Proteins deliver about the same energy value as carbohydrates, only more gradually. They are somewhat harder to digest, which may sometimes be an advantage: the work of digestion can help you keep warm when you are *not* exercising.

So how much food, in pounds, do you need to carry? You can probably reach your calorie target with 2 pounds a day of typical lightweight foods. Children and light eaters may be happy with less than that; in winter, everyone needs a little more. If you rely heavily on freeze-dried foods, 1½ pounds per person per day is an achievable daily ration.

Monitoring my own consumption, I find that I consume about 12 ounces of compact foods per day for breakfast and lunch combined, of which 3 ounces are breads or crackers, 6 ounces other carbohydrates like fruit, and 3 ounces protein and fat. That leaves about 12 ounces in the daily ration (measured before rehydration) for my share of dinner.

What about the finer points of nutrition: vitamins, minerals, balanced proteins, and such? By and large, on the trail, you can set such questions aside. Important though a finely tuned diet is over months and years, it matters little over the length of any ordinary wilderness excursion.

A few considerations do apply.

First, many people find that they function better in the mountains if their wilderness diet is not too different from what they eat at home. Sudden changes can upset the system and lead to diarrhea or, more commonly, to constipation. Foods with roughage are valuable in the trail diet. Some people carry laxatives as well.

Second, some people know they need to avoid certain foods. Some must watch their sodium intake—if you are one of these, read labels carefully, and consult your physician about your wilderness diet. If you're one of the people who have unpleasant reactions to monosodium glutamate, you'll be relieved to know that it's rarely found in freeze-dried food today.

Third, women who take long wilderness trips during their reproductive years may benefit from taking iron.

Planning Food: The Process

Who plans the meals? Only on large trips, like those sponsored by organizations, are you likely to find a central commissary. In a party of more than three or four members, it's customary to split into smaller cooking groups, each of which works out its own menu and carries its own stove.

Dinner, if hot, almost has to be a group project. The other meals are often handled individually. Each packs his or her own breakfasts and lunches, plus a dinner for the entire group on one or several nights. For example, if four hikers are going out for four days, each can bring one dinner to feed four, plus four personal breakfasts and lunches. If you do it this way, you may want to make sure that you don't wind up eating noodles and chicken every night; aside from that, little consultation is required.

Whether you're planning for one or for ten, the first step is to work out a *menu*. Some people think that they skip this step, but in truth they don't; they write the menu in their heads even as they push a cart down supermarket aisles. However, most of us have to be a little more methodical. You may find it useful to check books on backpack cookery for recipes and sample menus. One source is Sierra Club Books' *Simple Foods for the Pack*. Soon your own preferences and your own experience will take over.

Given a menu, you can proceed to figure the quantities of groceries you need. When in doubt, it's perhaps better to make the main, cooked courses a little scant and fill out with finger food. A big glob of uneaten stew creates a real disposal problem in the wilderness: in fact, somebody is going to have to pack it out (see Chapter 18).

Planning Food: The Wilderness Meals

At *breakfast*, some people like to fire up a stove and enjoy a full-scale meal with cooked cereal and bacon and eggs or pancakes. Others limit themselves to just-add-water foods, such as instant cereals, drinks, and concoctions like Instant Breakfast. Still others prefer cold foods like granola, crackers, cheese, and sausage. There is absolutely nothing wrong with cold cuts, at breakfast or at any other meal, but to some people they just don't seem like food. Coffee or tea is pretty standard; pick your form.

Lunch, on the trail, is not an event but an occupation. It should contribute about 40 percent of the day's calories. Some parties never do declare a particular refueling stop to be the midday meal, but others like to schedule a longer break for some dedicated eating. Some even fire up stoves for hot drinks, soup, or whatever. On an exceedingly strenuous trip you may need such a lunch stop just to make sure you are taking in the necessary fuel. Common lunch foods are breads and crackers with or without spreads (not dairy butter—it doesn't keep); dried fruit; nuts; candy; modest amounts of sausages and cheeses; and fruit-flavored drinks made from powdered mixes. Note that firm-textured cheese, despite what it says on the label about refrigeration, lasts well in a warm pack. Flour tortillas also travel well.

The classic trail mix—"good old raisins and pea-nuts"—usually has at least one additional ingredient, M&M's candies. Many, many other mixes are found, some of them in supermarket bins.

At higher elevations—say above 8,000 feet—many hikers find it best to avoid nuts, meats, and cheeses during the day. They find these fats and proteins hard to digest without a long rest after eating and don't want to risk exaggerating any queasiness brought on by unaccustomed altitude.

Dinner is almost always hot and is the largest meal. Commonly it begins with soup, goes on through a solid, one-pot main course, and ends with hot drinks, or dessert, or both. The main course usually follows the "macaroni and cheese" model: it consists of some-thing starchy—pasta, rice, instant potatoes, bulgur wheat, couscous, quinoa—and something rich in pro-tein and fat—cheese, meat, beans. Other ingredients add flavor. You'll often see vegetable stew with beef, instant rice with meat or fish or cheese, and such pre-fabricated main courses as beef stroganoff and chicken tetrazzini. Side dishes add calories. Puddings are a con-venient and popular dessert.

Ordinary dried beans will serve quite well on the trail; soaked a night and a day in an extra canteen, they'll cook up quickly when you want them. Dehy-drated vegetables can be reconstituted the same way.

If you're going above 10,000 feet, don't rely on spaghetti and such; because the boiling point is lower up there, pastas, especially thick ones, don't cook well. Quick-cooking freeze-dried versions avoid the prob-lem, and so do other carbohydrate bases, like instant couscous or mashed potatoes.

Food attracts bears. If you are going to grizzly bear territory, freeze-dried foods, which have less odor, are preferred. You'll have to skip cheese, fish, bacon, and sausage—all backpacking favorites—and anything you'd have to fry. Even where the only bear is the less danger-ous black, be aware that smelly foods can increase your problems. See Chapter 29.

Buying Food

In general, you must buy food in forms that are *light in weight, small in volume,* and *nonperishable.* Cans, as a rule, are out (except for certain compact and popular items like sardines). You also need dishes that are *easy to cook*—unless, of course, you pride yourself on camp-stove miracles.

You have several types of stores to work from. Sporting goods stores stock mainly freeze-dried dishes and ingredients. Health and organic food stores carry some useful staples that you may not find elsewhere (powdered hummus, for example). Asian and other specialty markets can add some zestful components. But the supermarket, in truth, can give you most or all of what you need. There is no reason in the world to pay premium prices for such products as macaroni, cereals, powdered milk, instant rice, or hard biscuits.

If you use freeze-dried foods, be prepared to pay $6 to $8 for a main course for two, about half that per dish for side dishes, desserts, and breakfast foods. The most expensive procedure is to buy all dinners and breakfasts in this form. More selectively, you can choose freeze-dried main courses for your dinners, and round them out with cheaper foods. Another course is to buy concentrated bulk ingredients, like dried eggs, dried peas, and diced beef, to use in your own recipes. (Few gear stores carry these, but you can order them directly from such makers as AlpineAire and Adventure Foods.)

One caution about freeze-dried foods. The instructions usually recommend preparing them in the package, simply by adding boiling water, stirring, and waiting a specified time. In my experience, though, these dishes do not get properly moist, soft, or even warm without a minute or two of simmering in a pot—even on the kitchen stove in my sea-level home.

Especially if buying at the supermarket, double-check the printed claim that such-and-such a packaged dish serves three, four, or six. With luck, a "serves four" carton from the market will serve two on the trail.

The labels on freeze-dried dishes state what the reconstituted weight will be: "two 12-oz. servings," for example; and of course the weight and volume of the finished dish are essentially the weight and volume of the water you add. Twelve ounces is actually quite a lot of food, and two solid 8-ounce cupfuls, whether of one dish or several, will satisfy most appetites at dinner.

Another form of compact food is the "energy bar," packed with all sorts of nutrients and costing between $1 and $2. Be sure to taste test before you buy any of the many brands and flavors in quantity. These bars have gotten tastier of late, but some versions are still pretty inedible.

Flavored drink mixes are also a form of food. Plain old lemonade is maybe the most refreshing. You'll pay much more for "sports drinks," specially formulated— the manufacturers proclaim—to give you energy and to replenish substances lost in sweat, known as electrolytes. The energy boost comes essentially from sugar, and for practical purposes "electrolytes" translates to salt. You need both, of course, but I find that there are more palatable ways of getting them.

Fresh foods do get taken on short trips, or for the first day or two on longer ones. Firm salad vegetables will travel well for a while; romaine is about the most durable of the lettuces. Apples will last if you can keep them from bruising, and you'll never taste anything so good as a great juicy orange, produced with a smirk on day five or six and shared around. Or not.

At the other extreme from the highly processed foods, many people concoct their own foods to eat on the trail. People bake journey-cakes and nutritional fudges; dry their own fruits and vegetables; jerk their own beef, chicken, turkey, and fish. A basic dryer combines a small heater and a fan and costs $50 or so.

How much should food cost per person per day? This can vary hugely. For its outings, the Sierra Club plans $8 to $12 a day. Buying for yourself or a small group, you may pay more, but $12 a day should cover it, even with considerable use of freeze-dried items.

Packing Food

There are several schemes for packing food and the ingredients of meals. One traditional method is quite elaborate: each individual meal is premeasured, pre-arranged, and packed in its individual, labeled plastic bag. Everything you need for that particular job of cooking will be there. Such packing can take a good deal of time at home, especially if meals are cooked from many bulk ingredients. It does save time on the trail, assures that you won't run out of food on the last day, and allows you to leave the menu at home.

A simpler method is to pack all the ingredients that will be used in dinners, throughout the trip, together in one large plastic bag (or several, to share the load). Needed directions, of course, go in the same bag, perhaps with a menu. Similarly, you can pack your lunch and breakfast foods in large bags of their own. Each morning before leaving camp, you extract the day's lunch and stow it where you can easily reach it.

Or, again, you can sort foods simply by day: a bag for Monday, a bag for Tuesday.

However you arrange things, you will have to do considerable weighing and repackaging. (It's nice to have two scales on hand: a postage scale for small amounts, a diet scale for larger quantities.) Get rid of cardboard containers (but not the directions printed on them) and other excess wrapping. Crackers, however, travel better in the original packages. Purists may want to get rid of foil wrappers at this point, but I don't go that far: just make a resolution not to litter with these and not to toss them into fire (they won't burn).

Most foods can be stored in stout ziplock polyethylene bags, the kind found in any supermarket. Powders and greasy things should be double-bagged. Cheese, which sweats, can be wrapped in butcher paper or cheesecloth, or dipped in paraffin, and then double-bagged or wrapped in aluminum foil. Still larger, thicker plastic bags, sold in gear stores, are good for keeping related items together. Heavier bags will last many uses, so wash and reuse them as often as you can. Carry plenty of extra ziplock bags in several sizes. Fruits and vegetables, on the other hand, last better in paper bags than in plastic.

You can also make some use of rigid plastic boxes and bottles; a few compact foods—meats and fish—are carried in their original cans. Butter and oils can't be bagged. Cylindrical potato chip cans and well-cleaned milk cartons have their uses. Especially fragile items can be tucked into pots.

Figure out your plan for protecting food from bears and other animals. What will you use for a bearbag? If you haven't bearbagged recently, practice the skill at home (see Chapter 18). If you will be using a solid-walled bear canister, make sure your groceries will fit in it.

You don't want to cut your food supply too fine. Throw in an extra dinner, or at least some extra finger food, for a possible added day. Some people like to carry a packet of concentrated energy food for an emergency; it can be largely candy, pemmican, jerky—anything that will keep a long time. Wrap it tightly in a couple of plastic bags (you might seal them shut with a hot iron), stick it in the bottom of your pack, and forget it. Once a year go ahead and eat such items as pemmican and dried meats, and replace them; they don't last forever.

Planning Fuel

How much fuel do you need to cook the meals you have outlined?

That depends on your stove (some are thirstier than others) and on your cooking habits. A standard if economical allowance for liquid fuel is ¼ cup per person per day. That's for quick-cooking dinners and minimal use at breakfast—say 30 minutes of daily running time. More extensive cooking ups the quota considerably. On a first trip, I'd recommend taking ½ cup per person per day and seeing how much you come back with. You do want to come back with a little—the reserve idea again. One person alone uses more than

50 percent of what a pair would use. On snow, where water must be melted, fuel needs will approximately double.

What about cartridge stoves? Again, consumption rates vary. With most models, 1 ounce of butane/propane mix runs the stove for 20 to 30 minutes. A typical large cartridge contains just under 7 ounces of gas. One such unit is adequate for two people for three days. If you use smaller cartridges or a lustier stove, adjust accordingly. Some small cartridges are nondetachable: once the seal has been pierced, they stay put until empty. If you've mounted one of these and it isn't brand new, bring a spare. You may also want to bring a duplicate if you're taking a cartridge stove into cold conditions: you can help the stove function by occasionally swapping a chilled cartridge with a warm one.

As noted, you can keep fuel needs low by choosing foods that need minimal simmering. For some other fuel conservation tricks, see Chapter 18.

Water

On most trips, water is taken for granted; there's no need to plan for it if it's plentiful along the way. But sometimes it is not so easily found. When a supply must be carried, it's important not to underestimate how much you need.

Even a person who isn't exercising needs 2 quarts of water a day, most of it in liquids, some of it in solid food. A hard-working hiker loses much larger amounts in sweat and breath. On a strenuous trip you require a full gallon a day or even more. That's more than you may find yourself prompted to drink by thirst alone. Though straight water is the very best thing to hydrate with, flavored mixes, hot chocolate, and such have the advantage of keeping you interested.

Most wilderness travelers today boil, filter, or chemically purify all water from natural sources. For the reasons and the options, see Chapter 20.

13

Packing &
Preparations

You've got your gear. It's lying in great disorganized piles all over the living room.

You've got your trip. You're leaving tomorrow morning.

How do you get all that junk into your pack without utter confusion? How will you know where things are when you need them? How can you make sure of leaving nothing essential behind, and of taking not an ounce more than you need to take?

These are problems that every backpacker must deal with. Every backpacker finds personal solutions, personal organizations, personal shortcuts, and odd arrangements. What follows here is a set and rather fussy procedure to make use of, if you care to, the first few times you put a packload together.

First Step: Make a List

When you make your first list of objects to be taken, divide it by category. List all items connected with food and cooking in one section, all items connected with shelter and bed in another, and so on. Think carefully about the places you are going. In such a month in such a spot, do you reasonably need to take a venom extractor? High-powered sunscreen? A spare pair of dark glasses? Hiking shorts? Long johns? Imagine the situations you may be facing. As a starting point, you may find it useful to consult the accompanying skeleton list.

When you're done packing, file the new list away. Later, as you walk the trails, you will be making notes—mental or written, conscious or unconscious—as you go along: "Flashlight should be in outer pocket . . ." "Didn't need down jacket this trip . . ." "Could have used a larger pot . . . ," and so forth. Remember which items you had but didn't need, and which you needed but didn't have. Then, when you get home, you can correct and rearrange your original list to make it a better guide next time you head into similar country at a similar time of year.

Skeleton Pack List

This is meant as a starting point for a precise packing list of your own. Ask yourself: Do I need . . .? and then: Do I have . . .?

Bed and Shelter
    sleeping bag
    pad or mattress
    ground cloth
    weather shelter (tent, tarp, bivouac sack)

Kitchen
    stove, cookware
    spare fuel as needed
    any needed stove accessories
    matches, fire starters
    personal utensils
    provision for dishwashing
    provision for food protection

Tools
    maps
    compass
    other navigation aids
    knife or multitool
    cord
    notebook/writing tools
    repair kit

Tools (continued)
    flashlight or headlamp
    spare batteries and bulb

Clothing
    basic outfit
    boots and socks
    spare socks and underwear as desired
    clothing for cold and wind
    clothing for rain and snow
    hat
    glasses or goggles
    bandannas

Emergency
    signals (whistle, mirror, bright cloth)
    emergency shelter provision
    matches/firestarters
    medical kit; venom extractor

Personal
    tooth-care items
    toilet paper
    insect repellent
    sunscreen
    other toiletries as needed

Haulage
    stuff sacks
    plastic bags and closures
    water containers
    daypack

Second Step: Assemble and Check the Gear

Here's one way. Get a big cardboard box. Locate the items on your list one by one, place them loose in the box, and check them off the list. Examine each item as you go for any needed maintenance that was missed the last time you got home. Fire up your stove. Run a quart through your water filter. Replace batteries as needed. (This is the point at which you find that none of your lights is working.) See that your first-aid kit is replenished and any medications up to date. If you have any brand-new gear, be sure to get familiar with it now.

Especially if you are heading for grizzly country, old gear, including tent and pack, should be gotten as clean as possible, and cooking gear rewashed.

Third Step: Combine the Objects in Groups

A typical pack may contain over 100 items, many of them small and losable. If you just dump them in, your confusion will be hopeless. Instead, handle them in groups. Keep all the kitchen items together, the medical kit together, the repair tools in their own small bag. Or forget superficial logic and work out convenient groupings of your own. Build a pattern that enables you to find what you need when you need it. In any case, avoid leaving tiny objects loose.

A typical frame pack, with its upper and lower compartments, suggests an organization. Almost everyone seems to use the lower level for clothing, for instance. In a pack with fewer built-in divisions, as in many internal-frame backpacks, hikers rely on cloth stuff sacks to organize their gear. If you use these bags, you'll find yourself leaving much of your gear parked in them between trips; this shortcut can make the final packing fairly quick and easy.

What about shared gear? In a group, items like tent and cookware must be allocated among the packs. If the hiking party is all from one household, this is easy. When people are converging from different places, the process is a shade more complex. The ideal is to meet beforehand, but it is more common to divvy up the community load at the last minute, on the road or at the trailhead. Each party member must be sure to bring the objects he or she is responsible for, and to leave space in the pack for a reasonable share of the combined community load.

Fourth Step: Pack It In

Now you start the pleasant task of loading the pack—the wardrobe and larder from which, in the next few days, everything you need for life must come. Especially if you haven't done it before, expect to load and unload several times before it seems just right. As you go, keep certain things in mind.

Consider the Distribution of Weight

Stuff sacks and other load components should be arranged to put as much weight as possible close to your back. Think of yourself as building a mortarless wall against the inner surface of the pack; if there's space outward from that to be filled, use it for clothing or other light things. If there are load-compression straps, loosen them before you start and tighten them firmly when you are done.

The load must also be evenly divided between the *sides* of the pack. You don't, for instance, want 2 quarts of water and fuel in one side pocket and nothing but a sweater in the opposite one.

It used to be conventional wisdom that a trail hiker should carry a top-heavy pack, with weighty objects packed high and close to the back. With modern load-carrying systems, however, this advice has been challenged. Some treadmill tests with variously loaded packs have shown no significant difference in ease of carrying. Try different arrangements and see what you think. Many women, notably, seem to prefer a somewhat lower center of gravity in the load.

Top-heaviness is definitely to be avoided when you are packing for cross-country hiking, for scrambling, or for travel over snow—especially if you are using an external-frame pack. Too high a load will move around disconcertingly on your back. Put heavy objects at about shoulder-blade height.

Consider When You Will Want to Get at Things

Try to cut down on the number of times each day you will have to burrow deep into your pack. Thus, there needs to be an accessible slot for the food you will eat for lunch each day. Water should be accessible. Camera and accessories, if you carry such, should certainly not be buried. Likewise sunglasses, sunscreen, hat, bandanna, bug dope, map and compass, toilet paper and trowel, and whatever else you are likely to want as you go. This will never work out perfectly, and on a leisurely trip it doesn't matter, but it's nice not to be rummaging all the time. In the least reachable regions (which vary by packbag design) you store the things you will not need till evening, like tent, dinner food, and possibly your stove (but see "Consider Special Problems" below).

Consider Special Problems

Fuel and water should, when possible, be packed outside rather than in the main compartments of a pack (and of course right side up). Any liquids carried inside the pack will be safer in metal, rather than plastic, containers, and should be further isolated by ziplock bags. Food should be higher up in the load than fuel. Then there are a few fragile or aggressive items to consider. Some stoves, for instance, won't take much mashing. Sharp objects like tent poles shouldn't be so packed that they could poke holes in a jacket, a food bag, or the pack itself. Any air mattress needs to be in a good, tough stuff sack; if carried outside the pack, it should ride on the top, not the bottom.

If you finish the trial packing job and find you have objects left over, or that the load is lopsided, or that things you want accessible are not, unload the stuff and try, try again. Often at this stage you change your mind about what is essential and what is a luxury.

Figure out how to manage objects that will only occasionally be carried on your back, like skis or snowshoes for winter travel. If there is a likelihood of rain, consider how you will protect pack and contents. If you have a number of items strapped onto the outside of your pack, will your pack cover or poncho fit over them? If not, how will you attach them outside the waterproof cover? It's easier to work through these complexities ahead of time than with water running down your neck.

When your pack isn't quite large enough for the load, you can make more hauling room by adding a frame extension or additional tie-on patches, as discussed in Chapter 6. Shock cords and straps with buckles are always likely to be useful and can be tightened better than simple cord. Little carabiners and pin-like clips come in handy. Additional carriers, like a beltbag or camera pack, may prove their usefulness here.

Unless you live just miles from the trailhead, the last packing job you do at home is still in the nature of a draft. Even if perfect, it won't stay that way. You may have to dig things out of your pack while on the road; you may have to add in some community gear at the end of it. If the basic fit is right, don't worry about a little sloppiness: the time for last-minute adjustments is still to come. And, no, you won't be the only one who has to make some.

What about boots and clothing you will put on at the roadhead? If there's a lengthy road trip intervening, it is convenient to put these items in a duffel bag alongside your pack, together with any items you'll want in transit. A generous daypack may also serve as road duffel. It's especially nice to have your stuff compact and self-contained if you're going to be a passenger in someone else's car.

Packing for Air Travel

If you are traveling by air, you'll have to rearrange your gear for maximum protection. Anything rigid or breakable should go in the middle of the pack, with lots of softer things surrounding it. Shorten up the shoulder straps and sternum strap. Wrap the hipbelt around the base of the pack (the opposite of the wearing position) and secure it with added straps or by passing it through any handy exterior tie-on loops. Make sure that every tag end is cinched, buried, or fed back through a buckle. Bind zipper sliders in place with wire ties. For more protection, you can wrap the pack in several thick garbage bags and secure it thoroughly with duct tape. (Carry more garbage bags and tape for the flight home.) Better yet, wrap your sleeping pad around the pack and put the whole thing in a hefty duffel bag.

Be aware that you cannot transport stove fuel by air: it will have to be purchased at the other end. Same goes for matches, butane lighters, and signal flares. Some airlines will not even accept camp stoves without fuel, and, if these are found, will destroy them. Find out your carrier's policy in advance.

Other Last-Minute Preparations

If your toenails are not already trimmed short, trim them straight across now. The last time you shower and wash your hair before you leave, forget conditioner and any scented lotions or deodorants. Such additives cause you to get grimier faster, and may even attract mosquitoes—or, more seriously, bears.

If you haven't already done so, this is the time to leave an informative note for a family member or friend, explaining your plans in some detail and indicating when you expect to be out of the woods or the hills. Include the license number and description of each automobile; names and addresses of other people in your party; and the phone number of the local office of the land management agency whose jurisdiction you will be visiting.

What about that date of return? Most hikers, in telling their friends when they plan to return, ask that the alarm not be sounded unless they are *well* overdue, say 24 or 48 hours. They hate the feeling that people will begin worrying immediately if they switch to a longer route or take an extra day at an irresistible campsite. (Yes, a cell phone would be tempting.) If you give yourself this margin, be sure you have food and fuel for the extra time.

As a rule, fill your water bottles at home. A 2-to-5-gallon water can is a handy thing to have in a road-head car.

Travel on the Trail

Followers of trails and of seasons,
breakers of camp in the little dawn wind,
seekers of watercourses over the
wrinkled rind of the world,
o seekers, o finders of reasons
to be up and be gone . . .

—Saint-John Perse, *Anabasis*

14

To the Trailhead

A considerable portion of every backpacking trip is spent, not on the trail at all, but on the road. And while getting to the trailhead is by no means half the fun, the drive to the edge of wilderness is certainly a pleasure in itself. On the road you are in between, anticipating, imagining, watching the land unfold around you. The work is done, the decisions made. You're both excited and relaxed. You're on your way.

I have said already: "the *drive* to the wilderness." As noted in the previous chapter, you might be getting there by some other means. But when trailheads lie, as they often do, on remote and rugged roads, there is really no other good way of getting there than on your own wheels.

Lost keys can produce major hassles. One ruefully experienced hiker suggests making extra copies and giving one to each member of your party; if you're driving a rental car, invest in at least one key copy. Also have a credit card along, or enough cash to get home on if a car breakdown or change of plans requires you to do so (if, for example, your ride has to leave the trip early).

Touching Base in the Region

Unless you have completed the paperwork by mail (see Chapter 11), you will probably have to stop at a local land agency office for a fire permit, a wilderness permit, or both. (Requirements vary and cannot be readily summarized.) In a few well-trafficked areas you may find registration booths near the trailhead; more typically the responsible office is some miles away. Wilderness permits can sometimes be picked up after hours at self-registration stations; fire permits, as a rule, cannot. Find these things out in advance.

Permits aside, it's an excellent idea to stop at a ranger station to ask some last-minute questions, or to double-check information received earlier. Are key roads in good condition? Have there been recent problems with trailhead crime (see "Trailhead Strategy," below)? What is the latest local weather forecast? How high are the creeks running? What about snow on the passes? How are the bears behaving? (You may be advised to rent a bearproof canister, or even offered a free loaner.) The less you learned beforehand by phone or correspondence, the greater the need to talk now to the local managers. There's a safety aspect, too: if a permit isn't required, it's a good idea to leave word of your projected route and schedule.

Most people have a last restaurant meal before they head in on a multiday wilderness trip. It's nice to do this in the town nearest the trailhead, and to let drop casually that you're in town because of the wilderness next door: a subtle message about its economic value. A decent tip never hurts. Repeat a few days later when you have the inevitable enormous "exit meal."

If you're in a very small town not geared up for tourism, be friendly to and respectful of local folk. Avoid crowding them out at stores or eating places. If you need to park, hike, or camp on private property, ask permission and offer payment. Make a point of buying some supplies locally.

Many wilderness roadheads lie at the end of long, rough roads, far from the nearest service station. You may have some trouble tracing the maze of branching routes to your destination. And dirt roads eat up fuel. Head into the hills with a full tank of gas.

Trailhead Strategy

This trailhead business is sometimes more complicated than it seems. At many trailheads, three possible concerns arise: first, impact and congestion; second, theft and vandalism; third, animal raiders.

Some trailheads are major parking lots, designed for the traffic they get. Others are wide places in the road. People sometimes insist on parking where there is no room, damaging roadside vegetation—and maybe getting stuck in ditches and mud. If there isn't room at the actual trailhead, park elsewhere along the road. Another half mile on foot won't hurt.

More troubling is the problem of roadhead crime. It is no longer unusual for cars to be broken into. Again, one solution is to leave the car elsewhere than at the obvious trailhead. For best security, park at a ranger station or in a patrolled camping area (if a small fee is charged, regard it as insurance). If you drive an expensive car or plan to leave expensive items in it, this precaution is thoroughly sensible.

Wherever you park, stash any valuable items in the trunk or securest area. Leave nothing visible. Empty the glove compartment and leave it open, unscrewing the little bulb so your battery won't drain. Wallets and such go with you on the trail. (Better to leave all but essential cards and cash at home.) Carry the keys. Though many people do it, it's hazardous to leave spares hidden around the locked car. If you arrive in the evening and sleep beside the car, do lock it for the night. To discourage theft, some people like to remove distributor rotors or otherwise disable their vehicles. In certain areas, it is unwise to leave a car with bumper stickers or decals that suggest conservation sympathies. It is also recommended that you not chat too casually about your plans with people met at the roadhead: thieves have been known to masquerade as hikers. It's all a damned shame.

If you are headed for bear country, which is most of our wilderness, you want to leave the car interior as clean as possible. Try not to leave attractants in it, like extra food or even cleanup supplies; any you're stuck

Travel on the Trail

with go in the trunk or most secure area. If possible, park in the shade so odors won't develop.

Then there are the porcupines, which have the odd habit of chewing on brake lines. This is such a problem in parts of Canada that people shield the undersides of their cars with chicken wire.

If freezing temperatures are likely, be sure to leave the parking brake off (a frozen brake immobilizes the car). Nor should you set the brake if you have recently driven through water; the problem here is rust. If necessary for safety, place chocks behind several wheels.

The Beginning

It always seems as if you could just start walking. Seldom does it work out that way. Unless you have done more planning, conferring, and prepacking than most hikers find time for, you will need to do some last-minute rearrangement before you hit the trail. Most important, you will probably have to redivide community gear—shelter, stove and pots, food, fuel—to everyone's satisfaction. (A family group, of course, will have had more chance to sort out such details at home.)

Changing from car clothes to trail clothes, and putting on your boots, is about the final stage. Many hikers apply tape or moleskin to their feet at this point, before the stresses of the trail begin. Chug some water now, too.

Should you stretch before you hoist your pack? Probably not—stretching cold muscles is not a good idea. Rather, plan to ease into the day with 15 minutes of not-too-strenuous hiking. If stretching is part of a regular fitness routine for you, by all means work it in later. Otherwise, this is not a good time for innovations.

One more thing as you set out: if a trailhead register is provided, take a moment to sign in. Even though you may have filled out a wilderness permit already, or left word with the office, the register is still the final record of who you are and where you are going. It also helps the agency gauge traffic on its trails. It may be objected that signing in provides more information for trailhead criminals; on balance, though, it's still the thing to do.

15

Life on Your Own Two Feet

When the last stray object is stuffed into the last bulging pack pocket, when the car is locked and the map refolded, when the boots are securely laced, comes an end—and a beginning. You've been a planner, a list checker, a filler-out of forms, a motorist. Now that's over with. Congratulations: you're just a backpacker, now.

Walking with a Pack

As one kind of weight comes off, of course, another kind comes on. By now you'll have put your pack on many times, but let's review some ways of getting the thing up there.

The natural but strenuous method is to grab the pack by the shoulder straps (or, perhaps, by an upper crossbar), haul it up the front of your body, swing it around to the back with your stronger hand, and wriggle your arms, first one, then the other, under the straps.

To reduce the strain, you can start in a crouch and hoist the pack first to a bent thigh, parking it there for a moment before completing the maneuver and straightening your lower body. Even better, you can create the transitional thigh platform by placing one foot on a low rock or log. It's a little hard to visualize, but try it and see.

Or you can park the pack on a convenient rock, fence, or tree limb, or have a friend hold it in position for you, and back into it.

Then there's the dramatic flop or inversion method. It requires a light, tight pack with no dangling accessories. You hold the pack in front of you, straps toward you, *upside down*. Then you lift it up, over your head, and down onto your back, sliding your arms under the straps as it descends.

In the worst case, when the pack is heavy and there's nothing in sight to rest it on, you may simply have to set it on the ground, sit down with your back against it, slither into the straps, and surge to your feet—strong leg muscles, and maybe the help of a stick, required.

Whatever method you use, don't lean over to pick up the pack, and don't bend your back to shorten yourself to the level of a low rock or other pack-supporting platform: bend your knees instead.

As you walk, you will occasionally want to adjust the way the pack rides on your back, for better comfort or simply for variety. You might tighten or loosen the hipbelt, ease up on load lifters, tug on the sternum strap to shift the harness inward on your shoulders. If you come to a section where you have to scramble over stones or plow through bushes, a looser hipbelt, and more weight on your shoulders, will reduce the lurching of the load. Too much shoulder carrying, however, can bruise the brachial nerves and give you what's called "pack palsy" or "trekker's shoulder," a numbness of fingers, forearms, or even the whole arm. Though temporary in most cases, it's best avoided.

The first time you carry a pack in a given season—and almost any time you carry an excessively heavy load—your hips will get red and sore. Aside from the slight discomfort, this does no harm, and will happen less as time goes on. Some people, early in the season, will put tape on their hipbones as well as on their heels.

All About Walking

Does anyone seriously need instruction in how to walk a trail? Probably not. Complicated though the art of backpacking sometimes seems, the *act* of backpacking—the moving along with a load—is almost too automatic to describe. Walking is what we're built for. There are, nonetheless, some points worth mentioning.

The most comfortable trail pace for most people is not fast—at least the legs are not pumping rapidly—but it is very steady. Some experts recommend striding out, taking the longest steps you can manage; others see more efficiency in a deliberately shortened stride. But your own legs will tell you how far they want to swing. Let your arms swing, too, in the natural way. If you're using trekking poles, you'll plant each tip as the opposite leg goes forward and use the pole to give an extra push to that stride.

A hiker in good condition can go up a fairly steep and sustained hill without either gasping for breath or slowing down to a crawl, though the stride will shorten. Avoid pointing your toes outward, which may seem easier but actually increases the strain on the knees. Tilting your pelvis slightly forward will bring the large muscles of the buttocks into play. Breathe deeply. Expelling the breath with a little effort through rounded lips gives you the sensation of getting more oxygen.

If the rise is severe, you may switch to the *rest step*. In the rest step, you simply pause briefly every time you begin a new stride, at that moment when the forward foot is planted but has not received any weight. Each leg thus gets a series of tiny rests. On a steep slope, heavily loaded packers may break stride in this manner for a second or more with each step.

Going downhill can be hard on the knees. Although it's natural to plant the foot heel first, with quite a jolt, it's gentler to descend almost flat-footed in what might be described as a fast creep. Keep your back erect and your knees slightly bent, unless you are plunging with straight legs down a soft surface like snow or volcanic ash.

You can adjust fit by tightening and loosening boot laces in different parts of the lacing pattern. You can loop laces around hooks to increase friction and maintain the adjustment.

Some hikers adjust the lacing of their boots depending on the slope they are facing. At the start of a climb, they loosen the lower or toe-end laces and tighten the upper laces to stabilize the heel, which tends to shift and chafe in uphill travel. On the down-slope they loosen the heel and tighten the toe, which prevents the toes from stubbing themselves against leather. Only your experience will tell you whether you need to bother.

In order to keep such customized lacing from evening out, you have to build in a high-friction "brake." Some boots have special clamplike retainers in the middle of the pattern for this purpose. You can get the same effect by wrapping opposite laces around each other two or three times in a hitch. Where there are hooks, rather than eyelets, you can also reduce friction by running laces around the hooks in loops ("mountaineer's lace") rather than simple curves.

Care and Feeding

You will need to adjust your clothing frequently. You may start out on a chilly morning with long pants, a heavy shirt, a stocking cap, even an insulated jacket, but be down to boots, socks, and hiking shorts by afternoon. You learn quickly that it makes sense to start cold; however chilly the air at breakfast, you'll warm up fast on the trail. If you start hiking in the clothes that are comfortable for puttering around camp, you will be hot and sweaty in a few hundred yards.

There are two competing principles here. One is: *keep comfortable*. The second is: *don't spend all your time fiddling with clothes*. With garments that you can adjust while you wear them, like shirts and sweaters with closures in front, you won't have to stop continually to add or subtract a layer.

But of course you can stop as often as you like. Unless you happen to want to make it one, this is not a marathon. There's always a picture to be taken, a snack to be eaten, or just something worth looking at. For hikers with a schedule, 10 minutes of rest an hour is a useful guideline.

When it is time for a stop, find a spot off the trail, on an unvegetated surface. A convenient natural pack table is nice, too. In grizzly bear country, don't linger where there's bear sign or a food source (like ripe berries). For more about bear safety, see Chapter 29.

Be sure to take in water or other drinks as you go, at the rate of about a pint an hour. We used to be urged to drink more than we really wanted, to avoid dehydration; now we learn that drinking too much can produce an equally undesirable condition called hyponatremia, meaning low sodium in the blood. Either will bring weakness and nausea. Dark urine is still a signal to drink more.

Intake of food is also continual. Ninety minutes, the nutritionists say, is as long as a hiker should go without eating *something*. Some people subsist on snack food all day long. Some like to stop and eat, in addition, a distinct midday meal. It doesn't matter how you do it, but get the calories—mostly carbohydrates—in. The hiker should also regularly get some salt, in food or perhaps in the form of a sports drink.

With nibbles of food in your mouth all day, you may wonder what's happening to your teeth. This is a sensible concern. It's not sugar and starch directly that do the damage, however, but rather bacteria in the mouth; the best defense is to brush and floss thoroughly in the morning, starting the day with teeth very clean. It also helps to slosh water around in your mouth after a snack. Tooth care in the evening is also as necessary on the trail as at home.

Hiking with Others

Almost inevitably, the members of a group will hike at different rates—some a little faster, some a little slower. A small difference in pace can produce quite a bit of separation. If this starts happening, talk about it. Spreading out may be quite all right, as long as the leaders wait at any trail junction, or it may not. It is miserable to be the one slow member of a group that is moving at racing speed: the only one who experiences as a struggle what should be pleasant exercise, who can't take the time to look around and enjoy. It's less of a trial for faster hikers to slow down or wait than for slower ones to puff and strain. Try to avoid the "Here you are, let's go" syndrome in which the stragglers, laboring up to the well-rested leaders, never get a proper rest themselves. It's important that fellow hikers be able to tell each other, calmly and fairly early in the game, what they want and need.

If you do allow yourselves to spread out, make sure the people at the end of the line know what the plan is. For a person who simply follows, blind to the choices and landmarks of the route, getting separated can mean getting lost.

At the other extreme of things, it's rude to follow the person in front of you too closely; unless you're in a long, slow line, leave 6 feet of elbow room at least. If you want to pass, ask. If a companion wants to pass you, watch for a place where you can step off the trail onto a hard or barren surface, not onto vegetation.

If you meet another party coming the other direction on a slope, it seems natural for the downward-bound hikers to step aside: their momentum is less hard-won. A party with stock, however, always has the right of way. Pedestrians should step well off the trail on the uphill side and talk softly so the animals aren't startled to find someone there. Whenever a meeting is imminent, look for a spot where you can stand aside without compacting soft ground or crushing vegetation. Backpacking parties that meet on the trail or in camp tend to greet each other cordially, chat a moment, and withdraw.

Be very careful about dislodging rocks along a steep trail. If you do, yell at the top of your lungs: *Rock!*

Foot Care

It's a good idea, circumstances permitting, to wash your feet thoroughly with soap and water once a day and let them dry thoroughly in the air. This does something to keep odor down; holds fungal infection at bay; and helps in the prevention of blisters. A soak in a cold stream is lovely, but all washing with soap gets done away from natural waters (see Chapter 20). A daily change of socks (with the spare pair washed and drying on your pack) is healthy, too.

The best way to deal with blisters is not to get them. Make sure your boots fit properly and that they are nicely broken in before you set out with them (Chapter 4). Do enough preliminary hiking to toughen your feet somewhat. If you aren't sure you're ready, or if you know you blister easily, you will want to cover the danger points with adhesive tape, duct tape, moleskin, or the stretchable moleskin called Spyroflex before you leave the trailhead. Likely problem spots are the heel, the ball of the foot, the outside of the big toe, and the sides of the foot at the base of the toes. For best adhesion, wash and dry the spot first (a premoistened towelette is handy for this).

If you feel a zone of irritation forming as you walk—a "hot spot"—take action. Sit down, pull off the boot, and find out what's going on. Put on a protective layer; if you have one on already, make sure that it has not developed wrinkles (they can cause extra irritation) and reapply if needed. Check the boot lining, too: if there's a rough spot there, tape that. Make sure that your socks aren't wrinkled, holed, or more than slightly damp, and change them if needed. Relace your boots snugly. If the trouble spot is a heel, tighten the upper part of the lacing pattern so that your heel is not rising too far inside the rear of the boot as you stride.

If you do get a blister, you aren't by any means crippled. Several treatments are popular. I prefer the simplest. First, wash the spot carefully with water and soap. Sterilize a needle by passing it through the blue part of a flame, and puncture the swollen area at one edge. Very gently press the fluid out. When the skin is dry, cover the blister with a thin sterile pad from your first-aid kit. (Some people apply antibiotic ointment.) Then put on a layer of moleskin or porous adhesive tape. If the blister refills, repeat the draining after about 6 hours and again after about 12 hours, lifting just a corner of the tape to do so.

Another treatment commonly recommended is the "donut patch." In this procedure, you place a ring of moleskin or tape around the drained blister but not on it, leaving the blister itself exposed. (An unmedicated corn pad can also be used.) Then you add a second layer of tape or moleskin, this time covering the entire area. In theory, this arrangement takes pressure off the blister and prevents further irritation. On the other hand, it gives you something of a lump in your boot.

And some people swear by still a third procedure, "de-roofing": you trim the skin above the blister completely away, apply a dab of antibiotic ointment, and cover the raw patch with 2nd Skin, the burn dressing by Spenco. A layer of porous adhesive tape or stretch gauze goes on top.

A day's layover will help the healing process, but if this is difficult to arrange, it is not prohibitive to keep going. Walking a long distance with such a patch can be slightly uncomfortable, but it is by no means agonizing. Though blisters very seldom lead to any further trouble, it's important to watch the spot for signs of infection.

Walking Softly on the Trail

Everybody knows it but it bears repeating: if you're hiking a trail, *stay on it*. Cutting corners, taking shortcuts, walking outside the treadway—all these break down trail edges and cause erosion, gullying, and perhaps rockfall. If you're using a staff or trekking poles, plant tips inside, not outside, the trail tread, or on rocks.

Not all trails are well designed, and rather few are actually well maintained. Some are laid out so badly that it is hard to avoid doing damage. For example, a trail may push straight through boggy meadows or head directly up erosive slopes. In such places, people tend to move to one side or the other to avoid the mud or the rocky footing of an incipient gully. This is one of the main causes of *multiple trailing*, in which five or six parallel tracks scar open slopes and meadows. Such damage is not, strictly speaking, the hikers' fault—blame it rather on bad trail layout and poor maintenance—but you can best help by gritting your teeth and keeping to the original line.

As a rule, you walk single file, not side by side, on a trail. A possible exception is the old road or other pounded track so wide that people can, and obviously do, walk abreast. In cross-country travel, where you wish to avoid establishing any visible track, you should almost always walk abreast, each hiker on a separate course. See Chapters 22 and 23 for more on these points.

Whether on a trail or on a cross-country route, you should restrain any impulse to build ducks (small rock cairns used as route markers) or otherwise to flag the path. Let the next travelers find their way as you did. Chances are they prefer it so

Wildflowers, as a rule, shouldn't be picked or even touched. Although the amateur botanist can't be faulted for taking a sample, even this is technically forbidden in parks. If you don't know exactly what you're doing, don't transport plant materials from one area to another: you might be helping an exotic and damaging species to propagate.

Party Splitting and Side Trips

There's no great harm in dividing your party—if you do it with some care, making sure that each splinter group has all the essential gear, and that everyone is clear about a place and time for coming back together. Note that in grizzly country there is safety in numbers—three or four are safer than two and much safer than one.

You may also want to vary a trip by taking side trips, even perhaps solo, with nothing but a daypack. If you take such an excursion, you must be certain to have some basic items with you. Always be prepared for an unexpected night away from your main camp (see below). As for your main pack, if nobody will be near it, protect it from animals by hanging it in a tree or over a rock face before you wander.

Nineteen Essentials

The classic list of Ten Essentials, established by the Mountaineers of Seattle, has grown a bit. It now includes these items:

Map. At least the local topographic sheet.

Compass.

Sunglasses. Advisable anywhere; doubly important above timberline, in the desert, and, most of all, on snow. Snow blindness is no joke.

Sunscreen.

Extra clothing. This may be as little as a sweater or as much as a jacket, parka, and rain pants. Just as you do when you're packing the main pack at home, think of clothes to keep you *warm* and clothes to keep you *dry.*

Headlamp or flashlight.

First-aid kit.

Matches. Waterproof/windproof matches are good for this purpose.

Additional fire starter.

Knife.

Repair kit.

Extra food. Perhaps nothing more than a generous lunch; perhaps an emergency packet of high-energy food. It's true that a person can survive for days, even weeks, without food, and take no permanent harm, but in an emergency you need energy to work with and, still more important, to think with.

Extra water, or water purifier. If you're treating your water (see Chapter 20), you won't want to stop now.

Provision for emergency shelter. If you don't carry a plastic sheet, bivouac sack, reflective blanket, or the like, consider how you'd improvise with natural materials where you're going. (Such techniques are not for everyday or recreational use.)

Depending on local conditions, you will probably find yourself adding to these fourteen. Here are some other items you may not want to be without:

Insect repellent. In some places, this seems like a survival item.

Toilet paper. Natural substitutes are possible.

Bandanna.

Notebook and pencil. You may need to leave a note somewhere.

Signal device. Mirror, whistle, brightly colored piece of cloth, possibly cellular phone.

Stream Crossing

On most well-traveled trails, at least in the regular hiking season, you will find simple bridges across large streams. More primitive routes, however, don't have bridges. Lacking stones that are dry and conveniently spaced, you wade.

Some people stride through such fords and keep walking, letting feet and socks and boots dry as they go. But wet feet in wet socks blister easily. It's a better plan to remove your socks and wade in boots alone, or in tennis shoes or river sandals if you have them. (Bare feet are too easily cut or stubbed.) Don't try to throw boots across a broad stretch of water. A staff or trekking pole, or a pair, can add to stability.

Once across, drain and swab out wet boots as well as you can, put your socks back on, and continue. When socks grow soggy, replace them with a dry pair;

your boots should now be fairly dry. (Dry the wet socks on the outside of your pack if the weather's good.)

Most fords are very innocent. But there can be genuine danger in crossing a high-volume, swift-running stream such as you may encounter at the spring thaw or in cross-country travel. You may have to spend some time looking for a good fording point. Often it is better to wait for better conditions or to turn back, even if it means abandoning a destination or going the long way around. Ask yourself what will happen if you are swept off your feet. An astonishing number of people have been carried over the terrible verges of Yosemite's thousand-foot cataracts after trying to cross the harmless-looking mountain streams above. Unless you know exactly what you are doing, it is not wise to tie onto a rope at a dubious crossing: the seeming protection can do more harm than good. For more about these tricky situations, rarely encountered in ordinary backpacking, see Chapter 22.

Lingering Snow

In many mountain areas early in the hiking season— and in the Northwest, the northern Rockies, and the mountains of Canada and Alaska at any time—you are likely to encounter snowbanks on the trail.

Old snow is slippery stuff when cold, and mushy stuff when warm. Either is difficult. Crossing a flat snowbank, lift your feet cautiously and plant them very flatly. On hard snow, come down firmly to establish your footing. On hard-crusted snow that conceals a mushy interior, come down very gently and test the footing as you go: this should reduce the number of times you plunge in, swearing, to your knees. Be aware that snowbanks may have melted cavities underneath, especially at the edges.

Spring hikers who encounter a small melting snowbank on the trail often detour around the retreating margin of the snow, not wanting to wade in slush. By the following weekend the snowbank has shrunk; more parties come through and detour along a different arc, and then a third, until a whole fan of tracks is worn in the moist earth. The problem is so acute in some areas that managers close routes to public access during the thaw. If you encounter such a snowbank, and can't avoid it on rocks or logs, the conscientious thing is to put on gaiters and slosh through.

For something more about negotiating steep snow slopes in summer, see Chapter 22.

In Thunder, Lightning, and Rain

The weather that hikers dread most is extended rain. Even rain, though, is troublesome only when it comes time to set up camp; walking in the rain, with the proper gear, can be a pleasure. If you have good water-resistant coverings for yourself and your pack, you will be relatively comfortable. With water-resistant boots and gaiters, even your feet can stay dry.

That is, if you're prepared. For the unprepared, there is real danger in wet, cool, windy weather. If you don't have the gear to stay dry and warm, you run the risk of losing so much body heat that you suffer the collapse called *hypothermia*. Common sense and proper clothing, however, are all that's required to prevent such situations. For more on hypothermia, see Chapter 28.

In brief, western-style thunderstorms, you may be able to wait out a swiftly passing shower under the shelter of a tree. But make very sure it's the right tree, and not a likely target for lightning. Lightning is a definite hazard in the American wilderness, much more to be feared than, for example, the rattlesnake. Yet, like most hazards, it's easy to avoid.

Lightning doesn't strike just anywhere. It is drawn to prominent objects: the highest outcrop on a stony peak; the sharp brink of a cliff; a tall, isolated tree. When the bolt strikes, the charge spreads out through the ground and can shock you badly many feet away from the original strike. The current tends to move along cracks in rock and down small, shallow watercourses, especially when water is running in them.

When you hear a thunderstorm working its way through the sky, stop for a moment and count the number of seconds that pass between a flash and the resulting thunderclap. Each 5 seconds that passes indicates 1 mile of distance between you and the flash. (Each 3 seconds indicates 1 kilometer.) If you are in a high or exposed place, don't wait till the last minute to start your retreat; thunderstorms typically move 1 mile every 2 or 3 minutes.

What are unsafe positions? A peak, of course, or a hilltop. A flat meadow or plain or rocky plateau where you yourself are a prominent object. The shore of a body of water. The foot of a prominent tree. The top of a cliff but also the *base* of a cliff. A shallow cave on a slope. You are much less vulnerable at the bottom of a valley; among low boulders or bushes or trees of fairly uniform height; or in a deep, dry cave.

If you have a choice of tree species to shelter under, avoid oaks. Favor spruces and beeches. Regard pines as intermediate. This bit of folklore has a sound basis: the trees most likely to be struck have deep roots that go down to groundwater.

If you're trapped on a mountaintop or out in the open, with no time to retreat, at least get back from the highest points and from cliff edges. Among boulders, you can crouch between rocks of similar size and low profile. Members of a party should spread apart, keeping 30 feet or more of separation.

Take off your pack, your pocketknife, your camera, and anything else with metal in it, and move well away from the pile. You want to stay low but also to minimize your contact with the ground. Assume a crouching position with legs together and hands not touching your knees. This posture tends to keep the electrical current out of the body core. If you hear a buzzing from metal objects, smell ozone, see objects rimmed in a blue glow, or feel your hair standing on end, make sure you're in position, and hope.

If a companion has been struck by lightning, your quick action may be lifesaving: see Chapter 26.

Wildfire

With the western fire season comes a disquieting thought. What if, in some summer-desiccated wilderness, you found yourself hiking in the path of a forest fire? While I have never heard of a backpacker being injured in this fashion, some advice from fire experts is worth noting.

If you become aware of a wildfire burning in your vicinity, you must try to stay out of its way. In general, move downslope; flames advance 16 times faster uphill than down. If possible, head for a cool stream bank or a broad, unvegetated opening. Stay away from draws, which provide natural chimneys. Given a choice, get upwind of the blaze.

If you realize that you can't avoid the fire, look for an area of relatively open ground. Remove all synthetic clothing, which melts or burns readily, and your pack. Put a dry bandanna across your mouth and nose; if you have a reflective blanket along, hunker down under that. When the fire front has moved past you, assess any burns or other injuries you or your party may have sustained, and seek help. By laying out three objects in a triangle, you can alert firefighters to your presence.

Needless to say, you don't want to be the source of a wildfire. For the all-important precautions in camp, see Chapter 18. If you're a smoker and find you must light up on the trail, be exceedingly cautious about it: stop in a broad, bare area, scatter ashes when cool, and pack out butts. When fire danger is high, don't smoke at all. In California and sometimes elsewhere, areas may be closed to access in the summer and fall, both for public safety and to reduce ignition. Respect such bans.

16

Finding the Way

Let's face it. Few corners of the typical recreational wilderness are so remote, so trackless, or so primitive that they afford us much excuse for getting lost. Not truly lost, not lost without a clue, not North Woods lost. Nor do we need very complicated techniques to avoid losing ourselves. Navigation these days is most often a simple thing, a matter of keeping track of where you are, how fast you are progressing, what landmarks you are passing. It's a matter of awareness: common sense.

Yet people do get lost, and even in serious trouble, in the most populous of wild areas. And it is a rare hiker who has not had moments of disorientation along the way. Did I miss the junction? When did we cross into the watershed of Limbo Creek? What are those cliffs doing up there? Or just: What happened to the trail?

Even for the hiker who never moves on anything but the plainest of paths, navigation can be fun, not so much to tell you where you are as to identify what you see.

The Topographic Map

The basic tool of navigation is the topographic, or contour, map. Add to it a compass and a little thought, and you can answer almost any question about your place in the land. These invaluable maps—many thousands of sheets in all—are created by the U.S. Geological Survey (USGS) and by Geomatics Canada but are sold largely through private channels.

In the continental United States, the basic map series uses a scale of 1:24,000. These sheets are also known as 7.5-minute quadrangles, "minute" being a unit of space, not of time. Each map covers an area of about 6 by 8 miles, though the field shrinks somewhat at northern latitudes.

In an older series of USGS maps called "15-minute" sheets, each map covered a region of about 14 by 17 miles. Today, only Alaska is mapped at the 15-minute scale; 7.5-minute quads exist as well for a few regions in the southern part of that state.

In Canada, the base maps of the National Topographic Series have a scale of 1:50,000, making them rather comparable to U.S. 15-minute sheets.

On a regular topo map there are several kinds of information. Most important are the thin brown lines called "contour lines," or just "contours." Each traces a given elevation above sea level. If you imagine the map as a three-dimensional model that could be flooded with water, the rising surface would first touch the 1,200-foot contour wherever it appears, then the 1,400-foot, and so on. On U.S. 7.5-minute maps, the interval between contour lines is usually 40 feet. Every fifth line is heavier and darker, and marks a gain of 200 feet from the last such emphatic line; these heavy lines have elevation numbers attached. On the older 15-minute maps, the basic interval is generally 80 feet, and 400 feet separate the heavier lines. A notice at the bottom of every sheet tells you what contour interval applies.

Topo sheets ordinarily have a pale green shading to show forested areas. Green stippling indicates brush or perhaps tundra; uncolored areas are grassy or barren. Sheets also may show overlying grids of several kinds; more about these below.

Canadian topo maps are generally similar. Older sheets show elevations in feet; newer ones use meters. Canadian topos also differ from USGS quadrangles in having a legend printed on the back; in the United

States, you need a separate brochure for maximum explanation. For the sparsely populated northern regions, Canadian 1:50,000 sheets are published in black and white only.

Maps organize the world by grids. The oldest, most fundamental grid system is latitude and longitude: every place on earth is a certain distance north or south of the equator and east or west of a prime meridian that runs through Greenwich, England. Latitude and longitude are expressed in units called degrees, minutes, and seconds (hence "15-minute" or "7.5-minute" maps). You will notice tick marks along map margins, with labels in the format 32'30". These are indications of latitude (on left and right edges) or longitude (on top and bottom edges). If you drew lines connecting opposite ticks, you'd have a tic-tac-toe grid. At each crossing, a tiny cross is already imprinted.

A newer grid, the Universal Transverse Mercator system, is already drawn for you, printed in faint gray on U.S. and Canadian topographic maps. Its lines are 1 kilometer apart. This grid is very useful if you are working with a Global Positioning System receiver (see "GPS and Other Tools," below).

In the United States a third grid system may demand your attention. Most of the country is divided into squares, usually 6 miles on a side, called *townships*. Each contains thirty-six sections of 1 square mile each, which are numbered within the township in an unvarying back-and-forth pattern. The basic purpose of this system is to track land ownership, and land agency maps almost always reflect it, cutting the territory up into stacks and rows of section squares. Hikers and other people who work with the land soon become familiar with the pattern and use it to identify points on the map: "Looks like there might be a waterfall in section 17!" There's more than one "section 17," of course, but you usually know which one you are talking about, since the nearest neighboring section with the same name will be 6 airline miles away.

Topo maps today are both more and less accurate than they used to be. They are more accurate because satellite technology allows topography to be established more precisely than ever before. They are less accurate because remote sensing has all but replaced the laborious fieldwork called "ground truthing," especially with regard to little, evanescent things like trails. Don't be too quick to doubt your senses if your map seems to be wrong about some detail that can't be seen from the sky. Also notice the date in the legend. Many trails shown on older maps have been abandoned or rerouted, and the road systems in the rugged mountains of the western United States and Canada have exploded in recent decades.

In the United States, topo maps are available by mail and over the counter at a few USGS offices; maps covering popular hiking destinations are found at many stores. In Canada, map distribution has been completely privatized. Many companies also publish derivative maps, drawn from the government bases but sometimes containing more or newer information. Sheet prices run $6–$10. A more convenient way of acquiring maps is to purchase them on disk and reproduce them on your own color printer. Map databases covering entire states or regions are available for $80–$100. You can also download maps from the Internet. Map kiosks in some gear stores offer a similar map-printing service at $8 a sheet. See the Resources section for a sampling of map sources.

Protecting and Manipulating Maps

Classic paper topo maps can be protected from weather in several ways. Several companies market liquid coatings you paint on map surfaces to keep moisture and mildew out; some hikers use mineral oil or acrylic varnish, or cover the working side of the map with clear contact plastic. Maybe the simplest precaution is to store each map in a ziplock bag.

It can matter how you fold a map. How big do you want each segment to be when you finish? If your pack has a special map pocket, how large is it? Your folded map should be a bit smaller. A common procedure is to fold twice in each dimension, dividing the map into sixteen fields. An "accordion-style" fold allows you to see more fields without opening out the whole sheet. Folds that run the long way should be kept very straight, helping you to eyeball north-south lines.

Many hikers trim the margins from their paper topo maps, retaining only the actual representation of the land. Before you snip, consider how much of the marginal data is valuable. You may want to keep the scale (though you can stick it onto an irrelevant part of the map surface). Do write down the name of the sheet (maybe on the back) and the declination number from the diagram at the bottom (more on this in "Compass Step Two," below). For use with a Global Positioning System receiver (see "GPS and Other Tools," below), leave margins intact.

Commercial maps, by contrast, are prefolded and printed on tough plastic or water-resistant paper, with margins you won't want to trim.

If you are printing your own maps from a computer source, you'll probably use the special water-proof paper now widely available for this purpose. You can also manipulate the information many ways. What you have tapped into is a huge database, a regional supermap, any portion of which you can view and print out for a specific trip. Accompanying programs may allow you to analyze and mark up the field you select. For instance, you can highlight a length of trail with a cursor and get an instant readout of its length; you can produce an elevation profile of a hike; you can insert symbols at planned campsites.

Other Kinds of Maps

Three other types of USGS maps are of occasional interest to the backpacker. Sheets of the 7.5-by-15-minute series have a scale similar to ordinary 7.5-minute quads (1:25,000) but are wider, covering twice the distance east to west. Moreover, they are metric, showing elevations and contours in meters. The 30-by-60-minute series is also metric, using a scale of 1:100,000 and portraying larger areas with less detail. Finally, the USGS still publishes the old 1:250,000 series, covering still vaster stretches; though not useful for close-up route finding, these maps can be fun to consult in the car, giving you a sense of what's topographically what in an entire region. Geomatics Canada has 1:250,000 sheets as well.

In addition to topo maps, you usually also want the maps published by the agency that controls the land you are hiking on—National Park Service, Parks Canada, Forest Service, Fish and Wildlife Service, Bureau of Land Management, or state or provincial agency. These agency maps, though mostly less detailed than topos, may reflect more recent changes in roads and trails, and they often have useful text on the back. For some designated wilderness areas, the agencies have prepared combination maps showing current roads and trails on a topographic base—ideal, if the base is sufficiently detailed.

One final point. On most maps, true north is at the top of the sheet, east on the right-hand margin, west on the left, south on the bottom. However, sometimes the field is tilted for some reason. Look for an arrow labeled *north* somewhere on the sheet and adjust your thinking if it doesn't point straight up.

Map Reading

The basic skill is the ability to build, from the map, a picture of the country—to translate swiftly, automatically, from map to land and back again. You can practice this skill most easily by getting a topographic sheet for a familiar landscape near home and spending some time with it. Soon you'll know without thinking what a particular shape of land looks like in contour lines: that an outward eddy of lines along a slope indicates a spur ridge; that an indentation means a gully or a stream course; that one valley is broad and shallow, a second precipitous and deep. You will distinguish a short, steep hill from a long, gradual one, and a plateau from a knife-edge ridgeline. It is a fascinating study. The map begins as a dead graphic, a mere representation, but it comes alive as you learn it and instructs you endlessly. The map *becomes* the country.

The backpacker's navigation, in its essence, is not a set of techniques but a habit of thought; a custom of awareness; a matter of keeping tabs on where you are, and what the land is doing. In typical wilderness landscapes, unlike those of the city, there is seldom anything really inexplicable or arbitrary; there are broad, discernible patterns—drainages running one way and another; major and minor systems of ridges; plateaus and deep-carved canyons. If you keep alive this sense of pattern, it is rather hard to become entirely lost, whether you have a trail to follow or are striking out cross-country on a route of your own.

Some landscapes, certainly, are easier than others to lose your bearings in. Most confusing are areas that are level, rather patternless, or chaotically jumbled, and places where timber or topography cuts off your long-distance views. Fog or low overcast can complicate matters, and every snow traveler knows that brilliant-white, opaque, and snowy mist called whiteout. These are the cases where advanced navigation techniques—and GPS receivers—really come into their own.

The Compass and How to Read It

The compass is the second fundamental aid in wilderness navigation. Its function is to help you place the map in the right position, so that the map's north and the world's north are exactly the same. This done, the compass helps you read the land, from the map, with precision.

Nothing is simpler, in practice, than using a compass. Nothing is more difficult than to describe this simple act without giving a largely spurious impression of complexity. I suggest that, after scanning the next few pages, you reread them with a good compass in hand.

The essential part of the compass is the magnetized *needle*. The needle does not, except in a few localities, point to the geographic North Pole (*true north*).

A simple orienteering compass, combined with a topographic map and a landmark or two, can tell you where you are and where you're going.

Rather, it aligns itself to point *generally* north along a wandering web of magnetic lines that converge in northern Canada, at a point (*magnetic north*) a thousand miles short of the true pole. Thus the actual direction indicated by the "North" end of a compass needle varies from place to place. It also varies slightly from time to time, but we won't worry about that here.

There are many kinds of compasses. The type most used in backpacking is the *orienteering compass*. The needle rides on a pivot inside a round, fluid-filled plastic chamber. One end of the needle—the end that points (more or less) north—is specially marked, often with red paint. The surface of the chamber is a *dial* marked with 360 degrees running clockwise. Though no small compass has room for a separate mark for each of the degrees, the better models mark every 5 degrees, or even every 2.

The needle-and-dial assembly sits on a rectangular *base plate* of clear plastic and can be rotated upon it. The bigger the base plate, the better for close navigation—5 inches is good. The plate is marked with a big lengthwise *directional arrow*; this extends partway under the dial and can be seen through it. There may also be two notched sights, one on each side of the dial, along the arrow's line. On many compasses the

Travel on the Trail

base plate is also marked with several *scales* to use in reading maps: inch, millimeter, and other intervals given because, on maps of different standard scales, they represent miles or kilometers.

One compass variation is often seen on the trail: the type that has a hinged lid and, mounted inside it, a mirror. This feature adds a little precision when you take a bearing (see "Compass Step Five," below).

Good orienteering compasses without superfluous extras cost $10 to $20. The prominent brands are Silva, Nexus, Suunto, and Brunton.

Compasses are confused by metal. You won't get an accurate reading from a compass held near a camera, a car, or other metallic object.

Compass work is rarely finicky. Most of the time you will be using the tool in a simple, casual way. Just a glance at the dial, now and again, can guide you when you are uncertain or keep you from drifting off an ill-marked route. If you know you are supposed to be heading essentially north, then something is plainly wrong if the compass shows you moving steadily east.

Now for the finicky parts.

Compass Step One: Understanding the Circle of Directions

Imagine yourself standing on a peak from which you can see a hundred miles in every direction. Imagine yourself turning slowly in one spot—facing north, then east, then south, then west, then north again.

How do you name the directions you have been facing? The cardinal points—north, east, south, west—are easy. For the directions in between, you can combine and say: northeast, southwest; then north-northeast, south-southwest; then north-by-north-northeast; and so on. But obviously you can only go so far with this elaboration. For greater simplicity and precision, we switch from names to numbers. The circle of directions is divided into 360 units called *degrees*: 0 degrees is north; 45 degrees, northeast; 90 degrees, east; 180 degrees, south; 270 degrees, west;

Declination East

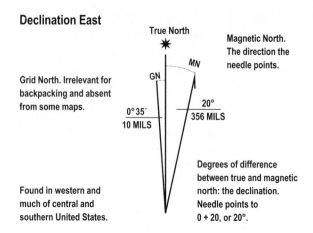

True North

Magnetic North. The direction the needle points.

MN

Grid North. Irrelevant for backpacking and absent from some maps.

GN

20°
356 MILS

0° 35′
10 MILS

Found in western and much of central and southern United States.

Degrees of difference between true and magnetic north: the declination. Needle points to 0 + 20, or 20°.

350 degrees, just a smidgen west of due north; and 360 degrees, north again (0 and 360 degrees, in the circle, being names for the same point).

Compass Step Two: Knowing Where Your Needle Points

In most of the United States and Canada, compass needles point either just east or just west of true north. To make good use of your compass, you need to know how much east or west. The name for this difference, measured in degrees, is *declination*.

Every topographic map has, in the lower margin, a diagram that purports to give this information. The vertical line with the star represents true north; the slanted line labeled "MN" indicates magnetic north, or the direction in which the needle is actually supposed to point (once the compass has been transported to the region depicted). The angle between these lines, expressed as a number of degrees, tells you how far you have to go left or right from zero on your compass dial to find the number that represents the point toward which your needle will actually aim when you are in the mapped area. If the declination is "west," you'll be going around the dial toward west—counter-

Declination West

True North

MN

GN

10½°
187 MILS

0°7′
2 MILS

Needle points to 360° – 10.5°,
or 349.5°.

Found in much of eastern
United States.

clockwise; if the declination is "east," you'll be curving toward east—clockwise.

Got that?

It has always struck me that the standard way of expressing "declination," as a deviation from an imaginary norm, is needlessly confusing. All that matters is that the needle, in a given region, points to a given spot on the circle of directions. Know that spot, swivel the compass dial until the needle points to that spot, and you're in business.

Compass Step Three: Orienting the Dial

Suppose the declination in your map area is 19 degrees east. This means, simply, that your compass needle will point in the direction represented by 19 degrees—about north-northeast. To orient your compass for that region, then, you rotate the dial until the number 19 comes into position at the tip of the needle. With your compass dial thus oriented, it has become an accurate guide to all directions. True north on the compass matches true north on the land; southeast on the compass is southeast in the outside world; and so on.

In the eastern United States, compass needles lean west from true north. Say the declination is 10 degrees west. Rotate the dial so that the needle rests at a point

10 degrees to the west of north. This point bears the number 350: 360 degrees (north) minus 10 degrees (declination west) equals 350 degrees. (To go west from north, counterclockwise around the dial, you have to subtract degrees.)

To make orientation easier, some compasses come equipped with a movable marker for your local magnetic north. By adjusting a tiny screw, you can create an obvious target for your needle to point at. Worth a couple of dollars? That's up to you.

Compass Step Four: Orienting the Map

Once you know how to orient the compass, the next big step is to get the map lined up as well. (Remember, you are doing this in the field, standing on the territory represented by that map.) The trick, essentially, is to go back one step and orient the compass again—this time *with* the map, as though they were one thing.

First, take the unoriented compass and rotate the dial until the directional arrow on the base plate is seen to pass through the mark on the dial that represents true north. Second, place the compass on the map, with the directional arrow in line with north on the map. (To line it up exactly, use a margin or an accurate north-south fold.) Third, hold this map-and-compass combination firmly in your hands and turn it as a unit until the compass needle points to the number on the dial that matches magnetic north. You have now oriented the compass and, with it, the map. The map now parallels the land.

Compass Step Five: Taking Bearings

Now that both map and compass are oriented, you can use them together to give you many kinds of information. Often a simple procedure will do. If you already know within a mile or so where you are on the map, it is easy to read the identities of prominent points. The big massif just east can only be General Steele's Backbone; the forested valley can only be the drainage

Travel on the Trail

of Horsethief Creek; what is glinting in the socket below can only be Hungry Packer Lake.

But sometimes you will need to read the land more precisely. Perhaps you don't know at all where you are; perhaps the topography is downright confusing; perhaps you must make a difficult choice of route. All these problems are reasons for taking *bearings*.

How is it done?

The idea is to find the precise direction from you to a particular object, say, a prominent peak. Raise the compass to just below eye level. Make sure it is correctly oriented. Now, keeping the dial in that same correct position, turn the base plate underneath it so that the arrow on the plate is pointing exactly toward the object you want the bearing on. Now look down through the transparent dial (or through sights if your compass is so equipped). You will see that the directional arrow is visible and cuts the circle of degrees at a particular point. Read the number at that point. This is your bearing.

If your compass is the kind with a mirrored lid, you'll notice a vertical line etched down the middle of the glass. There will be also be two sights, one taking the form of a hole in the lid, near the hinge. Adjust the lid so that the compass dial appears in the mirror, with the etched line crossing it at the needle's pivot point. Check dial orientation. Look through the sights at the object whose bearing you want. Note where the line cuts the mirrored dial. This is your bearing.

This information has many uses.

You know where you are and want to know what you're looking at. Take a bearing on the feature you want to identify. (Let's say it's a peak.) Note your own position on the map. Place the (properly oriented) compass on the (properly oriented) map with the center of its dial at your position. Say the bearing on your landmark was 120 degrees, or about southeast. Simply draw (or imagine) a line running from your position to the number 120 on the dial and on across the map. (The line printed on your compass's baseplate will do for a start. Swing the baseplate around to the proper position without disturbing the actual compass dial.)

The first height along that line that seems of proper elevation and distance is the one.

You know what you're looking at and want to know where you are. Take bearings on two known peaks (or any other prominent features). The farther apart they are, the more accurate your fix will be. Placing the compass on the map as before, draw (or imagine) lines running from those landmarks toward you at the proper angles. Where these lines intersect, you have your exact position. To double-check, you can sight on additional points.

Or perhaps you already know that you are on a certain *line* in the landscape: a major stream, a trail, a ridgeline, a road. This simplifies matters. Just one bearing, just one additional line on the map, may be enough to show you the single place where you can reasonably be standing.

You have the whole picture but want to find this place again. Say you've discovered something interesting, some distance off the trail: an old cabin not shown on the map, a hidden shortcut through a band of cliffs, a good fishing spot. You want to come back next year. But there's no obvious landmark along the trail to tell you where to leave it next time you come along. A bearing on a more distant landmark will do just as well. Write yourself a note: "Next time walk east along the Kangaroo Trail until Sawtooth Mountain is on a bearing of 315 degrees; then cut down the ravine to the left." You might further describe your cross-country route as a compass direction, or heading: "Then head downslope on a line of 125 degrees."

GPS and Other Tools

Many people today carry Global Positioning System receivers as an adjunct to map and compass. A GPS is a wonderful shortcut device for establishing your precise location and showing the way to other locations that are known.

The Global Positioning System is an array of 24 satellites launched and maintained by the U.S. military.

This Global Positioning System receiver is showing distance and direction to a "waypoint" previously entered, a desert spring.

By picking up signals from three or more such satellites, a little handheld receiver can calculate your position exactly, expressing it as a pair of coordinates. It can also tell you the direction and distance to any other point on the map whose coordinates you enter.

Coordinates? What coordinates? You can use either of two grids indicated on your topo map: latitude and longitude, measured in degrees, minutes, and seconds; or Universal Transverse Mercator (UTM), measured in meters east and north from specified master lines. The UTM grid is the one actually shown, in faint gray, across the map field. Of course, your target is unlikely to be exactly at a marked intersection of the grid, so you have to interpolate, something done far more readily with the metric UTM. It's helpful to have a UTM grid tool ($3), a transparent sheet that overlays a one-kilometer map square and divides it into a hundred smaller squares; see the Resources section. The language of UTM coordinates is slightly complex but quickly learned.

You can also enter, with a simple press of a button, the coordinates of the location you are standing in. Each point you have entered stays in the receiver's memory as a "waypoint." Once you've got the hang of it, you can map out a whole trail, or cross-country route, as a progression from waypoint to waypoint. To chart a curvy course using GPS, you have to break it up, establishing many waypoints linked by short, straight segments. (As far as the GPS unit is concerned, the only way between two points is a straight line.) In cross-country travel, you might get a bearing on your target from the GPS, head off in that general direction, and check again as you close on the destination.

Most of the time, the GPS does only what your compass could do. There are circumstances, though, where it works much better. In a snowstorm, or in heavy fog. On flat or undulating forested terrain. When you're closing in on a target that is not visible or distinctive—and not close to something that is. When you've found something you want to locate precisely and find your way back to. What GPS does not do, ever, is eliminate the need to think.

You can get a simple GPS, weighing just 3 ounces with AAA batteries, for $100. Bigger ones have larger screens, more memory, and interfaces allowing you to load and display map information. No need to pay for all this, however; you'll need your paper maps in any case. A more significant limitation of some cheap units is that they do not handle UTM coordinates; check this out before you buy.

When you get your GPS unit, play around with it for a while on familiar ground. Even a simple model has a panoply of menus and commands. You will need to give it certain instructions specified in its manual: tell it what time zone you are in, for instance; what units distance should be given in; and whether to indicate true, magnetic, or "grid north" (the first is the normal choice). You will also need to specify a "map datum," which varies according to the topo sheets you are carrying; check the legend at the bottom of the sheet. The 1984 North American datum is most common, but other datums can be selected at need.

A GPS that is left on all the time can provide a "breadcrumb trail," showing you where you have been as well as where you want to go. This is not a very useful function, however, and it wastes battery power. For practical purposes, a very occasional reading is really all you need.

Be aware that a GPS unit needs to "see" as much of the sky as possible; tree canopies and canyon walls can interfere with reception. Weather doesn't affect it, however.

For very fine navigation, especially on big mountains, an altimeter/barometer can be helpful. This is a device, mechanical or electronic, that measures air pressure. Because air pressure decreases rather steadily with height above sea level, this measurement can indicate your altitude. Air pressure also increases or decreases with the weather—falling pressure usually signals an advancing weather front. An air pressure sensor that simply tells you the local pressure, in a unit called millibars, is a barometer; if it expresses its data as elevation above sea level, it is an altimeter; many units do both. (GPS units also give you readings of elevation, but these are not very precise.)

Of course, the double meaning of air pressure readings can lead to some confusion. If you find your campsite has risen a hundred feet during the night, you may be in for a storm! The pressure changes due to weather, however, are usually both slower and much smaller than changes due to your own climbing and descending.

Some wristwatches now contain built-in navigation aids and weather-sensing tools: altimeters, barometers, thermometers, and compasses. None of these added tools, however, are as good as the stand-alone versions.

Low-Tech Navigation

Let's go to the other extreme. Far from having high-tech gadgetry, suppose you've even lost your compass? There are some rough-and-ready methods of determining direction. Except for the first, none of these tricks will do much more than straighten you out if you are grossly turned around.

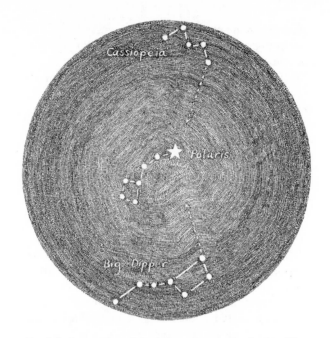

Two distinctive groupings of stars in the northern sky, Cassiopeia and the Big Dipper, point the way to the North Star. Polaris is part of a third less-prominent pattern, the Little Dipper.

Polaris

Our polestar isn't always at true north, but it's close enough for emergency purposes. To locate it in a clear night sky in summer, first find the Big Dipper. The two stars that form the end of the Dipper's "bucket," opposite the "handle," define a line pointing almost straight toward Polaris, a star of medium brightness.

If the Big Dipper is beneath the horizon, you can go by another constellation, Cassiopeia, which lies on the opposite side of Polaris and about the same distance away. Its five stars form a distinctive, flattened W. Whether the W appears right side up or upside down, its open, three-starred side points toward the North Star.

All stars, in fact, give directional clues. Here's a trick you can use without special knowledge. Pick any

Travel on the Trail

star (or planet) near the horizon and note its position relative to something distinctive, maybe a tree branch. Wait a quarter of an hour and watch how the celestial body moves. If the star rises, you are facing generally east. If it sets, you are facing west. If it moves to the right, you're looking south. If it moves to the left, you're looking north.

The Sun

It's useful to be aware of the arc the sun follows in the sky at a given time of year. North of the Tropic of Cancer, it is always in the south half of our sky at noon, but its rising and setting points vary. At the equinoxes, mid-March and mid-September, the sun rises and sets very close to due east and due west. In mid-June it rises somewhat northeast and sets somewhat northwest; in mid-December, it rises somewhat southeast and sets somewhat southwest. (Exact tables, organized by date and latitude, are available to pin this down.) Above the Arctic Circle, of course, there is a period at midsummer when the sun never sets at all.

You can use a watch or a stick to extract some of the directional information that's implicitly contained in the daily path of the sun. Though none too accurate, these methods are kind of fun and might provide some reassurance in a pinch.

If you carry a watch with hands, first set it to standard time (subtract one hour if it's on daylight saving time). Second, hold the dial flat and point the hour hand toward the sun (or the ground point that appears to be beneath the sun; you can align the hand with a straight shadow). South will be a point on the watchface halfway between the hour hand and 12, going in whichever direction the arc is shorter. (Before 6 AM and after 6 PM, you have to split the longer arc toward 12.) If it's 8 AM standard time, south will be at about 10 on the dial; if it's 4 PM, south appears at about 2 on the dial. If your watch is digital, you can translate, drawing the watchface on a piece of paper or scratching it on the ground.

Lacking a watch, you can read direction, roughly, from the shadow thrown by a straight stick. There are different versions of the technique. In the quickest procedure, you plant your stick in the ground, not straight up, but slanted toward the sun, so that no shadow is thrown. Then wait until a shadow appears. This shadow will mark an approximate east-west line. The reading can be taken at any time of day.

Signs in the Land

In the northern hemisphere, the north and northeast sides of objects are heated less by sunlight each day than the south and southwest sides. Other things being equal, then, moss *does* tend to be thicker on the northern side of trees; different plant communities tend to grow on north- and east-facing slopes; snow and ice linger longest on the northern sides of ridges. In rare cases, you may also be able to guess directions from the effects of a strong prevailing wind: lopsided trees, sand patterns, and so on. But all of these signs should be used with extreme caution. Local conditions complicate them, and, at best, they are crude.

"Sense of Direction"

Do human beings have a built-in "sense of direction"? Just possibly. It turns out that there is a bone between the eyes that is rich in iron; it may be a vestigial navigation device. But "vestigial" would seem to be the word. Study after study finds that people who try to walk straight lines without constant correction go around in circles instead.

Following a Trail

Ordinarily, there's no skill to following a trail. It's there, unmistakable, and you just plod. But even obvious trails grow faint at times. And in the United States there is a huge network of what might be called "ghost trails"; built in the 1930s under the New Deal, they have never been maintained since

Faint trails, especially above timberline, may be marked with small stacks of stones called "ducks" or "cairns" or "birds." Occasionally these piles are high, but most are just large enough to be clearly artificial. Often a single stone, placed at one side of the main stack, indicates the direction of the continuing trail.

In wooded country, indicators are found on tree trunks. These may be plastic tags, metal disks, paint spots, or the traditional ax cuts called *blazes*.

Blazes are usually shaped like a capital *T* or a dotted lowercase *i*, with a smaller separate cut above. Usually, blazes are placed at about chest height. Often they are stacked in groups of two or three; this stacking may or may not signal an impending turn. Blazes ordinarily face along the line of the trail, so if you see one facing sharply off to the left or right, it probably marks a bend in the route. However, blazes cut by different workers at different times aren't necessarily standard.

When the trail is clear, of course, you don't have to be too much concerned with these guides. But if the path starts going hazy on you—if it disappears under patches of snow, if it threatens to dissolve in a maze of deer trails, if the brush starts closing it over—begin watching the blazes meticulously. A surprisingly official-looking trail can be made by deer and bear. Be aware, too, that natural marks can counterfeit cut blazes.

When the ducks and blazes fail you, there are other signs you can look for. Have the branches of trees or shrubs been cut or clipped? Is there a terrace effect where the path was cut into a hillside? In a place where brush has obscured a route, the treadway itself may be free of new stems; plants are slow to root again on compacted ground.

If such detective work is required for long, though, you are probably no longer just bridging a difficult section of an otherwise plain path. Rather, you have to count the trail as defunct and regard the trip as a problem in cross-country route finding. Since the original trail builders may have found the easiest way across the landscape, though, you may want to stick to the mapped trail line as well as you can.

What if You Do Get Lost?

What *is* getting lost, anyway?

If you lose the trail in the undergrowth; if you hesitate at a junction; if you see a landmark you don't recognize; then you aren't lost. You're disoriented merely, and though disorientation can be the beginning of "lost," it is not the thing itself.

You are lost when you do not know how to retrace your steps to a place where you feel sure of your bearings. But perhaps even more than a situation, being lost is a state of mind: panic.

If you find yourself disoriented, whether you are "lost" yet or not, sit down. Get out map and compass. Think back on where you have been in the last hour. Think back to the last point at which you were sure of your position. Scan the landscape for features you can reason from. Consider the lay of the land—are you, for instance, in a valley that drains in a certain direction? If you find yourself initially too worried to think, start by making this a rest stop. Eat something, take a picture, have some lemonade.

If you have a Global Positioning System unit and a map, you can get unlost in a hurry. It will consult the satellites and give you your location; or you can enter the Universal Transverse Mercator coordinates of some spot where you've recently been, or where you'd like to be. The unit will tell you what direction to walk in. But of course if you have this gizmo and the skill to use it, you probably aren't lost in the first place.

Even just using your head, you should most of the time be able to reconstruct where you are, or at least how to get back to known ground. After all, a pedestrian moves only so fast. You won't be two counties away.

And if you can't reconstruct? Sometimes, especially on flat terrain, it is appropriate to walk a *search pattern*, a sort of rectilinear spiral widening out from

Travel on the Trail

your starting point. This can be useful if you are looking for something–say a trail–that is probably nearby. One caution, though: never lay down your pack or daypack while you search. You might not find it again, and this could turn a minor problem into a major one.

If you get lost on a side trip, away from your party, try to make contact with the rest of your group. Shout, blow your whistle, flash your mirror. Three signals of any kind are a distress signal; two signals of any kind indicate response–"We read you." Most stray people are collected, sooner or later, by their companions.

If none of this works, about all you can do is make yourself comfortable, keep signaling from time to time, and stay put until searchers turn up. Eventually your friends will report you missing, or an alarm will be sounded when you fail to return at an appointed time.

Your first priority now is *warmth and shelter*. If you are hiking alone with a full pack, you will have everything you need to make yourself cozy. Otherwise you may have to improvise.

If there is wind, getting out of it will be important. If you're on the windward side of a ridge, cross over to the leeward. Look for a natural barrier like a boulder or massive tree. A dense thicket of vegetation also cuts wind. If there's no easier escape, you can build a windbreak of stones or, if available, snow. For warmth, you can rake together a pile of forest debris and burrow into it.

If rain is a prospect, you need a roof as well as a wall. A cave or overhang is ideal; sometimes there are sheltered spaces among room-sized talus blocks. Lacking a previous tenant, a hollow log or tree will also serve. There may be a persistent dry zone near the trunk of a large coniferous tree.

If you have to build a roof, it needn't be fancy. The basic plan calls for a *ridgeline*, which may be a stout stick, a taut cord, or a fallen log; transverse *ribbing* of sticks or cord; and *thatching* of grasses, reeds, chunks of bark, fallen leaves, green foliage, or whatever else you can find. If there's a convenient fallen log or stone, the ribs can lean against that. Thatching 6 to 12 inches thick will keep out most of the rain. Build the shelter just big enough to fit into. Pile material under you, as well, so that you don't wind up lying in a puddle. If you need to cut boughs for your shelter, this is of course justifiable in a genuine emergency.

Though insulation is more important than the positive warmth of a fire, by all means build one if conditions permit. If you've found a semisheltered pocket at the base of a cliff, for example, a fire in front of you can make it downright cozy.

If you have to search far to find shelter, leave a marker at your first position, like a bright cloth or a circle of stones. Also leave a note saying who you are, what condition you're in, what kind of gear you have, what date it is, and what you're doing next. So that you don't get further lost, move with a plan, following a definite landscape feature or a compass line.

After shelter, the second survival priority (under some circumstances the first) is *water*. If you have to move around to find it, follow the precautions noted above. As for food, that can wait.

After basic comforts are assured, your job is to stay put. But it is also to keep trying to draw attention to yourself. And it is also very important to think.

Nothing attracts the interest of the authorities so quickly as a smoky fire. Distress or not, be careful how and where you light it. It isn't important to send up puffs in threes: just make sure the smoke is plentiful. This is one situation in which there is an excuse for putting green wood or foliage on a fire.

As time passes, keep pondering the land and your position in it. You may well sort it out yet. But don't strike out across country until you are quite sure of what you are doing (and then leave a note). Be cautious in following such traditional advice as "Follow water downhill." It all depends on what water and what hill. Sometimes a downhill grade leads not out of wilderness but deeper into it.

So much for the lost person. What should the unlost members of a party do when they realize someone is missing? The first rule is not to throw away your greatest asset, your known and inherently reasonable position in the neighborhood. Don't split up and scatter. Wait for a while at a distinctive point like a trail junction, stream crossing, or pass. Shout or otherwise signal, continually. Wait some more. If you think your partner may be behind you, send someone down the trail to a specified point or for a specified time. If you think the wanderer may be ahead of you, do the same. Pursue possible branching trails in the same way. (If you have the numbers, each search party should have two members.) If you are the only companion, don't move from your original position without leaving a prominent marker and an explicit note. If you think your friend may have left the trail, it may be appropriate to walk a search pattern, or a series of compass courses, across the area of concern. But return to your base by dark and stay there, signaling frequently with a flashlight. A campfire makes a good beacon, too. If the absent person doesn't show up by midmorning, you have to consider the possibility of injury and send for help. For related subjects, see Chapter 26.

To repeat, however: in summer backpacking, and in our modern wilderness areas, so small and so well mapped, nothing should be easier than staying out of this kind of trouble. And in fact it is fairly rare for well-equipped backpackers, traversing the deep backcountry, to lose their way. Casual hikers, wandering away from their cars without maps, are much more at risk. If you know what you are doing, and walk with a mind aware, the land should have no unpleasant surprises for you—or for your friends.

Making & Managing the Camp

It is legitimate to hope that there may be left . . . the special kind of human mark, the special record of human passage, that distinguishes man from all other species. It is rare enough among men, impossible to any other form of life. It is simply the deliberate and chosen refusal to make any marks at all.

—Wallace Stegner, *This Is Dinosaur: Echo Park Country and Its Magic Rivers*

17

Making Camp

Low-impact travel means many things. But among them, one is paramount: the proper making, managing, and breaking of the wilderness camp.

Camp is where we backpackers spend at least half the hours of the day. It's where we move around, mill around, stand and sit around. It's where we cook. It's where we sleep. Campsites are the bits of wilderness we use most intensely, and the spots most marked by our presence. It's not surprising that our camping habits draw the interest of officialdom, in the form of study— and in the form of rules or recommended practices.

There are two very different sorts of camping spots in the wilderness. First is the established site, unmistakably marked by use. Such sites have worn paths, fire rings, bare ground, perhaps even terraced tent platforms cut from a hill. Logs and stones may have been shifted to make tables and seats. Such camps, if you find them vacant, can be both convenient and charming. And from the point of view of low impact, they have a telling advantage: they are already barren. It is pretty hard to injure them further. The price has already been paid.

The second kind of camping spot is the pristine or wild site: the piece of unmarked ground that, for a certain time, you make your own. If you camp in such a place, you take onto yourself a large responsibility. It is your job to leave that land exactly as you found it: still unscarred, still unfrayed, recognizable to no one as a place that has been used. Some sites are much more vulnerable to scarring than others, and these the low-impact camper must be at pains to avoid.

What about the ambiguous case: a site that is just beginning to show wear and tear? Squint, and it looks pristine; look closer, and you see a little zone of trampled ground around a fire ring. This type of site, which can still melt back into its unaltered surroundings, should *never* be used; fire rings in spots like this should be dismantled.

Agency rules, by and large, are aimed at getting us to camp in established sites; to use wild sites very carefully; and to use ambiguous sites not at all. There are many refinements. Sometimes very specific campsites are assigned. Sometimes larger parties and those that build fires must stay at certain sites; smaller parties with stoves may camp at large. Sometimes particular areas may be closed, not only to fires, but to any camping—all the time or at given times of year, for various good reasons (wildfire danger is one; the welfare of vulnerable species is another). Local codes of conduct are generally printed on the back of wilderness permits or brochures.

In what follows, I may speak as if these regulations did not exist, as if nothing affected your choice of site but your own good judgment. This does not mean, of course, that official advice is to be ignored; on the contrary, I hope and assume that you will follow it.

Choosing the Low-Impact Camp

Where then *should* you camp? What standards do you go by—not only for low impact on the land, but for comfort and convenience as well?

Even among established sites, all is not equal; some should be avoided. In some alpine landscapes, you find many more fire spots and devegetated tent locations than anyone needs; the same may be true along popular forest trails. Many of these excess sites, built at random by the uninformed, could not have been worse chosen if the makers had drawn up a plan for maximum disturbance to land, wildlife, and the human experience. Then there are sites so punished by use that soils are badly eroded and tree roots exposed. Choose instead a spot that is still pleasant. You are not obligated to camp in the ugliest place!

Now the criteria.

Distance from Stream, Lake, and Trail

This is the rule that the land managers tend to put first, perhaps because it is easy to grasp. We are instructed to camp a given distance away from streamsides, lakeshores, and trails, or (in some areas) from private property. Meadow margins are sometimes added to the list. Specified setbacks vary, but 100, 200, and 300 feet are common. Two hundred feet is seventy to eighty normal walking steps.

The reasoning here is no mystery. Campers do tend to cluster needlessly close to water and to trails (and especially at points where trails approach water). Loss of privacy is one result. Increased pollution is a second. The formation of large trampled areas is a third. Perhaps most important, shorelines and other border zones—what ecologists call *ecotones*—tend to be key wildlife habitats. Loons, for example, nest on lakeshores and may abandon their nests if disturbed. In arid areas, where isolated springs are vital to wild animals, you can disrupt a whole web of natural patterns by settling down near the local waterhole.

Setback rules can make life complicated. In some wilderness areas, the majority of the existing campsites violate the letter of the law, and many of these are unobjectionable in every other respect. If it came down to a choice between camping at one of these technically illegal sites and bedding down on unmarked ground nearby, I would probably bend the rule.

Nonetheless, do your best to comply. If you want an established site, choose whatever available spot best fits the model. If an effort is obviously being made to "roughen" and renaturalize an old site, avoid the spot. If, on the other hand, you are camping in the dispersed style (which requires fanatical attention to low-impact matters), go much *more* than 100 or 200 feet from the trail or lake or stream. In the lake basins of western ranges, search for sites behind low trees on the hillsides, several hundred yards back from the water. Often you will find little terraces of twiggy soil, just the right size for a small party, or at least for a bed or two.

There are good selfish reasons for getting away from, and if possible above, the water. Since cool air sinks, it's going to be warmer up there. You will also have less dew, mist, and mosquitoes.

Ground Surface

The best kind of ground to camp on is forest duff—the springy cushion of needles, leaves, and twigs, free of green vegetation, that covers many woodland floors. The second best is bare ground: sand, gravel, rock, rocky soil, or an area already worn bare by human traffic. Deep snow is fine, too. Avoid damp places and don't camp on vegetated areas when it can possibly be avoided.

Not all vegetation, however, is equally sensitive. Low-growing leafy and woody plants, such as may be found on a shady forest floor or above treeline, are extremely fragile. Grasses vary in their vulnerability; although moist meadows can get scarred rather quickly, expanses of dry grasses and sedges are actually quite slow to degrade. In certain wilderness areas, campers who are not using established sites are positively urged to camp on such "shorthair" meadows.

Students of the matter make a distinction between resistant plants and resilient ones. Resistant plants can take a fair amount of pounding before damage begins to show; resilient plants are those that grow back quickly once the disturbance ends. Species may be resistant but not resilient; resilient but not resistant; both; or neither. Dry mountain meadows are of the first type: once they do wear thin, it takes a long time for them to recover. (So if you camp on such grass, do it for one night only.) The species that make up tundra, the low-growing vegetation found at heights where it's too cold for trees, may or may not be resistant, but, given the short growing season in this alpine zone, they are never resilient. (Thus, in some areas, camping above timberline is simply forbidden.) The cryptobiotic crusts that form on desert soils (see Chapter 23) are neither resistant nor resilient. (Stay off them completely.)

You might wish to find out from a local agency office which species and plant communities in its territory it is most concerned about. Failing that, you can fall back on the one-sentence rule: don't camp on growing things at all.

Size, Flatness, and Drainage

The site you pick must have not only the right kind of surface but also a sufficient expanse of it. A large party stuffed into a small site will naturally tend to trample adjoining, perhaps less suitable, ground. It is obviously also important that the site be fairly level; besides the comfort factor, steep ground, if it is anything but solid rock, is easily disturbed and easily eroded. On the other hand, if a site is dead flat, or actually concave, it may be a place where water pools or flows. Stay out of pockets that might become ponds; stay out of dips, or swales, that might carry runoff during a rain. In the desert, during the thunderstorm season, be careful not to camp in dry streambeds (called *washes*); arid though they seem, a flash flood can turn them into rivers deeper than a tent is high.

Safety

Be aware of other possible hazards: snags or branches that might break in the wind, cliffs from which stones might fall, and, in the winter, avalanche paths. If lightning is a possibility, you won't want to settle near an isolated tree or rock outcrop.

Various animal hazards may need consideration. If there are "bedding sites" where something large has slept and crushed the vegetation, move on. Abundant bear scat and obvious game trails suggest the same. You may also want to avoid a site that other campers have left dirty and thus attractive to bears; if you must camp there, clean it up. Also avoid an area where numerous burrows suggest a rodent colony: fleas or droppings may carry disease. Abandoned cabins are unsavory for the same reason. Steer clear of a hornet's nest. In bear country, your site must include a proper outlying tree to hang your food from at night.

Water Supply

Water somewhere near camp is pleasant but not essential. Given enough container capacity, you can fill up at a convenient stream in the afternoon, and then make your evening stop with no need for a local supply. Where good sites are few or crowded, this extra degree of freedom can help you find the best.

Privacy

Consider your own privacy and that of others. Researchers find that many backpackers prefer an uncomfortable but solitary camp to an ideal spot with neighbors. Even if you don't feel that way yourself, it's courteous to assume that others will. Try to be out of view and out of earshot of the next camp. Sound carries readily across lakes and meadows, less so through trees.

Local Climate

Cool air settles at night in basins; night breezes move downslope along ravines. A hillside flat or the top of a knoll may be as much as 15 degrees warmer than lower ground. Whether you want more warmth or less, you can take advantage of these variations. Consider also the wind; you may want to escape it behind a natural windbreak or use it to blow away mosquitoes. If you are hoping for an early start, a site with an eastern exposure, bringing early sun, will help.

Suitability for Longer Stays

If you are planning to stay in one place for several nights, you'll be somewhat choosier about the site. Now you consider the overwhelming view, the nearby swimming hole, the peaks to climb, the canyons to explore. But it is also important that you find a specially impact-free site for such an extended stay; vulnerable areas, if they must be used, should not be used for a long stretch.

Setting Up the Low-Impact Camp

Although experienced backpackers can settle in quite quickly, it is far better to allow yourself several daylight hours. Blundering around with a headlamp is no fun. And an early stop gives you time for good cooking, for relaxation, perhaps for a side trip, a splash in the lake, a boulder problem, or a few minutes with a camera or a natural history guide.

If your target campsite is very specific—as when a particular spot has been assigned—you're there when you're there. But if you have a choice of sites—and anytime you are camping on unmarked ground—you will want to reconnoiter a bit, comparing alternative locations before you start unloading.

What happens first when you've made your choice? In the rain, or late in the day, raising the shelter has to be the first job. Otherwise, water treatment and cooking may take first place; or the priority may be finding the bearbag tree. The weather, the time of day, the number of people, the site, and personal preference decide. A large group may have to organize itself to get things done; in a smaller party, there's nothing so formal about it.

A campsite has to contain these elements: a water source; a kitchen; a place to protect food at night; a place to sleep; and an area for sanitary needs. Depending on circumstances, all these components except the last may be within a small radius, or they may spread out quite widely.

Your water source may simply be a water bag hanging from a tree. If you will be going frequently to a lakeshore or streambank, choose an access spot where there is a clear trail, or rock and sand; avoid vegetated and undercut banks.

Should your hanging water bag contain water that has already been filtered or otherwise treated? Or should it contain "raw" water, a substitute creek? I've seen it done both ways. If your water treatment method of choice is filtration (see Chapter 20), you can spend a long time crouching on the bank before you have a bagful—but on the other hand, the job is done for a while.

If you build a fire, your kitchen will cluster around a fire ring. Even if you don't, the rocks of a ring may make convenient shelves and tables. In any case, the kitchen area must be on bare ground where trampling does no harm (this spot will get more traffic than any other part of camp). Then there's fire safety to consider (even a stove must not sit on twiggy duff!). If there is a constructed cooking shelter, use it.

Food storage may be a tree or a rock face from which bags can be slung; in some places, there are lockers or cables.

Sleeping areas may be one or several. Each bed should be sited on bare ground, duff, or possibly short-hair meadow grass.

A small group, especially at a little-used camp, needn't specify a toilet area, so long as everyone resolves to go well away from camp, trail, and water and uses normal care (see Chapter 20). But in a large group, it is wise to select a general area in advance, choosing a zone where no one else is likely to be camping.

It's natural to have most of these camp elements in a tight cluster; but campers in western Canada, Alaska, and the Rockies of Montana, Idaho, and Wyoming have formed other habits. To minimize the nuisance, or worse, that raiding grizzly bears may cause, things get spread. Beds are well separated from kitchens and night larders, and dishwashing is done at some remove from all the other elements. Wind direction is taken into account as well, with beds upwind and dishwater disposal down. Thus a bear pursuing food odors is less likely to stumble on a sleeping human being.

The perfect site is found, not engineered. Spend your time locating the right piece of ground, not reshaping the wrong one. Don't clear brush, drive nails, build cupboards, or move logs and stones. However hard you try, it is never possible to restore such objects so perfectly that the natural effect is completely recovered.

Living in a well-marked site, you limit your traffic almost completely to ground that is already bare, already stamped by human presence; a little more traffic won't alter it further. When paths and pads are there, use them. But avoid doing anything to extend that barren area. If you are at a pristine site, most especially if there is vegetation underfoot, the strategy changes. You try to avoid repeated traffic over any one piece of ground. In moving between kitchen and spring, or tent and toilet area, take a slightly different route each time, and try to walk on duff, rocks, and mineral soils. Try not to mill around too much in one place, as at the entrance of a tent or near the stove. If you go in soft camp shoes or sandals, you will automatically be more careful how you step. If you're wearing regular boots in camp, walk softly.

One final point. If you see a tiny tree trying to get started—even in what looks like a wasteland—improvise a fence around it and take care not to crush it. In the not-so-long term, many of our forest campsites are going be sun-beaten clearings, simply because no young trees are surviving to replace the old ones that will die.

The Pleasure of Wilderness Camping

Of necessity, this chapter has contained a lot of "don'ts." Because good wilderness practices often go against obvious convenience and the tradition of "woodcraft," it may take a little conscious effort to adopt them.

But soon enough, good practice is automatic. And you are free to enjoy each campsite you find for yourself—the smells and sounds of it, the views (short or long), the quality of its light, its trees and plants and birds. Every campsite, when you come onto it, seems strange and even a little unwelcoming (why just here and not a mile farther on?). Every campsite, once you have eaten and slept there, becomes a known place and a comfortable one. Your camps, after all, are the spots in the wilderness of which you have most knowledge; it is your campsites that you particularly remember.

The low-impact game has added to the pleasure of wilderness camping a new, keen edge. To wander through a landscape, never guessing that you could damage it, or that you have done so, is one thing. It is quite something else to know that you might have harmed a place and that you did not; to know that your skill and knowledge were great enough to let you use the wilderness without consuming it.

18

Fire & Food

Let's start with a piece of advice from the nutritionists: during the first half hour after you stop hiking for the day, take a moment to eat some carbohydrates—especially if you have big plans for tomorrow. In this immediate postexercise period, the body recharges its stores of glycogen, the muscles' running fuel.

Somewhat later comes the proper evening meal, and what is possibly the trickiest moment of your day: lighting the stove or fire.

Operating a Stove

Cooking on a portable stove is, at its easiest, almost like cooking on a range at home. Yet the use of stoves, like that of open fires, has its headaches, and even its hazards.

Stoves vary; no single procedure applies to them all. (For the kinds and their basic anatomies, see Chapter 9.) Consult your manufacturer's directions. But the following steps seem to cover most cases.

Stove Stage One: Preparation

First, pick your site: a level, wind-sheltered spot out of the line of traffic (so that nothing gets knocked over). The stove should be some distance from any other flame, from the rest of your gear, and from burnable underbrush. With luck, there may be a natural bench to sit on while you work and a nearby flat-topped rock for a counter. Few rocks are flat enough for the stove itself, though; it typically sits on the ground. If you are camping on snow, you'll need to place the stove on a scrap of wood or perhaps foam padding to prevent a fuel tank from getting chilled, or a warm burner from melting itself a pit, or both.

Second, check the fuel supply. With a bottled-gas stove, this may mean replacing a depleted cartridge with a full one; it may also mean prewarming a cold cartridge for better operation. Before use, you could carry the fuel next to your body; wrap it in insulation; take it into your sleeping bag; let it sit in the sun. Don't shake a cartridge, however. While the stove is running, you can warm the cartridge with your hands. You can also carry two cartridges and switch them each time the active one cools.

Follow directions carefully in removing and attaching cartridges. Some must be held carefully upright. Some can be removed between uses; others, once attached, must be left until they are empty. Some stoves use cartridges that screw on; others plug in. With screw-on cartridges, be careful not to strip threads. Especially with the screw types, a little fuel may spray out at the moment of connection: not a problem unless it persists (see below).

Older white-gas stoves with small built-in tanks should be filled each time you use them. An air space should remain under the cap (see your model's instructions). In moving the gas from storage bottle to tank, use a pouring cap or, better, a funnel with a filter. If you spill fuel, wipe it up and let the residue evaporate (it will do so quickly). If a spill has soaked into the ground beneath the stove, better shift the operation elsewhere.

If your stove is the common type with a pump that plugs into a larger fuel bottle, "refueling" may not arise; but on a long jaunt you will have to switch bottles or top up the current one from a reserve. Again, don't overdo it: with the bottle upright, an inch or so of air space should show at the top. Some bottles are marked with a fill line.

With two-piece stoves, you must next put the stove together by screwing the pump assembly into the fuel bottle and plugging the fuel supply tube from the burner into the pump assembly. Lubricate the end of the inserting tube with saliva or lip salve. Do not over-tighten any connection.

After refueling and assembly, close every cap and valve (firmly, not excessively) and check for leaks. A butane/propane cartridge that is losing gas will feel cold; there may be an audible hiss. Check that the burner is connected properly; if the problem persists, try another cartridge. Manufacturing defects are not unknown. If the stove is a liquid-fueled type with a pump, use that item to raise pressure in the tank (instructions will specify how many strokes). Then hold the whole stove upside down; check carefully for drips or wet spots. If there's a leak you can't troubleshoot, don't light the stove.

On a few old-fashioned pumpless stoves, the cap of the tank has a safety release valve; make sure this is pointed away from flammable objects. If you are using one of the older Optimus stoves that has a separate tank mounted behind a heat shield, confirm that the shield is clean and shiny and that it has not been knocked out of alignment.

Make sure that the burner plate (if there is one) is firmly attached (you'll see metal tabs that can be crimped to hold the plate more tightly to the burner head) and that pot support wires are firm.

With liquid-fueled stoves, this is a good point in the routine to clean the orifice where the jet of fuel issues. Older stoves may have separate cleaning needles that you insert by hand; on others you operate a built-in nee-dle by turning the fuel-flow valve control; on still others, you activate a built-in needle by gently shaking the burner unit. If a separate needle is used, be careful to come at the jet directly from above: a simple poke, not a reaming action, which can widen the opening and cause malfunction. If you're burning white gas, clean the jet every few days; if your fuel is kerosene, do so daily.

Stove Stage Two: Priming

Cartridge-stove users can skip this part, and so can owners of some liquid-fueled stoves. When a typical liquid-fueled stove is running, its own heat vaporizes the liquid fuel as it rises from the tank—a self-sustaining process. But in order to get the stove started, you have to apply heat to the vaporizing tube beneath the burner. You simply burn something—anything—in a little priming cup that is built in around the base of the vaporizing tube.

What fuel do you use? How do you get it into the priming cup?

It's traditional to make the stove cough up some of its own fuel for priming. On pump models, nothing could be simpler: just open the fuel-flow valve after pressurizing the tank, and the liquid will appear. With older, pumpless stoves you have a choice of methods. After opening the fuel-flow valve, you can warm the tank with your hands and your breath until the expanding fuel rises into the priming cup. Or you can leave the stove in the hot sun till the fuel expands; then open the valve and let it flow. There are other variations. Before pumps came along, priming was a whole conversation.

It's not so traditional, but often convenient, to put the priming fuel into the cup yourself. In that case, you use any burnable substance you like: white gas, drawn from the stove tank (or a fuel bottle) with an eyedropper; alcohol from a squeeze bottle; bits of woody or fibrous fire starter; or even toilet paper. The nongasoline alternatives have the advantage of producing less soot. If your cooking fuel is something other than white gas, you should definitely use a separate primer.

How much priming fire do you need? Under good conditions, a single eyedropperful of white gas, or the equivalent, may do it. But any amount is okay as long as the liquid fuel doesn't overflow the cup. Some bizarre accidents have occurred when people drenched their stoves with several cups of fuel. They were surprised at the resulting bonfires!

Before you put a match to the priming fuel, make sure that the fuel-flow valve is shut off, that the tank cap is screwed on firmly, and that all containers of liquid fuel are capped and set well away from the stove.

Then light. If you have primed generously with white gas, the flame may rise quite high before it fades; this is normal. By the time your priming dose has been consumed, the vaporizing tube should be hot enough to do its job, and (in pumpless stoves) the fuel tank should be warm enough so that vapor pressure within will keep fuel flowing upward toward the flame.

Stove Stage Three: Lighting

To light a butane/propane stove, hold a match to the burner; then and only then open the valve to let the gas stream out. Under good conditions, you'll have a strong blue flame from the start. If not, you may have a temperature problem. You may need to increase wind protection, or perhaps to warm the cartridge further.

Lighting a standard liquid-fueled stove is a matter of timing. Just as the priming flame fades, open the valve to admit fuel from the tank; it should catch. If you miss the moment, reduce the flow briefly while you apply a match. With luck you'll get a blue, clear crown of fire. If instead the flame flickers and wavers yellowly, you'll have to prime again. This is common, especially in the cold.

Certain white-gas stoves supposedly fire up without any discernible priming phase. Check directions. Under not-so-good conditions, however, you may get a weak flame or none at all. If this happens, the solution is not to pump up the stove further but to prime manually with a dab of paper or other solid fuel placed in the burner under the vaporizing tube. Then relight.

Stove Stage Four: Cooking

Once a stove is burning with a fine blue flame, arrange its windscreen for maximum protection and put on your first pot of water. If your white-gas stove is the older style

To handle hot pots, you need a metal pot lifter, light gloves, or a bandanna.

that has a metal valve key for flame adjustment, remove this between adjustments; otherwise, it gets too hot.

With pump stoves you'll need to maintain tank pressure by pushing the plunger a few times every 4 minutes or so. Also keep an eye on the temperature of a built-in fuel tank. If you find it getting too hot to touch, better shut down the stove and see what you can do to increase ventilation. Be alert to this problem if you have an improvised windscreen that encloses the tank or a broad pot or frying pan that overhangs it. With bottled-gas stoves, a cartridge should always remain cool enough to hold in your hand. Some stoves link burner and cartridge with a flexible hose; watch that neither hose nor cartridge rests too close to the flame.

Some white-gas stoves simmer well, and some, especially those with flat burner plates rather than ported burners, do not. Even these can be turned down somewhat after 5 minutes of full-bore operation. A half-empty fuel tank will dispense more evenly than a full one. You can also keep tank pressure on the low side, simply by pumping less than usual. Maybe the best solution is to place a metal plate between the flame and the pot, diffusing the heat, or to use a double boiler.

To conserve fuel, make sure you have something heating at all times; make sure the windscreen is effective; and keep lids on as much as possible. Often it's practical to stack your cooking, with a second pot of something warming on top of the first.

Even the smallest cartridge or tank of fuel will last through one meal, maybe two, except in a winter camp where quantities of snow must be melted.

Stove Stage Five: Shutting Down

When you shut down a standard liquid-fueled stove, a small flame will linger for a moment at the jet. Instead of letting this die, blow it out. The tiny puff of unburned fuel still in the pipeline will tend to clean the aperture.

If the stove is to be used again at the same site, you can leave it set up. If not, let it cool, wipe off any food spills, and pack it away. Loosen caps to let pressure out of tanks, then tighten them again. Close fuel-flow valves. Some cartridge-stove users report that partially used cartridges can leak in the pack; they suggest putting tape across orifices. Of course you'll pack your empties out of the wilderness with you. Bone-dry cartridges can be recycled with aluminum cans. Drive a nail through the opening to demonstrate that there is no gas inside.

Cooking in a Tent?

Cooking inside a tent is one of those things you're sternly advised against but may someday find yourself sorely tempted to do. If you think you may be tempted often, get a stove that can burn kerosene—or consider an alcohol unit.

Much safer than cooking deep within the tent is cooking just outside it, through the open door, under the sheltering roof of a vestibule. You can still work from a lying-down position, with most of you snug in your sleeping bag. Make certain the burner isn't too close to a roof or wall. Especially if you prime with liquid fuel, beware of a high-flaring priming flame; have a pan lid ready to interpose between the flame and the nearest nylon. If fuel spills on nylon, wipe it up, let it evaporate, and air the tent before you strike your next match. All fuels are bad for the waterproofing compounds on tent floors, as well as for clothing.

Stoves put out carbon monoxide, a poison that replaces oxygen in the bloodstream. If cooking inside, make sure there's *lots* of ventilation. Be especially on your guard at high altitudes, where there's less oxygen to begin with.

Fire

Campfires these days are not popular with wilderness managers. The impact of fires on the land—so many people have come to feel—is simply unacceptable: not because any single fire does much harm, but because so many campers are lighting so many. One fire ring may be welcoming, but twenty are obtrusive, and two hundred in a single camping area constitute a plague. The trampling caused by wood foraging in popular areas is itself significant, and if the wrong sorts of fuels are selected, real ecosystem damage is done.

But in this, as in so many impact questions, there's no substitute for common sense. A fire in an old ring of stones in a middle-elevation forest littered with down wood can't possibly be called an attack on the land. A similar fire built (illegally) of green wood on a peak in the crowded Catskills, or built (illegally) against a granite boulder in an unscarred alpine meadow, is an atrocity.

What makes a fire acceptable?

An abundance of appropriate wood.

An existing fire site in a good location.

And very great care.

If the cooking fire is in disfavor, still more, in some circles, is the pleasure fire: the comfortable blaze you sit around after the meal is done. Yet if fire has a legitimate use in the wilderness, it is not, in truth, for fixing food (stove cooking is simpler) but for fun. For fun and for something a little more than fun: for relaxation . . . for sociability . . . for the odd beauty of flames . . . as a special focus (*focus:* Latin *hearth*) of a place and time you enjoy. It may well be argued that the occasional small pleasure fire, lit as a deliberate luxury, makes more sense than a succession of cooking fires lit for a dubious utility.

Siting a Fire

The fact that you find a fire ring does not necessarily mean that you should use it. Lake basins in western ranges may contain several hundred rings, many of them badly sited.

Why so many fire sites? Partly, no doubt, because many people still put value on the *creation* of a camp, the carving out of a home in the wild world. But there's another reason. Established rings are often left dirty, unpleasant, full of cans, tinfoil, and organic garbage half rotted and half charred. You'll be doing a service if you choose one of these ruined rings, clean it up, use it, and leave it clean. This, in fact, is an argument for building a fire that you might otherwise forgo.

The ring you choose should be on bare ground well back from water. Make sure that there is nothing flammable within an 8-foot radius: no low branches overhead, no dry grass or brush close by, no duff through which worms of fire could burrow. Keep your other gear well away. Sparks make holes in synthetic fabrics.

If you have a choice of rings in otherwise acceptable places, you can afford to consider such things as sun (nice for cooking in the morning, sometimes too hot for cooking in the afternoon) and the direction of the wind (typically upslope during the day, downslope after dark).

If the ring you've chosen is choked with old ashes, remove them and scatter them widely, well away from camp, at several different locations. If the ring is huge, move its stones together until you have a hat-sized central chamber.

Now, fuel. If you have settled on a well-used site, the chances are good that the woods within, say, 300 feet will be pretty well picked over. Yet it is astonishing how much suitable wood you will find just outside that narrow circle. Scavengers have been lazy. In your own gathering, take a few pieces at a time from a considerable area. If you know you'll have a fire in the evening, it's smart to pick up a few pieces of wood along the trail late in the day.

Every stick of wood that you gather must pass three tests. Each piece must be *dead*; it must be *down* (not attached to a tree); and it must be relatively *small*. Avoid chunks that are green or rotten. Larger logs on the ground have special value in the ecosystem, and rooted snags are not firewood: they are habitat and hunting territory for owls, woodpeckers, and a whole community of critters small and large. Wood should be breakable by hand.

Operating a Fire

Gather a reasonable supply of wood, in various sizes, before you begin. Then take a final look at the weather and the site. (Has the day turned windy? Could sparks get into dry underbrush?) The risk of starting a brush or forest fire is not one you want to take. Always have water and a trowel at hand.

If yours will be a cooking fire, you may want to rearrange the stones and place a grate or perhaps a "dingle stick" (a sort of jib, braced at one end by stones, resting on a fireside rock or log) over the fire. From this you can hang your largest pot. (If you do much campfire cooking you may find it convenient to rig pots with bales of thin wire attached at *three* points around the rim, so that they do not tip when hung.) Any stick you use must be picked up off the ground, not cut or broken off a tree.

Starting a fire is both straightforward and slightly tricky; skills that were automatic to generations of firemakers may be less familiar in the age of stoves. Every fire starts tiny, with thin and very flammable materials; builds up to slightly larger kindling; and finally generates enough heat to burn whatever you offer it. Your starting point can be paper or knife-whittled, paper-thin shavings; fuzz sticks, sometimes useful, are shaved sticks with the shavings still attached. Some firemakers always lay the whole fire, small to large, before they touch a match to it; others start with the tiniest sticks, get them burning, and then add larger bits and pieces gradually and carefully. If you lay the fire in advance, leave lots of openings for air. Don't put on fragments of wood larger than you can reasonably expect to burn completely to ash or to very small coals.

What if it's raining? Here's where your fire starters come in. Fetch out your dry tinder or candle. Wax dripped on anything flammable makes a good starter. So does a fragment of porous wood, soaked for a few minutes in a pool of white gas. What does not work, though many people try it, is to pour white gas over a stack of wet kindling: the fuel just flares off, leaving the stubborn wood untouched. In a real emergency, you might sacrifice a nylon stuff sack—they do fine.

Traditionalists look for help in pitchy wood, which you can find as unrotted streaks in the decayed trunks of fallen conifers. This stuff burns delightfully. So, in a pinch, do the waxy needles of many trees. If it hasn't been raining long, you may be able to whittle away the damp exterior of a wood fragment and find dry wood at the center.

Once a fire is burning brightly, of course, it will dry and burn even the most sodden logs. But when all wood is truly waterlogged, as in rain-forest country, only the experts seem to get that far.

In more typical dry conditions, fire is a beast that has to be watched with the greatest care. Never leave untended one that is burning or even smoldering (though a low fire may be left to consume its embers on a windless night with sleepers close by). Whenever you leave camp, of course, the fire must be absolutely and unmistakably cold.

Fire at an Unmarked Site

There is rarely either reason or excuse these days for building a fire where none has been before. This is true without exception throughout the crowded wilderness lands of the East and in well-used areas of the Far West. In remote and little-visited sections, though, this principle may be slightly bent.

The ideal vanishing fire site is a sandy or gravelly spot where any mark that is made can simply be erased. Sea beaches and river shingles, washed periodically by tide or flood, are best of all. Given any kind of loose mineral surface, you can dig a small trench for the fire; when done, you can scatter ashes and smooth over the site with clean material.

Another option, for people who *must* have fires, is to carry a metal fire pan. River-rafting supply stores have them; you can also use a garbage can lid or an oil pan. Perch the pan on stones so that heat doesn't sterilize the ground. The result is pretty blameless, though the weight of the barrier is daunting.

For my part, I keep it simple. I don't build a fire except in a well-sited existing ring.

Food Handling and Cleanup

Food handling and dishwashing in camp must balance two concerns. The first is to prevent any transmission of disease from person to person. The second is to put as little soap as possible into the environment, and none at all into natural waters. Soap must of course be nondetergent, biodegradable, and phosphate-free. Washing is not done in, or even near, any creek, lake, or spring.

Hands that cook, or even pass food to other hands, must be as clean as possible. Wash them well with soap before dinner. Wash them with antibacterial gel after taking care of sanitary needs (see Chapter 20).

While you are cooking and eating, try to avoid wiping your hands on your clothing (use a bandanna instead). For one thing, the less your clothes smell of food, the less attractive they will be to small animals—or large. See Chapter 29 for more about these concerns.

Dirty dishes come in two divisions: pot or pots, and personal eating tools. You may be able to wash cooking vessels soapless. Fallen cones, fallen tufts of conifer foliage, and snow can supplement your scouring pad. (Sand and fire ash work too, but not on non-stick coatings.) Another trick is to finish your meal with a clear soup, which will pick up bits of food from the main course and leave surfaces almost clean. Conclude with a boiling-water rinse. As for cups and cutlery, each person in a small group might wash these separately, with minimal soap. Whenever a number of people's dishes are washed together, however, plenty of soap is required, or a boiling-water rinse, or both. In this case the largest pot can serve as dishpan, and will get cleaned up in the process. Let everything air-dry.

What about dirty wash water? Before disposal, it should be poured through a small strainer or a bandanna, and the solids added to your garbage. Then water should be scattered widely, away from your camp and other potential campsites, on porous ground among brush or stones, without dosing the same spot repeatedly. In grizzly bear territory, it's advised instead to pour wash water into a small pit dug in organic soil and filled in after the last use.

You would never think of dumping wastewater into a stream, but the authorities note a couple of situations in which it makes sense. If you find yourself on the bank of a large southwestern river, rolling cloudily along through a desert environment, go ahead and dump your (strained) wastewater right into the waves. It turns out that the river is better able to absorb it than is the adjacent, parched terrain. Again, if you're on the banks of a sizable stream in grizzly country, safety argues for in-the-water disposal; pots and utensils should be rinsed in the current as well.

As for solid garbage, all the old rules have given way to a simple, single principle: *pack it out*. The only exception, and then only if you build a fire, is material

The bare minimum wilderness place setting: bandanna, food cup, drink cup, spoon.

that can be readily, totally burned: paper and also plastic bags, which combust cleanly if they are fed, a little at a time, into a very hot flame. Aluminum foil won't burn: it only breaks up in fire. Watch out for packages that have a foil lining inside paper. Cans, if you have any, should be flattened, then washed or seared, and carried out.

What if you find yourself with half a pot of uneaten stew? See first if you can't finish it off; an excess of dinner may make a very good breakfast or lunch. Failing that, you simply have to take it with you as garbage. Neither burial nor burning is practical, and scattering, depending on the local wildlife, is somewhere between dubious and dangerous. You're training raccoons, bears, and other animals to scavenge and make camp nuisances of themselves.

What about fish viscera? In remote areas, away from trails, campsites, and the water's edge, they may be scattered on the ground. In high-use areas, or within day-trip range of the roadhead, they should be packed out. But if you are lake-fishing in grizzly bear country, the authorities recommend that guts be tossed into the water.

Protecting Your Food

Depending on where you are, you will have to take more or less elaborate precautions to protect your food from animal raiders. Procedures differ somewhat in regions without bears; with black bears only; and with both black bears and the more dangerous grizzly, or brown, bears.

Shelters and developed campsites especially attract animals. If you camp at a spot that has food lockers, metal hanging posts, overhead cables, or other built-in protective devices, by all means take the hint.

Many animals are inclined to piracy. In bearless country, you can protect open packages by putting them under pots or in pots with the lids wired on. Remove all food and crumbs from packs, and leave all zips and flaps open; otherwise, critters may gnaw right through packcloth to get at interesting smells.

In regions where bears are common, all food must be hung at night, or placed in bear-proof containers. Nothing short of that makes any sense.

To hang your food, you need two large stout stuff sacks, not less than 50 feet of strong cord, and the right kind of tree. Finding the last item may take a while. You need a tree with a living, spindly branch about 20 feet up—thick enough to support the weight of your food, but too thin to support the weight of a scrambling bear. Once you locate your branch, take a good length of cord, tie a rock to one end, and lob it over the limb at a point at least 10 feet out from the trunk. Place half your food in each of the two stuff sacks. Tie the first one to the line end where the stone was and haul until the bag is up close to the branch.

Next, attach the second stuff sack to the available line, not at the end but as high up as you can reach. Wrap the remaining free line around the load so that nothing dangles.

Finally, use your trekking pole or a stick to nudge this "counterbalance" weight as high as you can. The two bags should finally be hanging side by side.

To get your food back, you must reverse the

In counterbalance bearbagging, the load should be suspended some 12 feet above ground, 5 feet below the branch, and 10 feet out from the trunk.

process, pushing the first bag up toward the branch so that the second descends within reach. A loop tied in the line near the counterbalance is helpful at this point—you can snag this with your stick to pull the load down. (A hook or small carabiner taped to the end of the pole can aid the snagging.) It is also possible to wrap the extra cord in such a way that you can dislodge it with a poke. Another solution is to leave a dangling recovery cord of fishing line, too thin and slick for a bear to get a grip on.

Along with food, a number of other items in your kit should go in the bearbag. Include scrubber pads, any wooden utensils, and canteens that contain, or have contained, flavored drinks. Include also shampoos, soaps, insect repellents, sunscreens, toothpaste, and other scented personal products. Near the end of a trip, when your food is depleted, you may need to substitute a rock in one of the two bags.

Rainproofing your bearbag can be a problem; when a stuff sack is hung from its drawcord, water will get in at the top. The simplest solution is to wrap the contents in a large plastic bag and insert this, opening down, in the cloth sack that is actually suspended. Waterproof bearbags can also be purchased in stores.

Bears aren't rock climbers. In treeless areas, you may be able to hang food bags partway down a cliff.

An alternative to bearbagging is increasingly recommended, even required. This is the bearproof plastic canister discussed at the end of Chapter 9. In grizzly country, however, the authorities recommend that even canisters be suspended if possible.

What do you do if you actually see a bear investigating your suspended cache, or, worse, heading down the trail with your food bag in his jaws? If you're in Canada, Alaska, or the northern Rockies, and think the animal may be a grizzly, swear at yourself for carelessness and don't argue. But if it's a black bear—now the only possibility in most of the United States and eastern Canada—you can safely fight back by shouting, flashing lights, banging pans, blowing whistles, and such. It's okay to advance on the bear (but not too close and not in such a way that the animal is cornered). It's even okay to throw small rocks, not aiming at the face. Black bears are seldom combative and are likely to retreat or even drop what they have taken. Don't start picking up scattered food, however, until the animal is out of the picture. For more on bear concerns, see Chapter 29.

Keeping your food out of the jaws of wildlife is more than a selfish concern. Careless food handling causes animals to regard camps, packs, and even automobiles as sources of food; a bear that has gotten this message will probably end up being destroyed. ("A fed bear is a dead bear," the slogan goes.) The penalty for smaller mammals isn't so drastic, but our involuntary gifts of food can lead to local population increases that natural forage can't support.

19

Shelter & Bed

Do you really need to pitch a tent or other shelter? Weather and mosquitoes permitting, there's nothing like sleeping outside—really outside, with no cloth canopy between you and the big, brilliant dark. It's also far easier to choose a bedsite if you have no tent to consider. If the weather is uncertain, you have the further option of setting up shelter but starting the night in a bed outside.

There is, unfortunately, one excellent safety reason for preferring a tent: bears. Grizzly bears and even occasionally black bears have been known to investigate open-air sleepers; since the animals' investigating tools are teeth and claws, this can hurt. Bear experts recommend flatly that we sleep in tents, always. I refuse to take their advice in black bear country, the risk seeming too slight to matter; but in grizzly territory, I tent.

Site Selection

Sleeping sites get picked early in the process of making camp. The choice may be casual and obvious, or it may require some thought. The requirements are the same commonsensical ones that apply to the camp as a whole.

You obviously need a piece of flat or nearly flat ground: a narrow piece for one person sleeping out, a broader one for a tent and its occupants. You can settle for less than perfection: a gentle slope from head to toe won't hurt, but you don't want a roll-inducing sideways tilt. Lie down on the spot to test it for comfort.

A soft or malleable surface is nice. The most comfortable upholstery is fine forest duff; sand and gravel are also good, if smoothed and shaped in advance. Grassy ground is hard. All vegetation, indeed, is best avoided.

Good drainage is vital. Watch out for hollows and subtle drainage paths that might gather water in a sudden rain.

Take account of wind direction. Sleeping out, or in a flimsy shelter, you may want to look for natural windbreaks. With a good tent, this becomes less important. But if there is a chance of a considerable breeze, make sure you have room to pitch the tent parallel to the direction of the wind, rather than crosswise.

Consider what you'll use for anchors. With a tarp, the ideal is a pair of straight trees about 15 feet apart. For a regular tent you want ground firm enough to hold any stakes you use but soft enough to drive them into. Look also for rocks, trunks, and sturdy snags to which you might tie guylines. A boulder or big log may serve as one wall for a tarp shelter.

If cold is an issue, remember that high ground is warmer. Cold air flows downhill and gathers in moist and chilly pools. A site under trees will be warmer than one open to the sky, and will have less dew.

If your tent will be standing for several days in the same spot, look for a shady place, or plan to pitch an extra tarp or groundsheet above it, for comfort and to prevent premature deterioration of sunbeaten nylon.

Only after the basic requirements are met should you consider such luxuries as morning sun (a great help in prodding you out of bed) and the view.

Pitching Shelter

Once you've chosen a site, smooth and police the ground, removing sticks and loose stones. Unless you are working with something loose like leaf mold, snow,

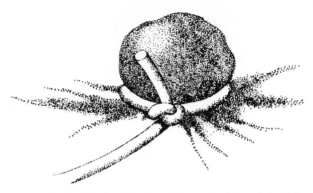

Need a tie-on point in the middle of a tarp? A smooth pebble and a knotted cord, or an equivalent commercial device, can be used to create one.

or sand, don't level or engineer. Drainage ditches are no longer dug; you don't need them, and they make lasting scars.

If you aren't pitching a shelter, you can proceed to making your bed. Spread your groundsheet—dirty side down—and mattress or pad. If the air is not too humid, unpack your sleeping bag and bivouac sack (if you use one) and lay them out. (You may want to let the bag fluff up for a while before inserting it in the outer cover.) If you've found a spot with a natural hollow for your hip, or if you can scoop one in sand or duff, that's fine. The digging of hipholes in hard ground is no longer recommended, and, with air mattresses, hardly needed.

Pitching a tarp is both simpler and more tricky than setting up a real tent: there are so many possible variations. You can arrange the tarp in an A shape, with a long ridgeline and sloping sides; like a lean-to, with one side high and one close to the ground; or even like a pagoda, with the center raised. Your choice depends most of all on the natural anchor points you find. Most tarps come with stout grommets built in at several points along the sides. Some have tie-on cords as well. If you need an attachment where none is provided—like the middle of the sheet—you can make one by wrapping a small, smooth pebble in the fabric and tying it off with a noose of cord. There are commercial devices that mimic this arrangement. A trekking pole can be a useful prop. If your tarp is a light one, you'd do well not to put too much stress on any one part. For instance, run a line under the entire ridgeline rather than attaching a short line at each end and letting the sheet pull taut between them.

Nine people out of ten, probably, will be pitching genuine tents. Before you start unpacking, make sure that the site is large enough and otherwise suitable. Decide where the main door is going to be; if there is any slope, you usually want the entrance uphill.

Now spread a ground cloth or a fitted tent-protection groundsheet. Make sure that the sheet does not protrude beyond the edge of the tent when you're done, possibly funneling rain beneath the floor.

Most tents these days are freestanding. Once you have slid various poles into various sleeves, or clipped various clips around the poles, or both, you have a stable structure you can lift and move around. (It can also blow away, so watch out if the wind is high.) A few light and popular tents, however, won't stand up until the corners have been staked and at least one guyline secured, providing tension.

In assembling shock-corded poles, unfold and join the segments gently. Resist the urge to "shake them out," whiplike: it works, but weakens the elastic and can damage metal. When you slide poles into or out of sleeves, be careful not to pinch fabric between segments. Always push from the base, rather than pulling from the forward end. At each end of its arc, a pole will seat in a brass grommet, usually marking a tent corner. Grommets are typically set in rows of two or three, permitting different degrees of tension; if your tent is new, don't choose the tautest placement now but save it for later years, when fabrics will have stretched a bit.

Next, position the tent as you want it. Before starting to drive stakes, lie down inside to see if a further shift is needed to keep you off roots, rocks, and such. Then stake the corners firmly. Given an assortment of stakes, choose the thinnest style that will hold in the

The tautline hitch is the best of several arrangements that allow a slackening tent line to be tightened without shifting a stake.

local soil. Where the ground is very hard, you may be able to improvise alternative anchors, like short lengths of cord tied to sizable stones.

A rainfly, if there is one, stretches over the structure last. It may have grommets in the corners that get impaled by the tent-pole tips, or "ferrules." Or it may attach to the lower edge of the tent body with clips, straps, or elastic cords. If you're pitching a tent in the rain, you can try keeping the fly draped over the inner tent, and even yourself, as you work.

The final action is to extend stabilizing guylines. As noted, some tents won't stand up until at least one of these is set. Even where they are not structurally necessary, guylines draw walls out tautly, help the tent shed wind, and may give you a little more room inside.

In low-impact terms, you might think it better to attach guylines to natural anchors rather than to stakes, reducing ground disturbance. That depends, however. In Rocky Mountain National Park at one point, so many cords were being tied around trunks that timberline trees were dying because of girdling. If you do run lines around young trees, provide padding against the bark.

Guylines tend to grow slack after they have been set. You can set them up to be adjusted without moving the anchors. To do this, pass the line through the loop or grommet where it joins the tent; then double it back and tie it to itself, using any of several knots that will grip under tension but slide when you loosen the strands. The most common is the *tautline hitch*. Some tents are pre-rigged in this manner; commercial gripping devices are sold to do this same job.

Housekeeping and Bedtime Precautions

Should you unpack your sleeping bag immediately, or leave it in the stuff sack? If the air is not humid, it's good to let the bag expand as long as possible. Down, particularly, takes quite a while to regain its maximum loft. But on a cool, damp evening, the bag may start getting clammy as soon as you expose it to the air; in this case, you're better off leaving it stuffed until you can get inside it. When you unpack a down bag, shake it out gently to fluff the fill.

Avoid bringing dirt, debris, and wet clothing into your tent. (This is less a concern beneath a tarp.) Muddy boots come off just outside. Dirt that does get tracked in can be left to dry and shaken out the next time the tent is struck. Snow, though, must be removed before it melts.

Whether you're sleeping outdoors or in, you don't want to be too interesting to the local wildlife. This means, above all, *not* taking food to bed with you: your evening snack has to happen before the bearbag ascends, not after.

Before you turn in, police the campsite. Loose objects, especially bright ones, are likely to be carried off by pack rats (in many regions). Various animals are also drawn to salty things. If there are porcupines around, packs, with their sweat-salty straps, should be indoors or hung out of easy reach; drying socks should hang well off the ground.

In a tent, your clothing and paraphernalia come in with you, with small items stashed in the handy netting pockets; boots can be left in the vestibule. If you're sleeping outdoors in the dew, stick small belongings in a "possibles bag." Turn boots sideways or put them in a bag as well. On a cold night, you can take removable insoles into bed with you for a warm start in the morning.

Balmy nights with mosquitoes can be troublesome for the tentless sleeper. For this situation you need a headnet, with a brimmed hat worn underneath to lift it away from your face, or a separate piece of netting to hide under. Repellent can prevent most of the bites, but it won't spare you the sense of being under siege. In desperation, lacking a net, you can breathe through a piece of clothing.

In the morning, shake out boots and clothes before dragging them blindly on; just occasionally you'll find some small crawling thing has found its way inside.

A Good Night's Sleep

Nothing should be more automatic than a restful night in the wilderness. The harder you have worked during the day, the more luxurious the warmth and softness of the sleeping bag become; the colder it is in the world outside, the lovelier the contrast feels.

Most people like to wear some clothing to bed. In a down bag, you should. Body oils gum up fluffy down; the cure, washing the bag, destroys some of the all-important resiliency of the plumules. Wear a stocking cap, or put a shirt under your head, to protect the bag from oils in your hair. Bags filled with polyester insulations, by contrast, aren't damaged either by dirt or by washing.

If you've planned well, you shouldn't find yourself in a sleeping bag too cool for the region you're visiting. But maybe you're testing the limits of a summer bag in winter, spring, or fall. If you do find yourself getting chilly at night, there are a number of things, some mentioned already, that you can do about it.

- *Speed up your metabolism.* Take a brisk walk or get some other exercise before you crawl in (some people do isometrics in the bag). If you feel warm when you lie down, your body will heat the bag quickly and give you a good start. When you're cold or likely to be, it's good to eat something last thing before bearbagging your food, preferably protein (the best fuel for warmth when you aren't exercising).

- *If tentless, move under cover.* Lying in the open, you radiate extra heat to the sky. Even the branches of a tree will cut that loss somewhat. And protect yourself from any chilling breeze; for instance, you can put your head downwind so that the cold draft won't enter the open end of your bag.

- *Put on more clothes.* The single most useful item is a knit cap; the head loses more heat than any other part of the body. Dry socks are also important. Then come pants, shirt, sweater, mittens, possibly a jacket—even, if required, your waterproof breathable rain gear—until your whole wardrobe is on. Or, instead of wearing it all, you can stuff some items into your sleeping bag, especially at your feet, to stop air motion and hold warmth in.

- *Build up the insulation beneath you.* A wind parka, a rope, an emptied pack—almost anything will help. Make sure there's something under your feet as well.

- *Bag hands and feet.* If you get seriously cold, you can try sticking your extremities in waterproof bags: moisture won't escape, but neither will the considerable warmth that is carried off with it.

Keeping dry is an important part of keeping warm. Sleeping gear always gets damp at night. Although synthetic bags will keep on warming you to some degree even when wet, down bags will not, so you have to fight any buildup of moisture. If the weather allows, you can dry a bag by hanging it on a branch, a ski, or over your pack as you walk. It will also dry well in a sunny tent on a layover day. Don't attempt to dry damp clothing by taking it into the sleeping bag with you.

If you should ever feel that you are dangerously chilled, make a fuss about it. If you act early, there is an easy corrective: strip and get into a warm sleeping bag with a companion. Hot drinks also help; alcohol, when you're cold, only does harm. If you recognize in yourself or in a companion the symptoms of what is called *hypothermia*, it's an emergency (see Chapter 28).

20

Sanitation & Clean Water

Time was when nobody dreamed of a wilderness being anything other than *clean*, clean beyond the measure of any city or town. One writer observed happily that wilderness dirt was "perfectly sanitary, being rendered so by oxygen and remoteness from human habitation." Then there was the notion that running water purified itself every 200 feet.

But gradually we began to hear a different, disquieting story. Backpackers were reaching home only to suffer punishing bouts of diarrhea, caused by any of several unpleasant organisms found in human and animal feces: notably the protozoa *Giardia lamblia* and *Cryptosporidium parvum* and the bacterium *Campylobacter jejeuni*. These organisms can be transmitted in water, and it was the water that was blamed. Those sparkling lakes and streams were declared polluted. From the 1970s onward, we were advised to boil, filter, or chemically treat every drop of wilderness water we drank.

Several things are fuzzy about this picture, though. It isn't clear whether we have seen a true explosion in infections, or rather a surge in reporting and publicity. Nor is the source of the problem clear. Are we really catching these ailments from untreated water? Or are we rather catching them from each other, in camp, because of poor sanitation, as quite a bit of evidence suggests?

Backpackers don't have to resolve the debate about what is going on. What we do have to do is defend ourselves, in two ways. First, and absolutely vital: each of us must be scrupulous in disposing of body waste, keeping all traces of it both far away from natural water and out of our food supply. Second, each of us has to know how to purify water taken from the land, and make an informed, case-by-case decision about whether and how to do so.

Sanitation

You need only spend a few days in a popular hiking area to know that some people still are careless in their toilet habits. Feces left on the surface of the ground, especially anywhere near water, can contaminate a large area. Some infectious organisms live in animal droppings as well, but many—including dangerous ones like hepatitis—travel only human-to-human.

So waste must be isolated, which means buried. What you do, when the need comes on you, is to dig a small, single-use hole, a "cathole," in a spot well away from trail, camp, and waterside. "Well away" is 200 feet at the very least. If your bodily schedule permits, it's good to take care of this chore during the day, when the party is between campsites; this prevents an overload in popular areas.

Around some camps, late in the season, you may find so many catholes that it's hard to locate fresh ground. This is a sign of too much use, but also indicates a certain laziness: walk a bit farther and you won't have this trouble. (Maybe you can collect some wood at the same time.)

Pick your site carefully. You want a deep-soiled spot that is neither too dry nor prone to waterlogging; the shady side of a log is good (all the better if the log provides a seat). With trowel, boot, or stick, excavate your pit, not deeper than 8 inches, but deep enough so that you can cover your deposit with a couple of inches of soil. If the soil surface is sodlike, held together with rootlets, cut out a slab and set it aside. Use as little toilet paper as you can. Bits of debris like fir cones can help with the preliminary wipe. When you finish, use a small stick to mingle feces with soil and drop the soiled stick into the hole. Then replace the surface plug, or rake in clean, scooped-out earth, and restore surface litter.

Toilet paper is slow to decompose. In places where natural processes are sluggish—in high, cold country or in barren desert—it might make sense to touch a match to the paper, reducing much of it to ash. But overenthusiastic TP burners have been known to start fires, so rule makers now frown on this practice. It is better, in these cases, to pack the paper out.

In a few heavily used mountain areas, more than that is asked of us. We are being urged, even here and there required, to pack out the waste itself. The essence of the system is an inner, biodegradable bag, a scoop of absorbent material (like powdery soil or kitty litter), and several plastic bags for a leakproof seal. Kits are offered at certain roadheads, sold commercially, and easily improvised. On exit, the paper bag and contents (never the plastic) can be dropped into any vault toilet. This practice is not likely to become general, though, and is hardly possible on the longer trip.

Having taken due care to keep the pathogens in human waste out of the larger environment, now take extreme care to keep them out of your immediate environment: by washing your hands scrupulously. How best to do this is a matter of some debate. Soap and water would suffice only if followed by a prolonged, copious rinse, and this can be hard to achieve on the trail. The authorities now recommend using a no-rinse antibacterial gel, or perhaps antibacterial towelettes, after catholing. Be sure to keep your nails clean as well.

It isn't necessary to be so fastidious about urination. In the way that matters most, the urine of a healthy person is quite clean: that is, it contains few or none of the organisms that can cause disease. However, the acid in urine does burn vegetation, and some animals like to nibble urinous leaves—yes, these matters have been studied! The ideal is to besprinkle barren rocks.

Washing and Swimming

In principle, all washing—of yourself, of your clothes, of your teeth, of your dishes—should be done well away from the water's edge. Save your use of soap for when it really matters. For general personal cleanliness, soapless cat baths make most people feel fresh enough. Some use antiperspirants. To get warm water, you can heat it on the stove, or leave it in a dark container in the sun; a shower attachment can be fitted to a water bag. Some find that a sponge with a scrubber pad, applied gently, cleans the skin better than a cloth. Pre-moistened wipes from your kit can be refreshing every once in a while.

Swimming is delightful and usually harmless. Stay ashore if you are ill, however, and make sure you aren't introducing any fecal traces into the lake or stream. It also does no harm to sponge off a few layers of sun-screen, bug dope, and general grime before you plunge. At the shoreline, avoid stepping on plants and under-cut or crumbling banks.

Two special cases alter these practices.

On the bank of a large, rushing stream, it may be just as well to wash clothes, soapless, in live water; in a remote area, you can even suspend them in the flow and let the current do the job for you. In grizzly bear country, streamside washing is positively recommended.

At the other extreme are water bodies so sensitive to contamination that you should make minimum con-tact with them. An example would be a desert pothole filled with rainwater. Generally speaking, wherever there is a little water in a harsh environment, better just keep your distance, or at most tap the source for drink-ing water only.

Water Treatment

The perceived pollution problem in the wilderness has led to a striking change in habits. We are now routinely advised that every drop of water taken from the land must be boiled, microfiltered, or treated with chemi-cals. I don't go that far (see "The Old Way," below); but plainly every hiker now must know to treat water and be equipped to do so.

Boiling

Boiling is the classic water treatment. Most experts feel that a momentary full boil is the maximum necessary for practical purposes, even at high elevations. A brief boil unquestionably kills *Giardia*. Suggested boiling times of more than a minute reflect bureaucratic caution and can safely be ignored. Boiling, of course, consumes fuel, and it can only conveniently be done when you are in camp. So other alternatives are more widely used.

Iodine Treatment

For many purposes, chemical treatment is most convenient. The recommended chemical today is iodine. Bleach and the old chlorine treatment, halazone, are not used any more. A new chlorine option, chlorine dioxide, is used in Europe but is not approved by all American authorities.

Iodine was long thought effective against all pathogens. It now appears that one organism of concern, *Cryptosporidium*, may resist this treatment. In the absence of more and better-focused research, I'd be slow to jettison my iodine kit; but people are wondering.

Iodine for water treatment comes in several forms.

Tincture of iodine. Tincture means a solution in alcohol; the bottle you buy must say "2 percent" or "USP standard." (It will also say "Poison," but don't let that scare you.) The standard dose is five drops of 2 percent tincture per quart of water. Let stand for half an hour. If the water is very cloudy, double the dosage; if very cold, double either the dosage or, better, the time. A much more concentrated tincture, designed specifically for water treatment, may be on the market soon.

Iodine tablets (tetraglycine hydroperiodide). Potable Aqua is the familiar brand. The recommended dose has recently increased to two tablets per quart. Give tablets 3 minutes to dissolve, then let stand for at least 20 minutes. Since tablets lose potency on exposure to moisture and air, keep them in a tightly sealed container; avoid opening the bottle with wet fingers. Potable Aqua kits are now available with companion pills of ascorbic acid—vitamin C—which can be added (after treatment is complete) to neutralize the iodine flavor. Discard unused tablets at the end of each season. Cost: about $5 without C tablets, $7 with.

Iodine/water solution. The kit consists of 4 to 8 grams of iodine crystals in a small, tightly capped glass bottle, capacity 1 to 3 fluid ounces (exact numbers don't matter, but a larger container is easier to handle). You can find the ingredients yourself or, easier, pick up the ready-made setup by PolarPure ($10 or so). When the bottle is filled with water and shaken vigorously, some crystals dissolve to form a solution. This solution—*not the solid iodine in the bottom*—is the treating agent. The recommended dose depends on the temperature and clarity of the water you are treating: check instructions. Each time you use some solution, replace the drawn-off water, twist on the cap, and shake again; more iodine dissolves, and the concentration stays the same. One caution: the solution is weaker when cold; in chilly weather, carry it in a shirt pocket or warm it before using. And store the unit in several layers of plastic. It tends to leak a little and turn things around it a violent purple.

Some tricks and precautions apply to all types of iodine treatments:

- If uncertain of the normal dose, remember that the treated water should look slightly brown and taste a little funny.

- There are trade-offs between time, temperature, and dosage. You can cut back on chemical if the water is warm; you can also use less if you're able to wait for several hours.

- Consider the treatment times recommended in kit directions to be the absolute minimum: there is evidence that *Giardia* cysts can hold out for several hours. Letting the water sit overnight before drinking is ideal.

- Thorough mixing helps the treatment. After adding the iodine, rattle the bottle with the lid slightly loose so that the threads are moistened.

- Cloudy water should be cleared by straining it through cloth or letting it stand for several hours before treatment.

- It's fine to add vitamin C or flavorings to kill the slight iodine taste, but only *after* treatment is complete.

- Iodine is slightly toxic in large doses; avoid ingesting solid iodine, and don't let kids play with the kit. Pregnant women, people with thyroid problems, and people allergic to iodine shouldn't use this method at all. And iodine shouldn't be relied on heavily during multiweek hikes.

Filtration

The most used water treatment today is filtration. Half a dozen makers now offer filters suitable for backpacking. Weights range from under 8 ounces to a couple of pounds; costs range from under $50 to over $100; selling points vary widely. What's to choose?

The main question is just what you want to filter out or kill. All reputable filters stop *Giardia*, *Cryptosporidium*, and other protozoa of concern. These also block bacteria. A smaller assortment of machines, known as water purifiers, take care of viruses as well. Finally, some filters use carbon to remove organic chemicals like pesticides or herbicides (but may or may not counter viruses—these functions are separate). Carbon can also remove the after-treatment residue of iodine.

In the North American wilderness, where the water is pretty clean by planetary standards, any filter that blocks the protozoa will probably serve you well enough. Indeed, there is some disadvantage to buying a

Two widely available water filters, the Sweetwater Guardian and the MSR Mini Works EX. Good against protozoans and bacteria, such models do not block viruses—and in the American wilderness, they don't need to.

more capable unit: it is likely to weigh more, cost more, require harder pumping, and clog more frequently.

Several options may come with your filter, either as part of the package or sold separately. Often handy is a *prefilter* that attaches to the intake hose and screens out coarse material. Another useful item is a bottle fitting that allows you to pump without spillage straight into a wide-mouthed bottle or water bag.

Filters of another type have no pumps but work by gravity. These are reliable and easy to use in camp but too slow for the trail. They are also notably heavy. Some regular pump models come with gravity-feed adapters.

Another variant is the in-the-bottle filter. Reversing the usual process, you put suspect water in the container and take clean water out, usually just by sucking it out of a spout. This is a personal, not a group item.

Filter technology keeps changing. If you're in the market, seek the current advice of stores, magazines, catalogs, Web sites, and friends.

With the advent of filters, a new chore has been added to the backpacking day: crouching by the water-side, pumping away. It's a slow business at best, and when your filter acts up, it gets slower. Indeed, water filters seem to be among the most troublesome and hated items of gear. To keep problems to the minimum, get to know your filter and follow its instructions carefully.

As with any treatment method, you'll start with the cleanest, clearest water you can find. Moving water stirs up sediments and contaminants, so draw from quiet pools if you can. Keep the intake hose off the muddy bottom (some models are usefully equipped with floats). Cloudy water should be dipped into a container and left to settle, an hour or two or even overnight, before filtering. (Glacial flour—the fine suspended rock dust found in some high-mountain streams—is almost instant death on filter elements.) If you have a prefilter, use it. Particularly ugly water can be filtered twice, or filtered once and then treated with iodine.

When water starts coming through the device, let the first few spurts hit the ground before you start collecting. Keep the outlet tube—the spigot where treated water emerges—scrupulously clean. Touch it as little as possible and keep it from flopping into the water source. After each use, pump air until the last drops are gone, shake out the hoses, and wipe surfaces dry. In the pack, keep the outlet tube in its own bag or wrap a plastic bag around it. To permit further drying, carry the filter as a whole in the mesh bag it came in.

When it's cold enough, ice forms in filters and slows pump action. Prevent this by taking the gizmo into your tent, or even into your sleeping bag, in a plastic bag. If a filter gets dropped onto the rocks, suspect the worst; any sudden change in its action probably means you need a new filter element.

If the filter seems to be gradually flagging, it's time to clean the works, a task that takes different forms; consult the directions for your model. At home after a trip, instructions usually call for sterilizing the unit by pumping a weak bleach solution through it. If so, repeat the operation at the beginning of the hiking season. In between, store the filter in a dry place in its netting bag.

After a certain number of cleanings, filter elements must be replaced. (On longer trips, take a spare.) Generally, ceramic filters have longer cleaning intervals and longer life overall. Replacement cartridges will cost somewhere near half the price of the complete original unit.

Combination Methods

Since each type of water treatment method has its drawbacks, many people switch off among methods. At dinner, for instance, they boil water; overnight, they iodinize at low concentration; on the trail, they filter. You can also combine methods in treating a given batch. For instance, water may be filtered first through a unit that stops protozoa and bacteria, and afterward treated with iodine at half the standard concentration to dispose of viruses. Or it may be treated with iodine first and then run through a filter containing carbon to remove the chemical residue.

One final caution: some water is dangerous because of naturally occurring chemicals like arsenic and won't be made drinkable by any sterilizing treatment; even carbon filters may not help. Suspect a spring without insects or signs of use by animals; avoid water draining from old mines or areas with hot springs, geysers, or fumaroles.

The Old Way

What if (like the author) you're unwilling to forgo the very special pleasure of drinking water straight from the country, flat on your belly, sucking it from a stream, or getting its tang across the cool rolled lip of a metal cup? Are you crazy? No: but be very careful about where you pursue your habit.

Giardia and *Cryptosporidium* can be found in just about any water; so the branchwater drinker is taking a certain risk. That risk, though, is much less than the authorities (and the pill and filter makers) would have you think. Repeated studies of actual lakes and streams find very low doses of pathogens, far less than the populations used to test filters and treatments in the lab. Many people have drunk natural waters for years, and continue to, without ill effect. And the penalty for guessing wrong is not prohibitive. Giardiasis is miserable but no disaster for a basically healthy person. Some other waterborne diseases, hepatitis E for instance, are far more serious, but these are derived from human contamination only, and typically via waters far more polluted than you'll encounter in the North American wilderness.

When you look for water, *think watershed*. Where does a stream come from? What pollution sources might there be in its drainage area? Don't drink downstream from a known camp or trail crossing; rather, go upstream, or find a smaller stream issuing from a basin containing no trail or major cross-country hiking route.

Lake water does not quite follow the watershed rule. Large bodies of water act as settling basins, and water from a lake outflow is likely to be safer than that from inflow streams. Where streams wander across meadows, something similar happens: they are likely to be cleaner where they leave than where they enter. Other things being equal, it's always better to drink from still water than from a current (which can stir things up).

Some otherwise wild landscapes are grazed or overgrazed by livestock. If you see many cows or much dung, better treat the water, period. Same goes for streams with beaver dams, a major source of contamination. (In beaver country, filters clog in a hurry.) Also boycott streams that have their sources outside wilderness, in civilized territory; this is a not-uncommon situation, especially in the Southwest and in the Ozark region. In the region bordering Lake Superior, including Isle Royale National Park on the lake itself, all waters without exception must be treated to kill a regionally ubiquitous parasite, *Echinococcus granulosis*.

Water fresh out of a remote snowbank is likely to be safe (as well as exquisite). Watch out, though, for colored "watermelon snow," tinted by algae that can give you indigestion or worse. Merely scraping away the pink layer isn't enough—the clean-appearing snow below it may also contain the organism.

What If You Do Get Sick?

Giardiasis develops five to seven days after exposure. Since most wilderness trips are shorter than that, sufferers tend to come down with it at home rather on the trail. The similar disease caused by *Cryptosporidium*, however, can develop in as little as two days, and so can diarrheas caused by bacteria. If you do get sick on the trail, make sure you keep up your fluid intake and get to civilization as fast as you can (see Chapter 26).

In all these illnesses, diarrhea is the main affliction; accompanying miseries vary. Untreated, you can expect to be laid up for a week or more (up to three weeks for giardiasis). There are drugs for giardiasis; bacterial infections can be treated with antibiotics. Cryptosporidosis just has to run its course. Only a stool analysis can tell exactly what you've got. By all means, seek your doctor's advice.

21

Breaking Camp

Some campers, very careful when they choose their campsite and organize their brief life there, are rather casual and careless when they depart. Yet breaking camp is a moment of special responsibility for the conscientious traveler.

Suppose you have camped at an established site. It is, inevitably, a beaten-down, impacted place. That is its great advantage. Even here you can look around before you leave and ask yourself: How much have we added to the problems of this place? How much can we undo?

There is no point in getting rid of a properly located fire ring that the next party may want to use. But if you see a ring where no ring should be—at the lake's edge on grass, for example—it can be a good service to remove the stones and disguise, as much as you can, the scar. Make sure that the ring you used yourself is completely clean, ready, and inviting. Otherwise you may be encouraging the next comers to construct a fresh one.

Your fire must, of course, be unmistakably dead. Stop adding wood to the flames well before you are ready to leave so that coals will burn into ashes. Never bury the fire with dirt; this may fail to kill it properly and also spoils the ring. Instead, douse a still-warm fire with quantities of water. Comb through the ashes with your fingers to make sure they are cold clear through. Be certain to pull out any unburnable fragments like aluminum foil (which should not be there in the first place) and pack them away with you. If, in spite of all care, you do have sizable chunks of wood left over, it's okay to leave them in the ring.

If a ring is choked with ashes, should these be scattered, buried, or left alone? There has been quite a debate about this, but the consensus now is for scattering to restore nutrients to the soil. Take cold, gray ashes away from camp and fling them widely in several places. Black, extinguished coals, however, should be left in place for further combustion.

There's a gracious old woodcraft tradition of leaving a cache of firewood for the next party. This is no longer the expected thing, but, if you do find you've collected excess wood, then certainly leave it by the ring rather than scatter it again.

Gather up litter—your own and as much as you can reasonably carry of what may have been there before. See how many bits you can find of "microlitter": twist ties, matches, torn-off corners of food wrapping, and the like. There are always more than you imagine. If there are young children in the party, you can recruit them for a treasure hunt.

So much for the typical, relatively civilized site. If, by contrast, your camp has been in a place not obviously used before, there is more to do. Your tracks must be made to vanish. Some instructors in wilderness programs like Outward Bound have made a game of it. They ask their students to imagine themselves fugitives, with hostile trackers behind them examining every yard of ground for signs of their presence.

If you have used only a stove at the pristine site, your job will be simple; if you have ventured a fire, it is more complex (see "Fire at an Unmarked Site" in Chapter 18). It is truly important in this situation that *all* charred wood be consumed to ash. Ashes pass quickly back into the soil, but charcoal lasts so long that archaeologists count on it for dating ruins. Avoid winding up with a big half-burned log, there being no good way of disposing of such an object.

Ashes, again, should be scattered, with even more determination to make them inconspicuous. If you've managed well, you won't have coals; if you do, these had better be buried. Exception: where wildfire has left obvious traces in the scene, a few more embers won't bother anyone.

If you cannot make all traces of a campfire disappear from the pristine site, the fire should not have been lit in the first place.

Renaturalize your sleeping spots. Restore any rocks you've removed. Ruffle the smooth surfaces you've made. Scatter twigs, leaves, or gravel to replace natural litter you've swept away.

In general, check the ground wherever you have stood, lain, or sat around and do what you can to remove signs of your presence. You won't succeed in eliminating *every* trace, but you should be able to restore the scene well enough to fool any casual eye. Weather, in a little time, will do the rest.

Variations

*At the same time that we are earnest to explore
and learn all things, we require that all things
be mysterious and unexplorable, that land and
sea be infinitely wild, unsurveyed and
unfathomed by us because unfathomable.*

—Henry David Thoreau, *Walden*

22

Ultralight & Other Variants

Every backpacker knows the tug-of-war between two desires: to carry the lightest possible pack, and to have everything we need, or *might* need, come out of that container. It's an ongoing negotiation within each of us. It is also, to some degree, a matter of fashion. When I started backpacking, the Spartan approach was in. Then more and more items came to be seen as basic. Thin foam pads were replaced by air mattresses, tarps by tents, and fires by stoves (on good low-impact grounds). Suddenly, everyone carried a water filter. Little amenities multiplied. And pack weights crept up and up—to the point where a 40-pound load for a short weekend might be described as light.

In the 1990s, a healthy reaction set in, pioneered by the iconoclastic Ray Jardine. The pressure is on again to get loads down, and a new branch of the sport has developed: the highly disciplined practice called "ultralight" backpacking.

Throughout this book we've envisioned packs of 30 to 40 pounds, of which 16 pounds or more is the hard-to-reduce "dry weight." It is possible, however, to get pack weights down to half those levels. This is accomplished partly by doing without things; partly by using stripped-down versions of things; partly by making things do double duty; partly by carrying rather small reserves of consumables like food, fuel, and water; and partly by sticking to fairly benign hiking climates and conditions.

Weight savings start with the pack. For small loads, it need not have high capacity or elaborate suspension systems. You find very good and rugged packs that weigh 3 pounds or so instead of the typical 5 or 6. Packs designed specifically for ultralight use, by Jardine's company GoLite and others, go as low as 1 pound. Ultralight packs may lack internal frames, getting their spinal column from a folded closed-cell pad instead. Even plain old rucksacks—shoulder packs without hipbelts—are once again showing up on multiday trips.

The next major point of attack is shelter. The ultra-lighter may rely on a bivouac sack, perhaps with a tiny tentlike roof at the head; or on a lightweight nylon tarp. If a tent is carried, it will probably be single-walled, without a fly; a trekking pole will serve as its support. A group might carry a double-walled tent of the lightweight hoop design. Weight per person sheltered will certainly be two pounds or less. The old multipurpose poncho—a square, untailored raincoat that overhangs the pack, doubling as its rain cover, and that can be rigged as a small tarp—is also getting a second look.

The sleeping bag in the ultralight kit is likely to be filled with high-quality down. The lower half of the bag, the part your weight compresses anyway, may be an empty sheath that you pad with clothing, or into which you slide your pad. (Couples have the advantage of staying warm in light bedding.) Some ultralight bags have sleeves or at least openings for the arms and drawcorded bottom openings for the feet; you wear your bed to breakfast, and leave other insulating garments at home. Or you go the other way and carry a sawed-off, hoodless bag ("elephant's foot"), which you supplement with a generous down jacket. Sleeping pads are minimal air mattresses, or closed-cell foam.

These three items—pack, shelter, and bedroll—can be gotten down to a combined five pounds. Even ten pounds for the trio, sometimes considered the threshold of ultralight, is way too heavy for the zealous practitioner.

The ultralight hiker may carry a half-length sleeping bag ("elephant's foot") supplemented by an insulated jacket. If the jacket would have been toted anyway, a weight saving results.

One of the lightest stoves will be carried; bottled-gas versions are now down to 3 ounces. To reduce the amount of fuel toted, campfires may be substituted. Some ultralighters simply eat cold. Some go fishing, with the lightest possible gear (12 ounces and about $250).

Other possible savings come in tiny increments, item by item. Ultralight hikers prepare master lists including the weight of every component to a tenth of an ounce, and scan each item ferociously: Do I have to have this at all, and can I buy or create a lighter version? Here's where the handles really do come off the toothbrushes. Basic dry weight can go as low as 8 pounds per person.

A very light pack has multiple advantages. It permits the hiker to move along in comfort, almost oblivious to the load. It brings a pleasant simplicity to packing and to making camp. It's an engrossing game to see just how much you can get along without. And for those so inclined, ultralight allows for much faster progress. There is currently a vogue for what is called fastpacking or speed hiking, in which the energy saved by toting a tiny pack is spent in multiplying miles traveled.

In trade, you undeniably do give up some comforts and conveniences.

Is this approach for you? Circumstances may decide. After a knee injury, I received doctor's orders to carry no more than 25 pounds. For me, the ultralight option came along just in time.

For others who don't take up this particular challenge, there is still a benefit: trend-conscious manufacturers are busy dreaming up designs that deliver comfort at the lowest possible weight.

The Very Long Trip

Another variation on the brief "normal" backpack is the trip measured not in days but in weeks. Such a journey may be within a single very large wilderness area; more commonly, it follows a lengthy trail that traverses both wildlands and regions that are relatively tame. Either way, the extended trek requires detailed planning and preparation, and it is likely to require resupply. The ultimate that can be managed without reprovisioning or living off the land would seem to be about two weeks.

Especially if the area traversed is isolated, food for the longer trip takes careful planning. Your appetite will grow as time goes on; experienced long-distance trekkers add about ½ pound per person per day to the normal ration of 1½ to 2 pounds per person-day. Just about everything must be dried or freeze-dried. High-calorie, high-priced "energy bars" make sense as lunch foods in this kind of travel. Balance in the diet—scarcely a consideration on the shorter jaunt—becomes important on a long trip. The ingredients for each meal may be packaged together in a sealed, informatively labeled bag.

At some point it becomes necessary to replenish food, fuel, and miscellaneous supplies. This may mean connecting with a cache you have placed in advance; hiking out to a roadhead to meet a friend; making your way to a town with a post office; having supplies packed in to you by friends or commercial outfitters; or in very remote areas receiving an air drop.

Supply caches take various forms. You can leave food on the ground in bear canisters or tightly sealed metal boxes or hang it from trees in boxes or in waterproof bags (as for bearbagging).

If your route passes close enough to towns, you can mail supplies via the U.S. Postal Service (ask for Special Handling, Insured). You can also buy groceries in town, including white gas, which can't be mailed. The Appalachian Trail, on the East Coast, the prototype of all the long trails, passes quite close to many settlements, and the Pacific Crest Trail, on the West Coast, approaches a few. Besides food and such, you may need to replace minor medical supplies and various small items of gear as the weeks go on.

Along trails like the Appalachian, climate will change as you hike, because of the passage of time and also perhaps because of progress north or south. You may want to ship a heavy jacket home, for example, and replace it with something lighter.

Most long-trail hikers favor all-leather boots of middling weight. A good pair of leather boots should make it at least 1,500 miles. Before you buy, find out what the store, or the manufacturer, will do for you if the end comes sooner. Veteran long-distance hiker Karen Berger recommends picking up two identical pairs before you start and breaking them both in, so that a substitute is ready. Just as your feet swell a little in the course of an active day, they seem to grow during a very long hiking trip. Some people report gaining a full size. So start with a marginally generous fit rather than a marginally snug one.

If feet are prone to grow, the rest of you is likely to shrink on a very long journey. This can affect the fit of your pack. Unless you're already pretty skinny, it's best to start with a belt that feels a bit tight when cinched in to the maximum. You may in any case wind up changing belts along the way.

Water treatment can be a challenge on the very long trip. Filters used week after week are prone to clog. The easy alternative, iodine, isn't recommended for long-term use, either. Boiling consumes fuel. Drinking water off the land is riskier in these busy trail corridors than it is in wilder zones. Most people seem to settle on a mixture of methods.

Cross-Country Travel

Of all the miles that backpackers travel each year, 90 percent are probably hiked in summer. And of that 90 percent, 90 percent are hiked by trail. Sometimes we speak of wilderness as "crowded," but for those who wish to take a further step into wildness—to leave behind the busy channels of the trails—the wild country has room and to spare.

Not that you could call these remoter lands underused. Wilderness serves purposes beyond recreation; the lands where the hiker seldom comes may be the best preserved of all for wildlife, for watershed, for scientific study. Wilderness itself should have within it a deeper wilderness—wilderness, so to speak, to the second power.

The hikers who take advantage of that deeper wilderness are not numerous. And here's a paradox: wherever they do become numerous, the experience they seek vanishes before them. Whenever a cross-country route begins to carry more than a handful of people a season, informal paths start to appear, and then to erode and deepen. When this point is reached, the land-managing agency has three choices: to restrict use, to build a formal trail, or (as happens too often) simply to let the land take scar upon scar. A well-built trail is not a convenience merely, but also a way of accommodating use without excessive damage to the land.

Meanwhile, the trailless outback is there. And for a certain number of hikers, it is irresistible.

Cross-country travel is typically slow. If 2 miles an hour is a lively pace with a pack on a level trail, 1 mile an hour is good progress through woods and brush. And yet not even this slowness of pace is predictable. There are open, parklike forests as well as thick and tangled ones. And on the smooth granite expanses of certain western ranges, it may be scarcely harder to move off-trail than on. In the desert, too, marked trails are rare and scarcely required.

To hike off-trail you need a serious backpacking boot, weighing 3 pounds or more per pair in an average size, and with a good high top; lighter boots, comfortable on easy ground, offer too little protection for rugged travel. Make sure you have plenty of adhesive tape in your kit. A sprained ankle, likelier out here, can often be stabilized with tape, allowing you to retreat under your own power (see Chapter 27).

For travel in rough country, you will be happiest with an internal-frame pack that rides close to the back. Before you wade into vegetation, make sure that zippers are shut tight, and get rid of any trailing loops or hanging objects where bushes and branches could catch hold.

When crossing scree and loose ground, as well as snow patches, you may be grateful for a pair of gaiters. These zip-on cuffs fit tightly over the gap at the top of the boot, preventing loose rocks and the like from bouncing in.

Certain animal problems become slightly more troublesome when you leave the trail. In brush country, ticks are hard to avoid. Gaiters help here, and so do dabs of insect repellent at neck, wrists, and ankles, but about the only sure defense is to strip and inspect each evening and get rid of the creatures before they get deeply attached.

Snakes—rattlesnakes and, in the East, copperheads and cottonmouths—are somewhat more of a hazard off the trail. Don't step down on the far side of a rock or log without first getting a look at the ground there.

You are no more likely to see mammals off-trail than on. But there may be more risk of sudden bear encounters. In grizzly country, be cautious about bushwhacking in dense vegetation; you don't want to stumble on a resting bear. Brushy avalanche paths are favorite bear retreats; before crossing such an opening, pause and look for moving bushes or other sign. For more about these concerns, see Chapter 29.

Walking Softly off the Trail

On established paths you deliberately confined your impact to places already affected. On the trail you walked single file. In camp you built fires (if at all) at old sites. You concentrated your traffic in the smallest possible area.

But in off-trail travel, exactly the opposite applies. To avoid leaving traces, you disperse. A party walking through the woods, or on any surface where a mark could be left, should always walk abreast, each hiker in a separate line, so far as the land allows. A little impact, spread over a lot of land, will simply vanish. To make sure this is the case, off-trail parties should be small—two or three is best.

Resist any temptation to leave cairns or ducks. Although they may know better, walkers on the trackless ridge or in the empty forest should be free to imagine that no one else has been in that place, at least this year.

What kinds of land are most easily damaged by cross-country hiking and camping? The types are familiar: leafy forest floor vegetation, timberline vegetation of all kinds, wet meadows and bogs, erosive slopes. Although subalpine meadows are proverbially fragile, woody shrubs and heathers at the same high elevations are in fact more vulnerable still. Dry mountain grasslands, though slow to repair themselves, are also rather slow to scar.

In some environments, feces actually decompose fastest on the surface of the ground, exposed to sun and air. In remote areas, especially in the desert, authorities recommend surface smearing as an alternative to the usual cathole. Look for a sunbeaten spot well away from water and from any likely travel route; spread excrement thinly with a stick or a stone; and pack out any toilet paper.

Route Finding and Navigation

Route finding—picking your detailed line through the landscape—is perhaps the central cross-country skill.

What is the least impossible way through this prickly brush field? Which of several gullies will lead us through this band of steep rock? Can we get around the head of this valley without losing too much elevation? Where is the safest spot to ford the stream? Decisions are made every minute. The cross-country hiker is constantly looking both near and far; the route that looks easiest in the short run may betray you in the long run.

It is always good to travel the wilderness with a mind aware, conscious of the shapes of the land, their correspondence to the map, and your own progress among them. Off the trail, this attentiveness becomes essential. Be sure to look behind you now and then, noticing landmarks as they appear in reverse, in case you must retrace your course.

In trail travel, it is rather hard to get seriously lost, even if you should lose track of your exact position on the map. You know, after all, that you are on a certain *line,* or at worst (if you think you have overlooked a junction) that you're on one of several lines. Either way, you have only half a problem to solve.

Even off-trail, you may at times be following a prominent linear feature—a major stream, a ridgeline without confusing branches, an ocean beach. In orienteering, they call such features *handrails.* But much of the time you'll have no handrail to hold to.

In rugged, mountainous country, topography—the lay of the land—typically tells you a lot. Shapes are bold and distinctive. Your problems start when you can't see to read the land—because of fog, or clouds, or darkness, or winter whiteout—or when what you *can* see is uninstructive. Some landscapes are like that, flattish and jumbled, or flattish and forested, with no particular pattern to go by. In featureless country, as in blind weather, navigation has to go beyond the obvious.

There is one situation in which even quite experienced backpackers can get lost: coming down from a height, particularly from a large, conical mountain. On the way up to such a summit, ridges converge; the terrain gathers itself together toward the peak; you can hardly go wrong. On the descent, however, the land

Using Deliberate Error

Destination: waterfall

Deliberate error
to ensure
arriving east
of car

Rejected straight-line course

Forest

Deliberate error to
ensure arriving
west of correct
stream junction

Car

If you lack a GPS or landmarks for compass work, you can use deliberate error, a low-tech navigation technique that can be a valuable fallback.

fans out in front of you. A mistake of a few yards, one way or the other, will put you on the wrong ridge, in the wrong drainage, or even on the wrong side of the mountain. Again, the vital thing is to have noted, *on the way up*, how things will appear on the way down. Where visibility is likely to be a problem, mountaineers may carry *wands*, light bamboo stakes to which flags of brightly colored plastic tape are tied; these can be placed at decision points to mark the proper way. They must, of course, be collected as you descend.

The Global Positioning System is a powerful tool for cross-country navigation. Reading satellite signals, your little receiver will tell you exactly where you are; it will also give you a bearing to any point whose coordinates you enter. In closing on an invisible target, you can head in that general direction without concern for minor deviations, getting a new bearing as often as you like. A complex cross-country route may be laid out as a series of short straight lines leading to a succession of targets, or "waypoints." See "GPS and Other Tools" in Chapter 16.

Lacking a GPS or landmarks for compass work, the cross-country hiker can fall back on certain dead-reckoning tricks. The most broadly useful is deliberate error. Rather than head straight for an invisible destination point, you angle somewhat right or left. Reaching a linear feature that includes the target point—the stream that creates the waterfall you want to photograph, for example—you will know which way to turn: right if you angled left, left if you deliberately drifted to the right.

Stream Crossing

One of the most difficult wilderness obstacles is the major, rushing stream. If you expect to be encountering significant creeks, branches, brooks, or runs on your cross-country trip, by all means ask the advice of the management agency and other local sources. As always, try to get through to rangers who know the conditions and won't just advise you to follow the crowd. If you expect many crossings, bring river sandals or soft shoes as well as boots. Where streams are very cold, consider wetsuit booties.

A fast, shallow stream is not a particular problem, though it can be tricky if the current is fierce enough, or cold enough, or both. A slow, deep river may be easier than it looks. You can usually swim across, floating your pack in front of you on an air mattress, or buoyed up by contents stored in airtight bags. As for powerful, foaming whitewater, you needn't worry about that either: you *know* you can't get across.

What makes you think twice is the swollen mountain stream, knee-deep to thigh-deep, fast moving and possibly murky. You can probably cross it, yet you may or may not want to try.

When you reach such a stream, stop and study it. Assess its temperature, speed, and depth. Can you see the bottom, and what it is made of? Gravel is the best footing to wade on; sand is often okay but may erode underfoot in a fast current; rocks are more or less slippery and can trap a foot. Will the opposite bank permit an easy exit from the water? Consider what would happen if you were swept off your feet. Downstream are there rapids, falls, or prolonged steep banks? Are there fallen trees—"strainers"—that might entangle a person caught in the current?

Unless the spot you've hit is obviously benign, reconnoiter upstream and down. (If you are just below a junction of tributaries, maybe you can make two easier crossings above.) Unless you find a natural bridge like a log or a beaver dam, the best spot will be a stretch that is wide, straight, and relatively shallow. The broken water of a submerged gravel bar, or shingle, is preferable to a deeper, apparently calmer area. In picking out a detailed path, take advantage of eddies, swirls where the current is weaker. Avoid pockets of deep water, often indicated by darker color.

Consider the time of crossing as well as the place. Streams fed by snowmelt will be lowest in the cool of the morning. Releases from upstream reservoirs may be a factor, too.

When you're ready to cross, change to your sandals or lighter shoes. (If you use your boots, retie the laces for quick release if needed.) Remove any bulky outer clothing that might impede your ability to swim. Repack your most vulnerable gear in several layers of plastic bags. When you put on your pack, loosen the shoulder straps and leave the hipbelt unbuckled (so that, if you must, you can easily shed your load).

Now for the actual crossing. If alone, you're best off facing upstream so that the current won't tend to buckle your knees. Set your feet wide apart and take short steps, moving one foot at a time and always leading with the same foot. Test each new footing before you shift your weight. A trekking pole or stick will give you a third foot and help you keep your balance against the tugging flow.

Several hikers, crossing together, can support each other in a circle of three, with linked arms; in a line, each gripping the waist of another, facing upstream but moving sideways; in a wedge formation, again facing upstream; or abreast, with arms linked and wrapped around a long pole, facing across the water. In this "line-abreast" method, all move forward at once; otherwise, only one person moves at a time.

What if you get swept off your feet? The proper reaction varies from case to case. If the current is not too deep and fast, you may be able to recover your footing. In the more potent stream, you're advised to shed your pack and go with the flow, floating on your back with feet pointing downstream to bounce you off obstacles. When you reach slower water, turn over and swim diagonally upstream toward shore.

Hazardous crossings are sometimes made in very cold water, or weather, or both. If someone takes a spill and gets dangerously chilled, he or she may have to be stripped, dried, and put into a sleeping bag, following the drill for hypothermia (see Chapter 28). Lacking a hypothermia crisis, though, the best post-immersion treatment is to put on whatever dry clothes you have available, eat starch and sugar, and start hiking, fast and hard, to produce a lot of body heat.

Steep Summer Snow

In the northwestern United States and alpine Canada, snow may linger on mountain slopes for most of the summer. A snowbank is only an interruption, but what if your route simply vanishes under a steep, white snowfield? Even if you were on a trail before, you are now facing a moderate cross-country challenge.

In climbing a gently sloping snowfield, walk flat-footed, taking full advantage of the friction provided by your boot soles. As the angle increases slightly, you can point your toes outward and waddle up duck-fashion (a maneuver that skiers will recognize as the herringbone). Steeper slopes are best ascended by traversing at an angle, making switchbacks as required. If the snow is at all firm, you will have to kick steps as you climb. Use a scraping, arcing motion of the boot, and make the step no deeper than you need to feel secure. On short, steep sections, head straight up the slope, kicking steps into it with your toes. If you are the first in a party, remember that other people will be using the footholds you create; if long-legged, make steps a little closer together than you need.

On any but very gradual slopes, a third leg is essential. It can be a trekking pole (or two used as one), a stout stick, or an *ice ax*. If nothing more suitable comes to hand, you can carry a tent stake or a shard of stone. Whatever the tool, it is used as an anchor as you move up or down and as an emergency brake in case you slip. You face into the slope and move one of your three points of support at a time.

If you know you're likely to face this situation, forget substitutes: you want the ax. This tool consists of a stout metal shaft fitted to a head with two blades, one narrow (the pick) and one wide (the adze). For occasional use, a rather long ax is best; with the tip of the shaft on the ground, you should just be able to rest your hand on the blade. A suitable tool will weigh under 2 pounds and cost at least $60.

Besides giving you more security in moving up slopes, the ice ax allows you to have some fun going down them, using such techniques as the *plunge step* and the sitting or standing *glissade*, which lie a little outside the focus of this book.

To travel across icy areas or frozen, hard snow, you need an additional item: *crampons*. These are sets of spikes that strap or clamp onto the soles of your boots. Though not something you'd think of in most regions, crampons have become almost standard equipment in parts of the northern Cascades, the Canadian Rockies, and Alaska. Even an iced-up grassy slope can be a slippery hazard. Partial or instep crampons or cleats will do for most situations. If you use full crampons, which have twelve spikes, make sure that you get the two-piece type that comes with a hinge under the sole and can be worn with your normal boots. Instep crampons cost $30–$60; full crampons run about triple that.

Lacking crampons, try to time your crossing of icy slopes for midafternoon, or whenever a particular slope has had sun on it for the longest possible time. Most summer snowfields will get soft as the day goes on.

For more on the skills of travel on steep snow and ice, consult the Mountaineers' *Freedom of the Hills* (see the Resources section).

On the Edge of Climbing

If you begin taking trips away from the trail, you may sooner or later want to learn at least the simplest of the mountaineer's methods. With a little gear and the skill to use it, you can deal with unexpected obstacles; more important, perhaps, you can plan trips in country where obstacles *are* to be expected. A rope-carrying party isn't balked if, hiking down some desert canyon, it comes to the brink of a steep, dry waterfall. It isn't precluded from crossing a stretch of crevassed glacier. Peaks that are out of reach to most hikers, because of a little steep rock at the top, are open to the party with a rope and some slings and hardware to use in setting up anchors.

The point of the rope between climbers is this: it allows one partner, braced (and usually anchored) in a strong position, to protect a second, who is moving on hazardous ground. As the moving climber advances, the stationary partner—the *belayer*—feeds out rope. If the climber slips, the belayer can stop the climber's fall.

Most climbers these days wear harnesses, securely encasing the pelvis, to which the rope is in turn attached. For occasional purposes, though, you can fall back on an older, direct method of tying in, wrapping the rope around your waist several times and securing it with the knot called *the bowline-on-a-coil.*

Another rope trick for cross-country travel is the *rappel*, a way of getting down a steep place. Running the line around a tree, knob of stone, or artificial anchor, with both ends dangling, you slide down it, slowly and safely. Then you recover it by pulling on one of the strands.

Such climbing basics are much too important to be learned from a thumbnail sketch. Consult a specialized text instead, get instruction, and practice again and again.

23

Desert, Canyon & Coastline Travel

In the forty-eight contiguous American states, more than half of the land open to recreation has one characteristic: it is *dry*. If you have or develop a taste for desert hiking and some skills to match, you'll have a world of wonderful destinations to choose from—and, except in a few iconic landscapes, you'll have very little company.

Geographers quibble about what "desert" means. The backpacker has a practical definition: you are hiking in the desert when you have to think routinely about *water*—when H_2O is not just a gift of the land, to be counted on, but the center of your plans.

Much hiking done in regions loosely called desert is not, by this measure, desert hiking at all. High mountains, however parched their foothills, almost always yield water. Hiking in the Toiyabe Range of central Nevada, for instance, you are *in* the desert only as an island is in the sea. Arid lands are also interrupted by perennial streams that flow in deep-cut canyons. Many famous "desert" treks follow these arteries: you wade the shallows and push through the green stream-bank thickets of an Aravaipa Creek or an Escalante River.

Take away the wet mountains and wet canyons, and what you have left is the desert itself, the real thing. It's true desert hiking when you park on the shoulder of a rugged road from nowhere to nowhere and head up a long alluvial slope toward the hard, stark summits of a mountain range that appears in no guidebook. It's true desert hiking when you clamber up the branches of a bone-dry, precipitous gorge. It's the real thing when you strike out across the feature-less expanse of a playa, one of those dead-flat, lifeless, cream-colored sedimentary plains that fill the low points of many desert valleys. And if it is solitude you are after—perfect, silent, almost scary solitude—these are the places to find it.

Planning and Caching Water

Your objective in planning desert travel must be to avoid being short of water—*ever*. Dehydration is not something you want to take chances with.

How much water does a desert hiker need? Not quarts, but gallons—at least 1.5 gallons a day, in liquid form and in food, and sometimes double that. Figure a 6-quart daily minimum and add a quart to that for every 5 miles to be traveled—in reasonably cool weather. In the heat of summer, figure more.

Water is heavy, 2 pounds to the quart. Two days' supply at 2 gallons a day would already weigh some 32 pounds (plus a few ounces for the containers). Of course, if you're hauling water anyhow, you hardly need to carry dried or freeze-dried edibles: you might as well get some of your moisture in real food, fresh or canned. The military's Meals Ready to Eat often turn up in the packs of desert hikers.

If you have to carry *all* your water, your hiking range is necessarily limited. Many desert hikers wind up taking a succession of short trips rather than one longer outing—going out just for a day or two and loop-ing back to the car between excursions. This type of travel—call it the cluster trip—is a desert specialty.

There are several ways of increasing your range. One is to find water on the land. Often it is there to be found. What you must not do, however, is to put yourself in the position of depending on a supply that may not exist. Don't count on local sources just because a map shows the blue squiggle of a spring. You may or may not find it; it may or may not actually be flowing. Plan your trip so that the presence of on-the-ground water will be good news, its absence not dangerously bad.

Converging animal tracks may help you zero in on a spring, and so may the movements of birds, which circle water at dawn and dusk. Look for wet spots below cliff bands and up shady side canyons.

In addition to permanent springs, you sometimes find natural catchments or "tanks" that hold water for several days after a rain. There may also be livestock watering troughs somewhere around. As an emergency measure, you may be able to reach water by digging into the gravelly floor of a streambed. Dig at the outside edge of a bend, at a spot where vegetation indicates that roots are reaching the water table. (Cottonwood trees are one good sign.) A hole that is dry in daylight may show some water after dark, when trees release some moisture into the ground. In winter in higher desert mountains, a ready source of water is snow.

Even prickly desert vegetation, and even desiccated desert soil, contain a trace of water. You can extract it, in a pinch. For instance, you can gather plant matter (the more succulent the better) and place it in a plastic bag that you inflate with your breath, tie off, and leave in the sun; moisture will evaporate from the green stuff, condense on the plastic, and pool. More elaborate is the solar still. You dig a hole in the ground and roof it with plastic, anchored at the margins and sagging in the middle, where it is weighted with a stone. Below the low point you place a container. Moisture will evaporate from the soil, condense on the ceiling, run down to the low point, and drip into the container. If you have vegetation to place in the hole, all the better. Think twice before embarking on this project, however; at best you'll get under a quart in 24 hours, and there might be better uses for your energy and time.

Most desert waters must be purified. Many are polluted by domestic stock or by feral burros. (You can count on one drowned scorpion per spring.) A few sources are so alkaline as to be obviously undrinkable; a very few contain poisonous minerals. These are usually identified on maps, but be wary of pools that have no sign of life whatsoever around them. Also don't drink water running out of mines or mine-disturbed areas.

Caching water is another way of extending your range. The process can be simple. For instance, if you will be hiking out and back on the same line, you can start out under a heavy load of water and plant a generous supply a few miles up the route. For a greater extension of range, you will have to do advance work by car, planting caches near (but not right next to) roads. Figure to place one cache for every day and a half of hiking. Plan locations and quantities so that, if you failed to find a particular cache, you would have enough water left to reach the next.

For containers, you can use solid plastic bottles (not gallon water bottles from the supermarket—too flimsy), or tough, collapsible water bags. Smaller containers reduce the consequences of a leak.

The ideal cache site is a place you can easily recognize, but that other people aren't likely to stumble on. It is good to choose a site near some prominent *line* in the landscape: a road or track or fence line, the toe of a mountain slope, or the bank of a dry streambed, or wash (but not down in the wash in the summer thunderstorm season). Avoid areas trafficked by off-road vehicles. Desert veterans take care to place caches unobserved. It is not unknown for vandals to steal or destroy supplies.

The tradition was once to bury cache containers or place them under massive cairns, but the resulting disturbance is now frowned upon. It is still fine to nest bottles in sand and perhaps to wedge them upright with stones. A site at the north side of an adjoining shrub or bush will get a little cooling shade. Attach to the cache a note stating when the stockpile was placed and when it is to be removed.

Food and other supplies can also be cached; any food that is not canned or freeze-dried must be contained in several layers of plastic, so that the odor doesn't draw rodents, coyotes, and foxes. Some people scatter cayenne pepper around as a further animal turnoff. The desert has no bears.

Before you leave the site, make absolutely certain that you can find the place again. Mark the spot on your map. Take at least three compass bearings and write them down. Make a sketch of local topography. If you're using a Global Positioning System receiver, note precise coordinates. Some people even document cache sites with photographs from several angles.

When you retrieve a cache, remove all trace of it, filling any hole, smoothing sand, and rescattering any rocks you have gathered. If you skip or miss a cache, go back later by road to retrieve it.

With due care it just won't happen. But what if the worst possible situation does somehow develop: you find yourself short of water and miles away from the next source? Research shows that a healthy person, not dehydrated to begin with, can walk about 10 miles in the desert in daytime without additional water. If it's hot, hole up in the middle of the day. Move at a steady, moderate pace. If help or water is more distant than that, walk at night. If you have any water at all, experts advise against hoarding it; it is better to drink as you become thirsty and keep your body functioning well at the out-set. To reduce water loss, keep your skin covered with clothing, even in hot weather. Do not smoke or drink alcohol. Eat only a little (carbohydrates), and avoid salt. A pebble in the mouth may make it feel less dry. Talk as little as possible and breathe through your nose. If you find water that is undrinkable, you can cool yourself with it by moistening the skin; urine, in a pinch, can be used in the same way. You needn't force yourself to drink urine, however; it does the body no good.

Other Aspects of Desert Hiking

We think of the deserts as hot, but that isn't quite right. The North American deserts stretch 1,000 miles north and south (even omitting the Mexican portion) and range 5,000 feet or more in elevation. Nowhere is it hot

Scorpions are common in the desert (and elsewhere), but most species are harmless.

all the time. Death Valley, where the summer temperature in the shade can climb above 120 degrees Fahrenheit, is chilly in the winter; January nights in northerly deserts may be deeply subzero. By picking your hiking season, you can keep to a comfortable range.

If you steer clear of the extremes, you will need nothing extraordinary in the line of gear. For shelter, a light tent will do and often just a tarp or poncho—or nothing at all. Cotton garments will do fine, and are even preferred. A sunhat with a neck-protecting "havelock" is essential, as are sunglasses and sunblock cream. Nights may require warm clothes. A light, three-season sleeping bag is fine. Do be prepared for rain (sometimes even for hail or snow).

If you want to hike hot desert country in the summer—as some do—special precautions are required. It is vital that you understand the process of overheating or *hyperthermia* (see Chapter 28) and know how to prevent and counter it. The body can acclimatize to hot conditions, and a summer desert hiker should allow time for this adjustment before beginning a serious trek. Water consumption, of course, must be very high; electrolyte replacement drinks can be helpful. Summer desert hikers often move at morning and evening—even at night—and take a long siesta in the heat of the day. They wear loose, light-colored clothing, not heavy but densely woven enough to block ultraviolet rays. For maximum eye protection, some choose wraparound goggles instead of mere sunglasses. They may also carry canopies to pitch for the midday stop, tent poles to pitch them with (since vegetation may be sparse and low), and thick foam pads to keep their bodies off scalding ground. (Avoid air mattresses in southern deserts full of prickly things like cholla cactus.)

Watch how you park your pack in desert heat. Left harness side up, it will be unpleasantly hot to put back on; harness side down, it may pick up spines. Better stand it up, being careful not to lean it against some thorny thing. To keep water (relatively) cool, carry bottles inside.

Perhaps the most vital piece of "gear" for the desert hiker is the automobile. Out here that vehicle is more than transportation; it is a vital home base. Make certain it has *lots* of water in it, together with food, stove fuel, and first-aid supplies. Desert driving is hard on cars. A little mechanical knowledge and a basic toolkit may serve you better than the fanciest backpack ever made. In remote areas, it is a good idea for even a small group to travel in two vehicles. If you are expecting to drive rough roads, your equipment should include a stout shovel, tire chains, a piece of plywood, and a pump—all aids to getting through sandy spots and other rough areas. Partly deflated tires traverse sand more readily, and of course need reinflation afterward.

Once you're on foot, desert travel is overwhelmingly cross-country, without explicit trails or reassuring signs. Formal trailheads are rare. Navigation, though, tends to be straightforward. Views are long; topography tends to be on a grand and simple scale. Often you are following an unmistakable ridgeline or canyon. Vegetation is seldom so thick that you cannot work your way through it.

But obstacles and confusions do occur: unexpectedly continuous bands of cliffs, thickets of fiercely spined cacti, labyrinthine canyon networks, jungles of streamside growth. Elsewhere you may encounter webs of abandoned, rugged roads, bewildering rather than helpful. A compass and perhaps a Global Positioning System unit come into play if you strike out across a featureless playa, or if you are homing in on a water cache.

You could drown in the desert. Flash floods, unleashed by thunderstorms miles away, can transform dry gulches into rivers. If near a streambed, consider how much land it drains and watch for thunderheads over that watershed. Avoid camping in stream courses, especially in the narrows of a gorge. Never try to cross, either on foot or in a vehicle, a wash that is filling with water. In the Southwest, July and August are the peak of thunderstorm season.

The desert has its rattlesnakes, but no more than the woods. Carry a venom extractor. Arizona and California desert travelers should inform themselves about one highly venomous scorpion, *Centuroides sculpturatus*. See Chapter 29.

Walking Softly in the Desert

Easily scarred, slow to repair themselves, America's desert lands are taking a beating. Desert hikers are not contributing much of the damage. It stems much more from overgrazing, from uncontrolled prospecting, from off-road vehicle use and proliferating roads. The conscientious hiker, though, will want to use care here as elsewhere. All the familiar low-impact principles apply, and a few extra ones besides.

You might think the desert soil invulnerable to any disturbance as tiny as a hiker's footfall; actually, it may be uniquely sensitive. In many areas, the ground is covered with a blackish coating of algae, fibrous cyanobacteria, mosses, and other tiny plants, together making up what is called *cryptobiotic* or *cryptogamic crust*. Undisturbed, this crust absorbs rainfall, limits erosion, enriches the soil, and encourages the growth of taller plants. Once broken, it is terribly slow to heal. Go to great lengths to avoid trampling cryptogamic surfaces. Walk as much as possible in washes or over areas naturally paved with embedded stones. If you must cross crusty soils, go single file; in this case a single footfall is as destructive as ten. At roadheads, avoid crushing the crust, or indeed any surface not already damaged, with a tire track.

Another key point: don't compete with wildlife for limited water. If you draw from an isolated waterhole or a short section of a perennial stream, don't then camp beside the source, but move a good distance away, say, ½ mile or more. This is crucial in desert mountains where bighorn sheep are struggling to maintain themselves. Leave watering spots before dusk, when the desert animal world comes most alive.

In desert wilderness, as at timberline, fires have no place. You won't find much burnable material anyway; what you do find belongs on the land. You might bring wood to the roadhead, though, and have a pre-trip fire in a pan or existing ring. Some people burn their toilet paper to speed decomposition, but fires have been set that way and the practice is now discouraged. Instead, pack out TP. Depending on the popularity of the area, feces may be buried or left on the surface for rapid degradation by ultraviolet light.

Historical or prehistoric artifacts you find in the desert must be left alone. Yes, this applies to arrowheads and chips! If simple respect is not an adequate reason, consider that all such objects, simply by being where they are and arranged as they are, communicate information. Rather few sites have been properly studied, and amateur pothunters are the bane of archaeologists. If you stumble on something attractive that seems likely to be scavenged by someone else, leave it alone but report its location to the authorities. Such cautions apply to all wilderness, but it's in the southwestern deserts that one's conscience is most likely to be tested.

If you encounter range fences across your route, don't climb the strands (which may break), but part them and slide between. If you go through a gate, leave it as you found it—open if it was open, closed if it was closed. Such courtesies lessen friction between hikers and the ranchers who utilize vast tracts of publicly owned arid land.

Wet-Canyon Hiking

Overlapping true desert backpacking is the sport of canyon travel. This can be a very dry business or a very wet business, depending on the canyon.

In a dry-canyon system, the major obstacles are likely to be dry waterfalls. Topographical maps may not reveal all steep drops. If you hike a canyon not known to be easily passable, take a rope and appurtenances for setting anchors, and know how to use these tools. In traveling multibranched canyons, keep track of the choices you make at each junction.

Many larger canyons of the Southwest have perennial streams in them. You walk beside water and ford it so frequently that your feet are always wet. Leather boots are no good for such travel; you want sneakers or cloth boots with drain holes that let water as readily out as in. Sport sandals work well if you're not rock scrambling or carrying too much of a load. It may be necessary to swim across pools, floating your pack on an air mattress. If you do a lot of this, you may turn to an inner tube, an inflatable miniature boat, or a drybag (a waterproof pouch with a rolled-over closure at the top).

In some wet desert canyons you may encounter quicksand, created where springs well up through fine sediments. Contrary to its reputation, quicksand does not suck you down; think of it as a kind of heavy water. You can swim the morass if there's no other way to cross.

Flash floods are a more serious danger. Just as in hiking a normally streamless canyon, consider what may be happening in the watershed and keep an eye out for escape routes. The stream may warn you by turning muddy and rising slightly in advance of the main surge.

Most challenging is travel in very narrow, very rugged "slot canyons" containing vigorous streams, high waterfalls, plunge pools, logjams, and boulders wedged between walls. Traversing such a slot may involve ropes, rappels, wetsuits, and all manner of special equipment. There is a sport of "canyoneering," combining elements of climbing, kayaking, and spelunking and requiring similar knowledge and preparation.

Coastline Hiking

Another unusual environment for backpacking—one that can be desertlike, at times—is the beach. On the Atlantic and Gulf coasts of the United States, hikers can walk for days along low barrier islands with the ocean on one side and protected bays or sounds on the other; in more rugged regions, beaches alternate with stony promontories.

Beach walking has its peculiarities. Typically, you'll choose to walk next to the waves, where the sand is wet and firm. Sneakers or running shoes are normal footwear. Water may be a problem; on an Atlantic barrier island, for instance, you may have to carry or cache your supply like a desert traveler. (In some areas you can find fresh water by digging in a pocket between dunes, well back from the beachfront.) For cooking, washing, and brushing your teeth, brine can be used. Salt on your skin and sand in all your gear will simply have to be put up with. Lack of shade makes summer an unpleasant hiking season on southern coasts; autumn may be ideal. In many regions, fall is also the best time of year to catch the spectacle of migratory birds.

In coastal walking, especially on rugged shores, a tide table and a watch are essential tools. If a coastwise route is punctuated by rocky points, the tides may control when you travel: although some headlands can be clambered over, some can only be rounded at low water. Be sure to check if the local land agency offers maps with route indications for the coastal traveler.

Ordinarily, the beach walker camps above high-tide line, as indicated by sandmarks and debris. But any fires should be built lower down, where the next tidal cycle will remove the traces. Managing agencies rarely object to fires so sited (inquire, of course), and you can count on driftwood for fuel. On coasts where grizzly bears roam, the whole camp should be in the intertidal zone so that odors are washed away.

A tent on a beach needs to be very well pitched, and that can be tricky. Skinny stakes won't hold. Snow stakes, broader in section, may work; or you can anchor with "deadmen," stakes or other objects buried crosswise in the sand. Stuff sacks, filled with sand and buried, also serve. Driftwood, too, may offer solid anchors. Salt air, by the way, is hard on metal tent poles, which must be rinsed and wiped down when you return home.

On a really wild shore, the disposal of human waste takes an unusual form. It is sometimes actually better to throw excrement into the sea, tossing it perhaps on a flake of rock, than to bury it in the sand. Choose a time when the tide is going out and lob your missile out as far out as possible.

Hiking on a little-visited coastline, you can live off the land, if you choose, to an unusual degree. Besides fish, there are all those shellfish, like mussels, crabs, and clams. Tide pools, of course, are for admiration only: you won't collect or even touch the living things within them.

On some beaches at some times of year, birds that nest on the sand may be vulnerable to disturbance. One such is the snowy plover, found on the Gulf of Mexico coast and on Pacific Ocean shores; it nests from April through September. Avoid disturbing the line of debris that marks the highest recent tide: it may contain plover nests. If you notice a small shorebird circling nervously, calling obsessively, or feigning injury, it probably has eggs nearby. Move on.

24

The Winter Wilderness

In snow the wilderness grows and is wilder.

Except in the South, in the deserts, and in the coastal West, most of our wild country is snowed in during winter. The new white surface covers scars, smoothes old mistakes, shelters fragile ground. It covers the trampled campgrounds, the beaten trails of summer. Most of all, it closes roads. Goals that were an hour away by summer trails become the reward of a three days' march.

Once the snowy hills were pretty much unpopulated. Even now, winter is, by comparison, the empty, spacious season. But the winter wilderness today is tracked by travelers out for a day, a weekend, or a week, and moving with the extra vigor that seems natural in cold places.

Some shuffle along on snowshoes; some slide along on skis. Some are climbers heading for remote winter summits. Some are downhill skiers weary of busy commercial slopes, come to labor up steep peaks for the long swoop down. Some are simply backpackers, moving, camping, enjoying, dealing with the white, crisp world. But these travelers have in common a shared problem and a fairly similar set of solutions to it.

The problem: How do you stay comfortable and safe in the beautiful, strange, and unforgiving country of the cold?

Getting into Winter

Winter is another planet. So different are its rules, so special its demands, that it would take a separate book to deal with them thoroughly—as several good books do.

On a typical winter trip you will be cozily warm while you travel, and cozily warm once you're lying in your sleeping bag, drinking soup. But the times in between are rarely perfectly comfortable. Fingers get cold and disobedient. Bare metal can be so frigid that it stings and sticks to flesh. Flashlights balk, cameras jam, water freezes solid in canteens. Everything you do takes longer—and there is more to do: more gear to deal with, more fixing, more finding, more figuring, more rigging to be gotten through. To add to it all, there may be less daylight to work with.

Then why camp in the snow? Because the world of the snow is endlessly, cleanly beautiful. Because the land is emptier, ornerier, wilder. Because you have, more than in any summer travel, the sense of being on a frontier.

It's a real jump, the move into winter camping— almost like learning to backpack all over again. Most people will want to break into it gradually, starting with day trips, and then short overnight jaunts not far from the road. Test all your gear where retreat is easy. If you need a heavier sleeping bag, if your summer stove is going to balk in the cold, you want to know about it before you're committed. It helps to travel, the first few times, with more experienced companions. Outings clubs offer very valuable courses.

For something about the medical problems that can overtake hikers in cold conditions, see Chapter 28.

Winter Gear

In winter the pack list grows. The obvious new require-ment is a pair of skis or snowshoes and compatible footwear; for the options, see "Snowshoes and Snow-shoe Boots" and "Ski Boots, Bindings, and Poles" below.

Winter clothing starts with long johns, wool or synthetic. Many people use long johns as basic trousers, with a pair of shorts on top for modesty; heavier tights, with outerwear features like pockets, are also worn. Looser specialty pants are also seen, some with elastic "powder cuffs" that fit snugly over the boot and eliminate the need for gaiters. Then come the outer layers, insulation and shell. For extreme conditions there are "bibs," shell pants that rise well up the torso and hang from the shoulders with suspender-like straps; worn with a parka, these give a degree of protection you can only exceed by going to a one-piece coverall.

Some combination of gloves, mittens, and shells goes on your hands. For instance, an insulated glove or mitten with a wind-stop layer can be worn over a very light inner glove.

You must have a balaclava, a knit cap that pulls down over the neck, leaving a gap for the face. For colder and windier places, you may need a cap with a built-in facemask to prevent facial frostbite. For warmer days in bright sun, an ordinary broad-brimmed hat is also essential.

You must have dark glasses or goggles—two pairs, in fact, in case the first goes missing. For the fierce, bright lands above timberline, you need glasses with opaque barriers at the sides of the eyes. Though glass lenses block ultraviolet light most completely, plastic lenses will do for altitudes to 14,000 feet. Sunglasses suitable for winter run from $40 to over $100.

Internal-frame backpacks are almost universally used in winter. A snowshoe traveler, however, might get by with an external frame. Make sure you can fit all your gear into the pack, or onto it, tied to the outside. If zipper tabs don't already have pull-loops of cord attached, add some; these make it easier to work stubborn zippers with cold hands or in mittens.

True winter sleeping bags are inevitably heavier than summer types. A bag with 7 or 8 inches of loft, in a mummy style, takes most sleepers down to about 0 degrees Fahrenheit in comfort. "Three-season" bags, a little lighter, can be made to serve, especially within the protection of a tent. If the insulation is waterfowl down, a waterproof breathable shell will keep it dry; a separate bivouac sack is a second choice. You also need more ground insulation: typically, a thick self-inflating air mattress, or two, or one such supplemented by a sheet of closed-cell foam.

For shelter you'll need a tent that can carry heavy snow weights and stand up in strong winds. Where snow is deep, you can build your own shelter—igloo, snow trench, or cave. You'll need a folding snow shovel ($40 or more) for this work; some igloo builders also carry light snow saws (another $20 at least). You also don't want to be without a shovel in avalanche terrain (see "Avalanche," below).

Doesn't all this add up to a heavier load in your pack? You bet it does. It is difficult, in winter, to trim your pack weight much below 40 pounds on an overnight trip. Winter mountaineers, adding ropes and other paraphernalia, seldom carry less than 60 pounds. This is a price you pay.

On flat or rolling terrain, there's an elegant way of handling all that extra stuff: you can haul it behind you on a sled. Many people make their own rigs with a narrow child's sled, about 30 feet of tough cord (5-millimeter nylon), several miniature carabiners, and a couple of 4- to 6-foot pieces of thin PVC pipe. The rope, a continuous loop, is attached to two points at the front of the sled and to either side of your pack's hipbelt. In between, it passes through the rigid pipe segments, which prevent the sled from running into you from behind. Commercially available sleds with these features cost about $400. Some can be adapted to carry children.

In packing a sled, heavy items should be placed low and toward the back. It's also important that the sled fit within your ski or snowshoe track. If it's too wide (or your stance too narrow), the load will ride up one edge or the other and tip over.

Snowshoes and Snowshoe Boots

For the person just getting into winter backpacking, the snowshoe is the simplest tool of travel. Wearing snowshoes, you walk much as you would on bare

Snowshoes are slow vehicles but easy to maneuver and just about maintenance free. If you are carrying camping gear, especially on soft snow, you need a shoe as much as a yard long. Built-in crampons found on some models are helpful on hills.

ground without them. At first you will step on yourself a few times and take some comical falls, but the skill teaches itself. Snowshoes suitable for backpacking cost $150 to $350.

Though some snowshoers switch to skis after a time, many retain the webs as their primary tool. It depends partly on personal taste and partly on the kind of country to be traveled. In lands that are largely flat and rolling, or steep but not densely forested, nothing moves like a pair of skis. Yet in rugged, timbered mountains such as the northern Appalachians or California's Siskiyous, snowshoes, being more maneuverable, may actually serve you better.

The classic snowshoe was a piece of basketwork: rawhide stretched across a framework of blond ashwood. It was possibly the most exquisite object used in wilderness camping. Its main function today, however, is to decorate mantelpieces.

The typical modern snowshoe has instead a metal frame and a mostly solid deck of neoprene, copolymer resin, or other tough synthetic material. A vast range of traditional shapes has resolved itself into the style known as the Western. Shoes of this type are rather long and narrow, 8 to 10 inches wide and from 2 feet long to a shade over 3 feet. Both front and back are rounded, and the leading edge has a moderate upward bend. A *binding* encases your booted foot. Your heel rests on a stout *hinge rod*; your toe dips into the snow through an opening in the deck.

The backpacker's snowshoes need to be at least 30 inches long and a shade wider than most. Toting a load and sometimes traversing untracked snow, you want big platforms to spread your weight and keep you from sinking in. If you are heavy to begin with, buy the most generous shoes you can find.

Toe styles vary somewhat. For flattish terrain and fairly firm snow, a fairly flat prow—one that curves up just slightly—will suffice; it is also good for kicking steps in crusty snow. On powder snow, such a toe will bury itself and trip you; you need instead a moderate upturn—say, 3 or 4 inches.

Some shoes are built to drag their tails on the snow; others get lifted off the surface with each step. The former is better in powder, where you're likely to acquire a load of snow on the deck behind your foot; the latter is better on packed trails. "Dual rotation" systems have it both ways: ordinarily the shoe lifts as a unit, but if snow has piled up behind, the weight overrides an internal spring and the tail drags, saving you pointless labor.

Bindings typically come with the shoe but may also be purchased separately. They usually incorporate *snowshoe crampons*, toothed or knifelike projections mounted below the foot, to help in climbing steep or icy hills. You

Very warm and waterproof boots with rubber lower sections and tall leather uppers are variously known as shoepacs, mouse boots, or Maine hunting shoes.

can also get bindings that release at a touch and bindings with insulation that double as foot warmers.

On snowshoes you need at least a third leg for balance. One or two ski poles, or trekking poles with large baskets, will do in most terrain. If you expect to cross steep, icy snow on snowshoes, you may want to carry a long-shafted ice ax as well, and switch from pole to ax when an exposed traverse begins.

The traditional snowshoe boot is simply a heavy hiking or light mountaineering boot, built of plastic or top-grain leather, weighing 4 pounds or more per pair. Somewhat lighter winter boots are now being made that incorporate high-tech insulating and waterproof breathable layers. *Much* lighter boots—even running shoes—can be worn inside an insulated *overboot* or *mukluk*. Then there are the high rubber boots known as *shoepacs, mouse boots,* or *Maine hunting shoes*. These cover most of the foot with a single piece of vulcanized rubber; the rest of the upper—ankle and calf—is leather; the interior is lined with foam or felt. L.L. Bean and Sorel make familiar versions. Cost of either overboots or shoepacs is near $100.

There are several ways to increase the warmth of any boot that you fear may be chilly. If it doesn't spoil the fit, you can add inner soles or extra socks—but don't overdo it (overstuffing risks frostbite by cutting off the flow of blood to your feet). Dry socks are important; take spares.

Then there's the vapor barrier trick, which can be done with a plastic bag or a special nylon liner. The impermeable layer, pulled on over a thin inner sock, blocks the evaporation of sweat and keeps the foot noticeably warmer. A second plastic bag, placed outside the main sock layer, can be further protection if you're working with an imperfectly waterproof boot. A more expensive solution for the chronically cold-footed is the waterproof breathable sock ($40–$50 a pair).

Some cold-footed people have recourse to chemical warmers, little packets that deliver heat when you break an internal seal and cause two substances to mix; placed in a boot (or glove), they can produce a lasting glow. These gimmicks can certainly be helpful to someone who has to sit inactive in the cold, and they might have a place in an emergency kit. They're no substitute, however, for the real winter furnace, your body's own metabolism.

To keep snow out of your boots, you wear tall, spat-like *gaiters*, usually of waterproof breathable fabric. Greater protection comes from *supergaiters*, which cover the entire boot and cling to the edge of the sole with elastic rims called rands. These coverings cost $50–$100.

Skis

Unlike the beginning snowshoer, the novice backpack skier definitely has some learning to do. The learning process starts with the subtle task of picking the right gear, and goes on to mastery of various strides, turns, and ancillary techniques. It's an excellent idea to rent several ski packages (skis, bindings, boots, and poles) before plunking down the $500 to $1,200 your kit will end up costing you.

You won't find a rack of skis in the gear store identified as for the backpacking skier. Most people buying skis will be going out on day trips only, and product descriptions are geared to this majority. Generally, you'll see *track* or *skating* skis, intended for fast work on groomed surfaces; *touring* skis, designed for movement across country in moderate terrain; and *telemark* skis, which are built for ski mountaineering, including steep, alpine-style descents. The backpacker will be looking within the last two categories.

At this point in ski evolution, two quite different formats coexist. "Skinny" skis, the norm of decades, are narrow, parallel sided, and long—traditionally somewhat longer than the user is tall. "Fat" skis, now prevailing, are shorter than your height and wide, up to 115 centimeters at the tip, but narrowing to a wasp waist under the foot. They look as if someone had given them a good squeeze and forced ski stuff from the middle into tip and tail. This pronounced "sidecut" makes them easier to maneuver on downhill runs. For the beginning skier, or for someone making the transition from resort skiing, they are easier to handle.

Skis are not just flat boards. Rather, they bow upward from the snow, resisting the skier's weight. Put a pair together, base to base, and you'll see daylight—the camber—between. Some curve decidedly and can be flattened only with difficulty; others are fairly limp and can be pressed together easily. Stiff, high-cambered skis glide better, perform better on icy or windblown surfaces, and generally reward skill. Softer skis are more controllable, especially in fluffy snow. The trend today is toward soft.

Skis suitable for backpacking have metal strips running down each margin of the ski. *Edges* assist greatly in crossing icy slopes, in making turns on downhill runs, and in keeping control while laden with a pack.

There's one more big choice to make in the ski department: the one between waxable and "waxless" skis.

In skiing cross-country on the flat, you fall into a steady, gliding gait called the "diagonal stride," which looks (and sometimes feels) practically effortless. For this technique to work, your skis must grip the snow at certain moments and glide freely forward at others. This magic can be worked in different ways.

Traditional cross-country skis have a smooth plastic undersurface or base. On the trail, you coat this surface with one or more layers of cunningly formulated waxes. When the ski is stationary, snow crystals press into this coating and grip the ski. When you push forward, the projecting granules melt and let the ski glide. When the stride is finished, the surface refreezes and the bond is restored, giving you a firm base for the next forward push.

One wax won't serve for all temperatures and types of snow. The classic wax kit included a dozen or more grades suiting the most varied conditions. To some people, the skill of choosing and applying the right waxes is at the center of the skiing experience. For most, it seems an awful lot of work.

That's where the popular "waxless" skis come in. Their bases have been impressed with tiny steps or other one-way patterns that permit the forward slide but catch in the snow whenever motion is backward. These skis don't move as fast or climb quite as well as perfectly waxed conventional models, but they certainly do move. The textured bases can make a clattering sound, a drawback in some ears. Despite the name, waxless skis do benefit from a little waxing: a slick wax, applied to tips and tails, helps them to glide; and if you're pushing their limits up a hill, a grip wax, applied to the zone beneath the foot, helps them to stick. Waxes for "no-wax" skis are differently formulated than those for conventional models.

Waxed or waxless, there are limits to the slope a ski can attack directly. After that, you have to zig and zag. Even on the flat, you may have trouble getting enough grip for the forward stride when you are first in line, slogging into deep snow, with a pack on your back. At that point, you pull out your skins.

Climbing skins are strips of fabric covered with stiff artificial hairs. To use them, you hook one end (equipped with a loop or ring) over the toe of each ski;

the rest of the skin is held to the ski with a layer of strong, temporary adhesive. The bristles of the skin point backward and resist any retrograde slide. With skins, you can shuffle right up a pretty severe slope. Skins cost something over $100.

Ski Boots, Bindings, and Poles

When you buy your first pair of skis, you'll buy compatible boots and bindings at the same time. In fact, it is common advice to start with a boot you like, let it dictate the binding, and finally settle on the ski on which the binding will be mounted.

The traditional binding for backcountry ski use is the three-pin type originated by Rottefella. The mechanism, purchased separately and mounted by the shop, consists of three short pegs, a toe clamp, and a ridged heelplate. The corresponding boot has three small pits in the sole under the toe, matching the pegs. To get into the binding, you press the square toe of the boot into position, fit pegs to holes, and close down a securing clamp (called a bail). It takes just a moment to step into such a binding (unless ice has built up in the holes). The heel of the boot rises freely, as it must for effective skiing on level or rising ground; the boot flexes behind the toe. All bindings and boots of this type are built to a width of 75 millimeters, known as the Nordic Norm.

The second major option, which provides more downhill control and is gaining converts today, is the cable binding. From the toe clamp at the front, stout cables run around the heel of the boot. Even Nordic Norm boots usually come with a grooved heel to accommodate a cable if desired. Combination bindings, pin and cable, are also made. Other boot-binding combinations exist. The one of possible interest to the backpacker at this point is the New Nordic Norm Backcountry (NNN-BC). Despite its name, this system is quite unrelated to the old three-pin setup: both binding and boot are different, and the binding, not the boot, does the flexing.

The cable ski binding (top) provides superior control and is growing more popular. The three-pin ski binding (center) serves best on moderate terrain. The New Nordic Norm Backcountry binding (bottom) requires matching boots.

Backcountry ski boots are robust and high-topped. Especially for use with "fat" skis, plastic boots now predominate; these look rather like downhill boots but have the necessary flexibility for cross-country use. "Skinny" ski enthusiasts may still prefer leather.

Of course you need *ski poles*. The best are aluminum, though fiberglass is also seen. The proper length is up to your armpit. (The ski poles you'd use at a downhill resort are too short to serve.) Backcountry

Top, plastic boot designed to accept a cable binding. Center, classic leather boot with 75-millimeter (Nordic Norm) toe. Bottom, the New Nordic Norm Backcountry boot, used with a unique binding.

poles may adjust to different lengths—a feature some people like and some don't—and they may also allow you to remove the baskets and screw the shafts together to create a long avalanche rescue probe. As a backpacker, you need pretty large baskets for soft snow.

Taken together, skis and the required accessories add up to a pretty pricey list. The naked skis run $130 to $450 in the types backpackers are most likely to use, with "fat" skis fetching the higher prices. Three-pin or cable or pin-plus-cable bindings cost $40 to $160, and boots, at $190 and up, might set you back more than the skis. Aluminum poles cost $70 to $140. Add something more for a wax kit and quite a bit more for skins. All in all, you'll be lucky to hit the snowy trail for less than $700, and it wouldn't be hard to double that. Special package deals, frequently offered in stores, may save you a few dollars; end-of-season sales in the late winter will save you a bundle.

While modern snowshoes are close to maintenance-free, the skier's repair kit includes a few extra items. A pair of pliers and an adjustable wrench are standard. If you use cable bindings, carry a spare cable; if you use three-pin, carry a spare bail. In case a binding pulls out, you need the appropriate screws and screwdriver (usually #3 Pozi), epoxy glue, and something to plug the holes with before reuse (steel wool or some form of wood). A spare ski pole basket will come in handy someday. A broken pole shaft can be fixed with a stiff wrapping material—a bit of sheet metal or a half-section of plastic pipe—bound on with duct tape. If you use skins, you'll want to have the specified glue and some stout wire in case the loop up front needs replacing.

Leather ski boots need fanatical waterproofing and seam sealing, especially around the welt and at the toe, where bindings may rub. Classic three-pin ski boot soles sometimes crack beside the pin hole, making the binding useless; if this happens in the field, your best bet is to improvise a cable binding with wire, cord, or an elastic band, and head for home (and a cobbler).

Skis take some home maintenance. Edges need sharpening, which you can do; bases need resurfacing from time to time, which most people delegate to the shop.

Travel in the Snow

How fast will you move over snow? One mile an hour is a good pace on snowshoes in open country; 3 miles an hour is excellent progress on skis. Often you will do much less. A 10-mile day on snowshoes, when you carry a pack, is an extremely long one, as is a 20-mile skiing day. In some situations, skis may be no faster than snowshoes. It's on layover days, when you're daytripping out of an established camp, that they shine.

Take into account how much, or little, daylight you have to work with. At the winter solstice near the United States–Canada border, the day lasts less than 9 hours. If you allow 2 hours after dawn for breaking camp and 1 hour, at dusk, for getting settled in, that leaves only 5 or 6 hours for travel. Farther north, the days are shorter still; at the Arctic Circle in midwinter, the sun does not rise at all. On the other hand, much snow travel is done in the spring, when daylight hours make up more than half the day; again, the effect grows stronger to the north.

The first problem of snow travel is keeping warm (but not hot) and, as far as possible, dry. Clothing adjustments will keep the balance of heat production and heat loss. Allow all the ventilation you can. If there's snow in the air, you need to be wearing smooth-surfaced fabrics from which the flakes will slide; brush them off when they accumulate. Knock snow from low branches *before* you pass under them.

The thermometer doesn't tell you everything about cold. What chills you is the loss of heat from the skin (as well as from the lungs), and warmer air that is moving will remove heat as quickly as colder air that is still. If you are wet, evaporation in the wind will still further accelerate chilling. Humid air, too, is effectively colder than dry air. If your body keeps on losing more heat than it can make, you will enter the dangerous and even deadly condition called *hypothermia*, described at length in Chapter 28.

Nibble starchy or sugary foods as you walk, and drink plenty of water. If it's cold enough that water freezes during the day, insulate the containers. For instance, you can pull a thick wool sock over a bottle. Fitted foam sleeves are also available. Pack canteens upside down, so that plugs of ice won't form in the necks. Mixtures like lemonade stay liquid longer than straight water.

A constant minor frustration in winter is the way your sunglasses keep fogging up. Antifog solutions are available, and they help a bit (by causing moisture to form drops and slip downward). Ventilation helps, but will be limited in glasses with side barriers. Double glasses are effective (but expensive). Wearers of prescription lenses may carry contacts instead, but this choice leads to other miseries. (Ever try to find a dropped contact lens in a world of sparkling snow?) This is one of those problems for which there is currently just no good solution.

In some areas, you'll follow trails in winter as in summer. Abandoned roads make good travel corridors in rugged country. Most of the time, though, navigation is cross-country, with the snow the whole new country that you cross.

Winter weather can make it hard to keep track of your position. Your views of distant landmarks will almost certainly disappear in any overcast. Under some conditions the outlook shrinks to yards. Sooner or later you'll encounter one of those opaque snowy ground mists called *whiteouts*. You can lose all sense of place and direction. Here as nowhere else the compass becomes your lifeline. You need to know, not only how to walk a compass course, but also how to plan a whole trek as a succession of compass lines, or *headings*, as they are called—so many paces on heading A, so many paces on heading B. This is the situation where a Global Positioning System receiver can really come into its own. See Chapters 16 and 22.

Your detailed route over snow depends largely on the skis or snowshoes you are wearing. Skis and snowshoes, and different models of each, handle differently; some are more able, some less able, to cross icy slopes, to float in deep, soft powder, or to climb steep hills.

Often the snowshoers in a mixed party will head directly up a soft slope while skiers will circle around, or climb in a series of switchbacks.

There are certain hazards in traveling on snow. Tree trunks, warmer than the surrounding snow, melt "tree wells" around themselves, embarrassing to fall into. More serious is the risk in crossing snow bridges over flowing streams: a collapse can dump a backpacker into bitterly cold, rushing water. Look for the thickest bridge you can find, and cross one at a time; the leader should probe ahead with a ski pole or ice ax. Very fresh, very light, very deep snow can also be dangerous: people have actually suffocated in it.

Avalanche

Here is the terror of the winter wilderness. About twenty-five people a year die in avalanches in the United States alone. There is a whole science of avalanche safety, and every winter traveler should know at least the rudiments.

Avalanches, or snowslides, are of several kinds. The most dangerous is the *slab avalanche,* the great mass of snow that breaks, all at once, from a mountainside and plunges into the valley. Slab avalanches are likeliest during, and just after, heavy winter storms. The more new snow that comes down in a storm—and the faster it comes down—the greater the risk. It's cause for concern if more than a foot is added, especially if it piles up at the moderate rate of an inch an hour, or more. High wind adds to the danger. Remember that it may be snowing and blowing much harder up the ridge you must cross tomorrow than it is at tonight's campsite in the valley. Rising temperatures during a storm should also make you worry, for they mean that heavier, wetter snow is being dumped on top of lighter.

Once snow has fallen, it immediately begins to change and consolidate, generally growing much more stable. If it's not too cold, this will happen quite rapidly, and the risk of massive slides may vanish within

In wet snow, the top layer can peel off and roll itself up in a cylinder, called a sunball; large sunballs suggest the risk of a wet-snow avalanche.

hours. In very frigid weather, however, the snow changes slowly, and danger can last for many days or even weeks; north of the U.S.-Canadian border, it can last all winter. Watch for tiny "sloughs," harmless slides of loose, powdery snow; they indicate that the snow is settling nicely.

Slab avalanches can also form without fresh snow if it's cold and windy enough. Winds over 25 miles an hour can build up dangerous hard drifts on the lee sides of ridges. These "hard-slab" avalanches of wind-packed snow are especially important as a danger in clear but windy periods following storms.

How prone a given slope is to sliding depends largely on the history of that year's snowpack. Thaws followed by freezes, to take a simple example, will create icy layers within the pack, on which later-deposited snow is prone to slide. The matter gets complex and subtle. In avalanche safety classes, you're taught to dig pits, analyze the strata, and test snow stability. For an inveterate winter traveler, such training is a very good investment.

Up to a certain point, warm temperatures mean less risk. There is, however, such a thing as a *wet-snow avalanche*. Such snowslides occur in warm conditions or late in the season, when snow becomes waterlogged and loses its grip on the surface below. They are especially prevalent in the mountains of the Pacific coast and as far inland as the Tetons of Wyoming. Watch for "sunballs," curious wheels of snow that run down the

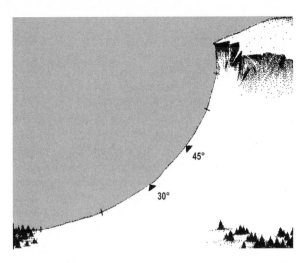

Avalanches are most likely on slopes of moderate steepness, between 30 and 45 degrees, as indicated by the small triangles and labels.

slope, rolling up the surface layer of the snowpack in a sort of scroll. Small sunballs don't signify much, but very large ones, several feet thick, suggest danger.

Before you head into the wilderness, inquire about current avalanche conditions. In some U.S. states there are avalanche information Web sites to visit or numbers to call, often at the Forest Service; the National Ski Patrol will certainly have information. The land agency office nearest your destination should know about local conditions. A national avalanche information Web site (www.avalanche.org) is an excellent place to start.

Whatever the type of avalanche, the danger is greatest on treeless slopes of middle steepness, between about 30 and 45 degrees. Gullies and open swaths in forested landscapes are especially risky. Dense timber provides some reassurance, but a few trees on an open slope don't prove a lack of avalanches there. Avoid the lee sides of steep high ridges. Keep out from under cornices, the solid waves of snow and ice that hang over the crests of windy ridges like paralyzed ocean breakers.

If an indicated avalanche path lies across your course, it's best simply to go around it. The safest course is to circle it on safe ground at the top; the second best, often more practical, is to bypass the swath on gentler terrain at the bottom.

If you find no way around an ominous path, try to judge the risk. Is it "avalanche weather"—has it been snowing or blowing a lot? Consider also what might happen if you were caught in a slide. A short avalanche path that widens at the bottom is not quite as bad as a long chute that funnels in. Are there rocks and trees at the base of the slope against which you would be crushed, or a cliff over which you would be carried? In some cases, by far the best choice is to turn back.

In crossing, move one at a time. Every member of the party should watch the crosser carefully; the last to go is in no less danger than the first. If you have a rope, by all means provide a belay. If the risk zone is wide, take advantage of any natural safety islands like clumps of trees and patches of bare rock.

If you do trigger an avalanche, things will happen terribly fast. On skis, you may just possibly be able to glide out to safety. If you're sucked in, survivors report, it's a little like being caught in a flash flood, but a flood at the same time fluid and solid. Don't just go along for the ride, but fight it. Immediately shed your skis and poles (there's not much you can do about snowshoes). Make the motions of a swimmer; try to keep on the surface of the tumbling snow, and to work over to one "bank" of the flow; grab onto vegetation. If you see the unmoving snow surface that underlies the avalanche, claw at that. If in spite of all this you feel yourself going under, cover your face with your arms to preserve a cavity of air. When you stop moving, make an attempt to widen that space in the moment before the snow hardens around you. There's no point in shouting; sound carries very poorly out of snow. If you can't dig, there's really nothing to be done but discipline yourself to calmness, and wait.

If you, the person spared, see a companion carried off in an avalanche, watch the process carefully. Your friend may appear and disappear several times. Note the last-seen point with reference to local landmarks. Then follow these steps:

1. Mark the point where you last saw the victim. Make a quick search down the apparent main line of the avalanche. Mark the location of any pieces of gear you find. Look carefully behind trees, on ledges and benches, and wherever any obstacle might have slowed or diverted the rushing snow.

2. Next comes the careful search. Probe systematically with skis, ski poles, ice axes, or avalanche probes assembled from ski poles. Reexamine the likely "traps" where the victim might have been stopped; then spread out to cover the whole surface of the avalanche.

3. When you find the victim, you may have to give artificial respiration. Get snow out of clothing and place the victim in a sleeping bag, head downhill. Treat, as needed, for trauma, shock, and hypothermia (see Chapters 26 and 28).

Should you summon help before finding the victim? If you have a cell phone, by all means use it now. But don't send a messenger. Unless you're right next to a ski resort, every member of your party should stay and search. Half of all buried avalanche victims die within 30 minutes. Keep looking for 6 to 8 hours: although very few victims last beyond the second hour, there have been astonishing exceptions.

In an attempt to improve the odds, many people now travel with special short-range radios called *avalanche rescue transceivers*. Every member of a party carries one. In a hazard zone, all units are turned on, set to "transmit." If there is an avalanche and someone is buried, the remaining members of the party switch their radio units to "receive" and zero in on the signal from the buried companion unit. Transceivers cost about $250–$300 and weigh 6 to 9 ounces. Current models, unlike earlier ones, are very easy to use.

Camping in the Snow

Camping in the snow is not nearly as uncomfortable as it sounds. While your comfort depends partly on things you can't control (like the weather), mostly it depends on your gear, your skills, and your common sense.

In some areas you can simplify camping by hiking in to established shelters. It's unwise, though, to count on finding the less elaborate shelters free of snow, and those that are open will sometimes be crowded. Even if your destination is a hut, you need to bring your own provision for shelter.

You generally have a wide choice of campsites in winter. The distinction between established and pristine sites disappears: you don't have to worry about trampling when the vulnerable earth is yards beneath your feet. It is polite, though, not to set up your tent right beside a route down which other travelers are likely to come.

If you don't find a level place, you can make one. The winter camp, of course, *can* be engineered without harm. Build a whole city, if you like—it will last, at latest, to the thaw. Make sure that you are out from under dead limbs and standing snags and, of course, away from avalanche paths.

One consideration is the availability of liquid water: not a necessity, if you have adequate fuel, but a luxury. You can lower water bottles to a stream rushing in a trench of snow, or maybe carve steps down to waterline. If you dig a deep-enough well, you can also get water from under the ice of any sizable lake. If you would treat this water in summer, treat it in winter too. Filters tend to freeze up, so boiling and chemical methods are more practical in the winter. Water melted from clean snow, however, can be drunk straight.

The first camp job is to pitch your tent. Without taking off skis or snowshoes, stamp out a level site. (If time permits, let the snow set for half an hour before proceeding; the platform will be less likely to get "postholed" by boots and knees.) To anchor guylines in snow, you need special, broad, aluminum *snow stakes*;

or you can use "deadmen," bits of wood or other small objects stamped into the snow and buried. Stakes and deadmen will quickly freeze into place, and you may have to dig or chop to free them when the tent comes down. Once the tent is up, you can unpack your sleeping bag and pad and let them fluff up inside.

Weather permitting, you may want to cook and eat outside before going in for the night. You can excavate a luxurious kitchen in the snow. Start with a natural depression, like a tree well. Straighten the vertical wall, and then dig out a waist-high "counter" for your stove and cooking gear.

Winter cooking can be something of a struggle. Stoves that worked beautifully last August may require multiple primings now. Propane/butane cartridges may have to be warmed to function. Even liquid fuels may give trouble in deep cold: frozen impurities can gum up stove passageways. Put insulation under fuel tanks. Be careful in handling fuel; besides being flammable, it can freeze the skin when spilled.

Winter dinners tend to be simple. The standard is the meaty one-pot meal, with hot drinks, possibly soup, and cold snacks on the side. If water must be melted, cooking only starts your evening in the kitchen: you may be at it for hours. Don't drink up the last of your old supply before you begin the melting process: you need a half cup or so to moisten the bottom of the pot. As you melt, keep drinking; have more tea, more fruit juice, more chocolate. If you wake up with a violent thirst toward morning, it's a likely sign that you've been shorting yourself. You need at least a full gallon of water, in food and drink, each day.

When conditions are less pleasant, hikers cook and eat inside, setting up the stove in the vestibule just outside the tent door. In truly awful weather, you may be forced to cook entirely inside, an intrinsically hazardous business. Watch out for any flare-up when you prime a white-gas stove. A pot with a bail can be suspended from a tab in the ceiling to minimize spills. Keep ventilation generous, to dissipate combustion gases as well as the copious steam you will produce. Be aware that a tent that has been cooked in will absorb food odors and should not later be used in places where grizzly bears are a concern.

The moment your tent is up, you begin to face the challenge of keeping it dry inside. Minimize trips in and out. Avoid bringing snow in with you. Keep a whisk broom and a sponge just inside the tent door. Brush yourself off as you crawl in; take your boots off at the entrance and make sure the snow is out of the laces and the spaces between lugs.

Depending on the weather and the capacity of your shelter, packs may stay outside. Certain objects, however, need to spend the night inside the tent and even inside your sleeping bag: your boots (in a plastic bag, or in your sleeping bag's stuff sack, turned inside out); your flashlight or headlamp; and batteries from any electronic gear like a camera. (To prevent damaging condensation, though, the camera body had better stay cold.) If the temperature is much below freezing, water bottles too will have to taken to bed or, at the least, tucked alongside your bag, on the side away from the tent wall. (Make sure the caps are on tight!) Alternatively, you can bury some of your bottles outside under several inches of snow—which, believe it or not, acts as insulation. (Make sure you know exactly where to dig in the morning. Fresh snowfall can obliterate all surface signs.) Fuel should be brought inside as well.

The ultimate luxury in winter is a warm, comfortable bed. Nights can be long; you spend a lot of time there. If your sleeping bag isn't really intended for winter, you may wind up wearing a lot of clothing to bed. Wet clothes, though, will only chill you; better to hang them from a ridge-seam clothesline. It's particularly important to put on dry socks at bedtime and, if you have them, insulated booties. If you're taking boots to bed, you can arrange them not too uncomfortably at your feet, behind your knees, or under your head as a pillow. Even if it's very cold, leave your nose and mouth uncovered in the hood opening; your breath shouldn't be trapped inside. (You can breathe through something like a stocking cap instead.)

Some people carry widemouthed bottles to use for indoor urination on nasty nights. On any clear night, though, the predawn stars when you go out are worth a few shivers.

Speaking of sanitation, the winter hiker obviously has a problem. Unless you happen to find a patch of clear, unfrozen soil, digging a "cathole" is pointless. In well-used areas, the packing out of feces (see Chapter 20) is becoming standard. In the cold, there won't be an odor. Failing that, all you can do is go even farther away from lakes or streams than you would in summer. Feces shallowly buried in snow will get an earlier start on decomposition. Kick fresh snow over the evidence, including urine stains. As for toilet paper, pack it out always.

Shelters Made of Snow

Although many never bother, every winter camper really ought to get some experience in building a shelter in the snow. These skills can be invaluable in an emergency, and quite a few travelers use snow shelters all the time, saving considerable weight. (The typical two-person winter tent weighs 8 pounds; shovel and snow saw for building a snow shelter, under 2 pounds.)

The simplest and quickest snow shelter is the *trench*. It's just what it sounds like, a moat, 3 or 4 feet deep, 6 or 7 feet long, and wide enough for a couple of sleepers (the narrower the trench, the easier to cover). In the old days you would make a roof of interwoven conifer boughs. That won't do now, of course, unless a life is at stake; instead, you use a tent fly, a tarp, or some such, laid on beams made of ski poles, axes, or whatever you have (downed branches, should you find them, make good supports). For insulation, cover the roof with snow. Be sure to leave an opening for ventilation.

More elaborate is the *snow cave*. To build one, you need soft to medium snow and a good thick snowbank. Suitable drifts often form near creek banks (watch out for any water flowing underneath).

There are at least two ways of digging a snow cave. The traditional method is simple to describe but difficult to carry out. You burrow into the snowbank, making an entry tunnel. About 4 feet in, you angle the tunnel upward; you then excavate a flat-floored, round-roofed chamber. The job takes 3 or 4 hours even with a snow shovel, and the excavators get soaking wet.

It is possible to shortcut the process a bit. The trick, essentially, is to dig the snow cave with an over-size entryway, so that you have room to work without burrowing like a mole, and then to close off the extra gap. Proceed this way:

First, cut away at your snowbank to make it as close as possible to a vertical wall.

Second, dig into that wall a horizontal shelf or alcove about 4 feet wide. Make the floor of this opening level with your belt; make its ceiling about 18 inches above. This alcove is the beginning of the inner room of the cave.

Now start expanding the alcove backward into the snow. Without expanding the initial opening, hollow out behind it as well as inward, sideways, and upward, but not at all downward. The floor should run back on a level.

When you've dug out all the snow you can get at from your first position, excavate a trench for your legs, cutting into the incomplete cave, so that you can stand up in there.

Now finish the cave. Make it as large as you like: a typical plan is more or less a rectangle, 7 feet wide, 5 feet deep (into the snowbank), and 3 to 4 feet high. It may be split-level, with a lower floor and a higher "sleeping shelf." Make the ceiling a smoothly rounded dome.

What you have now is a snow cave with one side gaping open to the air, a sort of cutaway model. It remains to close off the open side. You do this by cutting several big snow blocks and placing them in the now unwanted window. One of these blocks will bridge the trench you cut for your legs, turning it into a short tunnel—your permanent entry. Fill in the cracks and gaps between the blocks with loose snow.

Building block for an igloo. The smallest face will form part of the interior surface. Sides are beveled so that the blocks will tilt progressively inward as they are stacked upon each other, forming a dome.

Complex as it sounds, this method eliminates much of the misery of building a snow cave, and you don't get terribly wet (though it still is wise to work in waterproofs). Practiced cave-makers can do the job this way in an hour or so.

After the shelter is done, you "furnish" it. Cover the sleeping area with a groundsheet, and cut niches and shelves for a candle, your stove, and odds and ends. Punch a ventilating shaft up through the high point of the dome and a second above the stove. Narrow to start with, these shafts will widen as heat rises through them.

An *igloo* is something like a snow cave above ground. To build one, you need snow firm enough to hold its shape in blocks cut with your shovel (or shovel and saw). If loose snow is all you have, you can trample it down with skis or snowshoes, then let it set for 20 minutes or so. The bigger the blocks you work with, the faster the job gets done: 18 inches by 10 inches by 15 inches is typical. Because you're building a dome, the blocks must be beveled, with top and end surfaces sloping inward.

To guide yourself, outline the base of the igloo (round or oval—an 8-to-10-foot inside diameter). Then

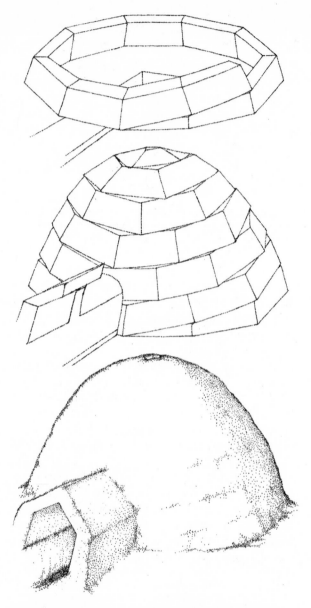

An igloo under construction. In the top view, a block bridges a trench that will serve as the entryway. Center, the tunnel is acquiring a roof. Below, the finished product.

Variations

choose the location of your entry. The best position is downhill and crosswise to the prevailing wind. Dig a trench from the center of your circle to the entry and several feet beyond. Remove the snow from this trench in usable blocks.

Trench dug, you begin laying blocks around the circle. (One of them will bridge the trench.) When you finish the first circuit, trim the first couple of blocks you placed to make a gradual ramp, and take the second course right on up over them, starting a spiral. Then just keep going.

Typically, one of the snow masons works outside cutting blocks while the second stands inside to take them, place them, and finish the shaping. Five or six courses will be required. Because of the beveled shape of the blocks, the walls will lean increasingly inward. If the blocks are regular enough and carefully beveled, they'll support themselves clear to the final large keystone block that closes the top. When it becomes convenient, cut an arched lintel into the block that spans the trench, making a better door.

At this point you have your basic igloo. For extra protection you can add a raised roof of blocks over the trench outside the wall, creating a longer covered entryway. Then coat the outside of the igloo with loose snow. You should be able to move inside, and out of the wind, in an hour. Punch a generous air vent at the peak. The structure will knit together quickly as it warms up inside.

There are things to be aware of in any snow house. Just as in a tent, you have to make sure your ventilation is good. See that air shafts stay open and that the entry doesn't get sealed by drifted snow; a low, outlying shield wall of two or three blocks may trap a drift where it does no harm. Then there's the moisture problem. When stoves are running, the snowy roof will drip. Since drops collect on projections, the smoother you've made the roof, the less drizzle there will be.

It is an excellent idea to practice shelter building near the road, when nothing at all depends on quick, successful execution.

25

Hiking & Camping with Kids

Many people take their young children on hikes. Many people take them on overnight car-camping trips. Not so many take them on overnight backpacks, but even this is quite feasible. And people who have done it—who have raised their children half in the wilderness, half at home—seem to find the process delightful.

True, you won't be able to go very far or very fast; true, you will have to carry a certain amount of extra gear and do some extra chores on the trail and in camp. But a slower pace can be a pleasant change in itself. And children who have among their earliest memories the woods, the streams, the far-off mountains, may well have gained an advantage that will last a lifetime. Even very young children, too, seem to value the sense of being part of the enterprise their parents are carrying out. Something important, pleasant, and adult is going on, and they are part of it, not excluded. To older children, the actual responsibilities of the trail—even scaled down to their size—are a firm link with the parents, and a kind of preview of growing up.

Parents who backpack with their children, and enjoy it greatly, warn that you mustn't expect the wrong things. A trip with kids is quite another experience than a trip with adults; it's another, more leisurely style of travel. It isn't just that children have shorter legs than their parents; up to a certain and quite variable age, they also have different attitudes. The trail, for youngsters, is not a stretch to be traversed but a kind of elongated playground and discovery zone to be experienced. Parents need to switch attitudes, too—and may find themselves charmed to do so.

Most kids are tougher, physically, than we give them credit for. They'll make out just as well in the wilderness as out of it—maybe better. They won't be as clean as they might be at home, but you quickly learn not to bother much about *that*. A couple of matters merit more concern. First, children, and even adolescents, are more sensitive than adults to certain environmental hazards, including altitude sickness and ultraviolet radiation. Second, there's no denying that you're far away from the doctor. If you've put off learning first aid on your own behalf, you'll definitely want to take it up when you begin traveling with the young.

When you're starting backpackers small, you want to start them slow—partly for their sake, even more for yours. All those special items, all those modified routines need shaking down. It's best to begin with day hikes, very short at first, then longer. Here's where you test (and inevitably add to) your list of necessary items; here's where you get the hang of familiar chores performed in unfamiliar places. It's also at this stage that you find out about temperaments and problems. How happy is the two-year-old in the baby carrier? How much walking does the five-year-old feel up to? Before you move on to overnight camping, you may want to test your methods on safe ground. Try cooking meals on day trips; try a risk-free camp on the back lawn or at an auto campground.

As you move on to backpacking, begin with trips in known territory. Make plans that don't put your group under pressure, and plan excursions you'll enjoy even if you don't make it all the way to such-and-such a pond or such-and-such a waterfall. Most people who hike with young children don't fight bad weather when it catches up with them; they just go home. You don't want a youngster to get the feeling that misery and wilderness belong together. Take it easy. Make it easy.

There is comfort in numbers. One veteran reports: "Hiking with children of all ages, a factor for success is including other children. Going with two or three families makes for a better experience for all. Children will compete with one another to get to the destination; they won't become bored and cranky. Once in camp, adults can take turns supervising the youngsters while others have a chance to hike or climb further. Including other kids of the same age group holds for 'kids' up to twenty-five!"

For backpacking purposes, you can say that children come in three sizes. There are the very small ones, the *portable* ones, who aren't able to walk much yet. There are the older ones, five years and above, who (if not exactly hikers at first) are more or less *hikable*. And in between are the youngsters of two and three and four—kids who want to do things for themselves but can't very well. Backpacking parents find it most challenging to travel with children of this age. But many people do it, and the young and the old both seem to enjoy it.

Portable Kids

How soon do you start taking an infant into the wild country? As soon as you like. Some families backpack with babies only a month old; most wait till about six months. In some ways these youngest children are very easy to manage. You will, of course, be slowed down somewhat by feeding and diaper changing, and most of the family's gear will have to ride in a single pack. On the other hand, the baby will go happily as fast and far as you feel able to manage.

Not all destinations are suitable, though. New human beings are not at all coldproof, heatproof, or sunproof. Sunburn can be very serious in a small child, and infants have practically no ability to adjust to thin, high-mountain air. Because babies won't stand for wearing protective glasses, they can't very well be taken onto snow or to elevations above timberline.

What do you carry your passenger in? The choice is wide. (The old leather papoose-carrier, lined with

Full-featured child carriers include comfortable suspension systems, kick-stands for standing up on the ground, retractable hoods for sun and rain, and lots of extra storage space.

sphagnum moss as an absorbent diaper, was elegant, but the materials are hard to find these days.) For very young children, you can use soft slings. These hold the baby against your chest, or on your back, or at either side. Expect to pay $80 for such a carrier.

As soon as the child can sit with head upright, you can begin using a backpack-style transport: a soft, padded seat, slung inside a metal frame, with the rider facing forward. The best models have high backs and sides, almost encasing the passenger. Different designs fit kids from 20 to 60 pounds; seats may adjust to provide differing amounts of support as youngsters mature. A carrier is first of all a pack, and must have comfortable, adjustable hipbelts and harnesses. There is typically a kickstand so that the unit can be parked upright on the ground. A sunshield/rain hood is a useful accessory. The more incidental storage room there is, the better. Good backpack-style carriers cost $100 to almost $300.

Most babies, delighted by the motion, ride well on parental shoulders. Not until a youngster has begun to walk does a prolonged ride seem confining and dull. A familiar toy, tied to the frame, makes a good diversion.

When you have a passenger perched behind your ears, you obviously have to watch out for low branches and be careful about leaning over. The rider, who isn't doing any work, must be dressed much more warmly than you are. If it's the least bit chilly, pay extra attention to keeping the baby dry. Make sure also that eyes and skin are protected from bright sun.

The same baby clothes used at home will usually do on the trail. Elastic one-piece garments, lighter or heavier or doubled-up according to the season, are good. Whatever clothing you bring, carry a *lot* of changes; you can hardly bring too many. Make sure at least one set is noncotton. Raingear? Standard waterproof "slickers" coated with vinyl, available in department stores, work well for most young children. Get rain pants as well as coats. Since youngsters perspire less than adults, and don't tend to drown inside their waterproofs, you won't need to scour the stores for miniature garments in Gore-Tex.

In camp, very young children aren't likely to crawl or toddle clear away into the forest. But they are quite likely to head for the attractive flames of a fire (stove cooking is a little safer; cooking with kerosene or alcohol is safest of all). A tent can serve as a playpen. You can also make a pen out of a tarp, hung low at the middle, raised around the edges. Some parents use a leash and a harness.

As for feeding, make it as simple as possible. Breastfeeding is of course the easiest all around. Whatever the child has been eating at home should be continued; this is no time to introduce big changes. Kids who are just learning to feed themselves need a deep, generous cup with a big graspable handle. Also bring the usual plastic cereal bowl, bib, and washcloth. You may be able to minimize your use of pureed baby foods: quite a few freeze-dried foods are fine-textured anyway, and you can always mash solid food to make a usable paste. You will of course avoid glass containers.

In diapering, most people continue whatever routine they use at home. This is not the place to revisit the debate about the environmental effects of using cloth versus disposable paper-and-plastic diapers. Whichever you choose, take plenty—more than you expect to need—along with all the incidentals. Stools, of course, should be carefully buried, but not even the liners of disposable diapers go into the ground—much too slow to decompose. You'll need a strong, leakproof plastic bag (or several, one inside the other) for carrying soiled diapers. Be scrupulous, of course, about washing your hands.

What about warmth at night? A baby can be tucked in (cautiously) with a parent, or between two sleepers in a double bag. You can also use the upper part of a bag built for an adult or larger child, doubling over the excess material and filling in with insulating things. Again, an infant, warmly dressed and wrapped in a fleece blanket, can be tucked into a stuff sack. With a little home effort, you can create a tiny tailored sleeping bag—for example, by cutting off the arms and stitching up armholes and waist of an old insulated jacket. Since down is damaged by repeated wetting and washing, synthetic insulations are naturally preferred in the infant bedroll; Polarguard is known for its durability. You'll also need a bit of plastic sheeting and a small pad of closed-cell foam.

In-Between Kids

It's not the infant—the object to be carried—that parents find most difficult to take to the wilderness with them.

Rather, it's the two-, three-, and four-year-old who is neither a mere passenger nor quite a self-operating human being. Too heavy and restless to carry for long, the child can't walk fast or far. A 4-mile day, with such a companion, is about the most you can plan on. At this stage quite a few people sign up with organized groups for aid and comfort and take mostly easy trips to accessible base camps.

In the earlier part of this period, youngsters are of course still mastering the basic skills of being alive: learning to walk with confidence, to talk, to feed themselves, to use the toilet. Wilderness toilet methods, in particular, can be upsetting. When you've just learned that virtue is the porcelain bowl, it may seem not just odd but even downright sinful to squat over a hole in the ground. Some families stay close to campground outhouses at this juncture; others ease the transition by bringing along light plastic toilet seats. When operations commence, a parent should stay with the youngster and be patiently reassuring. Make sure that hands get washed thoroughly afterward—in a basin, not in a lake or stream.

This is the time when kids are exploring, handling things around them, getting into trouble. There are plenty of dangerous objects around a camp to be concerned about. But there's also a lot of gear, soft, harmless, and fascinating, for a child to play with.

Clothing gets more ordinary at this stage. You still need generous spares but not quite so many. For the bed, pint-sized synthetic-filled sleeping bags with hoods are available in various lengths; most cost under $100. Though kids need insulation under them, they're generally happy without the generous padding that many adults require.

Hikable Kids

Once youngsters are able to walk at a fair clip, the problems change; some of them disappear. Older kids will wear what anybody wears on the trail. Footwear, though, can be a problem. Sturdy boots, even if you can find them in the proper sizes, are expensive overkill for rapidly lengthening feet. Well-padded athletic shoes or lightweight hikers will serve.

Few families are large enough these days for much "handing down" of boots or other wilderness gear, but sometimes several families can get together in a sort of pool. Then there are the invaluable thrift shops.

Most kids seem to enjoy carrying packs from an early age. The first "load" may be no load at all, or a favorite toy. Use a daypack with shortened straps. The next step is a frame pack, simple, cheap, and adjustable enough to stretch with a growing body over several years; one firm, Kelty, makes a specialty of children's frames. By the beginning of the teens, kids should have no trouble with a full load—that is, a load up to about one-fifth of their own weight.

Even after children can walk pretty well, they may think of it as a chore. It takes some encouragement to keep a young hiker going. Although your range will be longer now, you still don't want to be in the position of *having* to get to a particular, distant place. You'll need to take frequent breaks to rest, to eat, to play a game, to look at something entertaining like a stream. It can be fun to look things up in guides to flowers, trees, rocks, birds—if you aren't too high-handedly "educational" about it. (Do it for your own sake and let your enthusiasm spill over.) Some favorite playthings should be there to fall back on.

In matters of safety, your judgment will have to substitute for the youngster's, and that can take a good deal of your time. Give each kid a whistle, pinned to the shirt. (You'll have to convince them not to blow it for the fun of it.) Keep younger children in sight and middling ones within earshot. Older kids may want to run ahead, but have them wait at a given, not very distant point (a trail junction, the foot of a slope, whatever). If you're in an area where grizzly bears or mountain lions are of concern, don't let kids run ahead at all.

Tell them what to do if they lose you. The rule: sit down, blow the whistle a lot, and stay put. Talk to them also about the possible hazards of the land: snakes, bears, falling rocks, rapid currents, poison ivy, or whatever. It can be hard to do this without making the country sound forbidding, but it's not a step to be skipped.

At this stage kids can begin to use a map and compass, initially just for fun. A youngster can play leader for an hour, telling the group which way to go at trail junctions, scheduling rests and snacks.

Discourage kids from eating while they walk. (Some of them can't hike and chew gum at the same time, and there's a risk of getting a food fragment stuck in a windpipe. Having taken a first-aid course, you'll know exactly how to deal with "foreign body obstruction of airway.") You'll have warned them, of course, against munching the unidentified leaf or berry; still, a handbook on local poisonous plants is one good item to have along. The usual first aid for plant poisoning is to induce vomiting. For more on these matters, see Chapter 26.

In general, watch out for problems children may be having. Some, as you might expect, complain very readily; others, surprisingly, do not. Check now and again for developing blisters. You need to make sure that kids stay comfortably warm or cool; watch for signs of hypothermia and hyperthermia (see Chapter 28). Above 6,000 feet or so, be very alert for altitude sickness, and head downhill decisively if you suspect it. Fortunately, even relatively stoic kids don't push themselves as dangerously far as prideful adults may sometimes do.

When you get to camp, check the site for any particular dangers—a steep drop, a rotten snag—and point them out. Experienced parents set limits: kids don't go beyond that creek, that rock, that stand of firs. With especially adventurous youngsters, one adult may have to spend most of the time keeping watch.

Any animals you encounter will be fascinating to the young. Teach the kids to understand them, to like them, and to respect them. Teach equally firmly that animals must not be fed, or petted, or even approached too closely. Critters that seem oddly unafraid may have something wrong with them. *Hands off the cute and furry.*

Kids, being small, are more likely than adults to look like potential prey in the eyes of a mountain lion or (rare case) the genuinely predatory bear. In regions where these animals live, you have yet one more reason to keep youngsters with you and, especially, to prevent any kid from wandering off alone. The wild-animal hazard can be exaggerated, and almost always is; yet it is not zero. You should also check youngsters twice daily for ticks. See Chapter 29.

Many or most kids like to do small chores at camp. Wood gathering is a pleasant assignment, and so is help with tent pitching. If weather and wildlife permit, kids may want to lay out their own open-air bedsites. Older children get a lot of pleasure out of a tent of their own. Then there's help with the cooking—safest are those jobs, like mixing a cold-water pudding, that don't get the small-fry too close to fire or stove. Be sure to tie back long hair when there's fire around.

There's nothing special about backpacking food for these relatively grown-up children. If anything, the food you take on a trip with youngsters should be even simpler, even easier to prepare, than you would otherwise favor. Some foods—desserts, of course, individually packaged hot-cereal breakfasts, and such—have entertainment value. Happily, the problem of the fussy eater is likely to solve itself on the trail.

Walking Softly: Entertainment Versus Wilderness?

Although kids may enjoy a trip immensely, they aren't at first likely to enjoy it for "adult" reasons. They are more likely than adults to want to return to familiar ground. And when they're in a wild place, they look for the same sorts of entertainments they would find at home: things to *do*. Toys, cards, and games are valuable, especially for rainy days.

Since nothing can fail to be new to them, babies just coming alive to their surroundings are as fascinated by one place as by another. Older kids want places they can play in. Above all they like *water*: a stream (especially with a swimming hole), a pond, an ocean shore, mud, or—best of all—summer snow. They tend to be unimpressed by the subtle detail of the forest. The appreciation of wilderness as wilderness seems to come later in life, though you're establishing the basis for it now.

Kids' energetic playfulness can lead to certain problems, for some of the things that seem most entertaining are also hard on the landscape.

Children (and boys especially—by nature? by social example?) are engineers. The first thing they want to do when they find a stream is build a dam across it; the first thing they want to do with dirt is turn it into miniature roads, walls, and earthworks. Even when no special project is under way, children, moving around as much as they do, can accomplish much more than their share of vegetation trampling and path beating.

Though it may not come easily, it's never too soon to start teaching kids those wilderness manners that consist partly of courtesy, partly of safety, and partly of concern for the fabric of the country. During the day's hike, make sure kids don't trample down trail edges, cut across switchbacks, knock rocks down the slope. Discourage the random collection of plants. Making camp, select a suitable well-used site and explain why you choose the spot you do. Point out sensitive areas, like vegetation that shouldn't be trampled. Try to steer games in harmless directions. Low-impact methods, indeed, can be presented as a kind of game or entertaining drama. Even adults find it sometimes useful to think of it that way, and kids have the ability to throw themselves into a fantasy without irony. (*The bad guys are after me. Did I leave any marks they can track me down by?*) At any rate it's worth a try. You're showing tomorrow's wilderness user how to walk softly in the fragile wild places.

Time Marches On

By about age twelve, youngsters will certainly be wearing packs essentially like those worn by adults, though a little smaller and usually simpler. External-frame packs, with their greater adjustability, have the advantage here. Harnesses can also be swapped as bodies lengthen. Cost is under $100 for an external, over $100 for an internal frame. You'll need to monitor loads—kids, like some adults, may feel compelled to fill up every cubic inch they've got, not always with very light or very practical things.

When full-scale packs begin to be worn, serious boots with good ankle support become necessary as well. Kids tend to buy for looks and brand name; they may not be very attentive to fit, and it's your job (with help from a fitter at the store) to make sure they don't wind up in blister machines.

In the middle of all this there comes a time—a different time, for different youngsters—when the young person begins to regard the wilderness somewhat as the adult regards it. Reports vary, but clearly some children begin to show this change of attitude as early as eight or nine. Wilderness travel is, after all, more play than work, for anyone; the gap between child and adult is not so great here as it would be, for instance, on a visit to the office where a parent earns a living.

Somewhere along the line, youngsters start to see the land as a place to adventure in, to admire and value for its own shape, its own interest. At this point they have already begun to be "real" backpackers, and this is the time that backpacking parents especially look forward to. At this stage some parents (fathers especially) can't resist forcing the kids to walk farther, carry more, and achieve more than they may really enjoy. This is a mistake that can just possibly spoil things. But most kids who discover for themselves the pleasure of the wilderness seem to be addicts for life.

A few years further on, the situation changes again, and the kids, long-legged and energetic, will be waiting constantly for *you*.

Trouble & How to Deal With It

It must be poor life that achieves freedom from fear.

—Aldo Leopold, *A Sand County Almanac*

*But it is a characteristic of wisdom
not to do desperate things.*

—Henry David Thoreau, *Walden*

26

Trouble!

We may not admit it, but there's a certain peculiar glamour to the thought of facing danger, of defending life and limb, especially in remote and photogenic places. People *like* to read about wilderness hazards and narrow escapes, to listen to other people's "war stories." But the charm quickly vanishes when threats become personal and real. Spend enough time in the wild places, and you're going to have some part, sometime, in dealing with an all too genuine emergency— another person's, or your own.

It's not that the wilderness is more dangerous than tamer parts of the world. A couple of hikers may be killed each year by snakebite; a couple, in a bad year, by bears or mountain lions or lightning; perhaps a dozen by accidents or by weather they're not prepared to handle. Small numbers, as such sad numbers go. But wilderness dangers loom large in imagination, because they are less familiar than city dangers, and also—oddly enough—because they are more under our control. There is so much we can do to prevent them. The responsibility is ours.

The way to stay out of trouble is to think in terms of trouble. This doesn't mean a hypochondria, a fretfulness, or even a conservative unwillingness to take *considered* risks (that's up to you). What it does mean is awareness. Go out well equipped. Go out well informed.

On the trail keep a just slightly wary eye on the world around you and on yourself.

Be alert to objective outside hazards: the approaching thunderstorm, the loose rock ready to fall on companions below, the hazardous ford, the red-hot stove. Some of these you will avoid; others you'll have to deal with. Either way, the great virtue is simply to know what you're about. Most accidents seem to happen to people who take risks *without knowing it*, casually, carelessly, unprepared.

Watch also for physical problems in yourself, or in your companions, that could become serious if not attended to. Deal with nuisances promptly, before they become more than nuisances. A cold, drenching rain, for instance, is only an annoyance—if you handle the situation properly. If you don't, it can lead to a life-endangering chill.

First Aid

First-aid training is simply vital. Every adult or teenager in a party should have some. The shortest medical course in the world, 7 hours of Standard First Aid, is available through local Red Cross chapters for $65. It's ideal if at least one member has received additional instruction. Most useful of all (but not available everywhere) are courses in mountaineering medicine or wilderness first aid. However, there is a fair amount that the relatively unpracticed first-aider can safely do, and in a pinch you have to work with what you know.

One sometimes-useful item in the pack is a booklet setting out, precisely and in order, the steps to be worked through when you have a seriously ill or injured person on your hands. Several such guides exist; your prefabricated first-aid kit may contain one. Among more-than-minimal handbooks, William Forgey's *Wilderness First Aid Manual* is one good choice (see the Resources section).

If the emergency is fairly minor—and most are—you will have time to consider, to consult the manual, to talk things over with the cooperative victim. It is the major injury, or the physical collapse, that is most frightening. Such cases are rare in the extreme but too serious not to consider in advance.

Details vary, but in general there are three steps in dealing with a major wilderness injury or illness.

First, you *save life*. A few problems are so dangerous that action must be almost instantaneous.

Second, you *stabilize things*. Chances are you won't be able to treat a major injury in any fundamental way; all you can do is make the patient as safe and comfortable as possible and follow, with caution, the instructions in your manual and the dictates of common sense.

Third, you *get the victim home*. Sometimes a person in distress can get out under his or her own power, slowly, and with help. If not, you'll have to arrange for outside aid, or, in some cases, carry your companion out yourself.

The notes that follow here are not meant to substitute for a first-aid manual, still less for actual training. I've tried to select, from the long list of things the hiker needs to know, a few that seem absolutely basic. Please do learn more.

The First Stage: Saving Life

Let's say you find a woman, a member of your party or not, seriously hurt, or unconscious, or both. Go to her, if you can do so without danger to yourself. Speak loudly to her, asking her how she is; if there's no answer, touch her, not roughly, in a further search for response. Unless she's plainly "all right," consider her your patient and proceed.

As a rule, you examine victims where you find them. You don't try to move them. (There are exceptions. A drowning victim won't be left in the water; someone struck by lightning had better be moved from the vulnerable spot; any immediate danger, as from falling rock or avalanche, can't be ignored.)

First things first: establish that the victim is *breathing*. Look for chest movement; listen for exhalation; try to feel her breath on your hand. If you can't quickly

Anybody heading for the wilderness should learn CPR (cardiopulmonary resuscitation). The pulmonary part of CPR—artificial respiration—is of special importance.

confirm respiration, make sure that there is no physical blockage of the breathing passages or *airway*. Place one hand under the back of her neck to tilt the head back at a sharp angle—this keeps the tongue from plugging the throat. Note this, however: neck injury is likely in any accident involving force or impact. If you even suspect such a problem, don't press up under the back of the neck. Rather, place your hands along the side of the lower jaw and draw it forward, closing the nose with your two thumbs. This jutting of the jaw may also help whenever the airway remains stubbornly blocked by the tongue.

If some foreign object is blocking the airway, you should be able to dislodge it by fishing it out of the throat, by slapping the victim on the back, or by applying the thrust to the abdomen known as the *Heimlich maneuver*. In a first-aid course, you'll be taught how to do these things correctly, and in rotation, until the blockage is cleared.

If opening the airway does not restore breathing, you move on to *cardiopulmonary resuscitation*, or CPR. In the pulmonary part of this procedure, the rescuer breathes for the victim, mouth to mouth. Place your free hand on the victim's forehead and close her nostrils with finger and thumb. Seal her mouth with your own, and breathe deeply into her. Remove your mouth to let her exhale. For an adult, provide breaths at the rate of one every five seconds; for a child, every three seconds.

The CPR procedure can also provide—but only if needed—an artificial heartbeat, produced by rhythmic pressure on the breastbone. Full CPR is exacting and energetic, especially if performed by one person alone, and must be learned by practice under supervision. The Red Cross incorporates CPR in its standard first-aid course; the American Heart Association has similar programs. If you are traveling with young children, be sure to master the somewhat different version of CPR that applies to them.

If a patient isn't breathing but has a pulse, you must provide artificial respiration indefinitely. But what of the victim whose heart has stopped? In the city, the rule is to start the full version of CPR, including chest compressions, regardless of how hopeless the victim's condition may appear—and to continue it until professionals arrive. In the wilderness, the choice isn't always so clear. A badly injured person with no heart action is most unlikely to be saved by CPR this far from hospital care. The same is true for a heart attack victim. On the other hand, the technique can make all the difference to someone who has suffered a lightning strike or a near-drowning. If a life is to be saved, it will be saved quickly: a person whose heart is not restarted within 1 hour, at the very most, has lost the battle.

Should you wear a surgical mask when doing CPR? Due to our newly strong concern about diseases that may be transmitted in body fluids, some people think so. Prefabricated aid kits may include such masks. However, the risk of contagion in mouth-to-mouth contact is really very slight. As Dr. Gordon Benner, Sierra Club medical officer, puts it: "I personally would do it without a mask and I hope that you would do it, too."

Three other problems can be listed with the instant emergencies. One is massive *bleeding*. In almost every case, you can stop the flow simply by pressing on the wound. (In this situation, do protect yourself from infection with a surgical glove or by placing a thickly folded cloth over the site.) Ten minutes of firm pressure should allow clotting and prevent further hemorrhage. If the wound is on an arm or a leg, it also helps to lift the limb above the level of the heart. Rather than removing the blood-soaked cloth, make it the basis of the dressing you later apply.

A second problem that won't wait is *heat stroke*, the late stage of bodily overheating, or *hyperthermia*. The treatment is obvious: cool the stricken person down. For more on this condition, see Chapter 28.

The third hurry case is *poisoning*. No matter what was swallowed, the initial step is to have the victim swallow water to dilute the substance. The next step is usually to induce vomiting. Neither of these can be done, however, if the victim is unconscious, or having convulsions. For certain poisons—petroleum products (stove fuel!), strong acids, and strong alkalis—you do *not* induce vomiting. These substances may do further damage to the esophagus if they are vomited up; there is risk, too, of getting them into the lungs.

The Second Stage: Stabilizing Things

When the instant emergency is over, the next danger is *shock*. Shock is essentially very low blood pressure, and can be caused by trauma, blood loss, dehydration, pain, and emotional reaction. It can occur with any accident or illness, and is sometimes a sole cause of death. Thirst, nausea, and increasing anxiety are symptoms. The skin will grow pale, damp, and cool. Heartbeat will be rapid and weak, breathing quick and shallow. The victim may get dizzy or black out. In the last stage of severe shock, blood pressure drops toward zero.

Treat for shock whether or not it has yet appeared. Lay the victim flat on her back. Raise her legs 8 to 10 inches if practical (but not if there is severe injury to head or torso). Loosen constricting clothes, especially at the neck. Her body will have lost much of its power to maintain its temperature; depending on the weather, you must keep her either warm or cool. If she's aware, be certain to reassure her, to listen to her, to satisfy her requests where you can. If she's awake, give sips of cold water. If she can't keep it down, try again in a couple of hours. Don't give fluids to someone who's spontaneously vomiting or suffering convulsions.

Along with treatment for shock, do a second, more thorough examination. Look, touch, and listen. Check for all sorts of injuries: wounds, fractures, burns, dislocations, frostbite. (Sometimes the most dramatic problem is not the most serious.) Count heartbeats per minute and breaths per minute. Get all the information you can from and about the victim. Take notes. Even an amateurish medical history may be of value later.

Special precautions apply whenever someone has taken a hard blow on the upper body, especially if the victim loses consciousness. First, until you know otherwise, assume the person has a broken neck; make sure the back of the head is supported and pad the sides to prevent movement. Shift the victim, if at all, with extreme care. Always move the body as a unit, avoiding any twisting that might damage the spinal cord.

Watch the victim's state of consciousness. As time goes on, does she become more aware and responsive, or less? Alert, and then hazy again? If there is any pattern other than steady improvement, it's vital to summon a rescue.

Now decide, with deliberation, what happens next. That may be nothing more than signaling or sending companions for aid. Or you may need to apply whatever treatments you are fairly sure of, guided by common sense, a manual, the patient's own reactions, and whatever training you've had. (The idea is not to "fix the victim up," but merely to prevent further injury. Don't do a thing unless you can tell yourself why you are doing it.)

Keep paying attention to your patient after the first crisis passes. Keep on noting vital signs. Talk to her. Let her know what you're doing. First-aid experts remark that, if you don't talk to the person in your care, you're practicing veterinary medicine!

In the excitement, give thought to the welfare of the rest of your party. Among other things, it's often important to set up a safe and comfortable camp.

The Third Stage: Getting Out

In few of our wilderness areas is there much difficulty about swift rescue, at least in summer, and at least for hikers on busy trails. If the victim can't move under her own power, the problem is simply to attract the attention of rescuers, or of other hikers who can send for them. If there are several healthy people in your party, send one (or better, two) for help. Be sure the party you send out knows how to describe your whereabouts. If you have a cellular phone, you will of course use that.

If you can't send people to the outside world, or want to send an additional message, nothing attracts the attention of the authorities like a smoky fire. A triangle of fires, 50 feet apart, will certainly be read as "Trouble Here." There are also recognized ground-to-air symbols that you can form by arranging gear or objects on open ground. The most important one to remember is the simple vertical bar (|), which means "serious injury." Then there is the double L (LL), which means "all is well"—worth remembering in case there has been some sort of false alarm.

How do you decide if an injured person can walk out? This decision can be hard. On the one hand, you don't want to risk further injury. On the other hand, many accident victims *can* make it out, slowly and with assistance. Helicopter rescues are damnably expensive. (Who pays? Policies vary. In any case, such an operation should not be unleashed casually.)

Especially if you travel away from the trails, or if you visit remote areas in winter, it is a good idea to learn some rescue techniques yourself: how to make a litter, how to splint major body injuries, and so forth. These are set out in books and courses on first aid, rescue, and mountaineering medicine.

27

Some Common Medical Problems

Most of the time, medical problems on the trail take a form much milder than the accident or collapse that demands your fast, clear-headed action. The typical complaint is a nuisance, not a danger; even rather serious injuries usually allow you time to think. Here is a list, short and by no means complete, of problems you may face sometime—the common cases, and a few uncommon ones in which a little information may be reassuring—together with the treatments that wilderness medicine experts recommend for them.

Surface Wear and Tear

Cuts, punctures, and scrapes. You step on a porcupine quill; you skin your elbow; you gash a thumb with your pocketknife. If bleeding is copious, stop it by pressing directly on the wound. If the bleeding wound is someone else's, especially a stranger's, you may want to put on latex gloves from your first-aid kit, or at least interpose a cloth: it isn't paranoid to think of AIDS. If spontaneous bleeding has not completely washed out the wound, finish the job with plenty of clean water. A squirt bottle or a plastic bag with a pinhole in it will make a good "hose." You don't need antiseptic or soap. You also do not need to apply a dressing unless the wound would get dirty without one. A gaping cut can be kept closed with one or more "butterfly bandages," strips of adhesive cut in an hourglass shape, with the thin part over the cut. A minor wound is certainly not a cause to head for home; a larger one might be. (All hikers should be sure their tetanus immunization is up to date; one booster shot is needed every ten years.)

Burns and scalds. These account for a large percentage of backcountry injuries. Whether the affected area is large or small, your first priority is to *cool it as fast as possible.* Remove clothing first (if it isn't stuck on). Immersion in cold water is ideal. Cooling will quickly lessen the pain, inhibit further damage, and promote healing. Prolong the cold treatment for up to 2 hours if it continues to soothe. Then clean the site with soap and water and apply a water-based gel dressing, such as Spenco 2nd Skin. Some sources recommend an antibiotic ointment as well.

Minor burns—burns that raise few if any blisters—will probably require no further attention; but do watch for infection. Burns that raise numerous blisters, or that penetrate the skin, are more serious. Be especially concerned about any blistering burn on the face, hands, feet, or genitals; any *large* blistering burn elsewhere; and any blistering burn at all on an infant. If a person has burns about the face, be aware that the breathing passages may be scorched, and watch for any breathing difficulty. People with serious burns should be evacuated.

If first aid continues more than a day, dressings will need changing every 24 hours. If you're using ointment, flush off the old coat with a stream of water and apply new.

For *sunburn* and *snow blindness*, see Chapter 28.

Eye problems. Getting a fragment of the wilderness in your eye is annoying and can be hazardous. The first thing to remember is not to rub the eye, which will only add irritation. Instead, get a wooden match or a thin twig; place it horizontally halfway up the outside of the upper eyelid; then fold the lower margin of the lid upward around it, watching the maneuver in a pocket mirror. Foreign objects tend to stick to the inside of the lid and can be safely removed with the corner of a bandanna or a cotton swab. Sometimes the problem is no more than an inturned lash. Sometimes the irritating object has already floated away but leaves a scratch that causes the something-in-my-eye feeling. If this persists, soothing eyedrops may be helpful; seek a doctor's attention for a persistently inflamed eye.

If someone's eye is actually penetrated by an object, your immediate job is to calm the person and instruct him *not to move his eyes*. Do not try to remove the invading object. Cover both eyes (so that the injured eye won't move in tandem with the healthy one) and summon help.

Broken Bones

Broken bones are scary and usually painful. Broken arms and legs, fortunately, are rarely very dangerous in themselves. If you even suspect a fracture, assume there is one. Fractures are not always marked by obvious deformation; check also for discoloration, swelling, pain, and tenderness. Unless a life is in danger, never move a person until all fractures, known or suspected, have been splinted.

Splinting—binding the broken part to something solid—prevents motion, keeps broken bone ends from damaging adjacent tissue, and generally makes the victim far more comfortable. The details of this craft make up a large part of advanced first-aid courses. For starters, remember that a fracture of a bone in the arm or shoulder can usually be splinted by placing the forearm in a sling across the lower chest and binding arm and sling to the body; most fractures of leg bones can be dealt with by splinting the broken leg to the healthy one.

In some first-aid courses you may be taught to leave a broken limb exactly as it is and merely to immobilize it with splinting—"splint 'em as they lie." In the wilderness, where help is more than minutes away, you will probably have to modify this principle. The injured person will be more comfortable, and the broken bone more stable, if you restore the limb to something like its natural or functional shape. This means straightening to some extent. While one person cradles the limb, another can take hold of the hand or foot and pull, gently and persistently, parallel to the normal alignment of the bone. When the injured limb looks more or less like the healthy one, proceed with splinting.

A particularly worrisome case is the *open fracture*, in which a wound reaches the fractured bone, or a broken end of the bone pokes out through the skin. Should you try to clean such a wound, or scrub the bone end, before splinting? The consensus is that you should simply remove visible particles of dirt and then proceed with straightening by gentle traction, causing the broken end to retreat back under the skin. All such fractures must be examined and cleaned thoroughly in the hospital, anyhow.

Anytime you apply a splint, you must make sure that blood is reaching the region of the limb beyond the break. Locate a pulse in the healthy limb; then make sure you can find the same pulse in the broken one, both before and after you apply the splint.

Head, neck, and back. As noted in Chapter 26, injuries that may affect the brain or spinal cord need a special degree of care. A patient who has been unconscious more than momentarily should probably head for home; any delayed effects are better dealt with there than on the trail.

Sprains and Dislocations

A sprain is damage to the ligaments that bind bones together in a joint: depending on the severity of the sprain, tissues may be stretched, torn, or actually severed. A dislocation occurs when the bones shift out of their normal positions in the joint.

Ankle problems. The badly twisted ankle is something every hiker, especially the solo hiker, dreads. Fortunately, most ankle injuries are not immobilizing. Often the sharp pain that seemed to indicate a major problem will go away by itself. Even a moderately damaged ankle can be walked on—with adequate reinforcement. On the other hand, if you mistreat a minor injury, you can just possibly make a long-lasting problem for yourself.

You've "done something" to your ankle. Consider it. Where does it hurt? Most of the time the painful spot will be on the outside of the ankle, below the bony bulge that marks the end of the smaller leg bone (fibula). This suggests a sprain, or, at worst, a fracture of the fibula. These injuries will allow you to walk out, with proper support. By contrast, pain at the inner side of the foot indicates a more serious problem; you probably shouldn't plan to do any walking.

If the ankle joint is actually torn, the foot will flop at an odd angle to the leg. This is a worse injury. The foot should be restored to its natural position and splinted. Wrap a jacket or other soft object around the foot in a U shape and bind it around the ankle, not too tightly but firmly enough to keep the foot steady. In this case there is no question of trying to walk.

In the case of a typical sprain, the immediate treatment is to *cool* the painful area with a cold pack (snow or a canteen of cold water, wrapped in cloth). At the same time *compress* the area by wrapping it with an elastic bandage. Begin at the toes and wind it around and around the foot and clear up the ankle. Place some padding under the bandage right at the painful spot to increase the pressure there. The third element of the initial treatment: *elevate* the leg to keep blood from pooling in the foot. The objective at this stage is to limit swelling.

Keep this treatment going for at least an hour—up to a full day. Then you can wrap the ankle for walking. Start by cutting three strips of adhesive tape 1 inch wide and about 3 feet long. Next, make sure that the foot is correctly positioned, at right angles to the leg. Now run a tape strip down the inside of the calf, around the heel, and up the outside of the calf, pulling a little in the last stage to rotate the foot gently outward. Apply the remaining strips in the same fashion, each overlapping the last and a little farther forward on the foot. Over the tape layer goes the elastic bandage,

There are several systems for taping a sprained ankle, some quite elaborate. This method, recommended by the Sierra Club's Gordon Benner, is simple and effective.

and over the bandage go sock and boot. Lace the boot firmly but not ferociously. If you don't have a staff or a trekking pole, find a stick to be used as a cane.

At this point, most people with twisted ankles find it quite possible to walk without excessive pain. A small amount of pain does not mean that it is dangerous to proceed. Move along slowly. Check from time to time that the ankle is not swelling; if it is, loosen the elastic bandage slightly.

Dislocated shoulder. This is a rather common wilderness injury. It is relatively easy to treat a dislocated shoulder in the field, and there is good reason to do so, because it becomes much harder to deal with as time passes.

There are several rival methods of restoring, or reducing, a dislocated shoulder. This is about the simplest. Have the injured person bend over, resting her chest on an object or on someone's hands. The injured arm hangs limp. Now take that wrist and pull the arm first downward, then downward and forward, turning it slightly in such a way that the thumb moves toward the outside. The tug should be strong and decisive, yet not so abrupt as a jerk.

A slower method uses a weight instead of muscle power to provide the traction. Give the victim your best painkiller and have her lie facedown on a tablelike surface with the bad arm hanging. With tape, attach a 15-to-20-pound weight to wrist or forearm. In 15 minutes or so, the pull should exhaust the arm and shoulder muscles, permitting the bone to pop back into place. Give it 2 hours; if it hasn't worked by then, abandon the effort and seek help. Not many hikers with stubbornly dislocated shoulders can be expected to walk out—the jolting is too painful.

Dislocated kneecap. Another dislocation that can be dealt with in the wilderness is that of a kneecap (as opposed to a dislocated *knee*, which involves major damage to the whole joint). It is not uncommon for a kneecap to slide out of position, usually to the outside of the knee; you can probably make it slide back by straightening the leg and pressing the bone gently from the side.

Dislocated finger. This ailment is also pretty manageable. Have the person flex the finger slightly; pull on the fingertip while you press on the dislocated segment from the end nearest the wrist and from the backside of the hand.

Other dislocations. By comparison with these cases, most other dislocations are serious business—much more dangerous, in fact, than typical fractures. The rule is to splint them and leave them alone. But always make sure there is a pulse beyond an injured joint. (First locate the pulse in the healthy limb; then try to find it at the same spot in the injured one.) If you can't feel a heartbeat out there—say in the wrist beyond an injured elbow—it may be necessary to shift the joint carefully in the hope of unkinking an artery.

Strains are injuries to muscle tissue. Minor ones are common and not serious; occasionally, though, a muscle in the calf or back will tear so badly that it cannot bear weight. This may be a considerable injury requiring medical attention. First aid is much like care for a sprain: cool, elevate, and gently compress the injured area. Some people with seriously strained muscles can walk out; some can't. A crisscross layer of tape and an elastic bandage, as with a twisted ankle, may help.

With sprains and strains, as with most other problems, the injured person himself is your best source of information. Only he can tell you how bad it feels, and whether or not he can travel on foot after your best efforts at first aid.

Bodily Aches and Alarms

So far we've talked of problems that arise because you are where you are, doing what you are doing: hiking in the wilderness, or anyway on a trail. But other, homelier complaints can arise out here as well as anywhere else, and sometimes do.

Headaches can ordinarily be treated with your light analgesic; usually insignificant, they may be connected with another problem like altitude sickness (see Chapter 28). A headache that comes on during the hiking day may be due to dehydration or to its mirror image, the supersaturated condition called *hyponatremia*. If you've been drinking little, have some water. If you've been drinking more than about a pint an hour, have some salty snacks instead.

Earaches tend to be due to infection; antibiotics can be taken if they persist. *Nosebleeds* are best stopped by pressing a cold compress on the bridge of the nose for as long as it takes. *Sore throats* may be a sign of another illness or may occur at high altitudes for no discernible reason; pus on the tonsils suggests that an antibiotic be taken.

Garden-variety upper respiratory infections—*colds and flu*—are certainly not emergencies. They're no fun, either, and if you're really under the weather, you may want to creep for home. Considering the number of people moving around in wild areas, it is truly astonishing how rare it is to encounter these common complaints out there.

Chest pain is alarming—everyone thinks heart attack—but can have other causes. There is little first aid for genuine heart problems in a wilderness situation, beyond comfort and reassurance and, if required, basic life support. People with known chronic heart problems will have medication along.

Abdominal pain. A growing pain in the belly, and anybody who still has an appendix thinks *appendicitis.*

If the pain does not settle in the lower right quadrant (below the navel and to the right of the midline of the body), it probably isn't an appendix that's complaining. Abdominal pain that does not increase when you press on the bothersome spot is probably superficial, not involving an organ, and not worrisome. Simple constipation can produce a suggestive pain but not the other symptoms of appendicitis: nausea, loss of appetite, and mild fever. If you do suspect the disease, start taking the antibiotic in your first-aid kit and head for civilization with all deliberate speed.

Indigestion happens out here, too; if you know you're susceptible, or are responsible for a group, carry an over-the-counter remedy. Pink bismuth in tablet form is favored by many. *Constipation* is not uncommon; drinking lots of water helps prevent it. Some hikers carry laxatives. *Diarrhea*, if serious, is more of a problem. You are not very likely to come down with a serious case in wild country in the United States or Canada. (Giardiasis, the infamous "backpacker's diarrhea," will not develop for at least a week after exposure. If you do come down with it, you will need a doctor's care. See also Chapter 20.) The essential thing to remember about any severe diarrhea is that you must replace fluids. Some first-aid kits contain oral rehydration salts, designed to replace not only water but also other chemicals lost.

28

Threats from the Environment

New backpackers are often too much afraid of wild animals. They may be too little afraid of other, less obvious, yet far more prevalent dangers: the heat, the cold, the wet, the wind, the alpine sun, the lack of oxygen at altitude. All these things affect the hiker. Some of them can make you very sick and some can kill you. One of the "environmental" disorders, hypothermia, probably endangers more backpackers in a single year than animals do in decades.

The Body's Thermostat

To keep working properly, the human body has to stay near the normal 98 degrees Fahrenheit. A very precise balance has to be maintained between heat gained and heat lost. If the balance shifts too far in either direction, the hiker becomes a victim, a person in trouble.

You generate heat just living. The harder you work, the more you generate. At the same time, the body loses heat, constantly, in the breath and from the skin. Survival depends on conserving this body heat when your surroundings are cold and getting rid of it when the neighborhood is hot. There are natural mechanisms for doing each.

What happens when the problem is *cold*? First, the muscles tense just slightly in what is called preshivering tone; this burns calories and generates a surprising amount of heat. (So you may be exercising in the cold without knowing it.) Then comes shivering, an even more effective heat producer. Meanwhile, the small arteries near the skin, where heat is radiated to the outside air, close down. Less blood approaches the skin, and less heat is lost. In dangerous cold, the body may cut off a large part of the circulation to the arms and legs, risking the limbs to keep the head and torso warm. After that, the natural defenses are exhausted. To operate in cold climates, we depend on artificial ones. Clothing, our added insulation, has made us a species that can live in the Arctic as well as in the tropics, where we evolved.

If the problem is *too much* warmth, there are different mechanisms. Vessels in the skin and in the arms and legs expand, bringing blood to the surface, where its heat is lost. Perspiration begins, and sweat, evaporating, takes large quantities of heat away. Clothes only get in the way of the cooling, except when you need to block the direct heat and burning ultraviolet rays of the sun.

This, oversimplified, is the system. The afflictions of heat and cold—hyperthermia, hypothermia, and frostbite—attack when it is pressed too far.

Hyperthermia

Hyperthermia is what happens to you when your body is unable to dispose of heat as fast as it manufactures it and absorbs it from outside. As the temperature of the vital organs rises, you begin to be sick.

The overheated person may feel faint and nauseated. The heartbeat may be fast and irregular. Sweating is profuse, yet the skin may feel oddly cool. The face is likely to be pale. The symptoms are generally those of shock (see Chapter 26). However, they don't always appear in neat packages. The most important thing to watch for is a growing indifference to surroundings. ("Whenever a person says he wants to sit down and catch up with the party later," one MD remarks, "it's a worrisome sign.") In this early period, the disorder is often labeled *heat exhaustion*.

As the body's core temperature rises to high-fever levels, the system goes haywire. The body may lose its ability to regulate blood flow to the skin. There may be a pounding pulse, labored breathing, and seizures. In the textbook case, the victim stops sweating: skin will be hot and dry. But symptoms vary, and it is most important again to focus on the person's attitude: a severely overheated hiker will lapse from indifference into major confusion. At this stage, the disease is commonly called *heat stroke*. It can kill.

The treatment, early or late, is the same: rapid cooling. This is best accomplished by removing clothing, sprinkling water on the skin, and fanning to produce evaporation. The water does not have to be cool or clean; in a pinch, even urine can be used. Once the person is clearly aware and able to swallow, give plenty of water by mouth.

Once the crisis has passed, you face the decision of whether to continue the trip or head for home. Except in very mild cases, the latter is probably the better choice—especially if the weather continues hot. In any event, an attack of hyperthermia is a signal to take it easy: the body has tried to handle a taxing combination of effort and heat, and failed.

How did it fail? Probably by being unable to sweat profusely enough. That ability is partly a matter of hydration—you have to drink a lot to sweat a lot—and partly a matter of training. In hot-weather hiking, one may have to perspire 2 quarts an hour to stay healthily cool. Hardly anybody can do this on the first hot hike of the season. But as time goes on, the body adapts to heat stress, "learning" to sweat more copiously and with less loss of the salts called electrolytes. An otherwise fit hiker needs about a week of intermittent exercise in a hot climate to make this adjustment. If you plan to hike the desert in the warmer part of the year, bear this in mind. Really intense hot-weather work requires conscious effort to replace sodium, by munching salty food or by consuming electrolyte-replacement drinks.

When the air is both hot and very humid, however, no amount of training will help: sweat just won't evaporate. Under these conditions, don't hike.

Heat cramps—painful involuntary muscle contractions, usually in the legs—are another misery that may affect unacclimatized hot-weather hikers. Rest, rubbing, and stretching help. So does salt intake, in food and drink but not in tablet form (likely to cause indigestion).

Hypothermia, the Killer

Of all the diseases of heat and cold, hypothermia has the ugliest record. As in heat stroke, the body's defenses break down, struggling vainly not against an excess of heat but against a lack. The temperature of those organs that are vital to life—the organs of the head and torso—begins to drop. All the conserving mechanisms are tried. All fail.

How do you know when hypothermia is coming on? It can be hard to tell. Cold feet and hands are not hypothermia; neither is a generally "chilly" feeling. Take these rather as warnings: signs that you're in a hostile environment and that your guard should be up. Fumbling hands may make it harder, for instance, to adjust your clothing properly.

Real hypothermia begins when the body's core temperature drops below 95 degrees. Violent shivering, though not always present, is a classic early sign. The sufferer grows somewhat clumsy and may have trouble talking. And yet the victim may push on—toughing it out—when she should not, wrongly convinced that she is only a little chilly and tired. Deteriorating judgment is itself a symptom.

If the cooling process is not arrested, this borderline condition will tip over into *profound* hypothermia. Body temperature, now, has dropped to 90 degrees. Shivering has tapered off or ceased. Muscles are very stiff indeed. Most notably, the person will start acting very oddly: she will stumble, mumble, say and do peculiar things. No longer is she competent. Finally, she will simply fall to the ground. If nothing is done for her, coma will follow, and then death.

If you notice the early signs of hypothermia in yourself or a companion, you take the obvious action: stop the loss of heat and make it possible for the person to warm up again. At the very beginning, it may be enough to get out of the wind for a few minutes and eat some candy. If the problem has reached the serious shivering stage, stop and set up shelter. Get your friend out of wet clothes, under cover, and into a sleeping bag. It may be helpful, and it cannot hurt, for a second hiker to take off outer clothing and get into the bag with the victim, sharing body warmth. If the victim can swallow, give her sweet liquids—hot, if possible, though the sugar is the main thing.

Profound hypothermia is not so easily dealt with. What if you come across a solo hiker semiconscious, or even seemingly dead, on a snowbank? In this instance, the right kind of first aid can save a life, but the wrong kind can kill.

In deep hypothermia, the heart muscle is chilled. One result is that the heart is prone to go into ventricular fibrillation, a random fluttering that pumps no blood and leads quickly to death. Any shock to the system can trigger this condition.

In such a case, the sufferer must be handled *gently*, with extreme care. Do not allow him to stand up or walk. (Sudden effort will shock the heart by bringing cold blood back from the limbs to the body core.) Even rewarming, if done too rapidly, can deliver a fatal blow. Don't, for instance, place a hypothermia victim in a warm spring.

Having avoided these errors, your first task is to prevent the person from getting any colder, typically by placing him in a sleeping bag. Your second, much less urgent job is to help rewarm his vital organs *but not, initially, his arms and legs*. Hot water bottles can be applied to points where heat can go quickly to the core—at the scalp, the neck, the armpit, the groin. (Hot mush in a plastic bag makes a good head-warmer.) In a tent, light a stove and boil water; the warm, steamy air will get heat to his head and lungs while the rest of him stays cool inside the zipped-up bag. Once the victim can swallow, sugary hot liquids are helpful. (Never try to get food or liquid into an unconscious person, though—it may be inhaled.)

A deeply hypothermic person may not be breathing and may lack a detectable heartbeat. In such a case, you certainly want to give artificial respiration, the pulmonary part of cardiopulmonary resuscitation. (Along with its primary purpose, it will help with rewarming.) Professionals debate, however, whether the chest compression part of CPR should be attempted. A cold heart may in fact still be beating, terribly slowly; intervention could produce a fatal fibrillation. As an amateur, you'd better not chance it. Meanwhile, don't assume the worst. "They're only dead," the saying goes, "when they're *warm* and dead."

If someone in your party has a brush with mild hypothermia, that need not necessarily alter your plans. A hiker who has been definitely hypothermic should probably be taken home. In a case of *profound* hypothermia, move the victim as little as possible; summon a rescue.

It doesn't take bitterly cold air to make "hypothermia weather." The problem can arise even on a mild day that is both *windy* and *wet*. On New Hampshire's Mount Washington, four hypothermia cases once had to be rescued within 48 hours—in August! Washington, one of the most weather-beaten summits in the United States, is hardly typical, but there is some risk in any cool region or season.

Frostbite

Frostbite is, essentially, freezing: the freezing of a part of the body. Feet and toes are the likeliest parts, by far, to be bitten; most of the other cases are fingers and hands.

Unlike hypothermia, frostbite can only happen when the air temperature is freezing. That makes it mainly a winter problem (though on some peaks and at some latitudes it can happen anytime). Winter campers, the first few times out, may worry about frostbite every time their hands or feet get unpleasantly cold. With more experience, you learn that mere chilliness isn't frostbite. Still, it's better to be overly suspicious than to be complacent.

Frostbite can sneak up on you. The *typical* pattern—a cold sensation, followed by pain, followed by no sensation at all—doesn't always hold. The best defense is to ask yourself frequently whether you have full feeling in fingers and toes, and to do something about it if you don't. If your feet feel chronically cold, for instance, try easing up on straps and laces.

If you think a finger is beginning to be frostbitten, you can quickly warm it in your armpit. If you are worried about your toes, there's the belly treatment. You stop, strip off your shoes and socks, and plant your feet on somebody's warm belly—not nearly as uncomfortable for the companion as it sounds! Groins and armpits work, too.

A part that is frostbitten will look waxy, feel cool to the touch, and be numb. If it is still soft and movable, however, the damage hasn't gone too deep. It will hurt while you rewarm it, but there should be no permanent harm. Seriously frostbitten flesh is inflexible and hard. If your fingers or toes have gotten like that, what do you do about it?

Your instinct might be to warm things up, fast. But this is sometimes the worst action you could take. In deep frostbite, the real tissue damage is done during the initial freezing and again when the flesh is thawed. While the part is actually frozen, nothing much is going on. Moreover, it doesn't hurt. Thawed, it will hurt like hell. People can walk many miles, without discomfort or further damage, on frozen toes and even frozen feet; but once thawing has taken place, a seriously frostbitten person must be carried.

There's another good reason for not rewarming deep frostbite too soon, and this is the risk of another bout of frostbite on the outward trek. Thawing and refreezing can turn a minor case into a major and crippling one.

So if you discover, in the middle of a bitter winter day, that someone in your party has a frozen toe, don't stop. Head as quickly as you can for the roadhead, or to a place from which rescue will be easy.

If you must make camp, you can hardly avoid rewarming a frozen part. Authorities agree that this should be accomplished quickly rather than gradually. Soak the injured limb in a bath of warm water. Mountaineering doctors debate the recommended temperature, but the consensus puts it between 100 and 105 degrees Fahrenheit. If the water feels hot to the first-aider, it's too hot for the patient. Keeping the water at that temperature as nearly as you can, soak the part for 20 to 30 minutes. Never pummel the damaged flesh, rub it with snow, break any blisters that appear, or try to exercise the limb. Never apply direct heat. After rewarming, bandage loosely.

Deep frostbite is another of those subjects that *has* to be talked about, because the problem is so frightening and serious when it occurs. But frostbite simply won't overtake a well-equipped and knowledgeable backpacker.

Altitude Sickness

"Altitude sickness" is a name for several related physical problems. Naturally enough, it is mostly encountered in high western ranges. More people than we realize get sick at altitude, sometimes running considerable risk without ever knowing it. In one study, 84 percent of the people who climbed to the 14,410-foot summit of Washington's Mount Rainier were found to have at least some symptoms.

Altitude sickness is brought on by a rapid rise in elevation. Though symptoms rarely start below 9,000 or 10,000 feet, they can begin as low as 5,000. How fit you are doesn't seem to matter a great deal. Neither, surprisingly enough, does smoking.

Ordinary altitude sickness, the kind experienced by thousands, is known medically as "acute mountain sickness." Coming down with it, you will probably notice first a headache, mild or intense. If you're hiking, you'll feel exhausted and short of breath. You'll lose your appetite and may feel nauseated. In more severe cases there is vomiting. Many people get a few symptoms toward the end of a long first day that ends above 9,000 feet, feel better when they stop hiking, and wake up perfectly fit in the morning. Others are uncomfortable for several days.

All of this is a nuisance at worst—for most of us, most of the time. But acute mountain sickness can develop, on the second or third day, into one of two other conditions, both highly dangerous. For either there is only one cure: *pack up and get down the hill*—preferably while you can still move under your own power.

Cerebral edema, a rare but deadly condition, is an accumulation of fluid in the brain. The current belief is that ordinary mountain sickness is actually a very slight cerebral edema, but the more intense form is unmistakably different. The headache turns violent. The victim will be alarmingly weak. She may stagger, babble, hallucinate. If she isn't taken to lower elevations, she falls into a stupor, followed by a coma and then by death.

Almost as serious, and considerably more common, is *high-altitude pulmonary edema*, an accumulation of fluid in the lungs. Over a hundred people die of this disease every year, some at elevations no higher than 9,000 feet. The symptoms are somewhat like those of pneumonia. There is coughing, shortness of breath, quickened breathing, and fast heartbeat. The lungs feel tight, stiff, constricted. There will be creaking or bubbling noises in the chest, slight at first, and then increasing. As the victim gets worse, coughing will bring up a pinkish foam. The last stage is a stupor brought about by lack of oxygen.

Descent is the real answer. Sometimes a drop of a couple of thousand feet will bring a dramatic recovery. If you can't evacuate immediately, have the victim sit up, and try to keep him alert. Bed rest only makes the condition worse.

Pulmonary edema is by no means unknown in older adults, but the danger is much greater for people under twenty-one. Hikers who have had it once must be on the watch for it afterward. And here's a curious fact: people who spend a long time at high altitudes, return to sea level for several weeks, and then go up again, run the greatest risk of all.

The best prevention for altitude sickness is going up slowly. It's ideal to start with several days at 9,000 or 10,000 feet, and to increase the altitude of your camp no more than 2,000 feet per night. If you must start at a high roadhead, try at least to get a full night's sleep there on the eve of the trip, and schedule a fairly leisurely first day.

Several drugs have promise in heading off altitude sickness.

The first is acetazolamide, known also as Diamox. It works at least against mild altitude sickness and is also recommended for treatment. People who are allergic to sulfa drugs can't use Diamox, however: it makes them hypersensitive to ultraviolet rays and gives them severe sunburn.

The second is the herb gingko biloba. Studies are showing that it reduces the incidence of altitude sickness by about half.

The third is Viagra, and related drugs aimed at erectile dysfunction. Work in the Alps shows that these compounds stave off illness for nine people out of ten, though the side effect in men may be unwanted.

Sun Exposure and Snow Blindness

It's painful to admit it, but the case is clear: any more than minimal sun exposure must now be recognized as bad for human skin. Ultraviolet (UV) radiation contributes greatly to epidermal wear-and-tear, and skin cancer is on the rise. The risk is there even if you acquire a lovely tan, or do not noticeably burn. The eyes are similarly punished; several conditions, including cataract, are promoted by ultraviolet exposure. People up to about age eighteen are especially at risk for skin damage, and young eyes remain extremely vulnerable up to about age twenty-five.

The farther south you go and the higher you climb, the worse it gets: the more ultraviolet rays come through the filtering atmosphere. At 10,000 feet, ultraviolet dosage is half again as strong as at sea level. Moderate overcast does little to stop this radiation. Be aware that burning rays bounce up from glittering granite, sand, water, or snow.

Protection takes the form of clothing, hat, and sunglasses, and of sunblocking lotions for exposed skin.

Sunscreen lotions are graded according to "sun protection factor" (SPF), prominently noted on containers. Backpackers favor SPF 30, which theoretically allows you to remain in the sun thirty times as long, before burning, as you could with no lotion on at all. You don't need to splurge on preparations rated higher than SPF 30, which add little protection. Choose lotions billed as sweatproof—they do float off with sweat, but not too quickly. For lips, use SPF-rated waxy sticks containing sunscreen. Be aware that these products lose potency in the tube; look for and respect stale dates. Better yet, start every year with a new supply. Put on your sunscreen an hour before the sun hits you, and renew it from time to time. Be sure to apply a generous coat under your chin and around your nostrils, where rays bouncing up from below can burn you badly.

Beyond sunscreens are opaque sunblockers containing zinc oxide, like labiosan. Some people favor these for sensitive spots like lips and noses.

A single layer of thin cloth is surprisingly transparent to the sun; a T-shirt, for instance, gives you no more protection than a coating of lotion with an SPF of 7 or 8. Thicker cloth, or multiple layers, can block UV radiation totally, but may be too warm for the conditions you are hiking in. Gear stores now carry light, well-ventilated garments designed specifically to block ultraviolet and rated, like lotions, with sun protection factors. For very bright conditions, sunhats with neck cowls, or havelocks, are valuable.

Sunglasses are essential in the high country and recommended in low-lying regions. Suitable glasses block the entire ultraviolet spectrum, including what are called the *UVA* and *UVB ranges*. The apparent darkness and color of the lenses are unrelated to sun protection. Gray is a popular, nondistorting tint. Polarized lenses are useful if you are trying to spot fish in water. Glass lenses cost more than polycarbonate and break more readily, but they are clearer and less likely to get scratched: take your pick. Sunglasses for outdoor use need virtually unbreakable frames. For extra-bright conditions—altitude, snow, and ice—you will want "glacier glasses" with shields of some sort at the sides. Suitable eyewear can be had for $30 and up.

If you break or lose your glasses, and don't dare do without, you can peer through a tiny hole in a bandanna, or make slit glasses by putting tape across an empty frame.

If you already wear prescription lenses, the need for sun protection can complicate matters. The simplest solution is contact lenses worn behind sunglasses; prescription sunglasses can also be made at a price.

If you neglect your eye protection on the heights, you risk coming down with the frightening condition called *snow blindness*, sunburn of the eye. The first symptom will be a scratchy, sandy feeling. That's the time to hurry off the mountain. In another 6 or 7 hours the eyes may swell almost shut, and the touch of light will become a physical, painful thing. At that point, to get down the hill, you may have to be led. The first-aid treatments are cold packs, total darkness, and perhaps aspirin or codeine for pain. The condition should abate in 1 to 2 days.

What about ordinary, epidermal sunburn? In mild cases, your sunscreen lotion will also do for a salve. Creams with aloe vera seem unusually helpful. Really severe sunburn can be incapacitating, with blistering, severe pain, swelling, headache, even nausea, fever, and chills. Moist, cool dressings will help somewhat. So will lotions with cortisone.

29

Problem Animals & Plants

The animals of the mountains, woods, and deserts are among the things that draw us there. The word *wilderness*, in fact, comes from roots meaning "the place of the wild beasts." Still, animals (and some plants as well) can make problems for the hiker, or worse.

Mosquitoes and Other Insect Pests

The bugs have probably caused many times as much misery as the snakes and the bears combined.

Mosquitoes lay eggs in shallow water or damp soil and hatch when days are warm and moist. In the mountains of the Southwest, where the soil is dry by August, they vanish early. Elsewhere, and especially in wet lowlands, mosquitoes may swarm much longer. With global warming and the northward spread of tropical illnesses, mosquitoes in the United States and Canada are getting new respect as vectors of disease.

Then there are the various stinging or biting flies, a whole tribe of species going by variable common names. *No-see-ums* ("biting midges," "punkies"), found in low-lying areas over most of the country, are so tiny that they vanish in most lighting and can pass through all but the finest netting. The *black fly*, a famous torment in the north woods, is also known as the buffalo fly. There are horse flies and deer flies and sand flies.

The *chigger* is the larva of a mite (thus actually an arachnid, not an insect). Found in the southern United States, it lives in grass; digging into your skin, it can cause an infuriating itch.

You defend yourself against this army with physical barriers or with chemical repellents. In very buggy places, hikers wear head nets. For night protection, in addition to netted tents, there are specialized bug shelters to be had; these cost $15 to $120 and weigh from a few ounces to a tentlike couple of pounds.

Repellents, however, are the first line of defense. There is one chemical that really does the job: N,N-diethyl-meta-toluamide, known universally as DEET and found in numerous products. In recent years there has been some concern about the safety of DEET, which strips paint, dissolves plastic, and gets into your system through the skin. Considering the rivers of DEET applied each year around the world, the incidence of problems is tiny, but some caution is indicated. Buy DEET in lotion or stick form and in concentrations of 30 percent or less. On children, DEET should be used sparingly, and in concentrations under 10 percent. New formulations are now available that last longer and are less readily absorbed into the body. Apply it to clothing, when practical, rather than to bare skin; but remember that the substance can damage rayon, acetate, spandex, and urethane waterproofing. Avoid getting it into eyes and mucous membranes; keep it off cuts, scrapes, and irritated areas; don't rub it in. If wearing both sunscreen and repellent, apply the sunscreen first.

DEET has some competitors. One is a chemical known as IR3535, long used in Europe and now incorporated in repellents by Avon (whose Skin-So-Soft lotion had a following among hikers even before this recent reformulation). Other DEET rivals are botanical products: citronella, a lemony substance derived from an Asian grass; catnip; eucalyptus oil; and compounds derived from soybeans and from tomatoes. The relative effectiveness of these products is debated, though none yet appears to match DEET. Citronella has the further disadvantage of being a bear attractant.

Bees, Wasps, and Yellow Jackets

Bee stings, relatively harmless to most of us, are very dangerous to some. If you have an allergy to stings, you probably know it; if you even suspect it, be sure to get a doctor's advice on how to deal with it. Desensitization is possible for some people; the injection of epinephrine is often lifesaving. Kits with preloaded push-button injectors are now available.

If there is an allergic reaction, it will be unmistakable. In a few minutes the person will feel faint and giddy. The skin will be cool and moist. In severe cases the reaction will resemble an insanely exaggerated attack of hay fever. The tissues of the throat may swell so much that breathing is cut off. There is little the first-aider can do in such a case. If you have the allergy, carry a kit and be prepared to give yourself the lifesaving injection.

If you're stung by a bee, get rid of the stinger by scraping it off with a knife blade, grabbing it with tweezers, or just getting it between fingers. If you have a venom extractor (see "Treating Snakebite," below), use that on the site instead. After-sting treatments like Sting-Eze also help.

What about the notorious "killer" or Africanized bees? Honeybees of this strain, recently arrived in the United States from points south, are no more venomous than other sorts, but are uniquely inclined to attack by the swarm. However, being essentially domestic animals, they are not expected to show up in wild places.

The southern United States, including Southern California, is plagued by another dangerous exotic, the fire ant. If you disturb a fire ant mound, you'll draw a mass counterattack, and every ant is capable of multiple stings. Keep your distance.

Ticks and Tick-Borne Diseases

Ticks, like mosquitoes, are bloodsuckers, but they do the job slowly. Their bites are not to be taken lightly, as they can inoculate you with more or less dangerous disease-causing agents.

Two ticks that carry Lyme disease (magnified 15 times). The deer tick (left) is found in the eastern United States and adjacent Canada; the western black-legged tick is its Pacific Coast counterpart.

These unpleasant arachnids come in numerous species, colors, and sizes, up to ¼ inch long; but it is the early "nymph" stage, truly tiny and hard to spot, that is most likely to get you. Nymphs are abundant in spring and summer. They climb onto you from tall grass or other foliage close to the ground. After riding on you for some time, they find bare skin and attach themselves painlessly. Long-sleeved shirts and long pants protect you to some extent. Tucking pants into your socks helps. So do built-in elastic cuffs or slip-on gaiters. So does DEET, applied sparingly at wrists, waist, and ankles. Clothing can be sprayed with permethrin, which is not only a repellent but also a potent insecticide harmless to our species. Permanone is one of several brands of permethrin preparations.

Ticks tend to prospect for a while before staking a claim; you can often catch and kill them before they dig in. Examine your clothes every now and then for small, dark, crawling objects, and do the same for your companions. Light-colored fabrics make the animals easier to see. Check your skin for ticks at least once a day, especially where clothing has been tight, as at waist and ankles. Check also hairline and groin. On a brushy, off-trail trip, hikers often strip before bed and

Trouble & How to Deal With It

inspect each others' backs. Parents should similarly inventory children, twice a day. Very fine-toothed tick combs, sold for use on pets, also work well on human heads of hair.

Once a tick is well attached, remove it with sharp-pointed tweezers. Grasp it as far toward the buried head as you can. Pull straight outward firmly and steadily until the creature, or most of it, comes out. Don't rock, twist, jerk, or crush. It is no great cause for concern if the mouth parts stay in your skin. Several companies make specialty tools for tick removal.

When you have extracted the tick, wash the puncture with soap and water and watch the spot for possible infection. Apply a venom extractor if you've got one (see "Treating Snakebite," below). Keep the extracted tick as a possible aid in diagnosis if you should get sick. If it's alive, seal it in a bag or other container with a scrap of moistened toilet paper.

There is now a whole list of tick-borne diseases, the most notorious of which is Lyme disease. Lyme is known to be spread in the Northeast and upper Midwest by the deer tick, and on the West Coast by deer and western black-legged ticks, both quite small even as adults and poppy-seed sized as nymphs. Early indicators of Lyme may be flulike symptoms and a bull's-eye rash resembling ringworm; these won't appear until several weeks after exposure. If not treated properly with antibiotics, Lyme disease can take very nasty forms, including a severe chronic arthritis. Vaccines exist but are not recommended for general use. If a rash or sudden illness follows a trip, seek medical advice. Other serious tick-borne diseases are Rocky Mountain spotted fever, babesiosis, ehrlichosis, and tularemia. Scary but less dangerous is tick paralysis, a weakness that afflicts some people while ticks are attached to them but clears up when the animal is removed.

Spiders, Scorpions, and Centipedes

The one acutely dangerous spider in North America is the black widow, a name for several species in the genus

A black widow spider bite can make an adult very ill and can possibly kill a child. The spiders are found widely across the United States, especially in warmer climates.

Latrodectus. "Black" widows may also be red or brown; the famous red hourglass pattern on the abdomen may be pronounced or not. The head is small compared with the round body; front and back legs are markedly longer than those on the side. The smaller and inconspicuous male is harmless.

Many people bitten by this spider see no worse effect than swelling or redness at the bite; others suffer painful and prolonged muscle cramps. In severe cases, hospital treatment is required. In about one case out of twenty there is danger of death; most victims are children.

Another species of concern is the brown recluse spider, also called the violin spider because of a distinctive mark on its back. The bite of the female can produce a troublesome ulcer. Of no concern at all are the tarantulas, various species found in the Southwest and as far east as the Ozarks; though large, furry, and spectacular, they have an insignificant sting.

If you're bitten by any spider, use your venom extractor on the site. Cooling the spot can reduce pain. Also catch the animal if you can. If you're sure it's a black widow, it's prudent to head for civilization. If a spider bite raises a blood blister, puncture this, drain it, and apply antibiotic ointment. If the spot is slow to

The bite of the brown recluse spider, found mainly in the Midwest and South, can produce a troublesome, long-lasting ulcer.

heal, seek attention when you get home. With any bite, take precautions against infection. If flulike or other untoward symptoms follow a bite, seek medical advice.

Scorpions are spider relatives and sting with their tails. There are various species in North America; though most are found in deserts, scorpions occur in many environments and as far north as Oregon and Montana. All are at least mildly venomous. The dangerous one is the bark scorpion, *Centuroides sculpturatus*, found only in Arizona and immediately across the border in desert California. Though some scorpions are as long as 8 inches, *Centuroides* are less than half that length; they're colored yellow to yellow green and have long, narrow pincers. Scorpions hunt at night. It's a good idea in any region to shake out your clothes and boots in the morning, though you seldom find anything inside them. In the daytime be careful when digging in sand or lifting rocks and logs. Scorpion venom attacks the nerves; even a *Centuroides* bite is unlikely to kill a healthy adult but can threaten the very young, the old, and the allergic. If bitten by any species, apply a venom extractor.

The western diamondback rattlesnake is one of the largest and most impressive of the thirty rattlesnake species found across the United States and in southern Canada.

Centipedes—many species—live under rocks and in downed wood. Some have a pretty good sting. The harmless millipedes, sometimes confused with centipedes, have two pairs of legs growing from each body joint—the centipedes, just one.

Snakes

We have four kinds of poisonous snakes in the United States and Canada. Most important by far are the *rattlesnakes*, about thirty species, found somewhere in each of the forty-eight contiguous states and in southern Canada, but there are other types: the *copperhead* in the East; the *cottonmouth*, or *water moccasin*, in the southeastern swamps; and the *coral snake*.

Rattlesnakes, copperheads, and cottonmouths are all pit vipers. They inject through fangs a venom that attacks via the bloodstream.

The markings of rattlesnakes vary; actual rattles may or may not be present. The snakes seldom grow longer than 5 feet. Rattlers become scarce above 7,000 feet in the warm Southwest and aren't found much above 3,000 feet in areas near the United States–Canada border. In wet, cool regions, they prefer the drier sides of ridges, especially southern exposures.

The copperhead, found in the eastern United States, has the characteristic ropy body and diamond-shaped head of the venomous pit viper family.

The copperhead is found widely through the East as far north as New York State. It has, indeed, a copper-colored head, and hourglass markings along its body. The cottonmouth, or water moccasin, lives in wetlands from Virginia south, and west to central Texas. It is a thick, dark snake, up to 6 feet long, without obvious markings. Hikers aren't likely to see it, but waders and canoeists must be aware of it.

All the pit vipers have a markedly wide head swelling from a much narrower neck. The body is heavy looking, ropy. The pupil of the eye is elliptical. Snakes not of this family, by contrast, have slender bodies merging into narrow heads with little indentation at the neck; the pupil of the eye is round.

Among those American snakes that are not pit vipers, only one is venomous: the coral snake. The coral is rather small, 2 to 4 feet long, and thin of body and head; it secretes a poison that attacks primarily the nerves. Coral snakes are handsomely marked with rings of yellow, black, and red. To distinguish a coral snake from other, harmless snakes that have red bands, remember that only coral snakes have red rings adjoining yellow:

Red on yellow, kill a fellow

Red on black, venom lack

One species is found in the southeastern United States, another in southern Arizona and New Mexico.

The coral snake, a relative of the cobra, secretes a powerful venom that attacks the nerves, but the animal rarely bites unless handled. One species is found in the Sonoran Desert, another in the Deep South.

Avoiding Snakebite

Snakes of different species vary in their readiness to strike, but none is out to get you. Recognizing that you are far too big to eat, they don't regard you as prey. They may, however, perceive you as a threat. That's what you want to avoid.

Snakes, cold-blooded animals, are active only when it is pleasantly warm. In some regions and seasons, days are too hot for them, and they do their hunting at night. If only the morning and evening hours are temperate, snakes will be moving then. Torpid snakes, however, will still strike if stepped on.

Remember these simple precautions:

First, wear long pants and high-topped boots in snake country—and especially when you leave the trail. Heavy fabric gaiters are protective. Some people headed for snake-rich terrain make tubes of thin cardboard and tuck them around the ankles, under the trouser legs: clumsy but effective shields.

Second, make sure you can see where you're putting your feet and hands. Be especially careful in rock scrambling. Never thrust a hand over an unseen edge to grope for a hold. If you get up at night, put on your boots and carry a flashlight.

Third, if you hear a snake rattling, stop dead still until you see where it is; then move away. Meanwhile, the snake will probably be moving away from *you*.

Fourth, never pick up an unidentified snake. A large number of bites result from this kind of foolish provocation.

Treating Snakebite

There is just one tool for treating snakebite in the field: the multipurpose venom extractor, a pumplike device that can be used also on bee stings, tick sites, even mosquito bites.

If someone has been struck at by a snake, examine the spot. If there are one or two deep, widely spaced punctures—the fang marks—you know that a viper has struck. You do *not* know that it has left a dose of venom—in about half of all cases, none is injected. You proceed regardless.

Calm the injured person and put her in a restful position, keeping the bitten limb low (below the level of the heart). Use a razor (part of the kit) to shave skin if it is very hairy. Choose the suction cup that best fits the area of the bite. Pull the pump handle all the way out and place the cup on the bite site. Now press the handle in, creating a vacuum; at the end of the stroke you'll see the skin puff upward into the tube. Leave the pump in place for 3 minutes.

When time is up, pull the handle out again, gently. Any extracted liquid will fall onto the skin; wipe it off carefully and wash the site with soap and water. If there's nothing, or just a little blood, you know that no venom was injected. Wash the suction cup as well.

Extractors are not applied to eyelids, genitals, or other areas of very sensitive skin.

The same directions apply to bites and stings by insects, spiders, and scorpions, except that the time of application is shorter: 30 to 90 seconds.

If, despite your efforts, some snake venom has made it into the person's system, the unmistakable symptom will arrive in a hurry: violent, increasing pain. The bitten area will also swell and become discolored. The victim may sweat profusely, feel nausea, and perhaps vomit (though these symptoms are sometimes caused by anxiety alone). Keep her comfortable, quiet, and cool. Place a cold pack on the bitten limb. Do not give coffee, tea, or alcohol. Depending on the amount of venom she got, your friend may be very sick or scarcely sick at all. Reassure her, watch her, and guard against shock. If symptoms have appeared, arrange an exit from the wilderness.

Meanwhile, try to identify the snake, or at least try to determine whether it is a pit viper (or coral snake). Kill it, if you can safely do so, and keep the body. This may help a doctor to choose an antivenin later on. But don't handle a snake for an hour after its death: a reflexive second strike is possible.

A Couple of Lizards

The Gila monster, found in the Southwest, is an almost harmless creature with a reputation. Massive, colorful, and up to 2 feet long, it certainly has a formidable look; it has jaws like a pit bull; and its venom can in fact be dangerous. But the monster is not in the least inclined to attack, and almost every bite on record took place when somebody picked up a captive specimen. Incidentally, the Gila monster is an endangered species and has full protection. For its sake and yours, leave it alone. Same goes for the similar Mexican beaded lizard, occasionally seen in southern Arizona.

Bears

High on the list of worrisome wilderness animals in North America are the bears: common black bruins in most wild areas; and in the northern Rockies and Canada, the magnificent, unpredictable brown bear, or grizzly. Backpackers outside the high Arctic won't encounter the third North American bear, the polar.

The black bear, *Ursus americanus*, can in fact be almost any color in a range from black through brown to blond. It has a sleek, pointed head: think of a seal. Adult females average 140 pounds, males 220 pounds. Black bears in the eastern United States are heavier.

Black bears (top) live in many wilderness areas. The key to peaceful coexistence: keeping our food out of their reach. In the northern regions where grizzly bears (bottom) occur, additional precautions apply.

Blacks are found in every wilderness region outside the desert, but rarely appear above timberline.

The grizzly, or brown bear, *Ursus arctos*, is an altogether more formidable beast. (The Blackfoot Indians of Montana called it Real Bear.) A mass of muscle between its shoulders gives it an almost bisonlike appearance, and the muzzle forms an angle with the massive head: think of a chow dog. Its claws are often 4 inches long, more than double the length of black bear claws. Colors run in the same range as black bear hues, but solid black is rare. Many but not all *arctos* bears have white-tipped hairs that give them the "grizzled" look. Adult grizzlies average about 500 pounds.

Grizzlies are found throughout western Canada and Alaska, in several mountain ranges in northwest

Montana, in far northern Idaho and the adjacent corner of Washington state, and tenuously in the far northern Cascades. An isolated population lives in and around Yellowstone National Park. Grizzlies operate quite happily above, or north of, timberline.

Black Bear Precautions

The black bear is traditionally more nuisance than hazard. However, dangerous and even fatal attacks have occurred.

The essential strategy with black bears is to keep your food out of their reach, by bearbagging, perhaps the use of bear-proof containers, and general cleanliness in camp (see Chapter 18). If a black bear is haunting your neighborhood, the authorities recommend a policy of "mild aggression." A pesky black can generally be frightened off by shouting, banging pots, even throwing rocks. You will often read that a mother bear with cubs is uniquely dangerous, but the record fails to confirm this. Keep a reasonable distance, however, and never try to take food from a black bear or—even worse—*give* food to a bear.

In a few aberrant cases, black bears have turned predatory, coming after human beings themselves as food. If a black bear seems threatening, the record shows, the worst thing to do is to run. Stand your ground and make noise. If actually attacked, fight back with everything you've got.

Grizzly Bear Precautions

The grizzly bear is the more dangerous species. Rather like ourselves, it is dominant, unpredictable, and inclined to defend its turf. It is also interested in our food, but almost never in us *as* food. So the first rule of grizzly relations is to protect the larder, even more thoroughly than we do against black bears. The second is to avoid confrontation. The third and least intuitive rule is *not* to fight back if an attack seems to be in progress.

If you're headed for a region that has grizzly bears, it very probably has black bears, too. You need to learn in advance how to tell the species apart. As part of your planning, contact the managing agency in the area you are visiting and get its advice about the local bears. And any traveler to grizzly territory should consult Stephen Herrero's *Bear Attacks* (see the Resources section).

Recognize that there is safety in numbers. Groups of three and four rarely get into trouble, groups of six or more virtually never—provided that they stick together and preserve the advantage. Even if your ordinary style is more spartan, plan to carry a tent that encloses you completely with opaque walls and has plenty of headroom. Binoculars, too, become basic equipment now.

Plan to do your cooking on a stove, and choose and pack your food to minimize odors. In this case, freeze-dried foods are actually preferable to those that are otherwise preserved, or fresh. Some traditional but smelly items—sardines, tuna, bacon, cheese, and the like—should simply not be carried. If you are accustomed to catching fish to supplement your larder, reconsider here: both the act of fishing and the odors of fish are somewhat dangerous in grizzly country. Bearbagging, of course, must be provided for (see Chapter 18). If heading for a treeless area or a bear hotspot, bring bearproof food canisters. The more cautious authorities also recommend that you carry a separate set of outer clothing to use while cooking: perhaps a spare light cotton shirt and an apron (see "Camping in Grizzly Country," below).

When you get to that region, check in with the rangers. Land managers in grizzly country keep track of bears, especially aggressive ones, and close trails and campgrounds accordingly. Warning signs may be placed at roadheads, and wilderness permits will be used to steer people away from problem areas. Get the official advice, and follow it to the letter. Be ready to change routes or even destinations if you must. Rental food containers may also be available.

Two kinds of grizzly bear encounters account for most of the trouble: sudden, unexpected meetings, where the bear's defensive instincts are aroused; and cases where the bear is drawn to your food. Most surprise meetings occur on the trail; most food-related problems occur in camp.

You lower your chance of trail encounters somewhat by hiking in full daylight.

In grizzly country, safety requires noise. Hikers make racket as they move along, conversing loudly with companions; singing; banging a spoon on a metal cup; clapping hands; talking to the air; blowing a whistle. Some favor tin cans with pebbles in them. Jingling bells aren't loud enough.

Watch for sign. Every few minutes, stop and listen—bears are too big to move quietly, especially through brush. Watch for, and if going cross-country avoid, berry patches, cow parsnip thickets, fields of glacier lilies, streams where fish are spawning, and areas where nuts litter the ground. Also keep clear of carrion, which may be evidenced by smell or by circling ravens and crows.

Keep your party bunched together, retaining the advantage of your numbers. Children, obviously, must be kept close at hand. Make your rest stops in spots where there's a view; sit back-to-back and keep an eye on your surroundings.

If you see a bear before it has sensed you, stop your noisemaking and try to see which kind it is. Binoculars help here. If there's a grizzly cub in the picture, just leave. If a solo adult is a grizzly, look for a safe, wide detour (on the downwind side); if there's no way around, retreat or stay put until the animal has moved on.

If you see a grizzly that is already aware of you, it may soon retreat—this is in fact the most common outcome. In this case, you can continue, maybe with a cross-country detour if the beast seems to be using the human trail. Since the animal has already registered your presence and decided to avoid you, keep its sensitive nose informed by traveling *upwind* from the bear.

If a grizzly takes unwelcome interest in you, much may depend on how you read the signs present in its behavior. A bear that just looks at you, without making noises or laying back its ears, is checking you out. If it stands up on its hind legs, it is checking you out from a higher vantage. It is appropriate to stay where you are and make conversational noises. Watch the bear, but from a corner of your eye; in the animal world, a straight-on gaze is a challenge. Reduce your apparent bulk by turning sideways or flexing your knees.

If a grizzly stands crosswise to you and puts its head down, it is suggesting—so experts say—that you back off. Do so, not too fast, while continuing to face generally toward the bear. If your retreat seems to increase its agitation, pause for a time, then continue.

The threat escalates if a bear faces you squarely, lowers and perhaps sways its head, flattens its ears, and makes sounds—moaning, huffing, or clacking of teeth. All you can do is keep backing away. Never turn and run.

After the threat behavior, the bear may charge. It may veer off at the last moment. If contact seems inevitable, hit the dirt, facedown, with legs slightly spread and your arms protecting your face and the back of your neck. If the bear just cuffs you or bites you a few times, force yourself not to resist or to cry out. If it flips you over, flip yourself back; otherwise remain still. When the attack ceases, hold this position in silence for at least 20 minutes before peeking to see if you've been left alone. Repeat attacks are rare.

Remember: this passive strategy applies to grizzlies only. Faced with a menacing black bear, you would project dominance, not submission.

Camping in Grizzly Country

At the end of the hiking day, stop early enough to find an appropriate camp and complete your cooking and food storage in daylight. Alternatively, schedule an early dinner break on the trail a mile or more before your actual camp. The ideal site will be fairly open, with little cover for approaching bears. Avoid camp-sites right next to the trail (or any obvious game trail) or next to running or standing water. Avoid also berry patches and other ursine food sources; areas with bear sign; and of course areas that show evidence of earlier raids (like scattered garbage or scat with remnants of human food in it). Also be wary of dirty camps with garbage or trash; if you can't avoid them, clean them up.

The kitchen and food-handling area should be set up 100 yards away from your sleeping spot, and down-wind from it, so that odors blow away from you. Since breezes tend to blow downslope at night, beds on a slope should typically be uphill. Locate also a suitable tree for bearbagging, ideally near the kitchen, and in any case similarly far way and downwind from the bed. If lockers, wires, or elevated poles are provided, by all means use them.

Should you in fact, as some sources suggest, carry and use a special set of clothes for cooking, to be bearbagged after the meal? This idea seems to be more preached than practiced. Stephen Herrero, perhaps the most respected student of human-bear encounters, admits, "I almost never bag my clothes." But, he adds, he would do so on a visit to a place where the bears were recently known to have scavenged human food.

After the meal, clean up scrupulously. Replace all foodstuffs in ziplock plastic bags, completely closed. Washwater and excess cooking water should be strained and the solids treated as garbage. Small quan-tities of washwater may be evaporated at the edge of a hot fire; large quantities can be scattered on the ground at least 100 yards away and downwind from all other camp activities. Wash yourself well.

Now for the bearbagging. What gets bagged depends, once more, on the local situation. In a bear "hot spot," the authorities say, you should gather every-thing that has been in contact with food, including items you might not think of: stoves; clean pots and utensils; water and water containers, and maybe those cooking clothes.

Besides food, every cosmetic, skin cream, dentifrice, and medicine should be suspected as a bear attractant. So should canned food, pet food, used toilet paper if you are packing this item out, and feminine hygiene products. Some body odors may also attract the interest of bears. Wash up after sexual activity. Menstruating women need to take special care with their hygiene, though a controversial suggestion that they avoid bear country entirely during their periods has been withdrawn. Use tampons rather than pads; wrap used tampons in foil and then place in a plastic bag; clean up with moist towelettes.

If your camp is in an alpine or treeless region, like the northern part of Denali National Park, you should be carrying bearproof canisters. These can also be useful in regions where all the available trees seem to be scrubby lodgepole pines. Place canisters at least 100 yards from any bedsite, downwind, and also at least 100 yards away from your kitchen. If possible, place them in brush, pile rocks on them, or suspend them over rocky faces. If trees are available in grizzly country, authorities recommend that even canisters should be bagged and hung.

Packs should ideally be hung, especially if you suspect that they are odorous. If not hung, they should be placed on the ground well away from your tent, empty and crumb-free, with zippers and flaps open.

Sleep in your tent, period. By all means pitch the fly if there is one, and lie as far as possible to the middle. Passing bears have been known to sniff at, paw at, or nibble on open-air sleepers, and to make investigative holes in nylon roofs. Never take a snack to bed. Make sure there are no food fragments about. Have a light at hand and, if you must get up at night, use it.

In the morning, use caution when you leave your tent and when you go to retrieve your food; if a grizzly is investigating, let it. If the culprit is a black bear, however, be "mildly aggressive."

You might think that snow campers could disregard grizzly bears, but that's not quite the case. The animals may emerge in late winter and spring; they move just fine over snow. Inconvenient though it is, late-season winter campers should separate cooking and sleeping areas and in general take the usual precautions.

What about weaponry? Few backpackers will have firearms, but many now carry bear-deterrent sprays containing capsicum, the chemical that makes peppers hot. If charged by a bear, you lay down a cloud between the animal and you; at closer range, aim at the face. The stuff is not a repellent to be sprayed around in advance—bears even like the smell, in low concentrations. Make sure the product you buy is intended for bear, not just for urban use. Canisters cost $50 or more, holsters included.

All bear encounters, including benign ones, should be reported to the authorities.

Other Large-Animal Attacks

Mountain lions, long regarded as no threat to human beings, have recently injured or killed people in several western states. Children and smallish people, especially hiking solo, are most at risk. There is safety in numbers. If a lion attacks, it will have in mind eating you, not scaring you off; your response should be to threaten, not to reassure. Do not run or crouch down. Make yourself as formidable as possible: stand tall, raise your arms and wave them slowly, or open your jacket like wide wings. If you're wearing a pack, hoist it above your shoulders. If you have kids in tow, pick up any small child, not crouching down to do so; position older youngsters behind you. Face the cat and maintain eye contact; bare your teeth; speak loudly and firmly; wave menacingly with a staff or stick; throw rocks or anything you can reach without ducking down. If possible, back slowly to higher ground or around a boulder or tree. If the cat stops moving, looks away from you, and begins ostentatiously to wash, you're making your point; reduce your own aggressive behavior to match, but keep the animal in sight and make a dignified retreat. If a mountain lion actually attacks you, shield your head and neck and fight back. It should be emphasized that lion attacks, though impressive to read about, remain exceedingly rare.

Besides lions and bears, various other sizable critters have been known to threaten, bite, gore, or trample humans from time to time. The list includes bison, elk, moose, and alligators. Surprisingly, given the stories we all read as children, it does not include wolves, a species never known to attack human beings. With mammals, a perceived threat to their young is the most common trigger for trouble. For instance, moose cows, protecting unseen calves, very occasionally charge at hikers. In this situation, stand very still—moose have poor eyesight and may lose track of you. If that doesn't work, move away slowly, as you would when faced with a grizzly, talking quietly but looking to one side; seek shelter among trees. All problematic animal encounters should be reported.

We're accustomed to put ourselves in the middle of the picture: to regard other animals in the wild as elements in our experience, whether as problems, as dangers, or as entertainments. But of course it works both ways. Our presence affects them as well. A bear habituated to human food will probably wind up dead. A squirrel that grows up begging from campers may starve when we're not around. On another note, do not handle or disturb young birds or mammals that appear to be orphaned: they probably aren't, and your interference is likely to be unwelcome if not damaging. In general, leave animals untouched, unpetted, unharassed, and photographed, if at all, from a distance with long lenses.

First Aid for Animal Wounds

First aid for a person damaged by a bear or other wild animal is simply first aid: maintain breathing, control bleeding, protect against shock, and seek help.

Even a minor wound inflicted by an animal wild or domestic can bring three possible dangers. The first is *infection*; you fight it by ordinary care in treating the wound, and later, if they are needed, with antibiotics. Second is *tetanus*, a dangerous but completely preventable disease. An immunization shot, plus one booster every 10 years, protects you. Every hiker should maintain this insurance.

By far the most serious of the three dangers is *rabies*. Skunks are the wild animals most likely to transmit rabies; raccoons, foxes, and bats can also carry it. Beware of any animal that acts oddly, including one that seems overfriendly.

An immunization for rabies is now available and is recommended for people, like cavers, who come into frequent contact with possible carrier animals. The immunization can also be given after injury, preferably within 48 hours.

If you are bitten by an animal that may carry rabies, try to catch it and kill it, if you safely can. The immediate treatment for the bite is simple: wash the wound thoroughly with *copious* soap and water. This will flush out many of the viruses, and if a rabies infection does occur, it will be less severe. Do not close the wound.

The next step is to get to medical care as fast as you can. If possible, bring the animal's body, or at least the head, for lab analysis. Treatment involves vaccination or revaccination, and the injection of rabies immune globulin, a short-term immune booster, for people not vaccinated before. Unlike past treatments, modern ones are not painful.

Hantavirus

Most diseases that pass from animals to human beings do so through a bite or puncture, made either by the infected animal itself or by an intermediary, or vector, like a tick. A notable exception is the serious respiratory disease caused by the Sin Nombre hantavirus: you can catch it just by breathing dust where its rodent hosts have lived. Deer mice are the common vector. Originally reported in the Southwest, the disease has turned up in thirty-one states of the United States. The mice live especially in such protected places as old cabins, mine shafts, caves, and ruins. Stay out of such enclosures, and don't camp where you see mouse-sized burrows and droppings (resembling black grains of rice). Though rare, the respiratory disease caused by the Sin Nombre virus is no joke: about half the afflicted people die.

Human Predators

You can't quite overlook the risk from certain other mammals, those large bipedal ones. Crime is not much of a problem in the wilderness, but there are exceptions. As noted in Chapter 14, roadhead burglaries are not uncommon. In a very few areas, human hazards are found away from the road. Rapes are not unknown. There have been murders on the Appalachian Trail. Certain wild areas near the Mexican border may be traversed by smugglers of drugs and of illegal aliens, and by the aliens themselves. Occasionally, too, marijuana growers set up shop far back in roadless areas. If you encounter unfriendly folk in the backcountry who seem not to be just recreationists, avoid confrontation. Keep your distance, and, if necessary, change your route. Once out in civilization, let the authorities know what you saw. Whatever your attitude toward the social issues involved, the wild places are not the stage on which they should be played out.

Irritant Plants

There are many, many plants in the wild that are more or less poisonous if eaten. Know exactly what you're doing before you eat any part of any wild plant, including, most especially, any mushroom. The only general first-aid rule for plant poisoning is to drink water and induce vomiting (but see the cautions in Chapter 26).

Much more common is another kind of toxic reaction: the brief, inconsequential sting of nettle or the unbearable itch of poison ivy and similar irritant plants. Poison ivy is hardly a danger to life and limb, but it can certainly take the pleasure out of a wilderness trip or the first week home.

Various closely related plants within the genus *Toxicodendron* are known commonly as poison ivy or

"Leaves of three, let it be." Easterners who have grown up with poison ivy (right) may be slow to recognize the western poison oak (left), and vice versa.

poison oak. These bushes or vines are found at lower elevations across the continental United States and southern Canada. The best field mark to look for is leaves grouped in threes. Each group of three leaflets grows out at a different point along the stem: the clusters are "alternate," not "opposite." Sometimes the leaflets are hairy, sometimes smooth; their edges may be smooth, toothed, or lobed.

Poison sumac, though related to poison oak and ivy, is quite different in appearance. A shrub or small tree, it has smooth, pale-gray bark and alternate leaves divided into seven to eleven leaflets, with smooth margins and a reddish tinge. This species grows throughout the eastern United States and Canada. In the South it is a tree up to 25 feet tall, growing in swamps and river bottoms; in cooler regions it is shrubby and keeps to boggy places.

Trumpet creeper is a woody climbing vine that grows in woods and thickets throughout the eastern United States. Like the sumac, it has divided leaves, which, however, grow in opposite pairs. The leaflets are toothed at the edges.

All these species produce the same irritant, a chemical called urushiol, and cause the same miserable dermatitis. The oily sap, most plentiful in spring and summer, is the carrier.

Trouble & How to Deal With It

About two million people each year come down with cases of poison oak and poison ivy. Sensitivities vary, but most people are allergic to some degree, or can become so without warning.

Twenty-four to forty-eight hours after you brush a plant, your skin begins to itch and redden, and blisters rise. The affected zone may seem to spread, but this is an illusion: the eruption occurs only where sap contacted the skin. The problem will last for seven to ten days.

The best defense against urushiol-bearing plants is, obviously, to avoid contact with them. Keep an eye on the vegetation as you walk. Wear long pants and long-sleeved shirts. Hands are likely to pick up oil from clothing or boots, so try not to touch your face as you mosey along, and wash carefully before touching your genitals. If you're hiking in poison oak country with a dog, assume that the dog is "hot."

For people who can't avoid poison oak, there are protective creams. Several substances seem to intercept urushiol, binding to it before it can bond to the skin. The latest and most promising of several commercial products in this line is a formulation containing quaternium-18 bentonite, a modified clay.

Urushiol can also be washed from the skin within the first few hours. Plain water is far better than nothing, and generous rinsing in a creek can decontaminate you quite well. Soaps, detergents, abrasives, and hotter water do no added good, and scrubbing just spreads the bad stuff around. For more total removal, you need a solvent like rubbing (isopropyl) alcohol or acetone; white gas, much more likely to be in your pack, can hardly be recommended but will work in a pinch. Tecnu is a high-priced solvent found in gear stores. These substances are all more or less irritating to the skin, however, and strip it of its natural protective layer of oil. Use them with caution, and not at all if you're likely to encounter more poison oak on the way home—de-oiled skin is doubly vulnerable to urushiol.

For some people, urushiol dermatitis is really disabling. If you know you are one of these, and know you have just been exposed, head for the road. A cortisone shot, administered just after the first appearance of the rash, can spare you a week of suffering. For more typical cases, the old soothing treatment, calamine lotion, is better than nothing.

The saps of the urushiol plants are transported by anything they touch, including boots, clothes, packs, car seats, and dog fur. They stay potent for quite some time. To avoid infecting others or yourself at second hand, wash suspect items thoroughly with water or solvents.

The Places &
Their Future

*We are not fighting a rearward action, we are facing
a frontier. We are not slowing down a force that
inevitably will destroy all the wilderness there is.
We are generating another force, never to be wholly
spent, that, renewed generation after generation, will
be always effective in preserving wilderness. . . .
We are working for a wilderness forever.*

—Howard Zahniser, at the Seventh Biennial
Wilderness Conference, San Francisco, 1961

30

Where the Wild Things Are

Where you go as a backpacker is partly a matter of taste, and partly a matter of proximity. Is it mountain you hanker for, or desert, or lake and cool forest, or even the exotic world of the swamp? And how far are you ready to travel before your hike begins? Though very long trips and jaunts to far-distant areas are fun to think about, most of us don't do this sort of thing often. Dreaming aside, the typical outing is a weekend, perhaps a week, and it takes place within a few hundred miles of home.

The areas we use are found mainly on land owned by government—federal, provincial, or state. They may, for instance, lie within parks, though no park is 100 percent wild. They may lie within national or provincial forests, or areas set aside for wildlife habitat; or they may lie in the broad expanses of public land known simply as crown lands (in Canada) or the public domain (in the United States). They may in addition be protected under the formal label "Wilderness," or they may not. Wilderness travelers (and wilderness advocates) learn to ignore the jurisdictional labels and zero in on the condition of the land: If I go there, can I get away from roads and vehicles, buildings and crowds? Will my surroundings *look* and *feel* wild?

Sometimes the backpacker's interest lies not in a particular landscape but in a path or corridor: the *long trail*, the named pedestrian route that traverses both wild lands and tame, and even crosses (by arrangement with the owners) long gaps of private land. The Appalachian Trail is the most famous of these, and the great model, but there are now such trails throughout the United States. The famous ones—the Appalachian, the Pacific Crest Trail, the newer Continental Divide Trail—run north and south, with the grain of the continent's mountain ranges. Today the system is gaining east-west links; work is progressing on the 8,000-mile Sea-to-Sea Trail (C2C) just south of the U.S.-Canada border.

Not many of us, though, get the chance to walk even 100 miles at a stretch. We take even the long trails in short segments. And solitude-seeking wilderness hikers tend, if anything, to stay well away from the trademark paths.

The wild areas of the contiguous United States and southern Canada can be thought of as islands of primitive landscape in a sea of development and alteration. This archipelago has a structure. The islands appear in chains and clusters, separated by stretches that are pretty useless, from the wilderness traveler's special point of view. One series of destinations lies near the coasts of the Atlantic and the Gulf of Mexico. A second occupies the highlands of the Appalachian Mountains and related eastern ranges; the Ozarks and the Ouachitas are a satellite cluster. A third scatter of wild areas occurs around the Great Lakes. Just a few atolls of primitive land interrupt the long horizons of the Great Plains.

Most of the wilderness, by acreage, is out west and comes, broadly, in two forms: mountain, and desert. The high-mountain destinations line up along the Rocky Mountains band and again along the Pacific coastal ranges. In between are lower and varied areas of canyon, steppe, and outright desert, some of our wildest wilderness of all.

Eastern Beach and Wetland Wilderness

Along the Atlantic and Gulf of Mexico shorelines, wilderness is not just metaphorically islanded. Here the backpacker's destinations are barrier spits and islands, the continent's sandy breastworks against surf and hurricanes, often sheltering broad zones of salt marsh and mudflat behind them. Though much of the original fringe of beaches and wetlands has been profoundly altered, certain areas are still pristine. Some of the notable enclaves: Monomoy Island National Wildlife Refuge (NWR) in Massachusetts; Brigantine NWR in New Jersey; Assateague Island National Seashore and Chincoteague NWR in Maryland; Cape Lookout and Cape Hatteras National Seashores and Swanquarter NWR in North Carolina; Cape Romain NWR in South Carolina; Cumberland Island National Seashore and nearby wildlife refuges in Georgia; Cape Canaveral National Seashore on Florida's Atlantic shore; Gulf Islands National Seashore in Florida, Alabama, and Mississippi; and Padre Island National Seashore in southern Texas, with adjacent refuges.

Access to these places is often by ferry, kayak, or canoe. Once off the boat, you may find yourself sharing the long, thin territory with mountain bikes and even motor vehicles, which can drive on the firm, moist sand. Though adjacent marshes are frequently protected as formal wilderness, only a few beaches have this designation. Check in advance to find when and where you can be alone. Find out, too, what schedule the birds are on. The marshes, among the most biologically productive zones on the continent, are key habitats for species that breed in these places or stop there on long migrations: ducks and geese by the millions, shorebirds by more millions, herons and ibises and egrets, terns and eagles and ospreys, and hundreds of species more.

The climate of these coastlands is in general very mild, but of course it varies greatly from the semiarid southern tip of Texas to the lush shores of Florida and

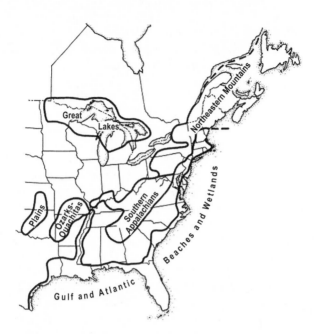

In the eastern United States and Canada, wilderness zones are scattered islands in a sea of modified landscape. You'll find the islands clustered within the outlined regions.

the hard capes of New England, where the coastal wetlands pinch out at last. Ordinarily, you will have to carry all your water. (See "Coastline Hiking," in Chapter 23.)

In the flat country inland from the coast, there is a parallel band of wild places. These are the swamps of the Gulf and Atlantic coastal plains, and of the lower Mississippi Valley: waterlogged forests of tupelo, bald cypress, and oak, hung with Spanish moss. Because logging was difficult in the swamps, a number of them have survived more or less intact.

Though some of the inland swamps are best traveled by boat, most are also accessible on foot. Some areas have raised boardwalks; in others, old railroad beds, dikes, and "ridges" (streaks of drier ground) provide dry-footed access. Away from such routes, you must count on getting your feet wet. Swamp hikers favor boots with mesh panels and holes in the sole through which water can drain. Landmarks are scarce, and skill with map and compass (supplemented perhaps by GPS) is essential for cross-country travel. Some swamps are habitat for bears, alligators, and cottonmouth moccasins; of these, the alligator is the most significant hazard. In southern states, the months from November to mid-March are the best swamp-hiking season: cool and insect-free.

Some of the better-known wild swamps are the (small) Great Swamp in New Jersey; the Great Dismal on the Virginia–North Carolina line; the Santee in North Carolina; the Congaree in South Carolina, with its record cypress trees; and the vast Okefenokee in southern Georgia, which contains over 500 square miles of protected wilderness. There are clusters of swampland wilderness areas in national forests on the coastal plains of North Carolina, South Carolina, and northeast Florida. The west coast of Florida has a big wild block at Chassahowitzka National Wildlife Refuge. West of Tallahassee in the Florida panhandle, you'll find several good-sized wilderness areas in St. Marks National Wildlife Refuge and an adjacent national forest. The Atchafalaya, Louisiana's best-known swamp, is drawing more and more hikers. In eastern Texas a few fragments of soggy forest in the Big Thicket region have been preserved.

The greatest of all the eastern wetlands is the Everglades, the enormous marsh and wildlife paradise that occupies much of southern Florida. Backpacking, however, is not what you come here to do.

Eastern Mountain Wilderness

The Appalachians, the Ozarks, the Adirondacks—all the mountain masses of the eastern United States—are wilder today than they were a century ago. Even the national parks in this region were repurchased from private owners after settlement and exploitation; the forests within their boundaries are largely young growth. Hiking through primitive woods, you may be surprised and charmed to discover old roads now gone to trails, old orchards still bearing fruit, even the stone foundations of old houses.

North Carolina's Mount Mitchell, the tallest peak east of the Mississippi and south of the Arctic, is just 6,684 feet high. Considering the moderate elevations, it is easy to underestimate the ruggedness of eastern highlands. Five-thousand-foot summits may still rise the larger part of a mile from valley floors below. Along with some gentle trails, there are many that are steep and roughly surfaced, especially in the Northeast.

The eastern ranges are almost entirely wooded, mostly with hardwoods—oaks and hickories, maples and beeches, birches and basswoods. When you travel under broadleaf trees in summer, you don't see out very often or very far. Under the trees, dense brush—dogwood, rhododendron, mountain laurel, wild rose—tends to confine you to the trail. Many hikers prefer fall and winter; when the leaves are off the hardwood trees and the stems of brush are bare, cross-country travel becomes more feasible. You see out, see for miles, see where you are. Besides, in cooler weather, you'll be better dressed for bushwhacking.

With a few exceptions, eastern mountain wilderness comes in rather small pieces. On longer trips, hikers may traverse several wild areas rather than choosing a single district to explore. This is the homeland of the long trail, the Appalachian and its numerous progeny and branches.

Anywhere in the eastern mountains, you will want a tent year-round. A tarp may serve for rain and dew, but not for the insects of summer. Gear must be moisture-resistant, boots well waterproofed, sleeping bags not of unprotected down. At lower elevations in the South, where summer nights are often uncomfortably warm, you may not want a sleeping bag at all in that season, but only something on the order of a wool blanket. Fires are widely restricted, and you will definitely need to carry a stove.

Throughout the region, and especially along the various long trails, you find simple, three-sided shelters. Although these can be handy at times, it is best to leave them out of your plans. They are often crowded and may be littered, dirty, or vandalized. Nuisance animals—bears, skunks, raccoons—naturally congregate at these sites. In some areas, rangers now discourage the use of shelters except on day hikes and in emergencies. In others, they are available to long-trail hikers only.

The Southern Appalachians

In this highest part of the Appalachian chain, the federal government has considerable wild holdings. The most significant is Great Smoky Mountains National Park in North Carolina and Tennessee, where roadless areas total 750 square miles. The national forests around the park and northward to the Potomac River contain numerous smaller wild areas. Notable southern Appalachian wilderness areas are the Sipsey in Alabama, the Cohutta in Georgia, the Southern Nantahala in Georgia and North Carolina, and the Cranberry and Otter Creek in West Virginia.

This is, above all, forest country. Appalachian Trail hikers grumble about weeks in a "green tunnel," but botanizers find endless variety in a hardwood forest of uncommon richness. Above 5,000 feet, fir and spruce appear. Summits may have "balds" of grass or heath, mostly rhododendron and mountain laurel.

Summers are warm and wet: days typically in the 70s or 80s Fahrenheit, though afternoon thunderstorms can cool things off; humidity is almost always high. The hiking uniform in such conditions is the minimum: shorts, perhaps a light shirt or net undershirt, and boots. (But you need long pants where poison ivy is dense along the trail.) On the lower slopes, nights may be only a little cooler than the days.

September, October, and November, the driest and clearest months, are really the best of the hiking weather. The trails are less crowded (except at times in popular hunting areas), the mosquito problem is past, and in cooler autumns the turning leaves can put on a good show.

In winter, snow is frequent but unpredictable. At middle elevations, rain mixes with snow and alternates with snow—it may snow at night and rain during the day. Freezing rain—glaze—is also fairly common. For all that, midwinter in this region is actually one of the drier times of year.

North and west of the loftiest ridges, the Appalachian highland continues as a plateau that reaches to and beyond the Ohio River in far southern Ohio, Indiana, and even Illinois. Hill country along the river in each of these states contains state parks, national forests, and some reverting-to-wild areas that are worth a visit.

Northeastern Mountains

Pennsylvania, with its low but still prominent ridges and plateaus, is a transition zone between southern and northeastern mountain landscapes. When the land rises again in New York State, the character of the mountains has changed. They are rougher, cooler, stonier; they bear the marks of ancient glaciation, evidenced also by the many lakes at their feet.

North and east of the Mason-Dixon line, the federal government is not the major landlord. Rather, states and even private owners control the wild land. In Pennsylvania, the state-run parks and forests are extensive; in New York, they are huge. Because the voters long ago forbade logging on state land in the Catskills and Adirondacks, great tracts of forest are more or less wild; the authorities have given explicit wilderness status to about 150 square miles in the Catskills and to 1,500 square miles, in several chunks, in the Adirondacks. In Maine, too, it is the state that is responsible for the wilderness and semiwilderness of Baxter State Park and the Allagash Waterway, together with "public reserved lands" open to various uses. In addition, thousands of square miles of private timberlands in northern Maine remain primitive in part and are the subject of a growing preservation campaign.

In New Hampshire and Vermont, in the White and Green Mountains, the U.S. Forest Service does control most of the public land. Even here there is an unusual setup. Much of the work of management—the trail maintenance, the staffing of backcountry shelters, even some of the planning—is done by private clubs, chief among them the Appalachian Mountain Club. In the White Mountains, the AMC runs eight backcountry huts, inns really, where meals are served—reservations, of course, required.

North of the Catskills, northeastern mountains are distinctly cool. Although some summer days may be hot, warm nights are rare, and cold storms can come in at any time of year. The 4,000-to-6,000-foot peaks of the White Mountains can get snow, high winds, and sub-freezing temperatures in any month. Hypothermia has killed many an unprepared hiker in these hills.

Early fall in the Northeast is an excellent time for the hiker, with many crisp, clear days and wonderful color displays if you time it just right; the notorious blackflies are gone. The peaks may be white by Halloween. Winter can be disconcertingly variable. Snow campers tolerate the cold but dread the occasional warm southeasterly rainstorm followed by a shift of weather, subzero temperatures, and northwest gales. Everything gets wet and then freezes solid. Travelers go home.

The original forests of these mountains were almost entirely spruce and fir. In the few unlogged areas, they still are. Elsewhere, deciduous hardwoods have taken over. Above the zone of full-sized timber, there may be a thousand feet of dwarfed birch and mountain ash; then, as low as 5,000 feet in some sections, only tundra and stone. Everybody wants to visit these alpine islands, which total only 13 square miles. Managers have their work cut out in protecting them from trampling and erosion.

The Appalachians don't stop at the Canadian border. The hills and plateaus of New Brunswick, southeastern Quebec, Nova Scotia, and even Newfoundland are considered part of the range. Though not lofty, these northern highlands may reach the arctic/alpine

The Places & Their Future

zone. National parks—Forillon in Quebec; Fundy and Kouchibouguac in New Brunswick; Kejimkujik and Cape Breton Highlands in Nova Scotia; and in Newfoundland, Terra Nova and the vast and primitive Gros Morne—protect some climaxes. There is a plan to extend the Appalachian Trail to Mount Jacques-Cartier on the Gaspé Peninsula of Quebec.

The Ozarks and Ouachitas

Between the Appalachians and the Mississippi, there is limited land in public ownership and not many backpacking destinations. But beyond the great river, in the knot of low mountains called the Ozarks and Ouachitas, wilderness is reappearing in national forests and parks. A couple of dozen small wilderness areas, scattered over southern Missouri, northwestern Arkansas, and far eastern Oklahoma, protect some 300 square miles of land.

In many ways the Ozark country resembles the southern Appalachian region, to which it is geologically related. It is a shade more continental in climate—the summer a little hotter, winters slightly less mild. Autumn is very pleasant. The wettest months are April, May, and June, and the driest (though by no means rainless) are December, January, and February. There's some snow, but it doesn't last. Because the high ground in these mountains tends to be rather flat and accessible to settlement, the primitive tracts are often found on steeper ground descending ruggedly to streams. When civilization lies above, water treatment is more than ordinarily vital.

Great Lakes Wilderness

Along the United States–Canada border, from the Adirondacks to the High Plains, extends a great, flat tangle of blue lakes, bogs, potholes, and circuitous rivers. Many American landscapes bear the marks of glaciation; but in this flat expanse, where other obvious landmarks are lacking, almost every feature you see is glacial: put there by the unimaginable weight and power of the ice sheets that, not long ago in geological terms, lay over it.

The ice laid down moraines and eskers and drumlins and erratic boulders; it shoved old rivers into modern courses; it scraped some landscapes bare and covered others with rich soil. Most of all, it made lakes: the five Great Lakes and uncountable smaller ones.

The result is a handsome country: mostly gentle in topography, mostly forested with hardwoods and various conifers, and in large part well settled. But near the international boundary are blocks of government land, set aside by the two national governments, several states, and the province of Ontario, where wilderness remains, or is being allowed to return.

The U.S. National Park Service has some of the larger properties: Sleeping Bear Dunes and Pictured Rocks National Lakeshores in Michigan, Apostle Islands National Lakeshore in Wisconsin, and splendid Isle Royale National Park in the middle of Lake Superior. In northern Wisconsin and Michigan's Upper Peninsula, there are numerous vest-pocket wilderness areas in national forests and wildlife refuges. Michigan, Wisconsin, and Minnesota have also delineated areas within their larger parks for protection as state-owned wilderness zones.

In Canada, hikers treasure the long Bruce Trail, which runs from Niagara Falls northwest along the limestone Niagara Escarpment, past metropolitan Toronto, to the end of the Bruce Peninsula in Lake Huron. Killarney Provincial Park, Ontario, holds a slice of the north shore of Huron. Near Sault Sainte Marie are the Algoma Highlands, a rare island of old-growth pine and deciduous forest whose fate is still to be determined. On the north shore of Lake Superior, Pukaskwa National Park is in the process of establishment.

The greatest lake country wilderness lies just west of the Great Lakes, in northern Minnesota and adjacent Ontario. On the American side is the famous Boundary Waters Canoe Area Wilderness within Superior National Forest, some 1,200 square miles of pines, portages, and labyrinthine waters. Adjoining the

Boundary Waters are parks in two nations: small Voyageurs National Park on the American side and the vast Quetico Provincial Park in Canada. Together these areas make up one of the major wilderness reserves of the North American continent. Despite the emphasis on water travel, lengthy trails wind among the lakes, and backpackers do find much to explore.

The climate of the lakes country is cold in winter and variable in summer, seldom punishingly hot and quite often damp and cool. In the eastern part of the region, late summer is the rainiest time; to the west, on the edge of the Great Plains, the rain peak comes earlier. The bugs diminish by August. Winter comes early. The Boundary Waters area gets six months of snow cover and some of the lowest temperatures in the contiguous United States.

Wilderness on the Plains

The Great Plains at the center of our continent are perhaps the most profoundly altered of all our natural regions. Of the original grassland ecosystems, only a few scraps and traces are left, these largely on hilly, nonarable ground. The limited protected areas are charming, though, and have the added fascination of the rare. Only a few of these sites are large enough to reward a long hiking trip, but there's a good deal here for the weekend visitor.

In western Oklahoma, Wichita Mountains National Refuge, an island of stony hills surrounded by farms, is habitat for the totem animal of the Great Plains, the bison. (One corner is classified wilderness.) Farther east, the Nature Conservancy has the Tallgrass Prairie Preserve in the Osage Hills. In the Flint Hills of eastern Kansas, Kansas State University maintains the Konza Research Natural Area. All these areas are open to some hiking but not to camping. Nebraska has fine small roadless tracts in its northern sandhills at Fort Niobara, Crescent Lake, and Valentine National Wildlife Refuges, and in Nebraska National Forest. Farther north in the plains belt, fantastically eroded regions called badlands interrupt the smooth skin of the prairie. In South Dakota, Badlands National Monument preserves table-lands, gulches, canyons and buttes, ramparts of colored and crumbling earth, and a couple of decent chunks of rugged, roadless prairie. One of these, the 80-square-mile Sage Creek area, is the largest designated wilderness on the plains. To the west, the Black Hills, a forested island mountain range, contain a bit of Forest Service wilderness. Theodore Roosevelt National Park in North Dakota, another badlands landscape, has smaller areas of grassy wild ground.

Near the Canadian border, lakes, rivers, and water-filled "potholes" are precious habitat for ducks, cranes, pelicans, and other birds. Several wildlife refuges here—Chase Lake and Lostwood in North Dakota, Medicine Lake and UL Bend in Montana—have hikable lands within them.

Near the western fringe of the plains, the grass grows shorter, the weather is drier, and the federal holdings are more extensive. Here there are many "national grasslands," terrain that was badly overgrazed in private ownership, then purchased by the government for restoration. In eastern Montana there are more than 1 million acres of rough-textured public domain land, wild in part, around the backed-up waters of Fort Peck Reservoir on the Missouri. Part of this region is managed as the Charles M. Russell Wildlife Range.

On the Canadian side of the border, several small, timbered mountain ranges, rising from the fields, are provincial parks: Turtle Mountain and Spruce Woods in Manitoba, Moose Mountain in Saskatchewan, Cypress Hills in Saskatchewan and Alberta. But the most significant preserve is Grasslands National Park in Saskatchewan, proclaimed in 1981 (but still in the process of creation as land is purchased from private owners). Its 350 square miles, in two chunks along the border with Montana, incorporate more relatively unaltered shortgrass prairie than all the U.S. areas combined. You'll find here such "un-Canadian" species as the prairie dog, the prairie rattlesnake, the sage grouse, and the pronghorn. You can prick yourself on a cactus.

Especially toward the north, the regional climate is rigorous. There can be a 150-degree range in temperature over the year, from 100 degrees above 0 degrees Fahrenheit to 50 or more below. In some areas, wind is all but perpetual. Early summer is the wettest time of year.

The Wild Rockies

When the first far ridges of the Rocky Mountains begin to detach themselves from the horizon—when the mountain-hungry eye spots solid peaks among the deceptive clouds—the westbound traveler is approaching the first of the real wilderness strongholds of North America.

The barrier ahead is no simple line of peaks. The Rockies are many ranges, tangled, branching, offset one from another—a world of mountains, not a chain. In central Wyoming they subside into a high steppe. This opening divides the Rockies into two very different regions: the southern, or Colorado, Rockies, and the northern U.S. Rockies of northern Wyoming, Montana, and Idaho. Nothing but a line on a map separates these from the Canadian Rockies, which run another 1,000 miles north through Alberta and British Columbia.

The southern Rockies begin just south of the Colorado–New Mexico border. When they do rise, they go up all the way: New Mexico has a couple of 13,000-foot peaks, and Colorado has fifty-four summits over 14,000. The wild mountain areas here are numerous and grandly scenic; often they clump together in larger complexes divided only by narrow road corridors. The Pecos Wilderness in New Mexico, the Sangre de Cristo Wilderness in southern Colorado, and the Flat Tops Wilderness in northwest Colorado each top 300 square miles; the Weminuche Wilderness near the southeast corner of the state is twice that size. To the west in Utah lies the very alpine High Uinta Wilderness, as large as the Weminuche and in need of expansion to include adjacent roadless lands.

The southern Rockies have a strong summer thunderstorm season; in the southern part of the region,

The western United States and adjacent Canada are rich in wild areas of the most diverse character, from desert canyon to alpine tundra to rain-soaked forest—sometimes just a few miles apart.

more rain may fall in August than in any other month. Mountain hikers are accustomed to scuttling down off these peaks, and out of the reach of lightning, by noon at the latest.

Winter in this part of the Rockies is an inviting season, with many clear stretches between storms. Though nighttime temperatures can go far below zero, the mountain climate is, if anything, a shade milder than that of the adjacent plains. Snow is that dry, cold, luminous stuff that skiers love—and fear, for this is the snow best suited to avalanche formation. Most areas can be hiked without skis or snowshoes by late June.

In the northern Rockies, beginning in Wyoming, the peaks are somewhat lower, the forest rather more lush, and the land considerably wilder. Yellowstone National Park is the center of one great complex of primitive lands. Two hundred miles to the west, the Idaho Batholith, a granitic region around the upper Salmon and Selway Rivers, is a stronghold of Forest Service wilderness. The Rockies of northern Montana, including Glacier National Park and the national forests to the south, is a third wild core. Individual roadless areas in these regions cover 1,000 square miles or more. One megawilderness is centered on the southeast corner of Yellowstone and includes the Washakie and Teton Wildernesses in adjacent national forests. In Idaho, two great wilderness units adjoin: the Frank Church–River of No Return, around the Middle Fork of the Salmon; and the Selway-Bitterroot to the north, separated from its neighbor by only the width of a road. In northern Montana, the fine wilderness in Glacier National Park itself is dwarfed by a national forest complex containing the Scapegoat, Bob Marshall, and Great Bear Wildernesses, adjacent to the south.

Wilderness areas on this scale have the splendor of the things within them—river gorges and fierce rapids, elk and grizzly, lakes and residual glaciers, deep woods, walls of granite and layered sedimentary stone. But most of all they have the splendor that comes simply from their size. Here, if anywhere south of the boreal forests, you can imagine yourself in the continent-spanning wilderness that was.

The hiking climate in the northern U.S. Rockies is distinctly damper and cooler than at points south. In the higher and wetter regions, the summer hiking season is July, August, and perhaps September; June is the end of one winter and October the transition to the next. Along with the usual summer thunderstorms, substantial frontal storms may blow in from the west at almost any time. The winter wet season is long and cloudy, though not without clear windows for the well-timed trip. As everywhere in the mountainous West, local climates vary with topography. Lower and east-facing slopes receive less precipitation than higher and west-facing ones.

Across the international border, the Canadian Rockies march onward toward the Arctic. One hundred and fifty miles north, a magnificent cluster of national and provincial parks—Banff, Jasper, Mount Robson, and others—blankets 10,000 square miles of glaciated scenery. Plans are afoot for a comparable cluster at the far northern tip of the range. Westward, across the trench occupied by the upper Columbia River, lies the Columbia Mountain System (including the Selkirks, the Purcells, the Bugaboos, and many other named ranges). Here too are several national and provincial parks; the provincial government of British Columbia has plans for more.

The Colorado Plateau and Canyon Country

From sources in Wyoming and Colorado, the tributaries of the Colorado River gather and converge. Flowing toward the Pacific, they encounter the Colorado Plateau, a great oval of highlands in Colorado, Utah, New Mexico, and Arizona. The result is a 10,000-mile web of precipitous canyons in rock now gray, now black, now yellow, now the famous southwestern rust or rose. Some of these gorges are gigantic, like the Grand Canyon itself, the mile-deep slot cut by the Colorado into the layered, colored rock of northern Arizona. Others are closed-in, convoluted, narrow. In the greater gorges, travel is by water; the lesser ones by footways. Above the canyons rise the mesas—isolated, flat-topped mountains left behind in the general erosion, many of them high enough to be forested, some of them partly wild.

Rivers in canyons make possible dam sites, enchanting to engineers. Several of the most exciting stretches of the Colorado and its tributaries have been flooded by government reservoirs. Even the Grand Canyon itself was almost so flooded. Much of the course of the main river is now included in parks or national recreation areas (the latter around the reservoirs); up the tributaries, the fate of large and fascinating wild areas remains to be decided. The new Grand Staircase–Escalante National Monument in southern Utah has plugged one of the major conservation gaps. The largest roadless expanse in the region—1,500 square miles stepping down with the strata from rims to river—is contained in Grand Canyon National Park.

The southern rampart of the Colorado Plateau is a long band of mountains called the Mogollon Rim, which swings across the Southwest in an east-west arc from the Rio Grande to the Colorado. Timbered, cool, incised from the south by dozens of canyon systems of its own, the Mogollon is prime recreation country. Several wilderness areas have been designated within the national forests here. One of these, the Gila Wilderness at the eastern tip of the rim, was the first such area ever explicitly set aside; it protects some 800 square miles of red rock and pine woodland.

On the Colorado Plateau, desert and mountain climates interlock. In the canyons, April and May, cool and clear, may be the best travel months. Water is comparatively abundant then, and the thunderstorm season, with its flash-flood danger, has not yet begun. When it does, be cautious about hiking a narrow, no-exit canyon, and above all of camping in a narrows.

The Deep Southwest

South of the Mogollon Rim and the southern tip of the Rocky Mountains, the land subsides toward the Mexican border. Along the Rio Grande in New Mexico and Texas is the U.S. share of the binational Chihuahuan Desert. In this region, the bulk of the year's precipitation arrives during the summer growing season, which makes for wonderful desert plants. The wildest corner is Big Bend National Park, in Texas, on a bight of the Rio Grande.

In southwest Arizona lies the U.S. portion of another primarily Mexican desert, the Sonoran. In this driest of the North American deserts, cacti are the big, dramatic growing things. The region contains the major cities of Tucson and Phoenix; numerous low, stark mountain ranges; and plenty of wild land. Of wilderness areas managed by the Forest Service, the Matzatzal is the largest and the Superstition probably the best known. The big Kofa Game Range is a refuge for desert bighorn sheep. Along the Mexican border, Organ Pipe Cactus National Monument and the enormous Cabeza Prieta National Wildlife Refuge enclose a magnificent desolation. A number of big chunks of desert controlled by the Bureau of Land Management have wilderness status as well. Only a few of these fascinating places get much recreational use at all, though certain corridors get lots of traffic by illegal immigrants from Mexico.

Backpacking in these regions is the purest desert hiking; winter, and at higher elevations spring and fall, are the comfortable seasons. But between the two deserts and on their fringes, a number of mountain ranges, small in extent but high in elevation, rise like seamounts into the temperate forest zone. Such national forest wilderness areas as the Chiricahua (Arizona) and the White Mountain (New Mexico) perch on top.

The Intermountain Region

West of the Rockies and the Colorado River drainage, and east of the lofty ranges that border the Pacific Coast, lies a vast interior region. Though on average low and dry, this is a very rugged section of the continent, containing many isolated mountain masses and rich in wild places.

On the north, this intermountain zone stretches right into British Columbia, where it is called the Interior Dry Plateaus. In Oregon, the Blue Mountains run east to west across the region, bridging the Rockies to the Cascades like the bar of an H. The Snake River cuts a path through this bar near the eastern end, forming wild Hells Canyon. The big Eagle Cap Wilderness is just west in Oregon, and the lava canyons of the Owyhee River, untamed but also unprotected as yet, lie nearby in Idaho.

South of the Blue Mountains is the heart of the intermountain west, the Great Basin. Here hundreds of separate mountain masses, oriented north and south, rise from a floor of cool sagebrush steppe. Despite the diligent scrapings of miners and prospectors, most of these rugged fault-block ranges have pristine country in them. Another, stranger kind of wildness is found in certain valleys, where streams that never reach the sea lay down their sediments to form the dead-flat, sterile, weirdly beautiful plains called playas. The Black Rock Desert of northwest Nevada is the biggest of these. Except in very wet years, you can walk across these expanses, keeping pace with mirages and sensing, as on a calm ocean, the curvature of the earth. Great Basin conservationists are having some success in getting protected status for areas both high and low.

Toward the south of the intermountain region, in southern Nevada and adjacent California, the elevations are generally lower and the vegetation different. This is the Mojave Desert, its signature species a lily that looks like a cactus, the curious Joshua tree. Death Valley National Park, Joshua Tree National Preserve, and Mojave National Preserve contain thousands of square miles of hikable wild land. A swarm of small wilderness areas, on land administered by the federal Bureau of Land Management, surrounds these vaster cores. Near the Mexican border, California's Anza-Borrego Desert State Park is a major holding, including state-designated wilderness zones.

In the lowest, hottest parts of the intermountain region, as in the Mojave, winter is the pleasant hiking season; spring and fall are reasonable; summer is impossibly hot. Farther north and at higher elevations, spring and fall can be delightful. From central Nevada north, summer in the valleys is merely warm; in the lofty, forested mountain masses, it is cool. Winter brings plenty of snow to the higher ranges.

The Pacific Ranges

Along the Pacific coast of the conterminous United States, just about all the remaining wilderness is found in mountainous country. These highlands rise in two parallel north-south lines.

Inland lies the greater mountain wall, the Sierra-Cascade chain. The southern half of this barrier is the Sierra Nevada. A single enormous fault block, it slopes gently on the west but breaks abruptly to the deserts on the east in a scarp as much as 2 miles high. The Cascades of northern California, Oregon, and Washington are built on a different plan. From a forested base of moderate height there rise, isolated and commanding, a dozen cones and spikes of lava: Mounts Shasta, Jefferson, Hood, and Rainier and numerous lesser-known cousins. The Sierra and the Cascades are cool enough, and wet enough, to carry glaciers—small remnant ice fields in the Sierra, impressive ice caps on the taller volcanoes and other high points of the Cascades. The far vaster glaciers of the past gouged out Sierra granites and Cascade lavas to make the sockets of hundreds of modern lakes.

Yosemite Valley in the Sierra and Mount Rainier in the Cascades, each now the centerpiece of a national park, were among the first western places to draw preservation campaigns. Today a hiker traversing these ranges on the Pacific Crest Trail, the western counterpart of the Appalachian Trail, will spend about half the trip in protected areas. These are largest and most densely clustered in the Sierra, crossed by no road for 130 airline miles, and again in the North Cascades of Washington, where several closely clustered areas encompass 3,000 square miles.

Nearest the ocean are the tangled, many-ridged coastal ranges, rising here and there to 8,000 feet or more. There is a constellation of wild recreation spots within view, on a clear day, of Los Angeles city streets. On the central California coast, the territory of the California condor, large blocks of brush and fire-tolerant forest are protected. The heavily timbered Klamath

Mountains region, on the California-Oregon border, contains generous wilderness, half of it in the Trinity Alps area; much more roadless land in the region is still at issue between preservation and logging. Olympic National Park near Seattle is essentially all wilderness, some 1,200 square miles in extent.

The hiking season in the Pacific ranges depends on altitude and latitude. In Southern California, summers are hot and dry; hikers head for the highest country then, saving lower-lying destinations for spring and fall. Some areas are closed to public use in the rainless months because of the extreme danger of fire. Only the highest peaks are forested; lower and middle slopes are covered with the complex and typically Californian brush fields called chaparral.

As you move north along either chain of mountains, the climate becomes steadily wetter and cooler, the forests greener, and the dry season gradually shorter. In the Sierra-Cascade chain (but rarely in the coastal ranges), summer thunderstorms are normal. In Oregon and Washington, serious summer rain can no longer be regarded as a surprise. The coastal side of the Olympic Mountains is the most sodden area in the forty-eight contiguous states: lavishly green below timberline and glittering with ice above. The North Cascades, inland across Puget Sound, are only a little drier. Hikers in this region, like hikers in the East, go ready for rain.

This pattern is varied by the usual local factors. Both the coastal ranges and the Sierra-Cascade chain cast rain shadows: their eastern slopes are markedly drier than their western sides. You can walk from glacier to desert in a day. Hikers on the immediate coastline learn to count on the persistent drizzle of summer fog.

Snow camping is at its best in the Sierra and southern Cascades, high enough to get lots of snow but southerly enough to enjoy clear spells between Pacific storms; farther north, such respites are rarer. All snow in the Pacific ranges is fairly wet and less ideal for skiing than the dry, loose powder of more continental ranges. It is also less prone to the formation of massive slab avalanches.

In British Columbia, the Pacific ranges are a great reservoir of wilderness. Between the Fraser River on the south and the southern tip of the Alaska panhandle on the north, a band of high country inland from the shore is predominantly wild in fact, if not yet in name. A few preserves exist, the largest of which is Tweedsmuir National Park; many more are under discussion by the provincial government, and, if designated, would constitute a true national treasure. The alternative to protection, for all but the most alpine areas, is clearcut logging.

Recreationally, this is wild and woolly country, a temperate coastal rainforest with only the ghost, if that, of a summer dry season. Trails are few; cross-country travel, in a sort of cool jungle defended by the prickly plant called devil's club, is hard; the higher country may require technical mountaineering skills.

Boreal Canada

Canada, unlike the United States, is still in large part a wilderness nation. Like the United States in an earlier period, it is laboring mightily to change that situation; at the same time, it is struggling to preserve a suitable chunk of its wild heritage (see Chapter 31).

The metaphor of the archipelago of wilderness continues to apply in the southern reaches of Canada. Agriculture, logging, and mining are the norm, wildness the exception, in the maritime provinces of Nova Scotia, Prince Edward Island, and New Brunswick. The same is true along the southern margins of Quebec and Ontario; and it applies in at least the southern halves of Manitoba, Saskatchewan, Alberta, and British Columbia. Much of the remaining wild land in this southern tier is contained in provincial and a few national parks; some of these are mentioned above in connection with the related regions of the United States.

For more northerly parts of Canada, however, and for the state of Alaska, we have to abandon the habit of thinking of wilderness islands in a sea of occupied land. Rather, the older situation prevails: developed

Canada is largely a wilderness nation—though you have to go pretty far north to find the widest primitive horizons.

areas are the archipelago, albeit a rapidly expanding one; wildness is the background, the matrix.

A few years ago, the frontier between the (mostly) settled and the (largely) wild lay near the southern fringe of the great coniferous boreal forest, or taiga, that arcs across the continent from Newfoundland almost to the mouths of the Yukon River. Now the Canadian taiga is everywhere invaded from the south by massive government-sanctioned logging operations. The new frontier approximates the sixtieth parallel, the north border of the prairie provinces. Canadian conservationists are working hard to preserve some significant fragments south of that line and to set limits on the scope of exploitation north of it.

Between the open prairies to the south and the boreal woods to the north lies a broad transitional zone where groves of trembling aspen mix with meadows of rough fescue, a charming, uniquely Canadian landscape of which little remains wild. Riding Mountain and Prince Albert National Parks protect remnants of the old scene.

Where the Wild Things Are

The boreal forest proper seems half woods, half water: thousands of miles of spruce and fir rather open underneath, lightened a little by aspen, birch, and willow; thousands of miles of mazy lakes and rivers. More than the rare trails, these waterways are the travel routes, traversed by watercraft in summer and in winter by over-snow vehicles, people on skis and snowshoes, and now and then a sled-dog team. Where roads have not yet penetrated, basic access is by small airplane. Canada's largest national park, Wood Buffalo in northern Alberta, protects a huge swatch of this country: it contains the world's most numerous herd of bison and the only known nesting site of the whooping crane.

North of the great boreal forest band begins the true Arctic, the treeless tundra region. Below a surface mat of lichens, mosses, grasses, sedges, heaths, and stunted willows lies ice, the frozen groundwater called permafrost. This never melts, unless the overlying vegetation is disturbed. However, with global warming, the permafrost zone is now retreating northward.

The Arctic tundra may be the most difficult terrain to travel in all North America. Trails, as such, don't exist. The ground is boggy and treacherous. You often progress by stepping from tussock to unsteady tussock of the ubiquitous cotton grass. Mosquitoes in summer make a kind of stinging smog. This is truly a wilderness for wildlife: habitat for vast herds of Arctic caribou and the wolves that prey on them, and vital breeding ground for half the birds of the Americas. Though people venture down the Arctic rivers in canoes, kayaks, and rafts, backpackers can best admire this region, and root for its preservation, from afar.

Still farther north, in parts of the Canadian Arctic Archipelago and on Greenland, lies the zone of permanent ice. Though travel here is expeditionary, the region actually sees a bit more recreational use than does the tundra to the south of it. Summers are full of cool light, with pale sunshine twenty-four hours a day around the solstice; the climate, for all its sometimes deadly rigor, is quite dry.

The Places & Their Future

In central and southern Alaska, auto, train, or ferry can get you to the wilderness. In the rest of the state, "the bush," access is by airplane.

Canada has many great national parks in the Arctic and is designating others as rapidly as negotiations with the aboriginal "First Nations" can be concluded. In most cases, traditional native subsistence hunting and fishing are to continue.

Wild Alaska

In Alaska, the North American cordillera, that washboard pattern of parallel mountains and valleys, makes a great left turn. Structures that ran north and south for thousands of miles are now oriented east and west. The several southern mountain masses of the state, including the high point of the continent at Mount McKinley, continue the general arc of the Pacific coastal ranges. The state's interior lowland, where the Yukon River flows west to the sea, is the last in a succession of intermountain troughs running all the way to Mexico. The Brooks Range in the north continues the line of the Rocky Mountains. Alaska is a continent in miniature.

At least 90 percent of the territory of the fiftieth U.S. state is in fact still roadless. Here wildness is indeed the matrix, the modern human imprint the exception. Well over a third of this matrix is protected in parks, wildlife refuges, and such; about 15 percent of it is actually classified as wilderness. More than half of the land thus protected in the United States, to date, is in Alaska.

For recreation purposes, the empire can be subdivided in various ways. By summer climate, for instance: moderate, damp, and maritime along the southern coasts; drier and more continental in the middle; still drier and ever chillier toward the north. Or by topography: mountainous in the south, flat in the middle, mountainous again north of the Arctic Circle, leveling out once more along the Arctic Ocean. By vegetation: rainforest in the southeast, windswept grassland in the southwest, boreal forest amidships, tundra to the north. Going up in elevation, as always, is like moving to the north: even in the southern forests, a modest climb will take you to tree line and tundra, and often onto permanent ice not far above that.

For the traveler, though, the state's terrain is best classified by access. There are areas (in the southeast) where your trip is likely to begin with a ride on a boat; areas (around the major city, Anchorage, and north to Fairbanks and Denali National Park) where your access can be by train or motor vehicle; and the great balance of the state, where you don't get far without a trip in a small airplane.

In southeastern Alaska, and in far northern British Columbia as well, the coast is a fretwork of islands, fjords, and headlands, with mountains banked enormously behind. Water is the only major highway. Regular ferry service takes you to towns that may adjoin wild forest or melancholy cutover land; Juneau, the state capital, has some of the most rewarding surroundings. In Glacier Bay National Park at the north, a local tour boat will drop you off anywhere. Floatplanes, though much more expensive, will get you to any southeastern Alaskan inlet you choose.

Most people are content to admire this coast from water level. A temperate jungle below tree line, a tangle of peaks and glaciers above, it doesn't exactly welcome

The Places & Their Future

hikers—but it rewards the ones who push their way in. There are rather few trails. Often the function of a formal path is to get you through rainforest and muskegs (peat bogs) to higher ground, tundra covered, where cross-country travel begins. There are over one hundred Forest Service cabins in the woods, mostly on shorelines, equipped with bunks and wood stoves and rentable for a few dollars a night; you don't find many purists scorning to use these.

The region's longest trail, the 33-mile Chilkoot, is more a historical artifact than a wilderness experience: in 1897–98, tens of thousands of prospectors took this rugged path across the coastal mountains from the northern port of Skagway to placer mines in the Yukon Territory in Canada.

The Alaska panhandle is almost all public land. Glacier Bay National Park occupies its northern end, Misty Fjords National Monument its southern. Most of what lies between is Tongass National Forest. Though the Tongass contains some large wilderness areas, Congress has followed the urging of Alaska politicians and earmarked it mainly for timber production. The magnificent cover of virgin cedar, spruce, and hemlock is fraying fast.

The Alaskan regions accessible by road include some of the state's best destinations, in the Chugach, Talkeetna, and Alaska mountain ranges. Immediately outside of Anchorage is Chugach State Park, as big as many a national park in the "Lower Forty-Eight" but in Alaskan terms a mere neighborhood playground. Nearby to the southwest is the Kenai Peninsula, a compact region that blends coastal, alpine, and forest Alaska in one. The Kenai has one of the state's best trail networks and one of its most welcoming hiking climates. The peninsula is more or less blanketed with state and federal parks and the Kenai National Wildlife Refuge.

A drive south and east from Anchorage will get you to the borders of the Wrangell–Saint Elias National Park and Preserve, the beginning of a binational arc of protected lands stretching along the coast to Glacier Bay and including Kluane Provincial Park in the Yukon and

Tatshenshini–Alsek Wilderness Provincial Park in British Columbia. The combined parks cover over 40,000 square miles, the continent's largest zone of preservation. This complex of volcanic and sedimentary mountains holds North America's most extensive glaciers, many of its highest peaks, and wildlife including three separate herds of caribou. The Alaska–Canada Highway skirts the northern rim of the region, and another road, the access to the village of McCarthy, penetrates it deeply from the west. Small planes ferry hikers into more remote regions, but there are peripheral hikes you can do without taking to the air. Your path will probably be an overgrown prospector's track, or a game trail.

North from Anchorage lie the granitic Talkeetna Mountains, a rather tame area by Alaskan standards but unusually well supplied with trails. Beyond in the Alaska Range looms Mount McKinley, which many prefer to call by its Athapaskan name Denali, "The Great One." The parkland around it, Denali National Park and Preserve, is actually fairly accessible. A major highway passes the east end of the park, and a road (for buses only) runs westward 90 miles along the north side of the Alaska Range. Hiking is fairly easy in the boreal forest and alpine tundra (encountered at about 2,700 feet). You have to be duly cautious about stream crossings, and about bears. A vast state park, also called Denali, abuts the national area on the southeast.

Alaska's great interior region is largely flat and largely wet. Northeast of Fairbanks, though, lies a hilly quadrant called the Tanana-Yukon Upland, very attractive for hiking. Here are the Chena River State Recreation Area, the White Mountain and Steese Mountain National Recreation Areas, the Pinnell Mountain National Recreation Trail, and the Yukon-Charley Rivers National Preserve. Developed to some extent with trails and cabins, areas like these—true wilderness to a refugee from the Lower Forty-Eight— might strike an Alaska hiker as rather tame.

North from Fairbanks the Elliott and Dalton Highways run with the Trans-Alaska Pipeline all the way to the Arctic Ocean. There is bus service, and passenger cars are allowed (but not recommended). Even in relatively civilized parts of Alaska, airplane access may be simpler, even cheaper, than travel by car.

The vast residue of Alaska, known simply as "the bush," is airplane country purely. There are now scheduled flights to many villages. In addition, bush pilots and air-taxi services, their vehicles equipped with wheels or floats or skis depending on landing surfaces, can get you just about anywhere, for a price.

"Anywhere" might be the western Alaska Range and the Aleutian Peninsula, where a chain of parks and wildlife refuges runs southwest toward Japan. It might be one of the parks or refuges of the boreal forest interior, along the Yukon and its tributaries, north of Fairbanks. It might be the remote west coast, on the Bering Sea, where the Yukon Delta National Wildlife Refuge is the largest of several land reserves. Perhaps the most enticing destination is the Brooks Range north of the Arctic Circle. Here, Gates of the Arctic National Park, the Arctic National Wildlife Refuge, and several similar units create a wall of wilderness broken only by the Trans-Alaska Pipeline corridor. Although there are no formal trails, higher and rockier sections are relatively easy to traverse; quite a few people also hike the difficult ground of the lower-lying tundras.

Travel in "the bush," obviously, is a step beyond backpacking as we think of it in tamer regions. You have to be well equipped, self-sufficient, and prepared for slow going and just about any kind of weather. Chartered flights take money, time, and a pretty flexible schedule—you'll be flown in, and out, when conditions permit. These challenges work to keep visitation pretty light. Vast reaches see hardly any use at all, unless by native peoples who continue to occupy their ancient lands (and strive to maintain some aspects of their ancient ways of living).

If your travels bring you near a native village, by the way, don't count on it for lodging or resupply, and seek permission if you want to linger in its neighborhood. It has its own life and business, which may or may not include catering to travelers. Inquire.

In this vast and demanding wilderness, is it really important to think about the impact of your travel on the land? Arguably, even more so than in the Lower Forty-Eight. Parts of the Alaskan bush are just now reaching the level of use at which the scars first start to appear. By the standards of the California Sierra Nevada, say, the signs are slight—a discernible use-trail along a stream, a bare dusting of litter. By the standards of Alaska, where people go to experience wilderness uncompromised, they are jarring. A choice lies ahead between sharply limiting use on the one hand and accommodating it, on the other, with formal trails and campsites, to which, however, the land is not well suited. Be glad it's not your choice, and seek advice from managing agencies about the practices they recommend. Unless otherwise instructed, behave as you would when traveling off-trail in any vulnerable terrain. Avoid trampling, especially repeat trampling, of any vegetation. Camp on durable surfaces, or move camp every night. Light no fires. Avoid spooking wildlife. Safeguard your food from bears. Take exquisite pains to pass invisibly.

By way of preparation for an Alaska trip, I especially recommend *Adventuring in Alaska*, by Peggy Wayburn. Drier but very useful is *Backpacking in Alaska*, by Jim DuFresne.

Some people count sheep. When I'm in need of a soothing mental exercise to go to sleep by, I sometimes count wilderness areas: list them in my mind, visualize their boundaries, imagine the hiking I might do within them. When I first fell into this habit, it didn't take me long to run through the roster of formally protected areas. Now the list is far too long for that, and I'm thankful. My acquaintance with most of these places will never go beyond this kind of somnolent touring. That's fine with me, too. These are treasures to be enjoyed in person; to be valued from afar: and to be preserved forever—if we can.

31

Toward a Wilderness Forever

The effort to preserve some of the wilderness of North America goes back more than 150 years. Along the way, we've several times redefined what it is we are doing. We've tried a succession of approaches, each bolder than the last. Now we stand at the beginning of a new campaign, the boldest of them all: one that goes beyond salvaging pieces and dares to seek the restoration of whole landscapes.

Roads to the Wilderness

In the beginning, there were the Native Americans, who lived lightly and thinly on the future territories of Canada and the United States. Though their presence modified the environment, perhaps profoundly, it did not make itself obvious. Away from the tiny zones of dense inhabitation—villages, pueblos, nomadic encampments—the land was what we would now call wild. Wilderness had no recognition: it was simply the way things were.

The Europeans who arrived on these shores from Columbus onward recognized wilderness, all right. For them it was first a storehouse to be looted and then a public enemy to be subdued, a vast force to be beaten back and down. They set about to do this with great courage and ever-increasing efficiency. At the same time, and from very early days, they expressed their awe at the magnificence they were invading. Almost in advance, they were nostalgic for wildness lost.

By the middle of the nineteenth century, people were wondering aloud if certain areas of wildland should not be left more or less alone. Calls for preservation came from such writers as frontier painter George Catlin, geographer George Perkins Marsh, and philosopher Henry David Thoreau. Presently this ferment began to have results. In 1864, Yosemite Valley in California was earmarked for preservation, initially through a grant to the state. In 1872, the Yellowstone region became the world's first national park. In 1894, the voters of New York State, appalled by the wave of deforestation sweeping over the Adirondacks, decreed that the remaining state-owned lands in the region be held unlogged, "forever wild."

Thus began what might be called the park model of wilderness protection. It aimed at preserving a few extraordinary areas, singled out for their scenery or (occasionally) their wildlife, and often compared to crown jewels. Since Yellowstone, a noble assortment of areas in the United States and Canada, and indeed around the world, has been set aside on this model. More recently, the emphasis has shifted from scenery to representation: national park systems are seen as collections, to be made as complete as possible, of a country's ecosystems and landscape types. Maintaining wilderness in the strict sense is not an automatic purpose of parks, and many roads and other visitor accommodations have been built in them.

For the United States, the creation of the first national parks marked something broader: a turning away from the policy of wholesale federal land disposal. Under policies going back to the Northwest Ordinance of 1787, most new lands annexed to the country became, not only federal territory, but also federal property. This, however, was regarded as a temporary and undesirable state of affairs. Barring a few shrinking and unstable allocations to Indian tribes, the goal was to have almost every acre in state or private hands, and yielding wealth somehow.

With Yellowstone, that policy began to change. Soon timbered areas were being withdrawn from the undifferentiated public lands and entrusted to a specialist agency, the U.S. Forest Service. Some key wildlife habitats became national wildlife refuges and ranges in the care of the U.S. Fish and Wildlife Service. Much later, the remainder of the public domain—mostly in the western deserts—was acknowledged to have value in itself and taken officially off the auction block. (No one has come up with a very satisfactory label for these lands, controlled by the Bureau of Land Management; they are usually just called BLM lands or public domain lands.) Again, wilderness preservation was not the object; but continued public ownership left that possibility open.

The notion of deliberately keeping certain areas free of roads can be dated to 1919 and to two rather low-level officials of the U.S. Forest Service, Arthur Carhart and Aldo Leopold. It was Leopold who really pursued the idea, urging his superiors to establish a system of wild recreational preserves. Starting with the Gila Primitive Area in 1924, the Forest Service set a number of such zones aside. In the 1930s a more upwardly mobile federal forester, Robert Marshall, made it his personal cause to multiply this system. In 1937, Marshall became one of the top officials of the Forest Service in Washington, D.C. Under his prodding, the list of protected areas was swelling fast.

But then, less than three years after his new appointment, Bob Marshall died. So did the job he had undertaken. In the ensuing decades, little new land was protected; indeed, much land in Marshall's primitive areas was reopened to logging and other incursions. Each time this happened, disappointed conservationists looked for another style of wilderness protection, one that could be counted on to stick.

The Wilderness Act of 1964

And so, after a decade of lobbying, came about the Wilderness Act of 1964.

The Wilderness Act is an extraordinary law. Before it descends into mechanics, and into the compromises that were necessary to its passage, it is readable, even stirring:

> It is hereby declared to be the policy of Congress to secure for the American people . . . the benefits of an enduring resource of wilderness . . . [a place] where the earth and its community of life are untrammeled by man, where Man himself is a visitor who does not remain.

In the act, Congress created what is called the National Wilderness Preservation System. Simply put, it is a national roster of protected wild areas on the public lands. Only Congress can place areas on that roster; only Congress can remove areas from it. The boundaries of each preserve are defined with legal precision: from this peak (for instance) down that ridge to this survey marker to that stream. Within those boundaries, wilderness is paramount. Roads may not be built; timber may not be cut; motorized vehicles may not enter. Neither may mountain bikes. (Grazing is permitted in certain areas, though, and even mining, where established claims exist.) Each such protected area is known as a "wilderness": "wilderness" in a legal sense, "wilderness" with metes and bounds, "Wilderness" with a capital "W."

When Congress creates a wilderness, the designated area remains part of the national park, national forest, wildlife refuge, or BLM district in which it lies. The same people continue to manage and control the land. Little changes. But changes that might otherwise take place are forestalled. Strict limits are set on what the managers can do with the land—or on what they can do *to* it.

The new wilderness roster started with a relative handful of areas inherited from the old Forest Service program. But it was open-ended. The law required not only the Forest Service but also the Park Service and the Fish and Wildlife Service to comb through their territories and recommend further roadless regions for the congressional imprimatur. (The fourth principal land agency, the Bureau of Land Management, was brought under the same mandate in 1976.) Several rounds of such inventories have occurred since 1964. And ever since the Wilderness Act was passed, local debates about the future of wildland have tended to be kicked up to Congress for their ultimate resolution.

Each case is something of a fight, of course. There are always people who want the largest possible amount of land placed in the formal wilderness system; there are always people who want the smallest possible allocation. Among the natural opponents of wilderness are the timber industry; the mining industry; the off-road-vehicle lobby; dam builders and power companies; chambers of commerce and local governments in rural parts of the Far West; and the aggressive pro-development lobby that calls itself the Wise Use Movement. Speaking for maximum wilderness are the various conservation groups, local and national, and the people they represent. In the end it always comes down to a simple test of public support: which side can pile up the most mail on the legislators' desks.

By the record, it seems fair to say that the pro-wilderness public is the larger. It may take time, but once a proposed wilderness begins to be seriously considered by Congress, the area almost always makes it into the system, though possibly trimmed by compromise.

Along the way the preservation project has expanded in scope and depth. At the beginning, most of the protected areas were alpine, recreationally attractive, and relatively uncontroversial. But gradually more varied lands—deserts and lowland forests, swamps and marshes—began to find their way into the system. There was a sharp debate as to whether or not to accept areas, especially in the eastern United States, that had recovered from past logging. (The eventual answer was yes.) Along the way, it began to be understood that wilderness was only incidentally a type of recreation land: that the goal was more fundamentally the preservation of the healthy, living fabric of the natural world.

With each new round of inventories, too, it became evident that there was considerably more roadless acreage left than we had thought. To the frustration of people who didn't like the idea in the first place, advocates kept raising their sights. At first, they thought 2 or 3 percent of the area of the United States might wind up in the wilderness system; a few years later, they were thinking in terms of a tenth—a tithe, as the eminent conservationist David Brower put it.

How large in fact could the wilderness system envisioned in 1964—based on the preservation of parts of the existing, shrinking stock of roadless areas—actually become?

The United States is a big country. Setting Alaska aside for the moment, we have, in the other forty-nine states, about 1.9 billion acres of land—about 3 million square miles. About one-sixth of that land is owned by the federal government.

Adding up the inventories made by the land agencies, we find that at least 120 million acres are still roadless and undeveloped. That sounds impressive, and it is. But compared with the total acreage of those forty-nine states, it's not quite so imposing—something under 7 percent of all the land, well under Brower's tithe.

By 2004, almost 50 million acres in the non-Alaskan states had actually been placed in the federal wilderness system. That's an area about half the size of California—and still less than half of the potential in these states. Many a sharp battle remains to be fought. The biggest potential additions to the system now lie in the Rocky Mountain and intermountain states of Nevada, Utah, Idaho, and Montana. And they lie, not in the national forests, parks, or wildlife refuges, but in the largely arid holdings of the Bureau of Land Management. The desert, for all its fascination and beauty, is always the last landscape to be appreciated.

Meanwhile, however, the game has continued to change.

The Fight for Wild Alaska

When the forty-ninth state was admitted to the union in 1959, nearly its entire area was federal land. As part of statehood, Alaska was due to receive a large grant of property. But here something new intervened: the indigenous peoples of the region, left out of the initial calculations in the best traditional manner, asserted through the courts their own land claims. The situation froze.

By the time it unfroze, in the late 1970s, the time was right for a grand allocation of public domain lands in Alaska—not only to the state, and not only to what became a set of native corporations, but also to the federal conservation systems on a scale never seen before. The American conservation movement realized that it had an opportunity that would never come again: the "last great first chance," as the slogan went, to preserve landscapes and wildlife wholesale.

The wilderness areas of the Lower Forty-Eight, for all their grandeur, are the uneaten scraps at a great resource consumption banquet. They contain more heights than lowlands, more rugged ground than flat, more deserts and tundras than forests and fertile soils. And in truth they are rather small. Though some wilderness areas bulk pretty large on the map of a national forest, very few of them look like much on the map of a state. In the United States south of Canada, you will be hard put to find a spot more than 20 miles from a road.

You will also be hard put to find a spot where all the plant and animal species present a hundred years ago are still around. This is especially true of what biologists call "keystone predators," animals like the wolf and the grizzly bear.

Henry David Thoreau, writing of New England in the 1840s, was already troubled by this impoverishment. "Is it not a maimed and imperfect nature I am conversing with?" he asks in *Walden*. And he adds longingly: "I want to know an entire heaven and an entire earth."

With Alaska, the United States had its great opportunity to preserve "an entire heaven and an entire earth": to secure—in single, unbroken, protected regions—natural units as vast as the whole watershed of a major river, or a mountain range from plain to peak, or the entire range of a migratory caribou herd. With a tremendous spasm of energy, on the eve of the conservative "Reagan Revolution" that would have doomed the effort, the challenge was met. In the Alaska National Interest Lands Conservation Act of 1980, the national legislature established parks and refuges and wilderness areas on a scale never seen before, and sufficient not only to safeguard scenery and recreation, but also to honor biological realities.

All is not well in Alaska. When it comes to formal wilderness classification, much land was left out of the system that should someday be in. In the Tongass National Forest, Congress has imposed the will of the timber industry on a temperate rainforest of planetary significance. Oil drilling is a perennial possibility in the Arctic National Wildlife Refuge in the Brooks Range, and will only be foreclosed when the land finally gets wilderness as well as refuge status. The expanded state, private, and Native corporation lands—sometimes constituting inholdings in the new federal preserves—are diversely managed. It will be a long time before the work of 1980 can be consolidated, let alone added to.

For all that, the outcome in Alaska is one to which the rest of the country, indeed the rest of the world, can only look in awe.

Bad News from Biology

In the years following the Alaska battle, there was a new recognition of the biological inadequacy of the system of land reserves in the rest of the United States.

Many animals, especially large mammals that rove, need extensive wild country for their survival. It is not coincidental that grizzly bears remain only in the wildest corners of the lower forty-eight states. Animal and plant species also need to be able to shift their ranges in response to changes in the environment—for instance, a series of warmer or colder years, or a vegetation shift due to natural succession. In addition, different local populations of a species need to be in contact to permit interbreeding, and to allow replacements to filter in if one local group is lost to an event like a forest fire.

Biologists studying oceanic islands have long noted a match between size and biotic wealth: the smaller the area of an island, the lower the count of species it supports. They have pointed out the troubling analogy: by our wholesale alteration of landscapes, we have made many wildlife habitats on the U.S. mainland into islands of a sort, surrounded by oceans not of water but of altered, biologically unusable land. Most of the islands have long since lost keystone species. The southern Rockies have no wolves; the Sierra Nevada, for all its grandeur, no grizzly bears. Between 1920 and 1976, thirteen mammal species disappeared from Mount Rainier National Park. Some other islands still support nearly their full complement of plants and animals. But can they continue to do so as decades pass and pressures natural and unnatural have time to work?

The by now undeniable process of global warming—the great climate change induced by deforestation and the burning of fossil fuels—can only add to the risk of extinction. If the last population of a certain plant of the tundra zone clings to the uppermost acres of a chilly peak, what will save it when the peak gets warmer and the forest closes in? How can a beleaguered species retreat to the cooler north when the way is blocked by a settled valley and a superhighway?

In 1960, at one of the conferences that generated the push for the Wilderness Act, the Wilderness Society's Howard Zahniser challenged his listeners to think in the very long term: "We are working for a wilderness forever." In the United States, with the Wilderness Act, we thought we had achieved that permanence. But by the 1980s we knew that mere legislated boundaries are not enough to make "a wilderness forever"—not if wilderness means something more than roadless recreation land. Most of the pieces of land we have protected, however beautiful and valued, are too small, or too far apart, or both, to make sense as biological reserves. And, certain whole ecosystems and landscapes are not represented at all.

Cores and Corridors: A Dream of Restoration

In the 1980s, alarmed by the prospect of species extinction on a scale not seen since the end of the dinosaurs, biologists proclaimed a new specialty called *conservation biology*. Increasingly, too, they began to speak out about policy. Studying the situation in the Cascade Mountains and elsewhere, they recommended that federal land be managed in a systematic way to preserve habitat, maintaining vital linkages.

This way of thinking cast a new light on roadless lands whose fate was still to be decided. Take the Klamath Mountains region of northwest California and adjacent Oregon, habitat for old-growth-dependent species like the spotted owl, the fisher, and the rare Humboldt marten (and also a planetary hotspot of botanical diversity). Here there are five important roadless areas, containing altogether about 1.5 million acres and more than a quarter of the old-growth forest remaining in the Pacific Northwest; a somewhat smaller classified wilderness area exists at the center of each. The roadless areas almost touch, creating corridors for species movement; the wilderness area boundaries stand well apart. If the connecting corridors are logged, as perennially planned, the biotic value of the entire complex will shrink disproportionately. In 1989, the California Wilderness Coalition urged that these corridors be protected, citing biological rather than recreational grounds. Their fate is still unresolved.

The Klamath proposal was the first of many. From coast to coast, the goals and arguments of wilderness defenders were shifting. Advocates learned to think less in terms of single wilderness areas, important though these will always remain, and more in terms of clusters, connections, specific wildlife needs: a wilderness *system*, not in the merely formal sense of a list of areas, but in the practical sense of a web of interrelated lands.

In 1992, an assortment of biologically oriented conservation veterans set out the boldest vision yet: the North American Wilderness Recovery Project (also called the Wildlands Project). A continental dream of biotic richness renewed, the project calls for a network of protected areas threading through every state and region. The system would be anchored by large, strictly protected core reserves, often based on existing wilderness and parks. These cores would be linked by narrower corridors, not necessarily pristine but sufficiently unaltered to permit the passage of moving animals and slowly shifting plant populations. Around the cores and corridors would lie buffer zones, in economic use but not too densely roaded and free of activities that would compromise the more strictly protected lands within.

The initial Wildlands Project manifesto offered pilot plans for the state of Florida, for the Blue Ridge region of the southern Appalachians, for the Colorado Rockies, and—most ambitious of all—for the northern Rockies of the United States, a region where past preservation victories provide a good foundation. The sketch plan shows core areas around Yellowstone; in the Glacier National Park–Bob Marshall Wilderness region near the Canadian border; and in central Idaho, where vast forest wilderness areas exist. Two more core areas would be created in the Hells Canyon region of Idaho and Oregon and in the Cabinet Mountains–Yaak Valley area of western Montana, where Canada's wild Columbia Mountains nudge south of the border. Primitive habitat corridors, mostly along mountain ridges, would interlink these cores.

It isn't hard to visualize such a system for a region like the northern Rockies (though political enactment is another matter). It's quite something else to imagine it on a continental scale. Obviously, such an achievement is the project of generations, maybe of centuries. The originators envision a long period of transition while we all get used to the idea. They foresee many compromises along the way, not in the goal but in the timing and details. They don't use the conventional heated rhetoric of "now or never."

Even in the very short term and the very small scale, however, the system idea reorganizes our thinking. It shifts attention from single wilderness areas to wilderness regions, wilderness sequences, wilderness constellations. It may suggest which fights deserve the most energy. It puts a new emphasis on the restoration of less-than-wild landscapes. And it provides a galvanizing, almost painful hope: for a future in which we are not (as Zahniser said) merely slowing down the forces of degradation, or even stopping them at certain lines, but beginning, here and there, to roll them back.

Canada's Great Opportunity

In Canada, the story of wilderness preservation has unfolded rather differently.

Here, too, it begins with parks. Banff National Park, in the Canadian Rockies, dates to 1885, and it has many impressive peers. But soon the paths of the two nations diverge. In the United States, the first park set-asides started a trend toward keeping all the western public lands in federal ownership. Canada, by contrast, chose to cede its public domain lands, known as crown lands, to the provinces. Since this transfer occurred, in 1931, public land policy south of the sixtieth parallel has been strictly the affair of the ten provincial governments. Their approaches have varied as much as might those of ten different nations.

North of the sixtieth parallel, where federally administered territories remain, less has changed; but even here land allocation is no longer accomplished, as often in the United States, by fiat. The Canadian central government just doesn't make major decisions here without the consent of territorial officials and of the Native groups that it recognizes as First Nations.

Given this institutional setup, the idea of a unified system of wilderness preserves, so central in the United

States, could not develop in Canada. Rather, the park model has continued to prevail, in its second, more sophisticated form: parks as a representative sample of natural regions rather than merely as scenic jewels. National parks are still being designated, mostly in the territories north of the sixtieth parallel, occasionally also in the southern provinces, in every case as products of elaborate intergovernment negotiation.

The great majority of Canada's parks, however, are creations of the provinces alone, and a varied lot they are. Some provincial parks equal in scope and grandeur anything found in the United States; others are not true parks at all but are rather akin to U.S. national forests—managed for timber harvest and all sorts of other uses and containing, at best, limited wild zones. At this writing, British Columbia is doing the best job of park building, both in quantity and in quality. The prairie province of Manitoba, where park status means next to nothing, is a notorious laggard. Conservationists and the federal government are encouraging the work through a high-level, low-pressure effort called the Endangered Spaces Campaign. Outside the parks, exploitation continues at a dizzying pace. As a 1997 federal report put it, "Little land exists now in Canada that does not have some kind of interest or commitment for uses such as oil and gas development, mining, hydro-electricity, forestry, agriculture, and private recreation."

Still, Canada has opportunities that the United States may envy. It has enormous amounts of land in government ownership, and it has truly vast tracts of de facto wilderness, especially in the Yukon Territory, the Northwest Territories, and the northeastern territory Nunavat. The door is still wide open to developing the kind of reserve system envisioned by the Wildlands Project. Already there is talk on both sides of the international border of a chain of linked reserves running up the line of the Rockies from Yellowstone country to the Yukon, and another sequence linking the New York State Forest Preserve in the Adirondacks with Algonquin Provincial Park in Quebec.

The Management Challenge

Meanwhile, in the old core wilderness areas—and wherever wildland is subject to recreational use—we face the more traditional question: How can we enjoy these places without causing them to deteriorate either biologically or aesthetically? That is, without making them less wild, either in function, or in feel?

It is easy to exaggerate the problem. We are not yet truly in danger of "loving the wilderness to death"—not much of it anyway. Some places look and seem wilder today than they did 30 or even 60 years ago. But if there is no longer a crisis, as there seemed to be in the 1970s, there is a challenge constantly renewed. How shall we act to maintain what has so nourished us, and maintain it not for a handful of years, not for a generation or two, but over centuries—a wilderness experience forever?

There is a whole science now of wilderness management. It concerns such matters as the reintroduction of fire to natural systems that cannot be healthy without it and fending off the exotic plant and animal species that increasingly threaten to displace native ones. Most of all, though, wilderness management has to do with us, the tourists, the visitors. It involves the building of facilities—starting with trails—to handle heavier use than the land could take without them. It involves education. It involves managing access, as in steering people to lesser-used areas (a controversial idea) or deliberately concentrating them in more heavily used ones (ditto). And it may involve quotas, formal limits on the number of people allowed in particular places at particular times.

Out of the complexities, two simple facts emerge. First, our own behavior, person by person and group by group, is key. The more intelligent responsibility we take for walking softly in the wilderness, the less reason (or excuse) the managers will have for heavy-handed actions. Second, bigger wilderness is better. A small, attractive alpine area, with good road access, is naturally going to come under great pressure. A large, forested wilderness, with high country nestled perhaps two days' march within it, is far less likely to be overrun.

So the problem of *managing* wilderness is in no way separate from the problem of *preserving* wilderness. The more we have, the easier it is to manage; the more the supply diminishes, the greater the manager's difficulties become. For eminently selfish reasons, we should insist on a generous wilderness, not a narrow, cramped, and superregulated one.

What You Can Do

If you've enjoyed the wilderness that is and would like to cast your vote for a "wilderness forever," there's no end to the ways you can do so.

One excellent and easy thing to do is to take a few notes. Wilderness managers and interested conservationists are far too few to keep track of the state of millions of acres of land. Backpackers can be their eyes and ears. Is a stretch of trail eroding? Are illegal vehicles crossing the wilderness boundary? Is livestock grazing where it shouldn't? Are exotic plant species—like spotted knapweed in many western areas—on the march? Armed with a camera, and maybe a little knowledge picked up at a ranger station, we can further document such problems.

A second simple thing to do is to write a letter, just one per trip. Every time I come out of a wilderness area, I like to send a note to the local staff of the managing agency. If nothing else, I compliment them on the beauty of the place and on their management of it (even if that management is merely benign neglect). I thank them especially for any assistance given. I report any concerns. And if the area is one whose fate has yet to be decided, I ask to be on a mailing list to learn of future plans.

If you visit an area that is not yet in a wilderness or equivalent protected zone, your written witness could prove very important. It can be vital, when push comes to shove, to demonstrate that specific people have stated concern for specific places, based on documented visits: that they visited Indigo Creek in May, or Silver Prairie in July, or King Lear Peak in September, and loved it there. Keep copies of such letters.

Not sure where to write? Get the address if you stop off at a local agency office—for instance, to pick up a wilderness permit. If you're using an agency map, you may also find an address on that. If you're missing the address, you can contact the regional or central office of the appropriate bureaucracy—see the Resources section. The Internet is a great help.

Beyond the simple letter, of course, lies a world of involvement, if you want to enter it.

- *Write your elected representatives.* In the United States, where the federal government has the largest role in public land management, that means your representative and your state's two senators, as well as the president and his or her top staff. In the less-centralized Canadian system, your first letter, at least, should go to your member of parliament on the provincial level. Tell them of your interest in wilderness in general and in such efforts as the North American Wilderness Recovery Project and Canada's Endangered Spaces campaign. If you've written to an agency regarding a particular area, send your legislators a copy of that letter, too. You may not get a very promising response, but don't let that bother you—politicians notice, though they may not read, their mail. (To reach a U.S. senator, write Honorable X, Washington, DC 20510; a representative is Honorable Y, Washington, DC 20515.) Phone calls and electronic mail, though better than nothing, don't carry quite the same weight.

- *Hook up with an environmental organization* that is interested in the same issues you are. If you don't have contacts in this direction, the central offices of the Sierra Club and the Wilderness Society can help; so can the Canadian Parks and Wilderness Society; so can some gear stores. A few addresses are found in the Resources section of this book. In a number of states and provinces, there are regional wilderness groups that follow issues jurisdiction-wide. Very local groups of wilderness advocates may concentrate on some single area. (You might contact such a group when planning a trip to its backyard.) Joining any of these organizations, for a few dollars, can be worthwhile. Hooked into a grapevine, receiving current information, you know, at a minimum, whom to write your letters to, and when, in order to get the greatest possible effect.

- *Locate a trails group.* In addition to the many organizations working to protect wild areas as such, many more exist to promote and to help maintain recreational trails. Some concentrate on the long, glamorous paths like the Appalachian and the Sea-to-Sea; others tend to the local trail networks where most of the day-to-day hiking gets done, and where the need is particularly great. In some parts of the United States, private organizations do as much to care for the land as do the government agencies that are in overall charge. Since agency budgets are perennially tight, such partnerships are gaining in importance everywhere.

Every conceivable kind of work is waiting somewhere to be done: exploring unprotected areas, bucking loads up trails, monitoring timber sales and mining claims, censusing species of concern, attending lengthy hearings, combing through government documents, and much, much more. You'll like the people you meet in these endeavors.

But the simple letter is where it all starts. And if a decent proportion of today's wilderness users did speak up to just that degree, their common voice would be very loud indeed.

There is more than a little satisfaction in doing something, however easy, to protect the future of a place you have enjoyed. It is as though you had paid a small and proper fee for the use of the land. If there is a tiny, unavoidable impact on the wilderness whenever a hiker goes into it, the hiker's letter written after the trip can more than cancel out that debt.

Permission
Acknowledgments

Thanks are due to the following authors and publishers for permission to reprint.

Anabasis, by Saint-John Perse. Translated by T. S. Eliot. New York: Harcourt, Brace Jovanovich, Inc. Copyright © 1938, 1949 by Harcourt, Brace & Co.

Gerard Manley Hopkins, Poems and Prose, edited by W. H. Gardner. New York: Oxford University Press. Copyright © 1953, 1963 by W. H. Gardner.

Homecoming with Reflections, by Jeanne McGahey. Princeton: *Quarterly Review of Literature.* Copyright © 1973, 1989 by Jeanne McGahey. By permission of the author's estate.

Mount Analogue, by René Daumal. Translated by Roger Shattuck. Baltimore: Penguin Books. Copyright © 1952 by Librairie Gallimard. Reprinted by permission of Random House, Inc.

Round River, by Aldo Leopold. New York: Oxford University Press. Copyright © 1953 by Oxford University Press.

This Is Dinosaur, by Wallace Stegner. New York: Alfred A. Knopf, Inc. Copyright © 1955 by Wallace Stegner. By permission of the author.

"Wilderness Forever," by Howard Zahniser, from *Wilderness: America's Living Heritage.* Copyright © 1961 by the Sierra Club.

Resources

Here are some starting points for your exploration of the wilderness of information about wilderness travel: a list of citizen organizations concerned with wildland; lists of government agencies in the United States and Canada that manage it; information on acquiring maps; a list of publications mentioned in the text; miscellaneous information sources accessible via computer; the names of a couple of roadhead shuttles mentioned in the text; and, finally, a selection of equipment makers and sellers. In the Internet age, the Web site of a group, firm, or government agency is almost always the place to start; it will yield phone numbers, addresses, and contact information for more local offices, areas, or dealers.

Conservation and Wilderness Travel Organizations

American Hiking Society
www.americanhiking.org. Advocacy group for hikers and hiking trails, especially long ones.

American Trails
www.americantrails.org. Industry-sponsored umbrella group for hikers and other trail users.

Appalachian Mountain Club
www.outdoors.org. Outings and conservation with a
New York–New England emphasis.

Appalachian Trail Conference
www.appalachiantrail.org. Umbrella group for thirty-
one organizations involved with the trail.

Audubon
www.audubon.org. Environmental action with a focus
on bird habitat.

Canadian Nature Federation
www.cnf.ca. Proponent of parks and protected areas.

Canadian Parks and Wilderness Society
www.cpaws.org. Wilderness advocate.

Federation of Western Outdoor Clubs
www.federationofwesternoutdoorclubs.org. Umbrella
organization in the West.

Leave No Trace Center for Outdoor Ethics
www.lnt.org. Public-private partnership promoting
low-impact practices.

The Mountaineers
www.mountaineers.org. Major outdoors/conservation
club in the Northwest.

The Nature Conservancy
http://nature.org. A leading organization among those
that preserve land by buying it.

Sierra Club
www.sierraclub.org. Powerhouse of environmental
action on many fronts; national and chapter-led wilderness outings.

Wilderness Education Association
www.weainfo.org. Educational programs for trip leaders on safe, low-impact travel.

The Wilderness Society
www.wilderness.org. Wilderness advocacy with a scientific slant.

The Wildlands Project
www.twp.org. Originator of the vision of a continental network of linked wild and semi-wild land reserves.

U.S. Federal and State Agencies That Manage Wilderness Land

Alaska Department of Natural Resources, Division of Parks and Outdoor Recreation
www.dnr.state.ak.us. Several Alaska state parks would be national parks in any other part of the United States.

Bureau of Land Management
www.blm.gov/nhp. The nation's biggest land agency manages 260 million acres, mostly arid, in the West and in Alaska.

California Department of Parks and Recreation
www.parks.ca.gov. Administers over a million acres. Backpackable parks include Anza-Borrego Desert, Henry Coe, and Humboldt Redwoods.

Maine Bureau of Parks and Lands
www.state.me.us/doc/parks. Administers 600,000 acres including the Allagash Wilderness Waterway; a separate Baxter State Park Authority runs the 200,000-acre park: www.baxterstateparkauthority.com.

Michigan Department of Natural Resources
www.michigan.gov/dnr; related information at www.ring.com/travel/parks.htm. Backpacking destinations include Porcupine Mountains State Park in the Upper Peninsula and the High Country Pathway in the Lower.

Minnesota Department of Natural Resources
www.dnr.state.mn.us. Backpackable areas include Big
Bog State Recreation Area and Beltrami Island State
Forest.

National Park Service
www.nps.gov. Controls 80 million acres of spectacular,
mostly wildland.

New York Department of Environmental Conservation,
Division of Lands and Forests
www.dec.state.ny.us/website/dlf/index.html.
New York State lands in the Adirondacks, Catskills,
and elsewhere contain over a million acres of state-
classified wilderness.

Pennsylvania Department of Conservation and
Natural Resources
www.dcnr.state.pa.us. Pennsylvania parks and forests
offer many wild corners and lengthy interconnecting
trails.

U.S. Fish and Wildlife Service
www.fws.gov. Runs 95 million acres of largely wild
national wildlife refuges and game ranges, including
large areas in the Southeast and West.

U.S. Forest Service
www.fs.fed.us. Some 188 million acres of national
forests and national grasslands include about one-third
of the nation's formally protected wilderness. The
agency's Aldo Leopold originated formal wilderness
zoning.

Wisconsin Department of Natural Resources,
Bureau of Parks and Recreation
www.dnr.state.wi.us. Kettle Moraine State Forest and
nine other areas allow backpacking.

Canadian Federal and Provincial Agencies That Manage Wilderness Land

Alberta Community Development
www.cd.gov.ab.ca. Alberta parks cover 5 million acres.

British Columbia Ministry of
Water, Land and Air Protection
http://wlapwww.gov.bc.ca/bcparks. The province is
busily setting aside reserves, which now total some 20
million acres.

Manitoba Conservation
www.gov.mb.ca/conservation/parks. Very large parks
include Whiteshell, Turtle Mountain, Duck Mountain,
Grass River.

New Brunswick Department of Tourism and Parks
www.tourismnewbrunswick.ca. Mount Carleton
Provincial Park is the big one.

Newfoundland and Labrador Tourism
www.gov.nf.ca/parks&reserves. Check out Bay du
Nord and Avalon Wilderness Reserves.

Northwest Territories Parks and Tourism
www.gov.nt.ca/RWED/parks. For major destinations
in this federal territory, start by consulting the
ParksCanada site below.

Nova Scotia Department of Natural Resources
http://parks.gov.ns.ca. Cape Chignecto is the principal
backpacking park.

Nunavut Department of Sustainable Development
www.nunavutparks.com. For major destinations in this
federal territory, start by consulting the ParksCanada
site below.

Ontario Ministry of Natural Resources
www.mnr.gov.on.ca. The province has eight large
wilderness parks, including Quetico along the
Minnesota border.

ParksCanada
www.pc.gc.ca/index_e.asp. Canadian national parks
are exemplary, totaling 67 million acres, but the bulk
of public land in the provinces is administered by
provincial governments.

Saskatchewan Environment
www.se.gov.sk.ca/saskparks. Major parks include
Moose Mountain, Cypress Hills, Wildcat Hill, and
Duck Mountain.

Société des établissements de plein air du Québec
www.sepaq.com/En/. Quebec manages 2 million acres
of parks, which it terms national rather than provincial.

Yukon Territory Department of Environment
www.environmentyukon.gov.yk.ca. For major destinations in this federal territory, start by consulting the
ParksCanada site above.

Maps

U.S. Geological Survey (USGS) topographical sheets
may be purchased at numerous private suppliers,
online at http://store.usgs.gov, or over the counter at
USGS Earth Science Information Centers in Anchorage,
Alaska; Denver, Colo.; Menlo Park, Calif.; Reston, Va;
Rolla, Mo.; and Sioux Falls, S.D. Current basic price for
all sheets is $6.00, plus a handling charge of $5.00 per
order. Also request the brochure *Topographic Map
Symbols, US.* Canadian topographical maps are available through private suppliers only. Private companies
also sell maps derived from the government sheets but
containing added information and often printed on
weatherproof paper.

Increasingly, maps must be seen not as separate publications but as local snippets taken from continent-spanning databases of geographic information. Private companies offer state or regional databases on CD-ROM disks at $80 to $100, as well as downloadable map-sized subsets available online. Satellite photographs are also available and fun to look at, though less useful for navigation. The U.S. Geological Survey is itself developing a database called the National Map, viewable online at http://nationalmap.usgs.gov, but still very much a work in progress. Some additional electronic sources for maps and aerial photographs:

http://maps.nationalgeographic.com/topo
http://mapserver.maptech.com
http://terraserver.microsoft.com
www.delorme.com
www.mapcard.com
www.topozone.com

Publications Mentioned in the Text

Backpacker Magazine
800-666-3434, www.backpacker.com.

Bear Attacks: Their Causes and Avoidance
by Stephen Herrero (Guilford, Conn.: Globe Pequot Press, 2002).

The Essential Outdoor Gear Manual
by Annie Getchell (Camden, Maine: Ragged Mountain Press, 2000).

Medicine for Mountaineering, 5th ed.
edited by James A. Wilkerson (Seattle: The Mountaineers Books, 2001).

Mountaineering: The Freedom of the Hills, 7th ed.
edited by Don Graydon and Kurt Hanson (Seattle: The Mountaineers Books, 2002).

Outside Magazine
800-678-1131, http://outside.away.com.

Wilderness First Aid Manual
by William W. Forgey (Seattle: HART Health and
Safety, 1999).

Selected Online Information Sources

Adventure Sports
www.adventuresports.com. A good general starting
point.

Appalachian Trail
www.fred.net/kathy/at.html. Information about the
trail.

Avalanche
www.avalanche.org. Links to local avalanche information across the United States.

Backcountry Toilet
www.uvm.edu/~rlachape/toilets.html. Wilderness
sanitation and related topics.

Backpacker Magazine
www.backpacker.com. The magazine's Web site
includes such things as a searchable database on current
gear and a bulletin board for locating hiking partners.

BackpackGearTest
www.backpackgeartest.org. A consumer-originated
testing organization with no ties to advertisers.

Great Outdoor Recreation Pages (GORP)
http://gorp.away.com. Portal for information on varied
outdoor activities, associated with *Outside* magazine.

Leave No Trace Outdoor Ethics
www.lnt.org. Detailed information on recommended
practices.

The Lightweight Backpacker
www.backpacking.net. Information and discussion with an ultralight emphasis.

Outside Magazine
http://outside.away.com. The magazine's Web site is a magazine in itself.

Slackpacker
www.slackpacker.com. Site aimed at the nonfanatical, comfort-seeking wilderness traveler.

Trailquest
www.trailquest.net. Information on the Appalachian, Pacific Crest, and Continental Divide Trails.

Trailspace
www.trailspace.com/backcountry. Moderated back-country newsgroup. Just go there and start reading and posting.

Wilderness.net
www.wilderness.net. Information about the U.S. National Wilderness Preservation System and related issues.

State and provincial tourism Web sites also frequently include information about backpacking destinations. For example:

> Arkansas, www.arkansas.com
> California, www.visitcalifornia.com
> Colorado, www.colorado.com
> Manitoba, www.travelmanitoba.com
> Minnesota, www.exploreminnesota.com
> Nevada, www.travelnevada.com
> New York, www.iloveny.state.ny.us
> Northwest Territories, www.explorenwt.ca
> Oregon, www.traveloregon.com
> Texas, www.traveltex.com
> West Virginia, www.callwva.com

Transportation Services Mentioned in the Text

Sierra Express Transportation
P.O. Box 8118, Mammoth Lakes, CA 93546-8118,
760-937-8294
www.mammothlakestransportation.com.

Transcanyon Shuttle
P.O. Box 348, Grand Canyon, AR 86023
928-638-2820.

Equipment Sources

There are hundreds of gear makers and major suppliers. This selection begins with firms that manufacture or retail a wide range of gear and continues with some prominent specialists, subdivided by the types of gear they make. Mailing addresses and phone numbers are provided where available, but many firms now prefer an approach via e-mail links on their Web sites.

Generalists

Bergans North America
1934 Flynn Street, Seattle, WA 98112-2618
206-329-2088
www.bergans.com
Packs, tents, sleeping bags, clothing from Norway.

Campmor
P.O. Box 700, Saddle River, NJ 07458
800-230-2151
www.campmor.com
Mail-order retailer with favorable prices. Good source if you need no advice.

Coleman Exponent
800-835-3278
www.coleman.com
Moderately priced packs, sleeping bags, tents, and stoves.

EMS (Eastern Mountain Sports)
1 Vose Farm Road, Peterborough, NH 03458
888-463-6367
www.ems.com
Major gear supplier for eastern United States.

Kelty, Inc.
6235 Lookout Road, Boulder, CO 80301
800-423-2320
www.kelty.com
Tents, sleeping bags, kid carriers, a major remaining
maker of frame packs.

Lafuma America, Inc.
6662 Gunpark Drive, Suite 200, Boulder, CO 80301
303-527-1460
www.lafuma.com/lafuma/us
Gear from France with a European touch.

L.L. Bean Inc.
Freeport, ME 04033
800-809-7057
www.llbean.com
Gear supermarket with many L.L. Bean items.

Marmot
2321 Circadian Way, Santa Rosa, CA 95407
707-544-4590
www.marmot.com
Broad-spectrum maker and retailer of high-end gear.

MontBell America, Inc.
303-449-7681
www.montbell.com
Japanese firm with ultralight emphasis.

Mountain Equipment Co-op
888-847-0770
www.mec.ca
The gear supermarket of Canada, with many branches.

Mountain Gear
2002 N. Division, Spokane, WA 99207
800-829-2009
www.mgear.com
Big store with online catalog.

Mountain Hardwear
950 Gilman Street, Berkeley, CA 94710
800-953-8375
www.mountainhardwear.com
Clothing, sleeping bags, tents.

MSR (Mountain Safety Research)
P.O. Box 24547, Seattle, WA 98124
800-531-9531
www.msrcorp.com
Distinctive stoves, tents, snowshoes, and much else.

The North Face
2013 Farallon Drive, San Leandro, CA 94577
800-535-3331
www.thenorthface.com
National chain with many North Face products.

Outbound Products, Infinity Sports Imports Inc.
E101-19720-94A Avenue, Langley, BC, Canada
888-718-2288
www.outbound.ca
Broad range of moderately priced gear.

REI (Recreational Equipment, Inc.)
P.O. Box 1938, Sumner, WA 98390-0800
800-426-4840
www.rei.com
Gear supermarket selling its own and other designs.

Salomon North America
877-272-5666
www.salomonsports.com
Ski specialist that now makes a range of general-purpose gear.

Sierra Designs
1255 Powell Street, Emeryville, CA 94608
800-635-0461
www.sierradesigns.com
Tents, sleeping bags, and clothing.

Sierra Trading Post
5025 Campstool Road, Cheyenne, WY 82007
800-713-4534
www.sierratradingpost.com
Mail order retailer with favorable prices.

Vaude
201-964-9292
www.vaude.de
Wide range of gear from Germany.

Ultralight Specialists

AntiGravityGear LLC
609 Hollingsworth Drive, Wilmington, NC 28412
www.antigravitygear.com

Exped Expedition Equipment
800-609-7187
www.exped.com

GOLITE LLC
P.O. Box 20190, Boulder, CO 80303
888-546-5483
www.golite.com
The firm founded by Ray Jardine to commercialize his
ultralight ideas.

Granite Gear
2312 10th Street, Two Harbors, MN 55616
218-834-6157
www.granitegear.com

GVP Gear
3764 Cavern Place, Carlsbad, CA 92008-6585
760-720-0500
www.gvpgear.com

LWGear
Lynne Whelden
1025 Shaw Place, Williamsport, PA 17701
www.lwgear.com

Nunatak Gear LLC
160 Twisp-Winthrop Eastside Road, Twisp,
Washington 98856
866-686-2825, 866-686-2825
www.nunatakusa.com

Stephenson's Warmlite
RD 4, Box 145, Gilford, NH 03246
www.warmlite.com
Unconventional sleeping bags, tents, vapor barrier
clothing, long considered eccentric, but in tune with
the ultralight age.

ULA Equipment
159 N 200 E, Logan, UT 84321
435-753-5191
www.ula-equipment.com

Footwear (Including Ski Boots)

Adidas America
800-448-1796
www.adidas.com

Alpina Sports Corp.
603-448-3101
www.alpinasports.com

Asolo USA, Inc.
139 Harvest Lane, Williston, VT 05495
800-448-8827
www.asolo-usa.com

Danner, Inc.
1319 St. Andrew Street, LaCrosse, WI 54603
800-345-0430
www.danner.com

Five Ten
P.O. Box 1185, Redlands, CA 92373
909-798-4222
www.fiveten.com
A pioneer of soles with "sticky" rubber.

Garmont USA, Inc.
170 Boyer Circle, Suite 20, Williston, VT 05495
802-658-8322
www.garmontusa.com

Hi-Tec Sports USA, Inc.
4801 Stoddard Road, Modesto, CA 95356
800-521-1698
www.hi-tec.com

Merrell Performance Footwear
800-637-7001
www.merrell.com

Montrail, Inc.
2505 Airport Way South, Seattle, WA 98134-2201
206-621-9303
www.montrail.com

Nike ACG
www.nikeacg.com

Raichle of Switzerland
800-451-5127
www.raichle.com

Salomon North America
877-272-5666
www.salomonsports.com

Scarpa
850 Summer Street, South Boston, MA 02127
617-268-5625
www.scarpa-us.com
Formerly Fabiano.

SmartWool
800-550-9665
www.smartwool.com
Specialty hiking socks of wool.

Teva
P.O. Box 968, Flagstaff, AZ 86002
800-367-8382
www.teva.com
Tough outdoor sandals.

ThorLo
2120 Newton Drive, Statesville, NC 28677
888-846-7567
www.thorlo.com
Specialty hiking socks of synthetic fibers.

Vasque
314 Main Street, Red Wing, MN 55066
800-224-4453
www.vasque.com

Clothing

Arc'Teryx Equipment, Inc.
2770 Bentall St., Vancouver, BC, Canada V5M 4H4
800-985-6681
www.arcteryx.com
Innovative (and expensive) clothing.

Columbia Sportswear Company
6600 N. Baltimore, Portland, OR 97203
503-985-4000
www.columbia.com

Helly-Hansen
P.O. Box 97031, Redmond, WA 98073
800-635-9595
www.hellyhansen.com

Lowe Alpine
P.O. Box 1449, Broomfield, CO 80038
800-891-7908
www.lowealpine.com

Moonstone Mountaineering Equipment
5350 Ericson Way, Arcata, CA 95521
800-390-3312
www.moonstone.com

Outdoor Research
2203 First Avenue S., Seattle, WA 98134
888-467-4327
www.orgear.com
Originator of various high-tech clothing designs.

Patagonia, Inc.
P.O. Box 32050, Reno, NV 89533
800-638-6464
www.patagonia.com
Originator of various high-tech clothing designs.

Royal Robbins
1314 Coldwell Avenue, Modesto, CA 95350
800-587-9044
www.royalrobbins.com

Sun Precautions
2815 Wetmore Avenue, Everett, WA 98210l
800-882-7860
www.sunprecautions.com
A pioneer maker of clothing designed to block UV
radiation.

Packs

Arc'Teryx Equipment, Inc.
2770 Bentall St., Vancouver, BC, Canada V5M 4H4
800-985-6681
www.arcteryx.com

CamelBak, CamelBak Products, Inc.
1310 Redwood Way, Suite C, Petaluma, CA 94954
800-767-8725
www.camelbak.com
Pioneer of "hydration systems."

Camp Trails, Johnson Worldwide Associates
P.O. Box 966, Binghamton, NY 13902
800-572-8822
www.camptrails.com
Frame packs.

Dana Design
333 Simmental Way, Bozeman, MT 59715
888-357-3262
www.danadesign.com

Gregory Mountain Products
800-477-3420
www.gregorypacks.com
A pioneer of the internal-frame pack.

JanSport, Inc.
P.O. Box 1817, Appleton, WI 54912-1817
920-831-2288
www.jansport.com
Some external-frame packs.

Lowe Alpine
P.O. Box 1449, Broomfield, CO 80038
800-891-7908
www.lowealpine.com
A pioneer of the internal-frame pack.

Mountainsmith
18301 W. Colfax Avenue, Bldg. P, Golden, CO 80401
800-551-5889
www.mountainsmith.com

Tough Traveler
1012 State Street, Schenectady, NY 12307
800-468-6844
www.toughtraveler.com
Packs for kids and child carriers.

Beds

Big Agnes
735 Oak Street, Steamboat Springs, CO 80477
970-871-1480
www.bigagnes.com

Cascade Designs, Inc.
4000 First Avenue S., Seattle, WA 98134
800-531-9531
www.cascadedesigns.com
Maker of Thermarest pads, the dominant air mattress.

Fairydown
www.fairydown.co.uk

Feathered Friends
1119 Mercer Street, Seattle, WA 98109
206-292-6292
www.featheredfriends.com

Moonstone Mountaineering Equipment
5350 Ericson Way, Arcata, CA 95521
800-390-3312
www.moonstone.com

Mountainsmith
18301 W. Colfax Avenue, Golden, CO 80401
800-551-5889
www.mountainsmith.com

Slumberjack
800-233-6283
www.slumberjack.com

Western Mountaineering
1025 S. Fifth Street, San Jose, CA 95112
408-287-8944
www.westernmountaineering.com.

Wiggy's, Inc.
P.O. Box 2124, Grand Junction, CO 81502
970-241-6465
www.wiggys.com
Unconventional sleeping bags with open-cell foam.

Shelters

Bibler Tents
5441-D Western Avenue, Boulder, CO 80301
303-449-7351
www.biblertents.com

Big Agnes
735 Oak Street, Steamboat Springs, CO 80477
970-871-1480
www.bigagnes.com

Dana Design
333 Simmental Way, Bozeman, MT 59715
888-357-3262
www.danadesign.com

Eureka! The Tent Company
Johnson Worldwide Associates
P.O. Box 966, Binghamton, NY 13902
800-572-8822
www.eurekatent.com

Hilleberg The Tentmaker
866-848-8368
www.hilleberg.com
Tents from Sweden.

Slumberjack
800-233-6283
www.slumberjack.com

Snow Peak USA
P.O. Box 2002, Clackamas, OR 97015
503-697-3330
www.snowpeak.com

Stoves and Kitchens

Backpacker's Cache, Garcia Machine
14097 Avenue, Suite 272, Visalia, CA 93292
209-732-3785
www.backpackerscache.com
The pioneer of bearproof food containers.

Bear Vault
5663 Balboa Ave #354, San Diego, CA 92111
866-301-3442
www.bearvault.com
A second-generation bear-safe design.

Brunton
620 East Monroe Avenue, Riverton, WY 82501
307.856.6559
www.brunton.com

MSR (Mountain Safety Research)
P.O. Box 24547, Seattle, WA 98124
800-531-9531
www.msrcorp.com
The pioneer and still-dominant maker of separate-tank liquid-fuel stoves.

Optimus. *See* Brunton.

Primus
Distributed by Suunto USA
2151 Las Palmas Drive, Suite G, Carlsbad, CA 92009
800-543-9124
www.suuntousa.com
www.primus.se

Sigg
www.sigg.ch

Snow Peak USA
P.O. Box 2002, Clackamas, OR 97015
503-697-3330
www.snowpeak.com

Suunto USA. *See* Primus.

Trangia AB
www.trangia.se
Alcohol stoves.

Ursack
P.O. Box 5002, Mill Valley, CA 94942
866-232-7224
www.ursack.com
Another food protection alternative: bear-resistant bags.

ZZ Manufacturing, Inc.
1520A Industrial Park Street, Covina, CA 91722
800-594-9046
www.zzstove.com
Unusual wood-burning stoves.

Tools

Gerber
www.gerberblades.com
Knives.

Komperdell
www.komperdell.com
Trekking and ski poles from Austria.

Leki
356 Sonwil Drive, Buffalo, NY 14225
716-683-1022
www.leki.com
Trekking and ski poles from Germany.

Petzl America
P.O. Box 160447, Clearfield, UT 84016
801-926-1500
www.petzl.com
Headlamps and climbing gear.

Princeton Tec
P.O. Box 8057, Trenton, NJ 08650
609-298-9331
www.princetontec.com
Headlamps.

Victorinox, Swiss Army Brands, Inc.
P.O. Box 874, Shelton, CT 06484-6226
800-442-2706
www.victorinox.com
One of two rival makers of the "original" Swiss Army knife.

Wenger North America
15 Corporate Drive, Orangeburg, NY 10962
800-267-3577
www.wengerna.com
One of two rival makers of the "original" Swiss Army knife.

William Henry Knives
2125-C Delaware Avenue, Santa Cruz, CA 95060
831-454-9409
www.williamhenryknives.com

Water Treatment

General Ecology, Inc.
151 Sheree Blvd., Exton, PA 19341
800-441-8166
www.generalecology.com
Maker of the popular First Need filters.

Katadyn North America, Inc.
9850 N. 51st Ave., Plymouth, MN 55442
800-755-6701
www.katadyn.com
Water filters and purifiers from Switzerland.

McNett
360-671-2227
www.mcnett.com
New chlorine dioxide water treatment.

MSR (Mountain Safety Research)
P.O. Box 24547, Seattle, WA 98124
800-531-9531
www.msrcorp.com
The former Sweetwater line of water filters is now combined with MSR's.

Polar Equipment
12881 Foothill Lane, Saratoga, CA 95070
408-867-4576
www.polarequipment.com
Inexhaustible crystalline-iodine water treatment kits.

Navigation Equipment

Brunton
620 East Monroe Avenue, Riverton, WY 82501
307-856-6559
www.brunton.com

Garmin International, Inc.
1200 East 151st Street, Olathe, KS 66062
913-397-8200
www.garmin.com

Magellan
800-669-4477
www.magellangps.com

Map Tools
1755 La Honda Road #95, Woodside CA 94062
650-529-9410
Information and aids for GPS users, including the
UTM grid tool mentioned in Chapter 16.

Silva Compass
Johnson Worldwide Associates
P.O. Box 966, Binghamton, NY 13902
800-572-8822
www.silvacompass.com
www.silva.se

Suunto USA
2151 Las Palmas Drive, Suite G, Carlsbad, CA 92009
800-543-9124
www.suuntousa.com

Skis, Snowshoes, and Winter Gear

Alpina Sports Corp.
603-448-3101
www.alpinasports.com

Atlas Snow-Shoe Company
115 Tenth Street, San Francisco, CA 94103
888-482-8527
www.atlassnowshoe.com

Atomic Snow
www.atomicsnow.com

Black Diamond Equipment
2084 East 3900 S, Salt Lake City, UT 84124
801-278-5533
www.blackdiamondequipment.com

Fischer
www.fischer-ski.com

Rottefella
www.rottefella.com/english.cfm
Maker of classic three-pin Nordic Norm bindings.

Salomon North America
877-272-5666
www.salomonsports.com
Maker of an alternative family of bindings.

Sherpa Snowshoes
444 South Pine Street, Burlington, WI 53105
800-621-2277
www.sherpasnowshoes.com

Tubbs Snowshoe Company
52 River Road, Stowe, VT 05672
800-882-2748
www.tubbssnowshoes.com

Voilé Mountain Equipment
2656 South 2700 West, Salt Lake City, UT 84119
801-973-8622
www.voile-usa.com

Index

Numbers in italic indicate an illustration

Grand Staircase–Escalante National Monument (Utah), 429

Grasslands National Park (Saskatchewan), 424

grates, 132

grazing. *See* cattle and sheep

Great Basin, 431

Great Bear Wilderness (Mont.), 427

Great Dismal Swamp (Va., N.C.), 416

Great Lakes (wilderness region), 279–80, *415*, 422–23

Great Plains (wilderness region), 423–25, *426*

Great Smoky Mountains National Park (N.C., Tenn.), 160, 418

Great Swamp (N.J.), 416

Green Mountains (Vt.), 420

grills, 132

grizzly bears. *See* bears, brown or grizzly

Gros Morne National Park (Newfoundland), 421

groundcloths, 96, 113, 202, 263, 264, 339

ground-to-air signals, 363. *See also* distress signals

guidebooks, 85, 155, 349

group. *See* party management; party size

Gulf and Atlantic beaches and wetlands (wilderness region), 311–12, 414–16, *415*

Gulf Islands National Seashore (Fla., Ala., Miss.), 414

hairbrush, 146

halazone, 273

hammocks, 98, 117, 136

handrails, 294

hand warmers, 320

handwashing. *See* sanitation; washing

hantavirus, 406–7

harness, 300, 346. *See also* packs

hatchet, 141

hats and caps: for sun, 48, *50*, *52*, 53, 306, 315; for warmth, 54, *60*, 267, 315

headache, 371, 384

head injuries, 362, 367

headlamps and flashlights, *139*, 140–41, 180, 201; uses of, 231, 336, 394, 403

headnets, 53, 266–67

heat. *See* hyperthermia

heat cramps, 376

heat exhaustion. *See* hyperthermia

heat stroke. *See* hyperthermia

Heimlich maneuver, 359

Hells Canyon (Idaho, Ore.), 430–31, 453

Helly-Tech. *See* microporous fabrics

help, summoning, 150, 152, 202, 206, 229, 230, 333, 363

hepatitis, 270, 279

Herrero, Stephen, 399, 402

herringbone, 298

high-altitude cerebral edema, 381

high-altitude pulmonary edema, 381, 382

High Uintas Wilderness (Utah), 425

hiking alone. *See* solo hiking

hiking clubs, 9–11, 154, 155, 314, 348, 420. *See also* conservation organizations

hiking pace. *See* pace

hiking staff. *See* trekking poles

hips, 193

historic artifacts, 309

hitchhiking, 163

HIV, 150, 364

Hollofil, 89

horses. *See* pack animals

hose clamps, 144

hostels, 101, 420. *See also* shelters

hot springs, 377

human waste. *See* sanitation

Humboldt marten, 452

hunting season, 158, 418

huts, 101, 420. *See also* shelters

hydration systems, 22, 70–71, *80*, 81, 83

hyponatremia, 22, 196, 371

hyperthermia, 306, 350, 361, 373–76

hypothermia, 204, 268, 298, 333, 373–74, 376–78, 420

ice ax, 299, 319, 329, 333
Idaho Batholith, 427, 453
igloos, 316, 339–41, *339, 340*
impacts of recreation on
    wilderness, 3–5, 309, 352,
    442, 456–57, 459; on
    ecosystems, 4, 160, 200, 251,
    309; on specific animals, 137,
    166, 236, 260, 312, 405; on
    soil and groundcover, 47, 116,
    190, 200, 203–4, 236–38,
    242, 251, 252, 291, 293, 304,
    308, 352; on trees, 117, 242,
    265; on tundra, 420, 442; on
    waters, 4, 236, 255, 270–72;
    on wilderness experience, 3,
    29, 117, 152, 236, 239
indigestion, 372, 376
infection, 199, 391, 405
inflatable boat, 310
injuries, 149–50, 358, 362,
    364–71, 386, 405
inner tube, 310
insects, 278, 385–87, 418, 423,
    436; and campsite selection,
    6, 237, 239; avoiding bites,
    51, 53, 184, 266–67, 292, 386;
    treating bites, 395
insect repellents, 145, 202, 259,
    267, 386, 388; effects on gear,
    78, 99, 114, 145
insoles, 35, 41–42, 44, 266
insulating garments, 54–55, *60*,
    61, 287, *288*
intermountain (wilderness
    region), 426, 430–31, 448
Interior Dry Plateaus (British
    Columbia), 430
Internet, 10, 20, 21, 85, 154–55,
    331; maps via, 157, 210, 211
iodination. *See* water treatment
IR3535 (mosquito repellent),
    386
iron, 169
Isle Royale National Park
    (Mich.), 279–80, 422
isobutane. *See* stove fuels
itinerary. *See* leaving word
Ivory Flakes, 61

jackets. *See* insulating garments;
    shell garments
Jardine, Ray, 286, 287
Jasper National Park (Alberta),
    428

jerky, 175
Joshua Tree National Preserve
    (Calif.), 431

Kansas State University, 423
kayaks. *See* watercraft
Kejimkujuk National Park (Nova
    Scotia), 421
Kelty, 349
Kenai National Wildlife Refuge
    (Alaska), 439
Kenai Peninsula (Alaska), 439
kerosene. *See* stove fuels
keystone predators, 449, 451
Killarney Provincial Park
    (Ontario), 422
killer bees, 387
kitchen gear. *See* cookware;
    stoves
kitchen in camp layout, 240–41,
    402
Klamath Mountains (Calif.,
    Ore.), 432–33, 452
Klimate. *See* microporous fabrics
Kluane National Park (Yukon),
    439
kneecap, dislocated, 370
knees, 13, 142, 194, 289, 370
knives, 138–40, 201. *See also*
    multitools
knots, 265, *265*, 300
Kofa Game Range (Ariz.), 430
Konza Research Natural Area
    (Kans.), 423
Kouchibouguac National Park
    (New Brunswick), 421

L.L. Bean, 319
labiosan, 383
lacing. *See under* boots
ladle, 133
Lake Superior, 279–80, 422
lakes, 4, 236–37, 239, 255,
    270, 279
land agencies, 184, 188–89, 234,
    235, 418; information from,
    7–8, 155, 157, 158–59, 160,
    189, 212, 238, 296, 331, 399,
    442; feedback to, 156, 404,
    405, 407, 457–58; history of,
    445–48
lanterns, 120, 141
large groups. *See* party size
laxatives, 169
leader line, 144, 259

Mount Hood (Ore.), 432
Mount Jacques Cartier
(Québec), 421
Mount Jefferson (Ore.), 432
Mount McKinley (Alaska),
437, 440
Mount Mitchell (N.C.), 417
Mount Rainier (Wash.), 380, 432
Mount Rainier National Park
(Wash.), 160, 432, 451
Mount Robson Provincial Park
(British Columbia), 428
Mount Shasta (Calif.), 432
Mount Washington
(N.H.), 378
mukluks, 46, 319
multiple trailing, 200, 203–4
multitools, 138–39, *139*, 143
muscle cramps, 376, 390
mushrooms, 407

Nalgene, 133
national forests (U.S.), 445, 446.
See also public lands; *named
forests*
national lakeshores (U.S.). *See*
public lands
national monuments (U.S.). *See*
public lands
National Outdoor Leadership
School, 7–8
national parks: Canada, 454–55;
U.S., 444, 446–47. *See also*
public lands; *named parks*
National Park Service, 155, 158,
212, 446–47. *See also* land
agencies
national preserves. *See* public
lands
national recreation areas. *See*
public lands
national seashores. *See* public
lands
National Ski Patrol, 331
National Wilderness
Preservation System, 446–48
national wildlife refuges (U.S.),
445, 447. *See also* public
lands; *named refuges*
native peoples, 443; in Canada,
437, 454; in United States,
441, 444, 449, 450
natural history, 349
natural waters, 4, 351–52;
avoiding pollution of, 255,
270, 272; camping away
from, 135, 236–37, 309;
judging drinkability of,
278–80, 303–4
Nature Conservancy, 423
nausea, 196, 372, 381, 384, 395
navigation, 10, 207–31, 293–96,
328, 350, 446; in desert, 305,
307–8, 310
Nebraska National Forest, 423
neck injuries, 359, 362, 367
needle, 142–43, 148, 199
New Nordic Norm-Backcountry.
See skis and skiing
New York State, wilderness in,
155, 419
New York State Forest Preserve,
455
Nexus, 215
Niagara Escarpment (Ontario),
422
Nikwax, 44, 61, 62
N,N-diethyl-meta-tolumaide. *See*
DEET
noise, 239
Nordic Norm. *See* skis and
skiing
north, magnetic and true, 211,
212, 216–18, *216*, *217*
North American Wilderness
Recovery Project, 453–54
North Cascades (Wash.), 299,
398, 432
northeastern mountains
(wilderness region), 160, 317,
415, 416–18, 419–21
Northern Rocky Mountains
(wilderness region), 330, 425,
426, 427–28, 453
Northwest Ordinance of 1787,
444
Northwest Territories (Canada),
455
nosebleeds, 371
no-see-ums, 385
notebook, 141
Nunavat Territory (Canada), 455

off-road vehicles, 158, 159, 304,
308, 446, 457
Ohio River, 419
oil and gas development, 455
Okefenokee National Wildlife
Refuge (Ga.), 416
older backpackers, 11–13, 142

Olympic National Park
(Wash.), 433
Optimus, 246
oral rehydration salts, 372
organizational trips, 9–10, 154,
314, 348
Organ Pipe Cactus National
Monument, 430
orthotics, 42
Osage Hills (Okla.), 423
Otter Creek Wilderness
(W.Va.), 418
Ouachita Mountains. *See* Ozark-
Ouachita
outings clubs. *See* hiking clubs
Outside magazine, 20
Outward Bound, 282
ovens, 132
overboots, 319
Owyhee River (Idaho, Ore.), 431
Ozark-Ouachita (wilderness
region), 279, *415*, 416, 421

pace, 161, 194, 197, 288, 291,
327; with children, 342, 348,
349, 353
Pacific Crest Trail, 290, 413, 432
Pacific ranges (wilderness
region), 330–31, *426*, 432–34
pack animals, 198
pack cover, 57, 82, 183
packing, 177–85, 316, 353; lists,
18–19, 177–80, 201–2, 288
pack loads, 25–27, 286–89,
316, 353
pack palsy, 193
pack rats, 266
packs: external-frame, 65–66,
71–73, *72*, 315; internal-
frame, 65–71, *68*, 292, 315;
travel, 81–82; ultralight, 74,
287; for children, 66, 72, 81,
349, 352–53; for dog, 165;
buying and fitting, 74–77;
care and repair, 77–79, 144,
184, 258, 266, 403. *See also*
child carriers; daypacks
Padre Island National Seashore
(Tex.), 414
pads. *See* sleeping pads
pain medication. *See* analgesics
pants, 48–49, 50–52, *50*, *52*, *60*,
418; for snow, 315; protection
against animals, 51, 388, 394
parkas, 58–39

parking at trailhead, 190
ParksCanada, 212. *See also* land
agencies; public lands
parovirus, 166
party management, 184, 197,
201, 231, 298–99, 349;
dividing gear, 180–81,
183, 191
party size, 10, 157, 235, 293;
safety aspects of, 201, 363,
399, 404
pathogens: via animals, 385,
387, 388, 406–7; via bodily
fluids, 150, 360, 361, 364; via
food or water, 269, 271, 273,
275, *276*, 279
Pecos Wilderness (N.Mex.), 425
pemmican, 175
pencil or pen, 141
Pennsylvania, state wilderness
in, 155
pepper, 135, 305
Permanone, 388
permethrin, 388
personal care products, 146,
184, 255, 271, 272; items to
bearbag, 259–60, 403
Pertex, 90
photographs, 305, 405, 457
physical fitness. *See*
conditioning
Pictured Rocks National
Lakeshore (Mich.), 422
pillows, 93, 98, 336
Pinnell Mountain National
Recreation Trail (Alaska), 440
pipe, plastic, 316, 326
pit vipers, 392–93, *392*, *393*
plains. *See* Great Plains
plants, 352; invasive, 160, 200,
456, 457; irritant, 407–10;
poisonous, 350, 407. *See also*
vegetation
plastic bags, 83, 135, 174–75,
210, 297, 303; as syringe, 150,
364; in bearbagging, 136,
184, 260
plastics, 133–34
playas, 302, 431
pliers, 78, 139, 143, 326
plover, snowy, 312
plunge stepping, 299
poisoning, 350, 361
poison ivy, oak, and sumac, 145,
350, 407–10

waterproof breathable fabrics. *See* microporous fabrics
water treatment, 176, 202, 240, 241, 269–70, 272–78; boiling, 273, 278, 290; chemical, 273–75, 278, 290; filtration, 180, 275–78, 276, 290; in specific cases, 279–80, 290–91, 303, 334, 421
Wayburn, Peggy, 442
waypoints, 221–22, *221*
weather, 189, 204–5, 223, 240, 254, 343; winter, 213, 229–30, 328. *See also* climate; hypothermia; hyperthermia
weather radio, 152
weeds. *See* animals and plants
Weminuche Wilderness (Colo.), 425
Wenger, 138
wetsuit booties, 296
wetsuits, 311
whisk broom, 113, 336
whistle, 150, 202, 349
white gas. *See* stove fuels
White Mountain National Recreation Area (Alaska), 440
White Mountains (N.H.), 101, 160, 420
White Mountain Wilderness (N.Mex.), 430
whiteouts, 213, 328
Wichita Mountains National Wildlife Refuge (Okla.), 423
wilderness: efforts to preserve, 6, 156–57, 158, 419, 443–59; inventory by region, 412–42; management of, 5–6, 456–57; values of, 3, 189, 291, 385, 449–51
Wilderness Act of 1964, 445–46, 447, 451
Wilderness First Aid Manual, 147, 357
wilderness land management agencies. *See* land agencies
wilderness permits, 5, 157, 163–65, 188–89, 399. *See also* regulations; wilderness, management of

Wilderness Society, 451, 458
wildfire, 206, 271, 282, 433, 456; and campfire safety, 252, 253, 254, 281–82
wildflowers, 200
Wildlands Project, 453–54, 455
wildlife. *See* animals; biodiversity
Wilkerson, James A., 147
windscreens, 128
winter. *See* snow travel and camping
wire, 79, 143, 144, 326
wire cutter, 139
Wisconsin, state wilderness in, 155
Wise Use Movement, 447
wolves, 166, 405, 449
women, 21, 146, 165, 169, 275, 403; boots for, 37, 41; clothing for, 49, 50, 54; sleeping bags for, 85, 91–92, 93
wood. *See* firewood
Wood Buffalo National Park (Alberta), 436
wool, 38, 48, 49, 52, 54, 417
wounds. *See* injuries
Wrangell–St. Elias National Park and Preserve (Alaska), 439
wrench, 326
wristwatch. *See* watch

yellow jackets, 387
yellow pages, 17
Yellowstone National Park (Wyo., Idaho, Mont.), 160, 398, 427, 444, 453
Yellowstone-to-Yukon plan, 455
Yosemite National Park (Calif.), 137, 160, 432, 444
Yukon Delta National Wildlife Refuge (Alaska), 441
Yukon Territory (Canada), 455
Yukon-Charley Rivers National Preserve (Alaska), 440

Zahniser, Howard, 451, 454
zinc oxide, 383
zipper problems, 78, 142, 143, 144
ZZ Corporation, 125